THE COMPLETE HOME RENOVATION MANUAL

THE COMPLETE HOME RENOVATION MANUAL

DRAGON'S WORLD

Dragon's World Ltd
Limpsfield
Surrey RH8 0DY
Great Britain

First published by Dragon's World 1992

Editor: Mike Lawrence
Designer: Bob Burroughs
Editorial Director: Pippa Rubinstein
Art Director: Dave Allen

The catalogue record for this book is available from the British Library

ISBN 1 85028 165 3

Typeset by Bookworm Typesetting, Manchester.

Printed in Spain

CONTENTS

Introduction

The challenge of completely restoring a dilapidated property into a home of your dreams is an exciting one. Just conjure up the scene. You are replacing the final roof tile while down below your partner is fixing ornate trellis work to help the roses trail around the door.

Then it's a quick wash followed by tea on the lawn, before returning refreshed to complete painting those gleaming white window frames. It's certainly a romantic scenario, but unfortunately not too realistic.

There may be times when things seem to be going well. But more often than not you are likely to find yourself up a ladder in the pouring rain struggling to get a tarpaulin on to a wildly leaking roof, while down below your partner is desperately trying to shut a warped window. At best, refreshment is likely to take the form of a mug of tea and biscuits as you sit on an old box with your socks and shoes still soaking wet from a puddle you stepped into.

A pessimistic outlook? Perhaps. But a large-scale house restoration job is not for the faint-hearted or the disorganised. But, whoever you are and whatever your capabilities, provided you know what to expect and have laid your plans carefully, you will be able to shrug aside the bad days – even enjoy them – as you get the satisfaction of succeeding with some other task.

This book has been designed to help you chart a smooth passage through the choppy and stormy waters that lie ahead. It will educate you in every aspect of house improvement so that you are fully conversant with each stage of the work. With its help, you will be able to formulate a strategy to take you from initial hopes to final realisation of the dream.

It does not matter whether you are a complete novice to do-it-yourself or whether you have already cut your teeth on home improvement work. In either case, you will find the information and advice in the following chapters invaluable.

Although, in essence, the book is aimed at helping you to do as much of the work yourself, it recognises that many people would prefer, for all sorts of reasons, to let professionals tackle certain aspects.

Whereas doing it yourself is the key to greatest economy, you may decide to employ a bricklayer, roofing expert or plumber to do individual jobs. Perhaps you feel incapable of achieving complete success, you want a job to be finished quickly or you have not got a head for heights. No matter what the reason, at the end of the day the decision is yours. The most important point to remember is that whichever way you go, the work must be done correctly.

Keeping complete control over the whole project means following an outline timetable and monitoring your budget throughout. Time and money are two of the most important elements of house renovation.

As you work your way through the initial sections of the book, you will become aware of how to assess the condition of a property, how to plan the work, how to establish what are the priority jobs, how to draw up a realistic timescale and how to decide on who is to do the work at each stage.

Before you go house-hunting, familiarise yourself with the initial sections. Take in all the advice offered so that you can come up with a practical judgement of what you are capable of or are prepared to take on. The idea of renovating a really run-down house has to be assessed alongside the alternative of improving a fairly respectable property.

Much depends on a whole host of individual factors, the most important surrounding your

own family and lifestyle. It is generally true that an individual or a couple without children to consider are going to be able to dedicate much more time and money to the task. A family obviously occupies considerably more time and tends to create unexpected demands on effort and resources.

If the objective is to make as much money as possible from your endeavours, then a really dilapidated property is the most likely bet – provided that the initial purchase price is right, the condition is evaluated correctly and you get all your sums worked out. However, a property in better condition, available at a bargain price, might be the more lucrative venture.

From the outset, treat the whole question of renovating as a business. Run the project on sound, practical principles. Keep a file, which should contain all correspondence with surveyors, architects, tradesmen, suppliers and financial establishments.

It may seem tiresome to do this, and taking the trouble to get everything down in writing can be time-consuming. But in the end it can literally save both time and money, particularly if a dispute should later arise over what was or was not said earlier.

Very often it is the small tradesman who is the least efficient with correspondence – usually because of pressure of work. However you must get all quotes and estimates in writing and if any amendments or alterations to the initial agreement occur then these must be formalised if disputes are to be avoided.

If a tradesman is reluctant to put it in writing, then find another one or type it out yourself and get him to sign it. It is much better to have a clear understanding at the outset.

Contact suppliers to find out how much notice you must give for a delivery and order everything – scaffolding, ready-mix concrete, timber and so on – in good time. Keep a diary to remind yourself to confirm necessary orders.

Once you have a thorough grounding in the planning work, then you can move through the rest of the book to find out what you might encounter in terms of repairs and restoration to walls, ceilings, heating and the rest. The sections are arranged in the order that they should be tackled, although there are circumstances where a particular property could suggest a slight amendment to the list.

There is also a section where you can gain sound advice on improving the quality of family living by up-dating those hearts of the home – the kitchen and bathroom – and finding ways of creating more space and generally improving the amenities in your new home.

GOODMAYES
GOODMAYES PARK
SOUTH PARK
FAIR CROSS
MAYESBROOK PARK
CASTLE GREEN
461
READ BEARING HERE
PHOTAX UV 52mm

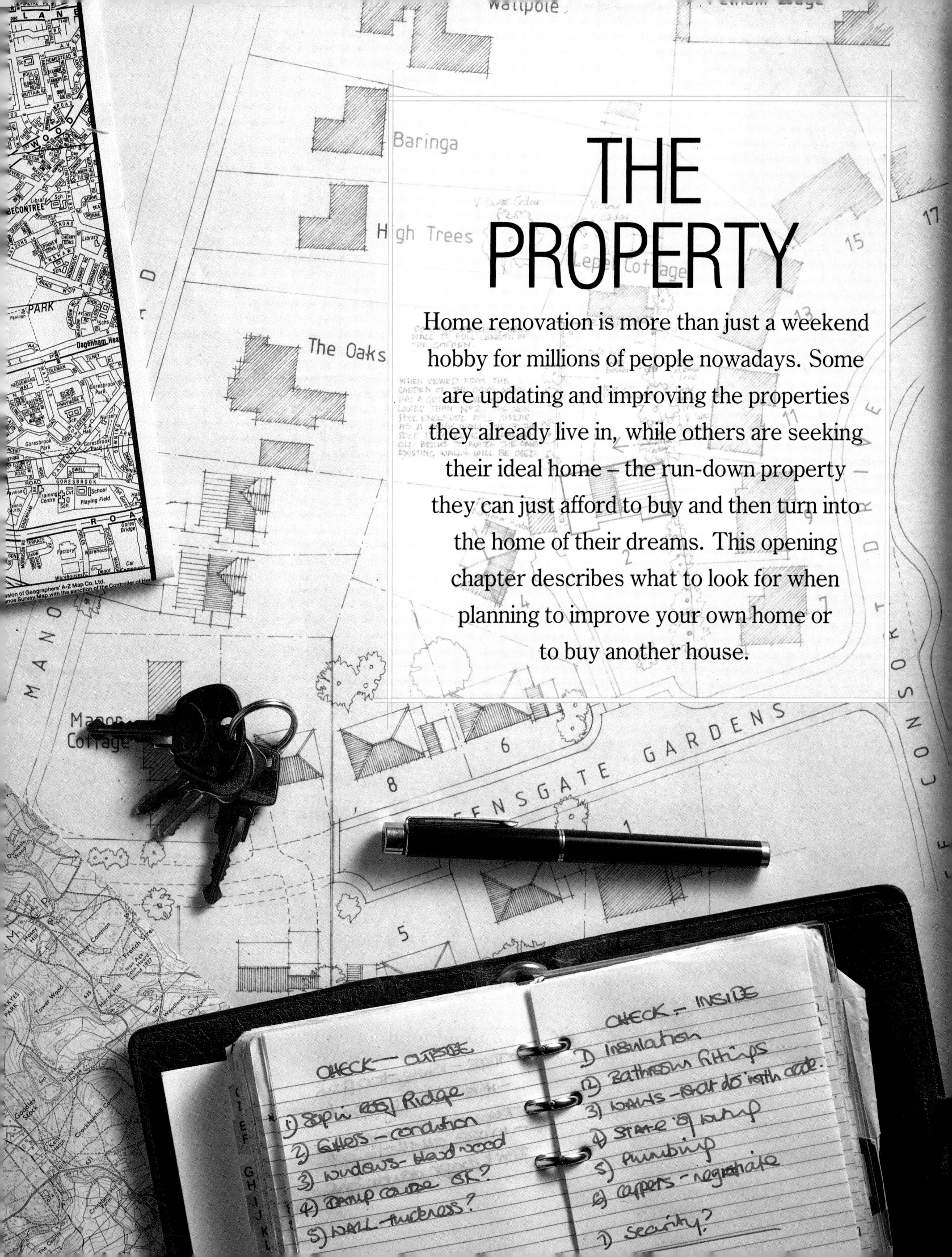

THE PROPERTY

Home renovation is more than just a weekend hobby for millions of people nowadays. Some are updating and improving the properties they already live in, while others are seeking their ideal home – the run-down property they can just afford to buy and then turn into the home of their dreams. This opening chapter describes what to look for when planning to improve your own home or to buy another house.

MOVING OR IMPROVING?

To move or improve – that is the question. It is a dilemma that most homeowners have to face at least once a lifetime. Comparatively few people remain in their initial house for ever; too many changes – expected or unexpected – occur over the years for that to be the rule.

We change our homes for many reasons – sometimes simply because we want to, sometimes because circumstances dictate. The traditional pattern (if such a thing exists) is for a couple to progress from a first-time buyer's property (a flat or small terraced house, perhaps) to a three- or four-bedroom semi or detached house as a family is started. If careers are successful or money is inherited, then for some there could be another move or two to more prestigious detached properties. Equally, a move to another home could be brought about by a change of job or location.

That, of course, is a carefully orchestrated scenario. For some, social circumstances, financial changes or simply the desire for a change of environment can be the motivating factors. Equally the prime mover could be investment with an eye to capital appreciation. Those involved in this activity are as much, if not more, concerned with houses as assets rather than as homes to live in.

In the past decade particularly, uncertainties in both national and domestic economies, coupled with the ever-rising costs of goods and services, have led to a large increase in another option – to stay put and add to the size and facilities of the existing home.

In the Sixties, the housing market was as stable and predictable as it had been for generations – and people could reasonably plan out the financial road ahead. They knew, for example, how much they were likely to be earning in, say five or ten years' time. Equally they knew that interest rates would increase roughly alongside their earnings and would have a fair idea of what their property was likely to be worth over that period.

It was a generally comfortable situation. If you aspired to a bigger or better home, then you knew what you had to find or sacrifice in order to get it. This created a stable market and a steady turnover of properties.

Today, the situation is totally different. No-one can possibly predict with any certainty what will happen to the economy in one year, let alone in ten. This naturally reflects on the housing market.

The result is a new attitude and approach, where homeowners now tend to look more at the possibilities of improving their existing home. And those looking to buy will pay greater attention to the potential of a particular property in terms of renovation or future extension to accommodate later requirements such as a growing family or ageing relative.

There are also those who are not necessarily concerned with extra space but who see the potential of an older property and want to enjoy the aesthetics and conveniences that come through renovation or modernisation.

Such people have to ask themselves a whole set of different questions in order to assess whether it would be financially viable to bring

■ Period cottages demand a wide range of renovation skills if their original features are not to be damaged irreparably, due to the wealth of different materials used in their construction. Sympathetic restoration need not, however, deprive the occupants of twentieth-century levels of comfort.

■ The terraced house is a common feature of both town and country streets, and as a first home gives many people an introduction to the whole business of home renovation on a manageable scale. A more substantial period cottage (below) may pose a bigger challenge, but in either case the structure is usually a good basis for sensitive restoration.

their existing home up to the desired requirements or whether a move would be more practical. They also have to bear in mind how much work they are prepared to do – or are capable of doing – themselves to keep costs within the available budget.

It is always far easier to assess how much it would cost to pay for alterations to your present home – especially if, as is likely, you have lived in it for a few years. You will already have a good idea of how you would change it, since you will know, for example, which rooms are the sunniest, which are an inconvenient shape, where there are awkward areas that could be put to better use and so on.

Possibly you have neighbours or friends with similar houses where improvements or alterations have already been made that you particularly like. Doubtless, with their help, you can also build up a fair picture of the kind of work and therefore budget involved.

Assessing a strange property is a different matter altogether. For a start, in a normal housing market you may not have the time to ponder carefully the pros and cons of a particular place or get builders in to give you quotations or estimates of what might be involved in improving it.

Unless the market is stagnant or the property difficult to sell for whatever reason, you will be fortunate to get even a week or two to make a decision. If the property is particularly desirable or priced as a genuine 'bargain', you will almost certainly find you have to make an instant decision. In this case, a good grounding in being able to evaluate property quickly could be priceless.

STAYING PUT

Assuming that your house is more or less suitable for your needs but you feel its layout or facilities could be improved – and it is in need of a good overhaul in certain departments – what are you going to do?

In general terms, there are some basic jobs that can be done immediately with few skills and a simple toolkit. Take the doors in a room, for example. Are there too many? Would it be more convenient if one opened outwards into a hallway rather than into a room? Could a sliding or folding door instead of a hinged one save valuable floor space?

Such jobs, involving some ability in the use of bricks or plasterboard needed to block off a doorway or basic screwdriver and chisel work to alter the type or operation of doors, cost very little to do. Even blocking off a window to create a complete run of wall for extra storage requirements is not going to over-tax your purse or your do-it-yourself skills.

The problem you will face in altering walls will depend on whether they are simply of a partitioning or load-bearing nature. The former, especially in a modern house, where many interior walls are of plasterboard construction, is simple to remove. On the other hand, a brick wall serving as a partition can be a daunting task for anyone not used to heavy work.

If the brick wall is load-bearing – that is, supporting part of the house structure above – then it requires expert building knowledge to decide on the correct replacement support to insert before it is demolished. With any work of this sort you must get professional, on-the-spot advice before you do anything.

Conversely, if you need an extra room, it could well be possible to partition off a large room to create two smaller ones. In this case, building a plasterboard wall is essentially a 'hammer and nails' carpentry job that most capable people should well be equal to.

The problem with planning alterations on this scale is being able to take a detached, clinical view of a house you have grown used to. It is sometimes impossible, for example, to imagine that cupboards or a large piece of furniture could be moved to an alternative location in a rearranged layout. We tend to become comfortable with familiar surroundings.

Before resorting to paying for the advice of an architect or surveyor, you need to get all your ideas down on paper. In other words, make a scale drawing of the complete floor area you want to alter. This does not have to be elaborate, but it should be accurate – so use graph paper and work to a convenient scale.

On the plan, mark the outside walls of the house and the position of all doors, windows, drains and other service pipes and cable runs. The interior plan should show whether walls are load-bearing or not. In addition, you must indicate precisely the position of doors and windows, pipes and cable runs inside – in fact, put down as much information as you think will be relevant.

It is only when you have the facts spread out in front of you that you can really begin to understand the existing layout of your house – and, most important, the possible opportunities available for change.

The relevance of marking on doors, windows, services and so on is to let you see at a glance where potential problems may lie and how difficult it is going to be to make particular alterations you may want. For example, a bathroom can pose problems since it has to function entirely around the supply and disposal of water. You cannot simply move it to the other side of the house as you might, say, with a dining room.

Even at the end of this exercise, you may still be baffled as to what can be done. If so, a professional should be able to come up with a series of possible options. Architects and surveyors usually work within a similar scale of fees and at least you should be able to get an idea of what the cost is likely to be simply by making a telephone call either to individual practices or to the head office of the relevant association or society.

■ The Regency influence brought a sense of lightness and frivolity to house style, with decorative features such as canopies and broad overhanging eaves masking the cheapness of the basic house structure

■ Georgian style in the late 18th and early 19th centuries favoured ornate entrances and multi-paned sash windows, scaled down in size as the storeys rose.

■ The Georgian style also spread to smaller homes, allowing the porch to become the focus of the façade. Windows are still carefully placed to enhance the overall symmetry.

■ In the country, simpler building styles prevailed, designed for practical purposes as much as for architectural merit.

You are unlikely to be charged an enormous amount for an initial visit, consultation and outline suggestions. Should you decide to take the matter a stage further and have proper plans drawn up for yourself or a builder, then you must ask what the fee for this will be.

You can run through the same process if you are thinking of buying a property and there is no pressure on you to make a quick purchase. However, you may not have sufficient appreciation or knowledge of building work to make a swift, accurate assessment on a particular property where there is a queue of interested parties considering buying as well. In this situation, you can take your professional adviser with you to get an immediate expert opinion on the property.

Your initial response to such a suggestion may be that this is a waste of money. But imagine what it could be like to buy a house believing it to be possible to make certain alterations or improvements, only to find out a few months later that you cannot do what you want – or that the cost of what you plan is prohibitively expensive.

Even in a lively market, most vendors understand that a potential purchaser will want a surveyor's report on the building. You can take this opportunity to get the surveyor to include renovation or alteration possibilities in his report. This could involve an additional fee, over and above the survey charge, which again you can ascertain in advance.

CHECKING IT OVER

The advantage of planning wholesale improvements to a house in which you have lived for a couple of winters is that you have a pretty thorough knowledge of its hidden weaknesses and problems.

You cannot, for example, spot a really cold, draughty corner when making an inspection of a strange house on a hot summer's day. Equally you will not know that the boiler makes strange hissing sounds as it warms up or that mould tends to grow on the wall inside a fitted wardrobe in the middle of winter.

When you inspect any property, you will be looking for the same things and searching for the obvious faults. But it is only with your own home that you will have a complete picture.

In some cases first impressions can be a good indication as to the overall state of a house. Although it is not uncommon to see somewhere with gleaming paintwork and a neatly tended garden that is in need of vast improvement inside, it is rare to see an eyesore with an

extent of which will only be revealed by expert inspection and specialist evaluation. If such conditions exist and prove to be serious, you will almost certainly be looking at a non-starter.

FIRST IMPRESSIONS

When you go to look at any property you are considering buying, the first and most obvious thing you will notice is its general decorative state. Peeling paint from walls, doors and windows, exposed woodwork, rusting gutters, cracks in the rendering or patches of missing pebbledash or algal growth – all these will be clearly visible. They are also familiar signs of a neglected property and possibly the greater problems of damp and rot.

No straightforward decorating job is beyond the capability of anyone prepared to wield a paintbrush. All the preparation work, such as removing rust, filling cracks, replacing putty and so on just requires a little easily gained knowledge, a modicum of patience, and no great degree of skill.

The only possible drawback for some people is that you will probably have to scale the heights to do part of the work. Not everyone is happy working from a ladder. Nowadays, fortunately, you do have the option of hiring a scaffold tower from which you can work safely and comfortably at heights.

You may decide it is worth buying such a kit if there is a lot of work to be done and you are prepared to undertake it on an on going basis. Rather like the Forth Bridge, decoration can be a never-ending task. You could even share the expense with a friend or neighbour.

Scaffold towers are not only exceedingly practical for this type of work – and to gain

overgrown garden that is immaculate and fully modernised inside.

If the house is run-down outside, expect the worst inside as well. You will probably find an antiquated electrical system and plumbing to match, few modern services and a lot of damp. Estate agents often describe such a property as being 'in need of some improvement'.

What they are in fact saying is that there is an avalanche of work to be done and it would cost a small fortune to employ builders to tackle the jobs required. If you are capable of doing some or all of it yourself and the house is being sold reasonably cheaply, then you could look forward to some return for your labours in the years to come.

Unless you are up-to-date with materials and their prices, then you should take a trip to a builders' merchant or speak to a few manufacturers to see how much, for example, a new garage door would cost – or new plastic guttering, a replacement window, a bathroom suite or fitted kitchen units.

Make a list of all the obvious, larger items you think you are going to need and then add on an extra 50 per cent for smaller items, decoration materials and so on. At least this will give you a rough figure to work on. It is not going to be totally accurate, but it will prepare you for the worst. And it should avoid the nightmare of seeing, halfway through the work, your budget turned on its head. If the cost of the improvements you would like to see is then reflected in the price you are paying for the property, then you can consider yourself as having got a definite bargain.

None of this, of course, takes into account such major faults as subsidence or dry rot – the

■ Terraces soon became the accepted form of building in towns, whether adorned by all the trappings of Regency style (above) or more simply broken up with projecting bays in Victorian times. Basements reached from below the front steps were a popular way of creating extra living space within a restricted floor plan.

The Victorian semi-detached house reflected the pretensions of its owners, who referred to them as villas rather than houses. Stock features were the projecting two-storey bays and the recessed arched entrances, often featuring decorative stonework.

access to the roof – but they are also quite quick and easy to put up.

If you feel reasonably confident about decorating yourself, then do it. If you need persuading, then just get a quote from a professional company and you will see the reason why!

'All that glisters is not gold', wrote William Shakespeare. And that could well apply to a house with shining paintwork. A quick spruce-up before placing a property on the market is an established practice. It is also one way of covering up a multitude of problems, including rotting wood.

You cannot, of course, inspect every inch of exterior woodwork. But a strategic prod here and there around door and window frames with a sharp penknife will reveal if there is a trouble spot lurking behind a fresh coat of paint. And if you find one chink in the armour, then look further, since there are bound to be more.

If, of course, the problem is limited to just a few frames, these can be replaced for a moderate outlay. And if you have already decided you want to install double glazing, rotting windows will cease to matter.

LOOKING UP TOP

You can check the condition of the roof and chimney stack at a glance – and the age of the house will help you complete the picture. A tile or slate roof should last around 50 years without any major trouble – apart from the inevitable handful of tiles that will have cracked or slipped. Such a roof is likely to have failed within that period only if the structural timbers have decayed badly.

Late 19th-century mansions began to develop decorative idiosyncrasies of their own, from decorative bargeboards to ornate chimney stacks. The more complex the detail, the more difficult authentic renovation can be to carry out.

With older roofs, you may find weak spots where rainwater and snow are getting through. On a slate roof, for example, a condition known as 'nail sickness' could have developed. This means that the nails holding the slates to the rafters have corroded and whole areas of slate could have slipped or may be ready to move.

The real key to knowing whether an apparently sound roof is watertight is whether any damp patches are showing up on ceilings or whether loft timbers or insulation are wet. The best time to detect this is obviously on a rainy day. Get into the loft and use a torch to search for any leaks. Make sure you trace them back

to the trouble area, since water will often drop some distance from where it gets in.

You can make a reasonably thorough inspection of the roof from the ground, using a pair of binoculars. Look for broken or slipped ridge tiles; loose or damaged flashing, where the base of the chimney stack meets the roof; and damage in valley gutters. The chimney itself, especially if disused, can be a prime source of dampness. So check that the brickwork pointing and rendering are sound and the pot itself is solidly fixed in mortar (known as flaunching).

You need to have a good head for heights, a proper roof ladder and, if necessary, correct scaffolding to get on to a roof for a closer inspection or to carry out repairs. There is no reason why you should not be able to complete most remedial work, although many are understandably reluctant to take it on. If you are prepared to, you will save yourself a lot of money. If not, get a reputable builder or roofing contractor to do the work.

■ Private speculative building after the first World War gave rise to a huge range of building styles, drawing on features of the late Victorian and Edwardian periods. The projecting bay was still a popular feature along with mock Tudor-style timbering, while pebbledash began to appear as a cover-up for cheap bricks poorly laid by unskilled labour.

Flat roofs are notorious for leaking. Unfortunately a visual inspection may not reveal anything untoward, even though the roof leaks like a sieve. Loose or missing flashing will be self-evident, as will cracks in the felt. But if a felted roof is, as it should be, covered with chippings, only the occupier will know whether it is sound or not. Age is a clue to condition. With a flat felted roof, after 10 or 15 years you are generally living on borrowed time.

If you are happy to work on a flat surface, then it would be worth your while to re-felt a small roof yourself. Leave large roofs to a professional contractor.

TAKING A SIDE VIEW

Normal cracks and holes in walls are cheap and simple to fill in. However major cracks could indicate some much more drastic problem, such as the need for underpinning foundations. Very often this is covered by house insurance and you can then call in professional experts to do the job. It is one type of work that could prove costly and very disruptive.

Patches of loose rendering or pebbledash can be tackled quite successfully by the amateur. Larger areas or complete walls, however, really need good building skills.

The job of replacing doors or windows is relatively straightforward, provided you are using the same size units. If you want to enlarge

■ The post-second World War period saw the development of modernist styles for both detached and terraced homes (left and below left). The main features were bland picture windows and the absence of any relieving features save for a boxy front porch. Occasionally, architects would hark back to more traditional styles (below), using features such as decorative tile hanging and modern sash windows to disguise the basic box structure of the house.

an opening, then you need to know what you are doing. It is quite possible that you would have to install a longer lintel to support the wall above, which is a major operation.

Metal guttering and drainpipes that need replacing should not pose any particular problems. The former are held in place with brackets screwed to the fascia boards (in the case of gutters) or to the rafter ends, while the latter are fixed direct to the wall. Using the plastic versions, which do not suffer from rust, you can put up a new system in a matter of a few days, possibly in just a weekend. Care should be taken with metal guttering however, since it is fairly heavy and quite awkward to handle when working at a height.

If you detect only the odd leak or patch of rust in your metal guttering, a little first-aid work will give it a new lease of life.

STEPPING INSIDE

It is most unlikely that you will move into a house and like the decor sufficiently to leave it as it is. So it is of no great concern if the wallpaper is shabby or the paintwork faded or chipped. Nine times out of ten you will want to strip the paper off or paint over the walls or woodwork.

As a general rule, however, the shabbier the existing decorations, the more preparatory work you will have to do to get things ready for redecorating. And it is also possible that behind old wallpaper lurks another problem, such as deteriorating plaster and possibly damp.

Whatever the overall condition, however, this is not normally an aspect of a property that should cause too much worry. The one advantage here is that if you can live with the existing decor, initially at least you will be saving yourself valuable time and money to spend on other more important or urgent jobs.

It is far more crucial to look at the services, starting with the electrics. An inspection of the understairs cupboard should reveal all, since this is where old systems normally originate. Tell-tale signs include the old-fashioned fuse box and probably a jumble of cables, which may even be rubber-covered. Look around the house for sockets that take round-pin plugs, are mounted on skirting boards or are broken or scorched. Switches mounted on wood blocks are another sign of old age, while ceiling lights suspended on frayed flex provide another clear warning sign.

If any of these conditions are present, then you need to have the old wiring ripped out and new power and lighting circuits installed. These should run from a modern consumer unit to an adequate number of 13 amp square-pin sockets in each room, switched fused units for kitchen appliances, flush wall switches, plastic-coated ceiling rose flex and so on.

This is expensive but essential work, which requires expert electrical knowledge plus some basic preparation – such as chasing out walls for cable runs, lifting floorboards and making holes to receive socket outlets. If you are competent, you can undertake your own rewiring. But you must get the local electricity board to make the final inspection and connection to the consumer unit. You cannot do this yourself.

Plumbing covers not only the pipework but the units themselves – sink, bath, wash-basin, toilet etc. If you find modern units, then you can reasonably assume that any old lead piping has been replaced by new copper and plastic versions. A look under the kitchen sink unit, in the airing cupboard and below the bath will tell you all you need to know.

If the house has central heating, find out its age. You cannot tell by looking unless you are an expert, since radiator designs have not changed much in 30 years and even boilers look more or less the same; the only real difference is that they tend to be smaller and sleeker now.

Once a boiler has been in service for 20 years, its days are numbered. There may also be corrosion in the pipes and radiators, something that can happen to an unprotected system in a matter of a few years.

Not too many people would take on the challenge of installing their own central heating or replacing a boiler, whereas repositioning or changing the odd radiator is only a day's work.

GETTING THE WRONG FEELING

If you detect a musty smell in any of the rooms you visit, if the air feels moist or there are stains on walls or ceilings, then dampness is getting into the house. This could be caused by rainwater penetrating porous walls, particularly adjacent to leaking guttering, in which case the problem is quite easily remedied.

Rising damp, on the other hand, is much more serious. This is caused by a faulty or non-existent damp-proof course (dpc). If you come across damp on the ground floor above skirting board level and spreading upwards,

■ The kitchen is the hub of both domestic and family activity, and will most strongly reflect the taste of its occupants. Cottagey homeliness or the clinical style of the operating theatre are largely matters of personal taste; what is more important is whether the kitchen functions well from a practical point of view.

■ The entrance hall of any house makes an immediate impact on the first-time visitor. Its size and shape are less important than the sense of providing a welcome, which depends more on factors such as lighting and decoration than on shape and size.

then you should call in an expert to check the extent of the problem.

Dampness can, in turn, lead to the even more serious problem of wet and dry rot. The former is not quite as bad, since the rot remains localised. But dry rot can find its way through walls and ceilings and eventually attack all the structural timbers in the house.

Dry rot is identifiable by a fungus growing on the wood. Further evidence is provided by cracks both with and across the grain, where the timber literally crumbles away when touched. It can be devastating – and so, too, can be the cost of eradicating it. Normally any work should be left to a specialist company, since it must be totally cleared and all affected areas sterilised.

Nearly every property is, to some extent, affected by woodworm. Unpainted structural timbers – floorboards, loft beams and so on – are the usual places to search for those tell-tale pin-prick holes made by the emerging beetle.

You can treat localised woodworm attacks quite easily yourself by applying a proprietary woodworm killer. You simply brush or spray it on to all unprotected timber in the vicinity of the attack, including of course the affected area.

■ The bathroom has come a long way from its early Victorian beginnings, when space for bathing and washing was not regarded as a high priority. As a result, much ingenuity is often devoted to cramming a quart into a pint pot during later renovation work.

PLAYING SAFE

All this may give you the feeling that suddenly viewing a house you are considering buying has become a daunting prospect. What you must remember is that, whatever its age, no property is going to be in perfect condition. What is important is that you are able to recognise what is serious and what is acceptable – and, of course, have a reasonable idea of what costs might be involved. Only then can you put a realistic value on the house and decide what it is worth to you to buy.

It is an obvious word of warning but one that can all too easily be ignored that 'when in doubt, walk away'. You may, for a variety of reasons, feel you have found the 'ideal' property and therefore try to convince yourself that any problems can be overcome – or, worse, that they do not exist. But it pays to be critical and careful. And if, by doing so, you fail to make the purchase, don't despair. There will always be another 'ideal' property round the corner.

CASIO
HS-8G
32" DOOR
GARAGE

PLANNING THE WORK

Once you have chosen the course your home renovation project is to follow, you need to decide on job priorities so you can start drawing up detailed plans, schedules and timetables. At this stage you must also decide whether you will need some extra help from the professionals in the home renovation business – people such as architects, builders, plumbers, electricians and other specialists.

The value of careful appraisal and ascertaining exactly what renovation work has to be done to a property will be reflected in both time and money saved. But even those can be wasted if you do not plan each stage properly. Without organising the correct order of jobs, you can easily find yourself having to cover the same ground over again.

An obvious example is with electrical work, where you may decide you want to install wall lights after you have decorated a room. Since this involves channelling into the wall to run cable to the lights, you will have to decorate the wall again afterwards.

Equally, in the kitchen it makes no sense to move a plumbed-in appliance to the other side of the room after you have discovered it is not in the most convenient place. To change the siting at this stage will involve extending the run of both supply and drainage pipes.

So you need to take your time to decide exactly what you want and then to draw up a blueprint of when and how each job is to be tackled. Unless you have very fixed ideas of what alterations or improvements you want to make to your 'new' home, it will certainly pay you to live in it for a few months until you get to know it a bit better and can be sure of what you want to be done and where.

Even after a short period, you may well alter your views considerably. You will also then be in a much better position to judge existing shortcomings or problem areas.

There are many factors that can influence how you arrive at your final plan. Is there major building work to be done? At what time of year is it best to do a particular job? Should you start inside or outside? Are there priority jobs? Are there any financial restraints? If you have had a surveyor's report carried out on the house, what were the findings and were there any comments within it that would affect your own preferred timetable?

■ Making sure the house is weatherproof is always a top priority. Loose or missing roof tiles allow water to get at the roof timbers and penetrate ceilings below, while blocked gutters will cause damp penetration lower down the building. Outside walls in poor condition will also allow rain and wind to penetrate the house structure.

MAKING IT SOUND

The first essential is to ensure that the roof is waterproof and free of rot. If the roof is leaking or the gutters are overflowing, causing damp in any of the rooms, or there is serious wood rot or woodworm to treat, then make these the main priorities.

In the case of anything involving structural timbers in the house, upheaval is unavoidable. Rooms will probably have to be cleared of

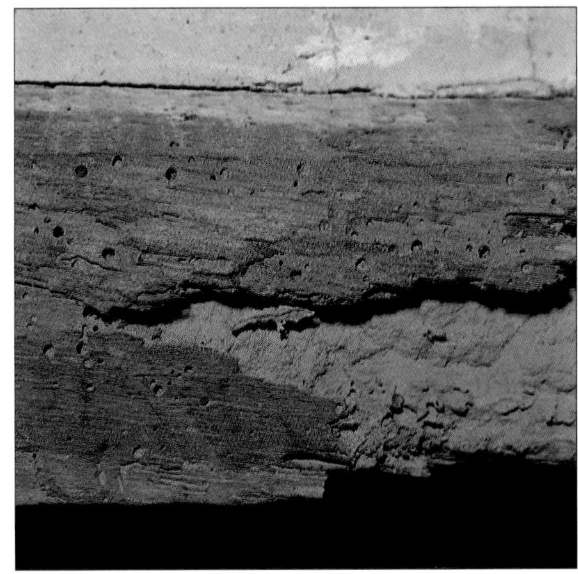

furniture while floorboards are taken up. The loft may have to be stripped of its insulation and all the items in it stored somewhere else while the woodworm treatment is applied.

Dealing with a bad attack of dry rot can cause an amazing amount of devastation, with plaster being hacked off walls and complete floor structures being replaced.

So this type of work is something that must be done immediately – even if it means having to put up with makeshift accommodation for the duration of the job.

It goes without saying that these jobs are always better done during the summer, since the house inevitably becomes a building site and doors and windows have to be kept open all the time. If you have to schedule it for the winter, get it done as quickly as possible.

■ Rot is public enemy number one, closely followed by infestation with woodworm. Both can cause extensive damage to timber.

■ Total demolition may be the only cure for internal structure defects.

WORKING ON THE INSIDE

Where the house is basically in sound condition, it is a good idea to turn your attention first to any interior structural work you want done. Alterations affecting the inside should ideally all be done together to minimise the unavoidable inconvenience.

If you are knocking down walls, replacing ceilings or installing doors to the outside, for example, get the work out of the way so that all the resultant rubble can be dumped and then cleared in a single operation. This can be done through the hire of a skip, which you will want filled and removed as quickly as possible – not hanging around for weeks on end.

Equally, thinking ahead, you may have some outdoor or garden projects planned where hardcore will be needed for the foundations. Therefore you will want to save any bricks you are removing and store them in a convenient pile somewhere outside.

Should you be planning any major building work, than it would obviously be an advantage to have this completed early on. Putting up a single-storey extension, for example, does not necessarily mean that too much mess will spill into the house itself. But it is still better to get the major upheaval over as soon as possible. One advantage is that it would then provide you with valuable temporary living accommodation

■ Many older homes have bathrooms and WCs that have gone unimproved for decades. Not only will the visible components need replacing; the underlying services such as water supplies and waste disposal may well need full-scale modernising too.

■ Similarly, the revolution in interior design may have passed the kitchen by, with washing, food storage and preparation facilities a picturesque relic of a bygone age. One particular need is often for a better electricity supply to cope with the multitude of gadgets now regarded as essential in a modern kitchen.

when working on the main rooms in the house.

On the other hand, a loft conversion or a double-storey extension will certainly affect the inside of the house, since walls must be knocked through, windows blocked up and staircases built.

Any alterations or additions to the essential services – water, gas and electricity – will inevitably result in considerable disturbance to floors and walls. Such work should therefore be planned with this in mind and all of it completed at the same time. Pipes and cables are the lifeblood of any home and their efficient operation will add enormously to the well-being and peace of mind of the occupants. Plenty of hot water, warmth from radiators and ample sockets and light switches that work will justify the necessary inconvenience any installation or repair work causes.

All these jobs take time – weeks and possibly months, depending on their extent, the ability of the individual and what time is available to carry them out.

Since you really cannot move on to general improvements and decorating before they are complete, you might decide that employing professionals for all or part of the work might be the sensible option. On the other hand, you may be happy to live with any inconvenience for as long as it takes to complete all the required stages of the work.

As far as services are concerned, the most important rooms in the house are the kitchen and bathroom. Cooking, washing and bathing facilities are essential and you will need to have at least the basic minimum services in operation while the work is going on.

If you have to replace the wc, bath or cooker, then make sure everything is arranged so that the work can be done speedily. You cannot afford to have these vital facilities out of action for any length of time.

If you have a family, particularly with babies or young children, it may well be sensible to

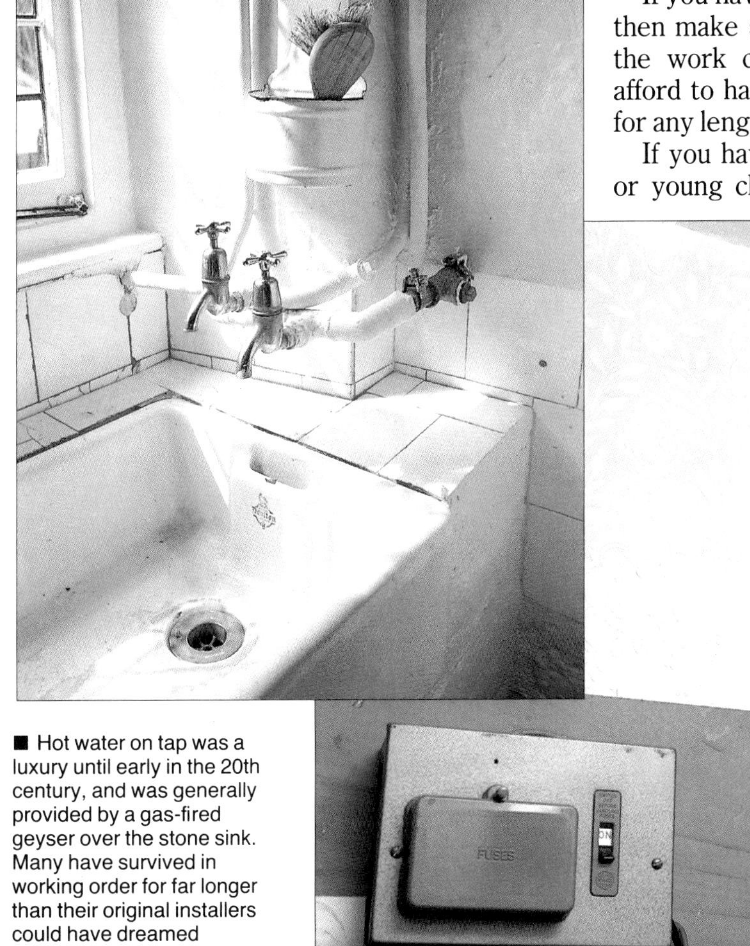

■ Hot water on tap was a luxury until early in the 20th century, and was generally provided by a gas-fired geyser over the stone sink. Many have survived in working order for far longer than their original installers could have dreamed possible at the time.

■ The inexorable rise in demand for electricity has in many older homes led to a piecemeal extension of the original wiring system well beyond the bounds of safety. Installations such as this must be a top priority for total replacement.

arrange for them to stay with friends or relatives temporarily while the work is being carried out.

Cooking facilities are, perhaps, the least critical in this situation. Arguably they can be out of action for a few days without causing too many headaches. Cereals, salads and fruit, for example, form a perfectly acceptable diet. Alternatively, should there be a convenient takeaway, you can at least make use of it for the short period necessary. Whatever arrangements you can make, never forget to have hot drinks readily available, either by use of a camping stove or a regularly filled flask, which hopefully you can get a neighbour to supply.

It is always a good idea to have at least one room set aside where the family can escape to and relax in some degree of comfort, especially in the winter. As long as it is furnished to a degree and has a carpet – however temporary – it will provide a welcome sanctuary.

WORKING ON THE OUTSIDE

Apart from any essential repairs you need to carry out to make the fabric of the house sound, you can leave exterior decoration until last – unless you cannot stand the idea of your place not looking as good as the house next door!

Remember, however, that if you intend any alterations that will affect the exterior later on, such as changing the position of windows or doors, this could upset any work you do now. You may, for example, have to apply fresh rendering around the new frames to make good any damage caused when the old ones are removed, and then repaint the affected areas.

For anyone who has not tackled exterior decorating before, be warned! Depending on the size of the house, its design and overall condition, it can involve you in months of work. Bearing in mind that most people will only have summer evenings and weekends at their disposal, to paint a large semi-detached property with wooden windows can take all summer.

Estimating how long a job is going to take is never easy, especially with larger projects where so many unexpected problems can arise. The sensible approach is always to overestimate – and be realistic. Nothing is worse than falling behind your schedule. This can cause a feeling of anxiety to creep in needlessly and encourages jobs to be rushed, so that standards of workmanship fall badly – and possibly disastrously.

The best advice is never to plot an exact timetable. Your plan should basically give you an order in which things are going to be done and the optimum time of year to tackle them. Illness or family and work commitments, for example, can all conspire to throw your schedules into disarray and interfere with progress from time to time.

FINANCING THE WORK

Not everyone is in the fortunate position of having sufficient funds readily available to provide them with complete freedom of choice over when particular jobs are going to be done. Some will have to plan what they are going to do around savings and future borrowing.

The ideal solution is to borrow sufficient money when taking out a mortgage to cover the cost of essential improvements as well – and all of them if this is possible and practical. So you must first find out what arrangement your building society or bank manager is prepared to offer you. It is absolutely essential that you allow for the availability of money to cover every stage of your work plan.

In certain circumstances, of course, you may well be eligible for an improvement grant – for insulation, for example, or if you have bought a listed property. Obviously you will need to check this out and determine when any money is going to be available. This will equally have an effect on your timetable.

Careful budgeting and purchasing can save you a lot of money, particularly if you are renovating a large proportion of your property. The overall cost will run into thousands – at least – so any savings along the way can help significantly in relation to the final total. There are several useful principles you should get into the habit of adopting.

First, especially in times of inflation, buying as soon as possible should represent a considerable saving. Buying in bulk is sensible, too. Even tiny items such as nails and screws should be bought in large boxes, rather than in expensive little packets.

Shop around for the best prices. Builders' merchants and DIY superstores are normally very competitive. But do not forget the small corner shop, where there are bargains to be had as well.

Finally, if you are going to employ an architect or surveyor, you must first consider what you want to do. Even better, prepare a rough drawing – however simple – since this should greatly reduce the final costs involved. If you can at least give an overall picture of what you want, it will save a lot of time and money paying the professional to experiment with different ideas.

DECIDING WHETHER YOU NEED EXPERT HELP

Assessing the job

Whether you decide to tackle a particular job or project yourself will depend on a number of questions which only you can answer, since they relate to individual factors such as the nature of the work, your personal level of skill and technical knowledge, the time and money you have available and your level of personal commitment to getting the work completed. Check how each of these points applies to the project you are tackling before making your decision.

Personal skill

Start by deciding whether you have the *ability* to tackle a particular job. You may have done it before with considerable success, or you may have watched someone else do it and felt that you could soon pick the skill up. Be honest with yourself about your ability, however; contractors hate having to undo someone else's bodged work, and would rather have been called in at the beginning.

Remember that larger projects will often require a range of skills. In this case, break the job down into its component parts and assess each one individually. For example, you may decide to leave the structural part of, say, a loft conversion to a contractor, but to do all the internal fitting out yourself. This is a perfectly acceptable way of tackling many projects, so long as the contractor is aware of your intentions at the outset.

Technical knowledge

Next, ask yourself whether you know what is involved in carrying out the work from a technical point of view. For example, jobs such as doing your own wiring or plumbing work or creating a new opening in a wall are not difficult in terms of the level of skill needed, but it is essential that you have sufficient knowledge to ensure that you make the right electrical connections, choose the correct pipe sizes or use the appropriate type of beam to bridge the new opening you are constructing. In some cases, getting expert advice may be all you need to do before you actually carry out the work yourself; in other situations the whole job may simply be too complex for the layman to tackle without enlisting some professional assistance.

Rules and regulations

Many home improvement projects have to comply with the requirements of various pieces of legislation that are intended to ensure that such work is carried out safely and to satisfactory standards. These rules obviously apply mainly to major structural work, but alterations to things like staircases or the disposal of waste water may also be covered. It is therefore vital, before even planning or starting work on any home improvement project, to ascertain whether any official permission is needed and also whether the work must comply with any technical regulations. Just because a job needs official permission or approval does not mean that you cannot do it yourself, but you must obtain permission first and ensure that what you do complies with the rules throughout. Contact your local planning and building control departments for further advice.

The time available

Next, consider how long the job is likely to take to complete. You will usually take longer that a contractor to carry out a particular task, and on larger projects you must weigh up the advantage of calling in an expert and getting quicker completion – at a price – against saving some money but having a longer period of disruption around the house. Other factors, such as having the house open to the elements during the winter, may also be relevant when you are deciding which course to adopt.

The cost

Cost if often the most important factor in deciding whether to carry out a particular job yourself. At first sight the thought that your own labour is free seems very appealing, and onn many jobs the cost of materials represents only a tiny fraction of the overall real cost. For example, having your house painted by a contractor will cost between five and ten times the price of the paint and other materials; the rest is his labour charge. However, you must be sure not only that you can finish the work in a reasonable time, but also that you can do it properly.

When you are pricing a project with a view to doing it yourself, remember that professionals can buy materials at lower prices that you can, as well as working more quickly. Balance these points against the cost of your own time. To get a proper picture it may help you to have a couple of quotations from professionals (see below) which will cost you nothing and will help you arrive at a decision.

Choosing a contractor

Personal recommendation is the best way of finding a contractor. Otherwise, it is safest to pick individuals or companies with membership of the relevant professional or trade organisation, and to check that the membership is genuine. Once you have found two or three suitable contractors, get written quotations so you can select which firm to employ on the basis of the materials specified, the time the work will take and, of course, the price. When you have made your choice, accept the quotation in writing so that you have a legally enforceable contract should any future dispute arise.

Standard Form
Abbreviated
Front
evation
INSPECTION CHAMBER
kitchen
utility room
BREAKFAST RM.
CASIO
HS-8G
COLOUR
742 FH Pebble Grey
Winter White
dove grey

THE STRUCTURE

Before you can start work in earnest, it is vital that you have a clear picture of what you are up against, by finding out all you can about the structure of the building and examining it closely for obvious and potential trouble spots. A guided tour round the house is the best way of assessing what is there and what needs attention.

TYPES OF HOUSE

Whether you are thinking of improving your existing home or considering purchasing a house in need of renovation, you must check out the basic fabric of the property to appreciate what essential repairs might be required. Once the structure is sound, you can start making whatever other alterations and modifications you want to carry out.

Houses are very individual, even on a purpose-built estate. Each one has its own unique set of circumstances that could result in specific structural problems. For example, a house on a corner plot could be more susceptible to problems caused by the weather than an identical one in a sheltered situation.

Each house has its own set of ground conditions, too. Tree roots in the foundations and back filling of the site can make one house more prone to subsidence and settlement than a similar neighbouring property.

Probably the most important factor in the structural stability of any property is the actual type of construction itself and the materials used. This section is dedicated to looking at the various types to help you make a quick assessment of the property you either own or are considering buying.

Apart from the period and style of the property, which may carry their own interest problems, there are other factors to watch out for. Unseasoned timber, for example, can make one house deteriorate much quicker than another. Dampness in a wall and an unsuitable choice of material can lead to spalling brickwork, where the surface of the bricks crumbles away due to frost attack.

Of course, a house is very much a hand-made construction. As such, much of its structural stability depends on the quality of the work involved. Two builders working from identical sets of plans can produce two very different buildings. So you must be on the look-out for faulty construction, such as poor quality brickwork and pointing or inadequate or non-existent damp-proofing.

Understanding the type and style of property is critical in trying to analyse possible faults. You must be able to know what you are looking for and recognise trouble when you see it.

Cavity brick wall

Houses built of brick since about 1920 are almost certain to be of cavity wall construction. Except at the corners, only stretchers (lengthwise) bricks will show on the surface of the

The Victorian Villa

■ The Victorian villa evolved steadily throughout the latter part of the 19th century, collecting details from earlier styles while trying to comply with the demands of ever-increasing building regulation legislation.

The roof was traditionally of slate, mined in Wales, the West Country and the Lake District and transported across the country first by coastal shipping and canal and then by railway. Ridges and hips were protected by moulded tiles, often with decorative finials, and valleys were lined with lead or zinc gutters.

Projecting bays with gables above provided extra floor area in the primary rooms, as well as giving the façade additional grandeur.

External walls were generally of solid brick, often laid in ornate banding and intricate patterns with decorative terracotta plaques and other features built in.

Sash windows were still the norm, with lintels and sills generally of stone in better properties; brick soldier arches bridged window openings in many more humble dwellings.

Entrance doors were generally recessed within an open porch, which was often surmounted by a decorative arch or portico.

■ A fireplace in every room was commonplace, so the roofline often boasted at least two chimney stacks, often carrying elaborate terracotta pots. Lead flashings waterproofed the join between the stack and the roof slope.

Internal walls were of brick if loadbearing, or of lath-and-plaster on a sturdy timber framework otherwise. The foundations were also generally of corbelled brickwork; concrete did not come into common use until around 1900.

Floors were generally the suspended timber type to keep damp at bay, although kitchens and sculleries at semi-basement level usually had solid direct-to-earth floors of necessity.

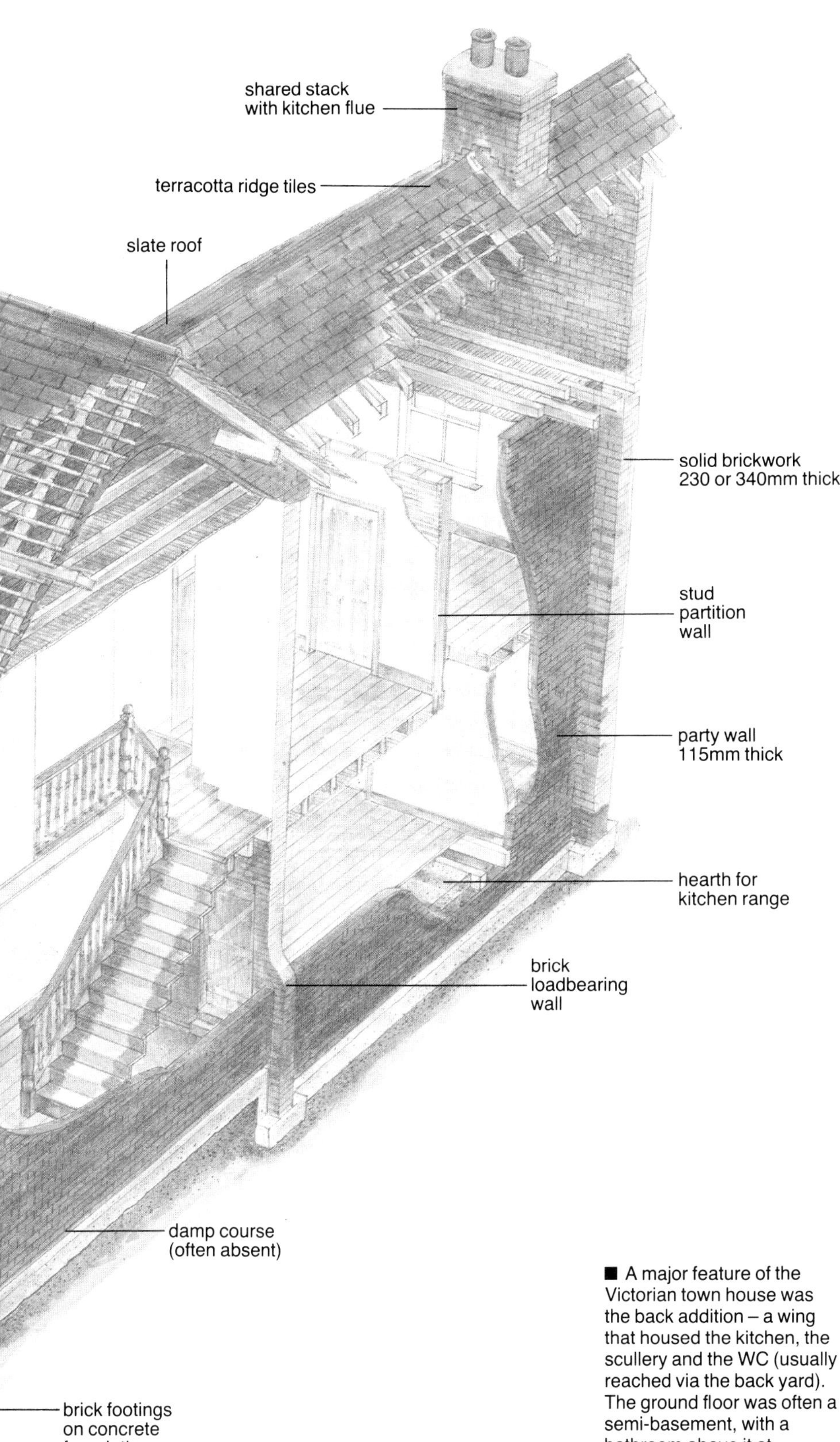

■ A major feature of the Victorian town house was the back addition – a wing that housed the kitchen, the scullery and the WC (usually reached via the back yard). The ground floor was often a semi-basement, with a bathroom above it at mezzanine floor level and a boxroom or staff bedroom above that.

wall. If the walls are rendered or pebbledashed, you will probably be able to tell if it is a cavity wall by measuring its thickness at a doorway or window opening.

Originally cavity walls were about 280mm (11in) thick (not allowing for the internal plaster) and consisted of a 115mm (4½in) thick facing brick outer wall, a 50mm (2in) wide cavity and an inner wall of 115mm (4½in) thick common bricks.

If the house has been fully insulated, it is likely that the cavity has been filled with insulation material. This could be urea-formaldehyde foam (although this is no longer popular because it can cause dampness in a wall), blown loose mineral wool or polystyrene beads. You may be able to see this insulation by looking into the cavity from the loft, if it has not been properly sealed.

In more recent houses, the inner leaf is likely to be constructed with load-bearing insulating blocks. In this case, the wall may not be to the normal full 280mm (11in) width. Furthermore, if the house was built within the last four or five years, it is likely that the cavity would have been filled during the construction with mineral wool insulation batts (slabs).

If built properly, cavity walls suffer few problems. The wide cavity provides sufficient circulation of air to prevent penetrating dampness. Such walls should be warmer than solid walls, particularly if some form of insulation has been installed.

Cracking and bowing can occur (see below) and if damp patches appear on the wall after rain, this can indicate that the wall has been badly built, possibly where mortar has been allowed to fall into the cavity and form a bridge by which damp can cross the wall ties.

Solid brick wall

Solid brick walls are the type found in older houses (pre-1920) and are distinguishable by having headers (half-bricks) as well as stretchers in the face of the wall. This type of brickwork is usually 230mm (9in) thick, although a 340mm (13½in) thickness is also quite common.

You can check the thickness of the walls at door and window openings. But remember to make allowance for the thickness of the internal plaster – usually from 9.5mm (⅜in) to over 25mm (1in) thick.

Old solid walls can give quite a few problems, particularly with regard to dampness. Many were built without a damp-proof course (dpc), which allows dampness to rise from ground level, and foundations were often rudimentary.

Such foundations could be stepped bricks laid directly in a trench, in comparison to the concrete footings used nowadays. If these footing bricks have crumbled due to the length of time they have been underground, then the house may have settled. This is evidenced by out-of-square door and window openings and cracks in outer walls.

However, this kind of settlement often occurred many years ago and has since ceased. So it is quite common to find out-of-true walls, floors, roofs and ceilings in old properties where movement has stopped and there should be no danger of further troubles.

Dressed stone

Houses built of stone will vary both in appearance and durability, according to the type of material used – usually of local origin. It can range from hard stone such as granite and flint to softer material like limestone and sandstone, which has a tendency to crumble.

Dressed stone blocks have a regular outline, rather like brickwork. In high quality houses, the stone can be very carefully cut with a dressed flat face called ashlar. More commonly, it has a split or rough projecting face.

Ashlar stone blocks are often backed with bricks and are plastered on the inside. Dressed stone walls are usually built in courses, like brickwork, and are normally of solid stone, bonded together with lime mortar (which is very soft) and plastered on the inside.

Modern 'stone' houses may be built using pre-cast reconstituted blocks. In this case, the construction and any subsequent problems are exactly the same as with a modern brick cavity wall. The only difference is that, instead of an outer brick skin, stone building blocks are used.

Stone walls frequently suffer from damp problems, while dressed stone has a tendency to crack along the mortar joints, like brickwork.

Natural stone

Many old cottages and houses are built with natural or 'random' stone walls. The material involved is used as found and is not dressed or cut to make uniform blocks. The stones are placed in a random style and the way the individual stones are keyed together depends entirely on the skill of the builder.

It is common for the spaces between the stones on the inner and outer walls to be packed with rubble. It is also quite usual for squarish stones to be selected to form corners – or sometimes dressed stones.

Bricks may be used with natural stone walls where a regular building material is needed,

The 1930s Semi

■ The 1930s semi is a hybrid of many architectural styles, but the features common throughout the boom housebuilding period between the two World Wars were the hipped main roof, the symmetrical pairs of bay windows and the recessed porch. Inside, the biggest change from Victorian times was to an essentially square floor plan, with a rear living room giving onto the garden instead of the bleak back addition looking onto an enclosed yard.

The roof was generally tiled, initially in plain clay tiles but increasingly during the 1930s in curved pantiles. Hips and ridges are finished with plain half-round tiles, with lead still used for flashings and valley gutters.

It is still built in the traditional way with rafters, purlins and struts, allowing loft conversions to be carried out relatively easily.

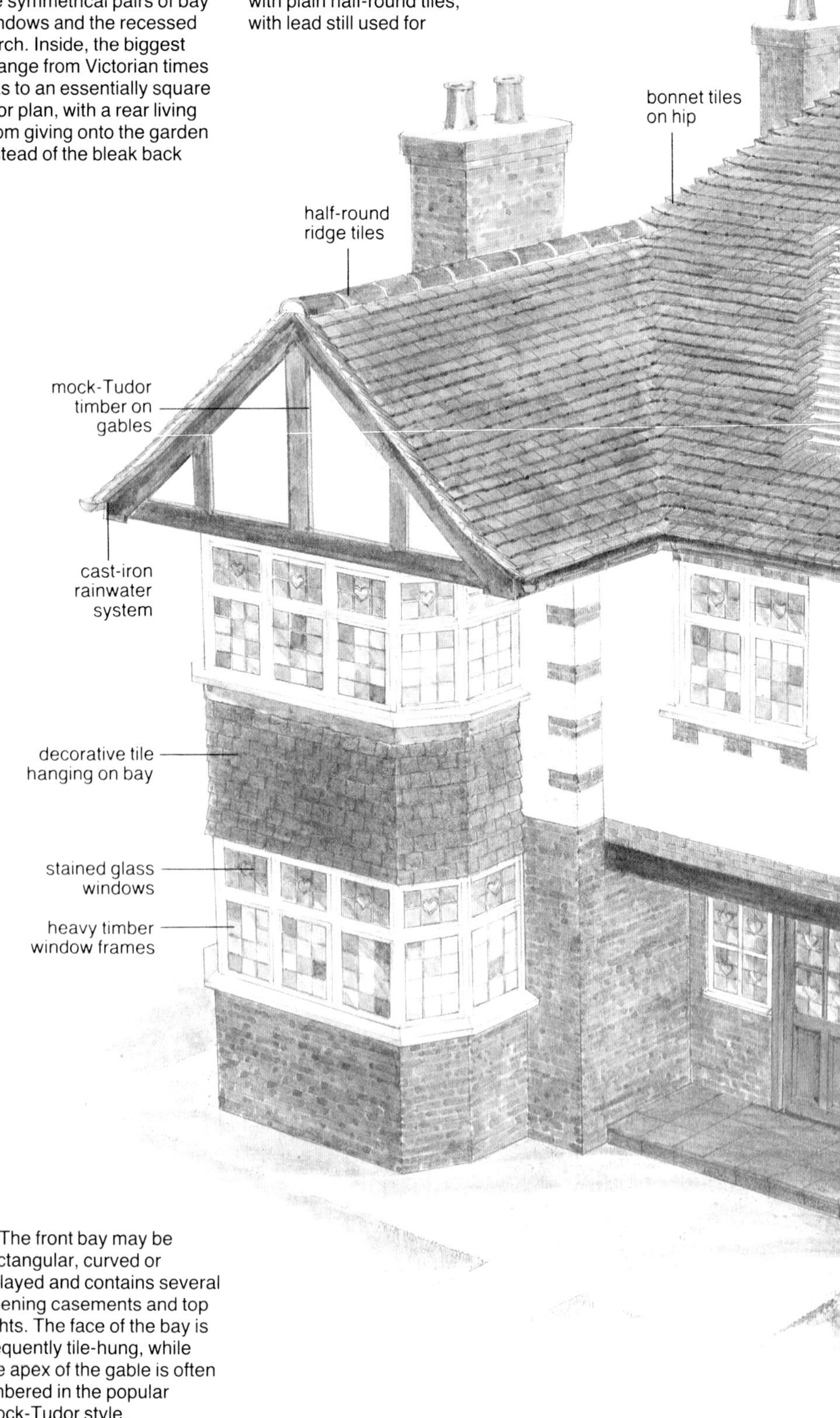

■ The front bay may be rectangular, curved or splayed and contains several opening casements and top lights. The face of the bay is frequently tile-hung, while the apex of the gable is often timbered in the popular mock-Tudor style.

The porch is generally recessed, with a stout front door and glazed side light.

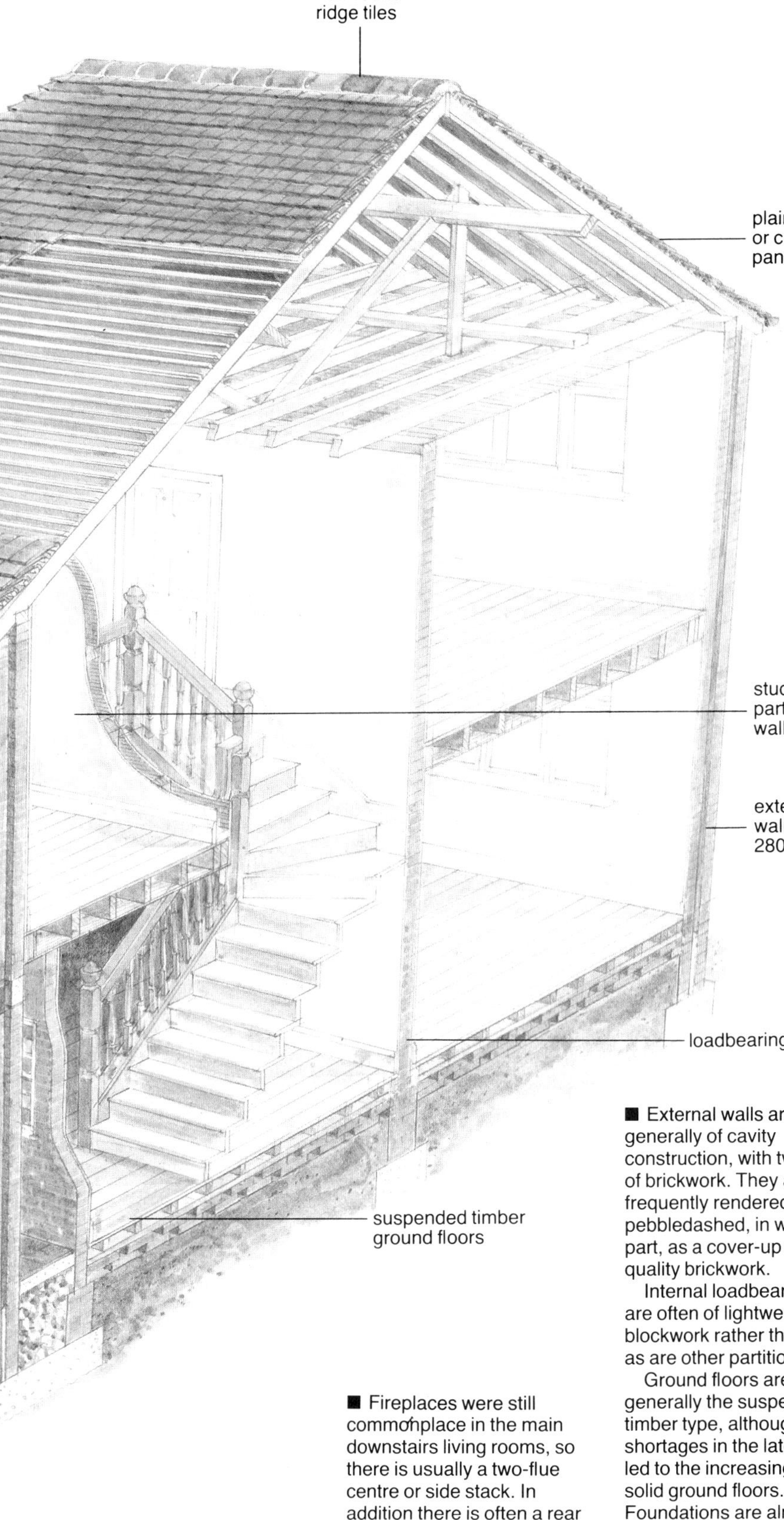

■ Fireplaces were still commonplace in the main downstairs living rooms, so there is usually a two-flue centre or side stack. In addition there is often a rear stack with a single flue for a kitchen boiler.

■ External walls are generally of cavity construction, with two leaves of brickwork. They are frequently rendered or pebbledashed, in whole or in part, as a cover-up for poor-quality brickwork.

Internal loadbearing walls are often of lightweight blockwork rather than brick, as are other partitions.

Ground floors are generally the suspended timber type, although timber shortages in the late 1920s led to the increasing use of solid ground floors. Foundations are almost universally the cast concrete strip type.

such as at corners (quoins) and for chimney stacks. In some cases, such mixtures of building material can look attractive. Often, however, they do not. In this case, it is likely that the building will be rendered with a lime and sand or cement mortar. So if you find a rendered stone cottage, you can reasonably assume that the rendering is hiding areas of brickwork.

Invariably, natural stone buildings were built on a foundation of stepped stones without a dpc. So rising dampness will be a likely problem and a definite candidate for early treatment.

Tile and timber-clad walls

The walls of both old and new houses can be tile-hung or clad with various other materials, such as slates or timber weatherboarding. All of these claddings are applied to make the walls weatherproof and to give protection against driving rain.

In some areas, cladding is a definite style of building. Often the ground floors of older buildings were built of brick and the upper floor was clad with clay tiles or timber weatherboarding. Sometimes you will find the whole building is timber-framed and then clad with tiles or weatherboarding.

In traditional building the tiles were hung on battens nailed to timber studwork, which formed the frame of the walls. These were finished with lath and plaster on the inside. Where weatherboarding was used, this was nailed directly to the studwork. Such walls are usually uninsulated and draughty, so any renovation work should include packing insulation blanket between the studs, protected by a layer of waterproof building paper under the cladding.

In newer buildings, tiles and other cladding can hide various types of wall construction. Where this is not used solely for decoration, such as under a bay window, it can be covering up problem walls, usually those prone to damp penetration during driving rain.

Cladding can be used over concrete block, brick or timber-frame walls, so careful inspection will be required to ascertain the exact type of building construction.

Traditional timber frame

The traditional timbered country cottage has a substantial timber frame and the areas between the timbers may be filled in with a variety of materials.

The beamed Tudor type has a box-frame post-and-panel construction in which main structural timbers, invariably of oak, are pegged together to form a complete loadbearing frame. The spaces between the frame supports are not loadbearing and are simply filled in with bricks, wattle and daub or lath and plaster. Alternatively, the frame could be covered with timber cladding.

This type of construction is popular in the Midlands and Southern England, while in the North and in Wales, the 'cruck' frame is favoured. Here curving matched cruck beams, which rest on the foundations, are taken right to the ridge of the roof. Sometimes the crucks are taken from stone walls and form the roof timbers only. With this type of construction, the walls are usually made of stone or brick and tend to be less substantial than a conventionally built house.

With either of these types of timber-framed building the beams form an essential part of the structure, so cutting a beam away to make an alteration can lead to all sorts of problems. You must bear this in mind if planning alterations to this type of property. It is essential to take the advice of a qualified building surveyor before starting any work.

Modern timber frame

A modern timber-framed house is strong and well-insulated, but has as much in common with a traditional timber frame building as chalk does to cheese! From the outside, it can look exactly like a conventional modern brick, stone or block-built house. Alternatively, it can be wholly or partly tile-hung or weatherboarded.

The main structural frame of this type of house is made of softwood studding – usually of 100 × 50mm (4 × 2in) timber – faced with sheets of plywood, which provide the wall's stiffness and strength.

The spaces behind the plywood sheeting, between the timber studs, are filled with non-combustible blanket insulation and the inside is faced with plasterboard. A moisture and vapour barrier of building paper is fixed to the face of the plywood sheathing and the exterior brick, stone or block cladding is built on the outside with galvanised metal ties screwed to the plywood sheathing to maintain a 50mm (2in) cavity between the two. This cavity ensures that if the brick outer skin becomes wet due to driving rain, any penetrating moisture does not reach the dry inner leaf.

If the exterior is tile-hung or weatherboarded, the cladding may be fixed to insulating building blocks or direct to the face of the timber frame.

Because plasterboard is used for lining a timber-framed home, tapping the inside walls

■ **Below** The roof of a 1960s house is commonly finished in interlocking tiles. Its structure will probably consist of pre-fabricated trusses, making for ease of construction but causing difficulty in creating loft conversions.

External walls are of cavity construction with a blockwork inner leaf, set on concrete trench foundations. Parts may be covered in cladding or tile hanging, or may have a plain rendered finish in part as a contrast to the exposed brickwork.

Internal walls are of blockwork if loadbearing, or timber studding clad with plasterboard otherwise.

Ground floors are almost always solid, with suspended upper floors often covered in chipboard rather than timber planking.

There are generally no chimney stacks or fireplaces, thanks to the widespread use of central heating.

The 1960s House

■ The commonest features of the 1960s house are its low-pitched roof and the widespread use of bland picture windows. Garages are now an integral part of the design, frequently with a flat felted roof linked to a boxy front porch.

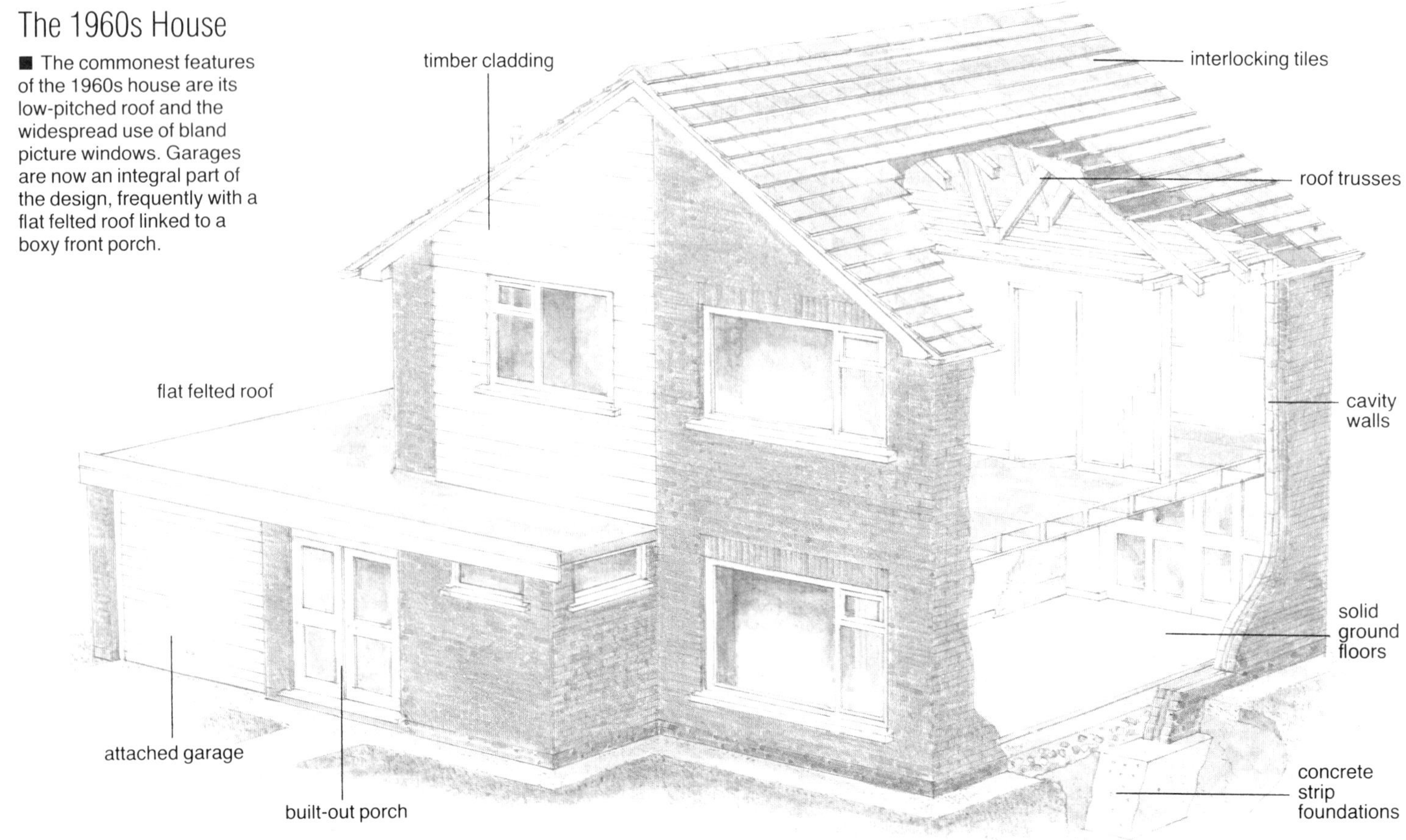

The 1980s House

■ **Above** The 1980s house is in direct line of descent from its 1960s predecessors, with its basically square plan. There is less external adornment for the most part, and more widespread use of woodstains instead of paint on external woodwork.

The roof is covered with interlocking tiles, on a structure of prefabricated trussed rafters with a pitch generally steeper than that of 1960s houses. Gabled and hipped styles are popular.

The external walls are either of cavity construction, with an inner leaf of insulating blockwork and insulation in the cavity, or are load-bearing timber frames with a decorative brick or stone outer skin. The cavity of a timber-frame house is not insulated.

Internal walls are generally of blockwork downstairs and plasterboard on a timber frame upstairs.

Floors are solid or suspended concrete rafts downstairs, and suspended timber upstairs.

and listening for a hollow ring is one indication of this type of construction. Other tell-tale signs to look for are wide timber boards around window and door frame openings, while a visit to the loft may allow you to see the plywood-sheathed timber frame on the gable walls.

In the case of a semi-detached or terraced home, the house is almost certainly timber-framed if the party wall in the loft is plaster-board-faced. The easiest way to establish the type of construction used is at an electrical wall fitting. With the power turned off, remove a light switch plate or socket outlet in an outer wall and unscrew the metal socket box.

In recent years timber-framed houses have earned a mixed reputation due to poor building practices. If correctly built and maintained, however, such properties are economical to buy and to run. There are examples of softwood timber frame houses 150 years old!

WALLS AND THEIR PROBLEMS

Certain basic criteria apply to the walls of a house, whatever its construction, and you should check that your walls meet these requirements. For example, they should be straight both vertically and horizontally. Equally, there should not be any cracks or major deterioration of the building material from which the walls are made.

Make sure, too, that door and window openings are square. You can check this by measuring the diagonals. They will be equal if the frame is square.

Of course, with an old building like a cottage, you can expect the walls to be slightly out of true. But there should not be signs of recent movement, such as fresh cracks. If you are considering a particularly old building – the typical 'country cottage' – it is certainly worth getting it checked out by a fully qualified building surveyor.

Bowing walls

If walls are bowing outwards, this can indicate a serious fault. At ground level, it can mean that the foundations have moved, possibly due to settlement, and therefore underpinning could be required.

If the bowing is in the middle of the wall, then the problem is a weakness in the wall itself, probably caused by an excessive roof load. Either the bricks or mortar used for the walls are not sufficiently substantial or the loading of the roof may be excessive. In the latter case,

The Stone Cottage

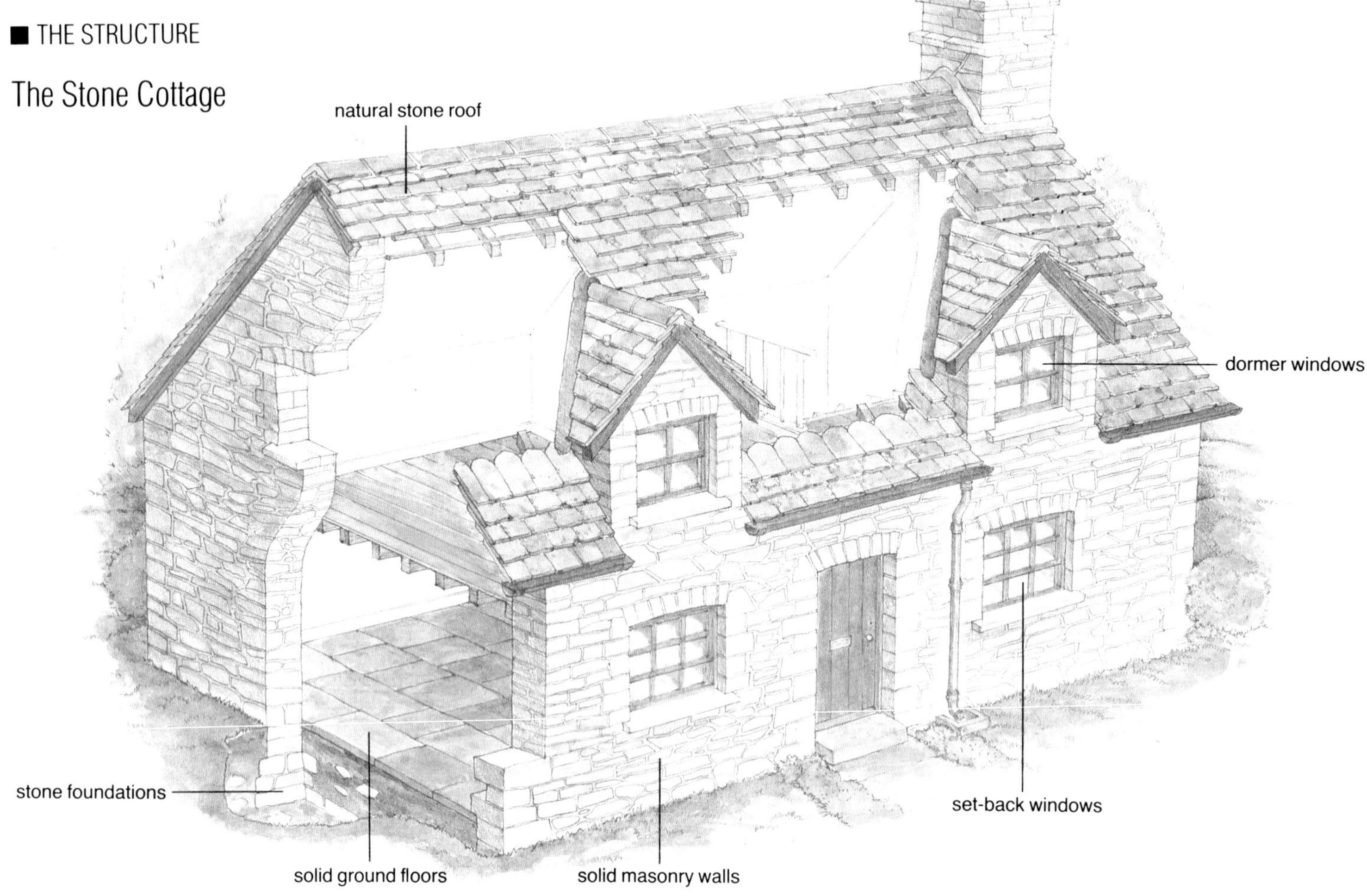

this could be caused by the use of concrete tiles in place of slates, for example.

You can usually detect a bowed wall by sighting along its surface. Because it tends to fall away from the ends of the first-floor joists, another sign is a gap between wall and skirting – or wall and floor – on the first-floor level. Specialist treatment will be required here, perhaps the insertion of steel tension rods at first-floor level or even the complete rebuilding of the wall involved.

If the bowing is outwards at the top of the wall, the problem is likely to be caused by a spread in the roof timbers, perhaps because the ties – that is, the ceiling joists – linking the rafters at loft-floor level or collars linking the rafters in the attic space have failed. This is usually associated with a sag in the ridge, so look for this fault too.

Again, this is a problem about which you must take specialist advice. Partial rebuilding of the roof and walls may be required. This could be a good time to see if such repairs are covered by the building's insurance policy.

Cracking walls

If you discover any cracks in the exterior walls, you must first decide whether the cracks are in the wall itself or are just in any decorative covering on the wall, such as cement rendering.

In the latter case, it is best to chip off a section of the cracked rendering to see if the crack extends to the brick or stonework. Cracks in rendering are not too serious and can be repaired.

Fine hairline cracks that follow the mortar joints in a stepped diagonal line are usually unimportant, especially if they radiate from the corners of door and window openings, which are often weak points in a wall.

Cracks more than about 2mm wide could be significant and may be an indication of more serious structural damage, such as settlement of the foundations, vibration from traffic, mining subsidence, heave caused by tree roots or drying out of the subsoil.

Such cracks could indicate earlier movement which has now stopped. But if they re-open after they have been filled with mortar, this indicates that movement is still taking place. This can be confirmed by fixing small strips of glass, about the size of microscope slides, across the cracks at two or three positions, using an epoxy resin adhesive or putty. The glass should be fixed just clear of the wall. If it cracks after a few weeks or months, this indicates continued movement in the wall.

Seek the advice of a building surveyor as to

■ Traditional cottages come in many styles, but most have several features in common. The external walls are of solid masonry, with small windows set back in the wall face for protection from the weather. Internal walls may also be solid, although lath-and-plaster partitions may also be found. Ground floors are laid direct to earth, and frequently have no damp course.

Rooms upstairs are often housed partly within the steeply-pitched roof, which may be covered in slate, tiles or split natural stone. A sturdy chimney stack completes the structure.

the cause and cure of the problem. If the trouble is due to roots, the offending tree must be removed. If the problem is inadequate foundations, then underpinning is required. This is an expensive job involving excavation of the foundations section by section and the casting of a reinforced concrete beam or other support under them.

The type of crack is often a useful guide to the problem. A stepped diagonal crack along the mortar line, for example, often indicates comparatively harmless general settlement, while a near-vertical line can mean more serious problems like subsidence. And a horizontal line can be a sign of sideways movement and is often accompanied by bowing.

The length and depth of the crack can also help to indicate the seriousness of the problem. Long cracks are usually more serious than short ones. Those that are visible both on the outside and the inside of a wall can be a sign of major structural faults.

The location of the cracks can also have a bearing on the likely cause of the fault. A diagonal crack running down the wall from high up on a corner can indicate subsidence of the foundations at the end of the building. Cracks that start at the base of a wall and converge upwards can indicate localised subsidence between them. A vertical crack down a wall close to a corner can indicate a failure of the roof ties, allowing a section of the wall to fall outwards.

A straight crack between terraced or semi-detached properties can be a sign of subsidence, while cracks along the join between a building and an extension can indicate inadequate bonding of the new wall to the old. Another cause can be a failure in the foundations of the extension. A vertical crack down a wall containing a chimney can indicate problems with the flue, possibly due to the drying of the internal brickwork and damage to the flue lining. The flue may need to be rebuilt.

Bulging walls

If you suspect a bulging wall, check first that it is not bowed. In the case of a bulge, this is normally where the wall is rendered and the rendering is coming away. Tap the affected area to see if it sounds hollow and test the rendering over a wider area to ascertain the extent of the problem. Look also for cracks in the rendering.

There is always the danger that rainwater will get behind the rendering, making the wall damp and the problem worse. The rendering should be chipped away and the wall re-

The Timber-framed Cottage

■ Old cottages, especially in country areas, may have a timber main frame infilled with stone, brick or cob under a thatched or stone roof. Their restoration is a major challenge, even to the experienced craftsman.

rendered after being allowed to dry out. This is certainly a job for a specialist if a large area of repair is involved.

Damp walls

Dampness in exterior walls can be due to penetrating or rising damp – or it could be due to condensation.

You can eliminate or confirm condensation by taping a piece of aluminium foil to the wall. If water droplets form on the surface of the foil, condensation is the problem. This can be reduced by improving ventilation and heating. Water droplets on the underside of the foil indicate that there is dampness in the wall.

If the dampness is near the bottom of the wall, perhaps shown by a line of white efflorescence along the lower part on the outside and damp and peeling wallpaper inside, the problem is rising damp due to the absence of a damp-proof course (dpc) – or a faulty one. Old brick or stone properties are most commonly affected.

Look for the dpc, which is visible as a thin black line between brick courses. If you find one, make sure it is at least 150mm (6in) above ground level and is not covered by soil. If there is no sign of a dpc, you may have to have one put in to keep damp at bay.

■ Many old buildings have rudimentary stone or brick foundations (1). By Georgian times more solid foundations were used, with solid exterior walls faced with stone (2). The Victorians favoured solid brickwork, with timber ground floors (3). The brick cavity wall prevents damp penetrating through solid masonry (4). Later insulating blockwork replaced the inner leaf, and the cavity was often filled with insulation(5). Timber-frame construction features insulated load-bearing wall panels (6).

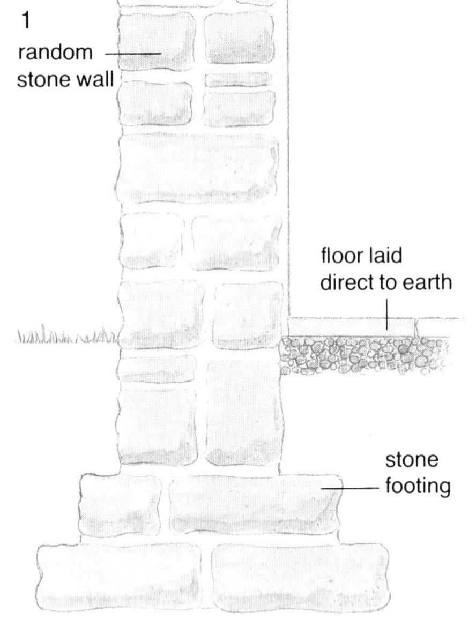

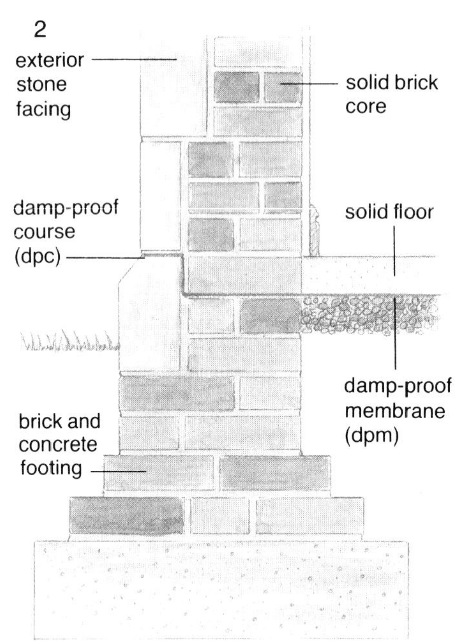

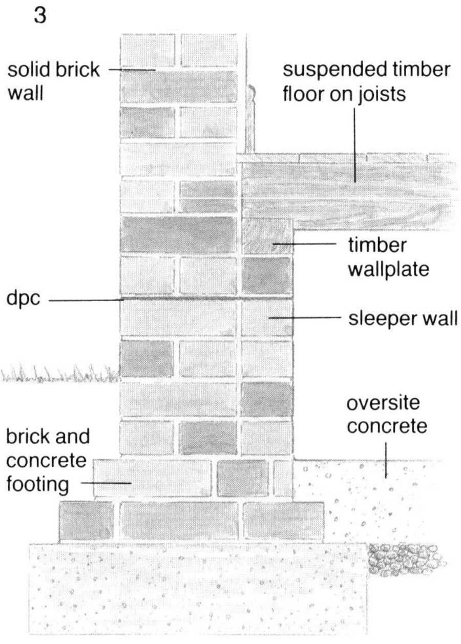

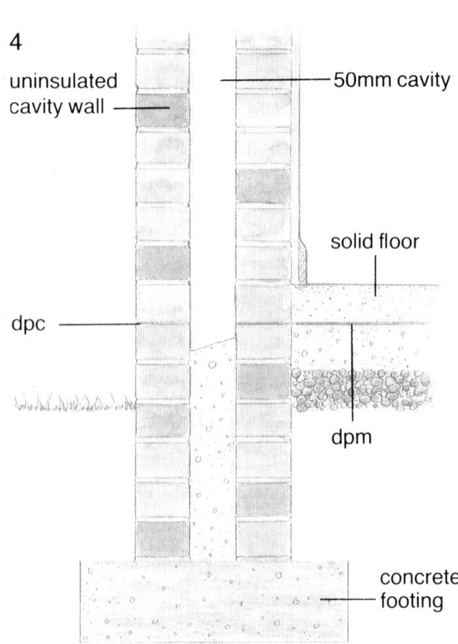

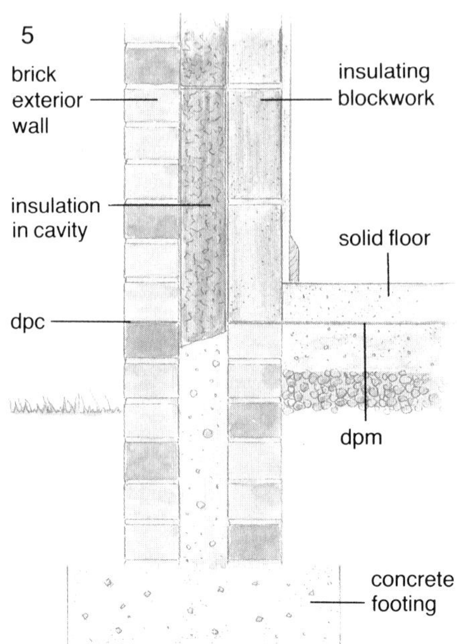

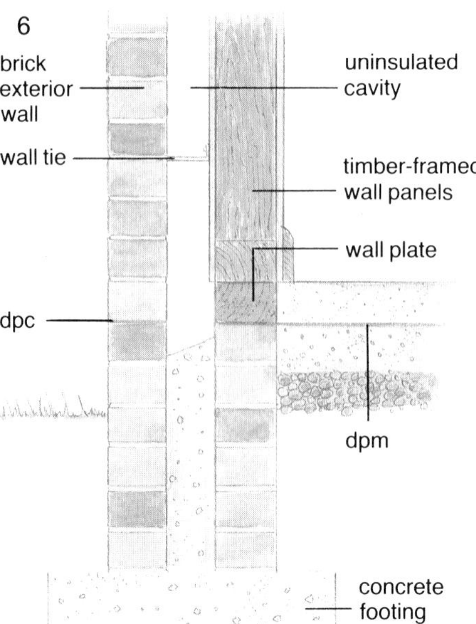

A conventional dpc can be inserted in a slot sawn in the bottom part of the wall. Alternatively a chemical dpc can be injected into the masonry. This work is usually best left to a specialist, although it is possible to insert a chemical dpc yourself.

Penetrating damp is usually a problem with older brick or stone-built properties with solid walls and will show up worse after heavy rain. It can occur at any height. Look first for a leaking waste pipe or rainwater downpipe and repair the fault where necessary.

Isolated damp patches are easily cured by painting the outside of the wall with a clear silicone water-repellent sealer. Larger areas, on the other hand, may require rendering, or a cladding, like weatherboarding, could be fitted.

Rotting wood

With outer walls, rotting wood is obviously only a problem where you have a timber-clad or timber-framed building. The rot-affected timber must be removed and replaced with new wood, treated with preservative. If the rot is extensive, it is probably advisable to get a timber specialist to make the repairs.

Missing claddings

Whether tiles, slates, timber or plastic are used for cladding, any missing sections should be replaced without delay or serious damp problems and wood rot could occur.

The damage could be the result of storms or other severe weather conditions. More likely, however, it is due to general deterioration, such as corrosion of the fixing nails (called nail sickness in the trade). So be prepared for the fact that even a small amount of damage could indicate major renovation work.

Fixing up cladding is a task that a competent handyman could quite easily tackle. If, however, large areas are involved, it may be better to call in a builder or specialist contractor.

THE ROOF STRUCTURE

There are three aspects of the roof structure to consider – the shape, the carcassing framework (which you can see from inside the loft space), and the external roof covering.

The roof shape

Basically roofs are either sloping (pitched) or flat, the latter having just a slight slope to throw water towards the gutters. The majority of houses have pitched roofs, since these perform best in potentially wet climates.

Flat roofs are cheaper and easier to build and

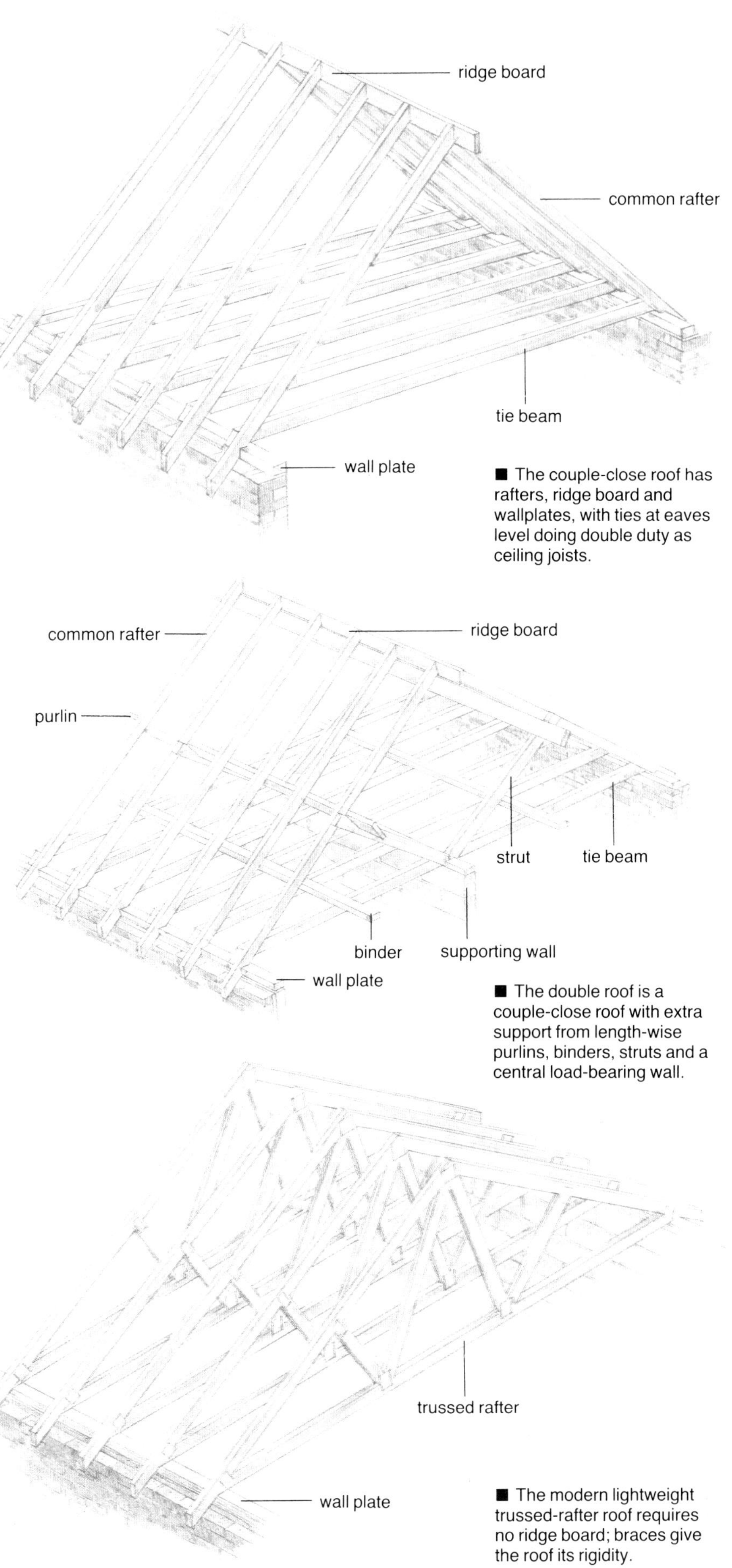

■ The couple-close roof has rafters, ridge board and wallplates, with ties at eaves level doing double duty as ceiling joists.

■ The double roof is a couple-close roof with extra support from length-wise purlins, binders, struts and a central load-bearing wall.

■ The modern lightweight trussed-rafter roof requires no ridge board; braces give the roof its rigidity.

tend to be used mainly for garages, home extensions, porches and some low-cost homes. Water does tend to collect on this type, however, and leaks are common. If you have a flat-roofed house, be prepared to spend quite heavily on maintenance.

The most common pitched type is the gable-end, where two sloping roofs meet at a central ridge which runs the full length of the roof. At each end a gable wall is built up to the ridge. On terraced houses it is common to have continuous pitched roofing running from one end of the terrace to the other.

With a hipped roof, the ends as well as the sides of the roof slope to the ridge, and the roof sections come down to the gutter level – that is, the eaves – all round. With a jerkin roof, the hipped ends do not come down as low as the eaves and a part gable wall is formed.

A mansard roof has a double pitch on each side of the ridge, thus forming a roof with two distinct slopes. Gables are formed on the end walls. With a mansard hipped roof, the ends as well as the sides have a double pitch forming a mansard roof all round the building.

A type of roof very rarely found on houses, but quite common on sheds and garages, is the monopitch. Here the roof slopes from one side to the other. Lean-to roofs are found where one building, usually an extension, joins on to a larger building. The conventional lean-to is a monopitch type, but lean-to hip roofs are also found where the sides of the roof are inclined in the same way as the main roof section.

Carcassing framework

Flat roofs are usually formed by timber joists spanning two side walls with a decking of chipboard or plywood on which a weather-proofed surface such as mineral felt is laid. The basic problem here is damage or deterioration to the covering surface. If left for a long period without treatment, the resulting water leaks will cause crumbling chipboard decking and rotting joists.

Many methods of building pitched roofs have developed over the years. Cruck, single and double rafter roofs are found in very old houses and cottages. These roofs were carefully made using substantial timbers and, while it is possible to replace damaged wood, it is usually out of the question to contemplate a loft conservation in historic roofs of this type.

From about the 19th century up to comparatively recent times, the traditional method of building ridged roofs with rafters supported by purlins and struts was used. With this type, it is possible to move the struts to allow for loft conversions, although the work must be carried out by specialists.

Such conversion is also possible with a trussed purlin roof. This type already has a clear space in the loft since there are no sloping struts obstructing the floor area.

A collared roof is also built with rafters butting on to a central ridge. In this case, however, there are no trussed purlins. The rafters are supported by collar ties which brace the rafters quite high in the roof to give extra height to bedroom ceilings. In a roof of this type, there is usually insufficient headroom to allow for a loft conversion.

Modern houses are usually built with trussed rafters, where the trusses are prefabricated in a factory. There is no ridge board and no purlins. Diagonal braces are nailed (using metal plates) between the underside of the rafters and the top of the ceiling joists and the tiling battens are nailed directly to the upper surface of the trussed rafters. This type of roof is not suitable for a loft conversion because the trussed rafters cannot be modified.

ROOF COVERINGS

Depending on the age and style of the property and the type of roof construction, there is a whole range of covering materials you may find. So check what type you have, since the inherent problems can vary widely from one material to another.

Plain tiles

These are sometimes used on new houses, but are more commonly found on older properties. Usually made of clay, but sometimes of sand-faced concrete, they have two projections at the top (called nibs) for hooking over the tiling battens. To form a watertight seal, each row is overlapped by two rows of tiles above it.

In very old houses, peg tiles are common. Here hardwood pegs are used in place of nibs to hold the tiles in place on the battens.

Ideally a plain tile roof will be lined with bitumen felt to prevent draughts and water leaks into the loft space. Watch out for cracked, broken and spalling tiles. These indicate that re-roofing is required.

Interlocking tiles

These tiles are widely used in modern housing and for re-roofing, especially as a replacement for old slate roofing. As the name suggests, the sides of the tiles – and sometimes the heads – interlock. Laid in single layers, the tiles have nibs which hook over widely spaced battens.

■ The roof coverings on older properties show far greater variety than is found on modern buildings, and often reflect locally available materials such as thatch or slate (top). Even handmade clay tiles differ widely in colour and texture from one area to another (centre). Only with the advent of the machine-made and mass-produced tile of today have roofs tended to monotonous uniformity.

Usually, alternate rows of tiles are nailed to the battens to prevent high winds lifting them.

A fairly recent roof of this type will be lined with underfelt to eliminate draughts in the loft space. Old roofs with many missing, cracked or broken tiles will need re-roofing.

Slate

Natural and modern imitation slates are the other common type of covering found. Although very satisfactory when sound, slates can give problems when they get old. Nail sickness causes them to slip out of place, while natural ageing will give rise to delamination.

Slates may be nailed to battens or, in better quality housing, the roof may be boarded and the slates nailed directly to the boards. Old roofs are rarely lined, which causes the loft space to be draughty, dirty and cold. If you are intending re-roofing, you can fit underfelt to cure this problem.

It is worth re-roofing with natural or imitation slates to maintain the original style of the property. In recent years it has been popular to replace an old slate roof with interlocking concrete tiles. These often spoil the look of the house and are frequently out of keeping with adjacent ones.

Other coverings

There are several other coverings available for roofs. Pantiles, which are usually made of clay, are a form of interlocking tile and are similarly laid in single layers. They also have the same faults as interlocking tiles.

Shingles are made of wood, usually cedar, nailed in place to battens in the same formation as plain tiles. Untreated cedar shingles have a life of about 30 years, but if pressure-treated with preservative when new they should last more than 50 years. To maintain air circulation around the shingles, underfelt is not used.

They can be treated with cedar wood preservative from time to time to maintain their original colour. Without treatment, they will weather to a silvery grey after a few years.

Thatch has tremendous visual appeal but is costly to maintain and is also a fire risk. True reed, which is expensive, can last for 50 or 60 years. Combed wheat straw, often called wheat reed, will give an effective life of 30 or 40 years, while ordinary long straw will generally last only 15 to 20 years.

Make sure the roof is closely wrapped in small-mesh wire netting to keep the birds out. Fortunately thatchers are still available in most rural areas where thatch cottages are found, since this is definitely not a job for the amateur.

Corrugated roofing sheets, which come in metal, fibre/cement or plastic, are mainly confined to use on outbuildings, although occasionally they are used for houses. Although functional, if found on a house they would be better replaced with another type of roofing material more sympathetic to the surroundings.

Roofing felt is widely used for waterproofing flat roofs. Usually three layers are used. The first is nailed down to the roof boards, while the second and third are bonded to the first using hot bitumen. The surface is liable to blister and crack and after about 15 years the roof may need to be re-felted.

Asphalt can be used as a covering and is

felt verge drip
cap sheet
second felt layer
first felt layer
angle fillet
verge drip batten
decking
firring
return joist
fascia board
solid bridging
joist
felt eaves drip

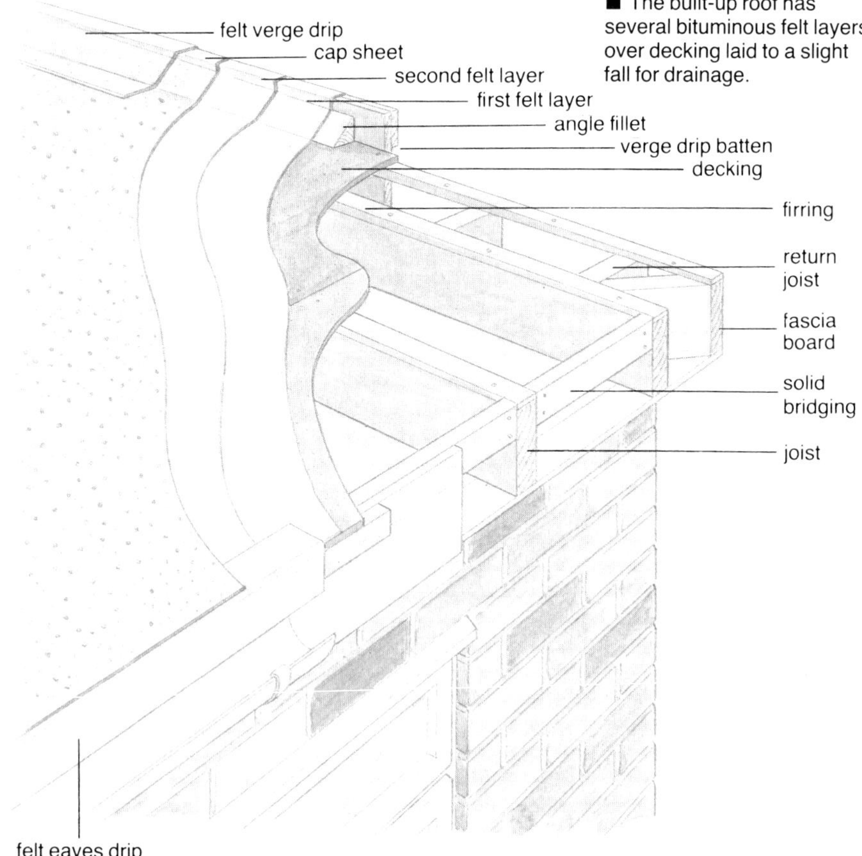

■ The built-up roof has several bituminous felt layers over decking laid to a slight fall for drainage.

cover flashing
lead tack
drip
angle fillet
cover flashing
overcloak
wooden roll
undercloak
sarking felt
overcloak
splash lap
anti-capillary groove
undercloak
parapet wall
box gutter

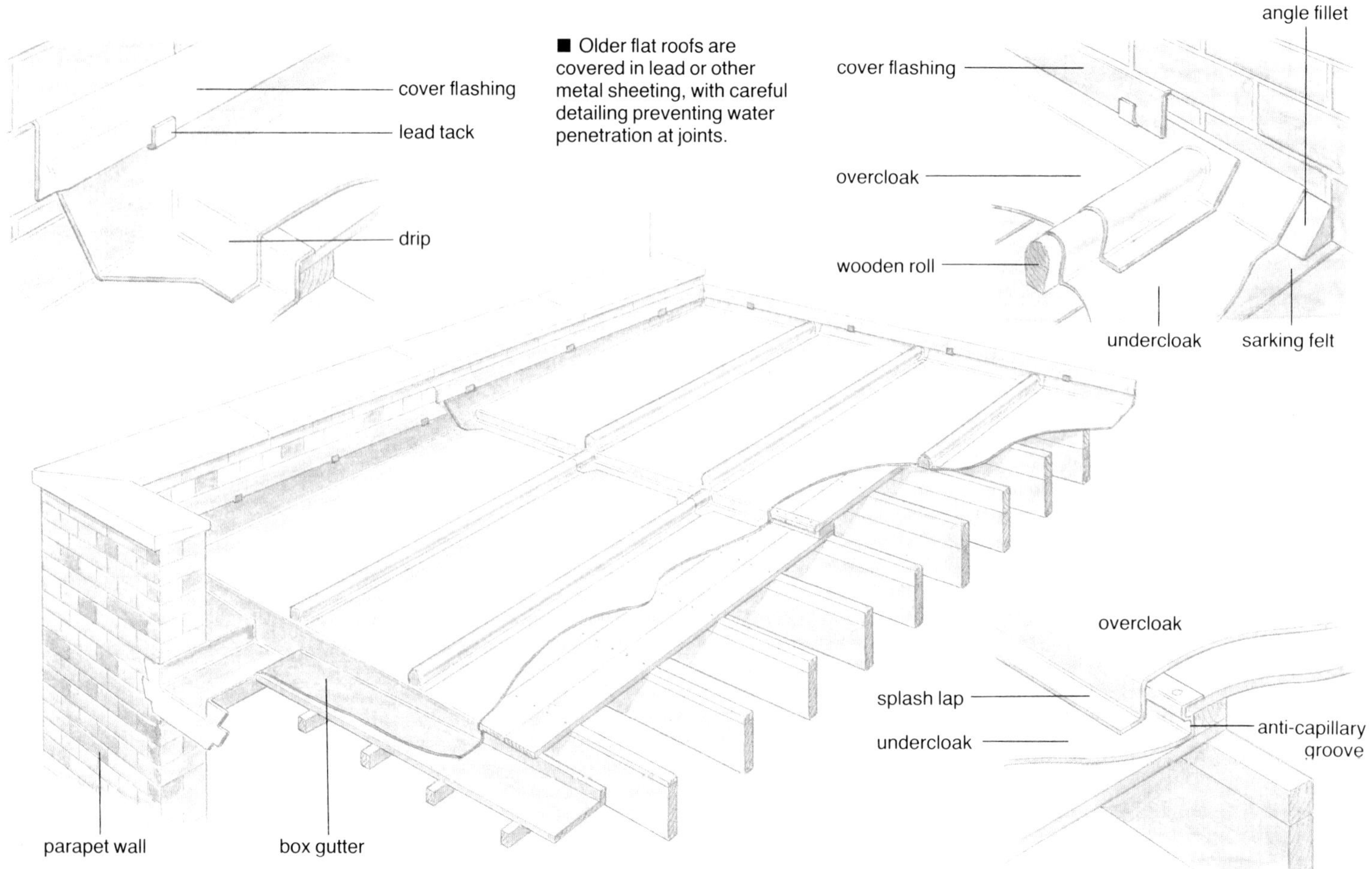

■ Older flat roofs are covered in lead or other metal sheeting, with careful detailing preventing water penetration at joints.

normally applied in a layer about 19mm thick over underfelt. Working with hot asphalt is a skilled job. Although cracks, if they form, can be repaired with cold mastic, it is best to get a flat-roof specialist to carry out any major repairs with this material.

ROOFS AND THEIR PROBLEMS

Whatever type of roof you have or find on a property you are considering buying, there are some basic problems you should be aware of and look out for. They will, of course, depend on the construction itself and the covering used.

Sagging roof

If the roof is sagging, this could indicate serious problems, unless the property is very old and the original cause has settled down.

If the ridge is straight and the sag is confined to a saucer-like depression in the roof covering, it is likely that the trouble is the result of poor construction of the part of the roof. Probably there are insufficient purlins to support the rafters or the strutting is insufficient. It is also possible that the rafters are too weak, so check that they have not rotted or been severely attacked by woodworm.

It may be possible to strut the roof to prevent the trouble getting any worse. In some cases it may even be possible to jack the roof back into line before re-strutting it.

If the ridge itself is sagging, and perhaps the roof covering too, then the trouble is likely to be more serious – and so more expensive to put right. It may well be that the roof timbers have been affected by rot or woodworm attack. Examination in the loft should reveal the extent of this problem.

If there is no sign of rot or insect attack, then look for possible insecure fixing of the roof timbers, which would allow the roof to splay outwards, or even movement outwards of the top of the wall. The latter is particularly serious. By dropping a plumb line down from the top of the wall at the eaves, you may be able to highlight the problem, which may well have been evident when you checked the exterior walls for bowing.

Hogged roof

This is a fault common to terraced and semi-detached houses. The roof falls away from the party wall, leaving the roof tiles or slates along that wall sticking up, with large gaps under them. It is due to settlement of the foundations and, as long as the settlement has ceased, should not give cause for concern.

Rippling

Slight undulations along the ridge are sometimes difficult to spot, but they are a sign that the rafters have been spaced too far apart. If the rippling is in the roof surface, this also indicates that the rafters are too widely spaced, combined in this case with the tiling battens being weak.

A check in the loft space will confirm these faults and reveal whether rot or insect attack in the roof timbers is the cause. In the latter case, take steps to eliminate the trouble. Not much can be easily done about over-wide rafter spacing and there is no need to do so unless the trouble gets worse.

Deteriorating coverings

If tiles or slates have cracked, slipped, delaminated, spalled or are missing over a wide area, you have no option but to recover the roof. This is expensive, but does give you a chance to line the roof with underfelt, which will make the loft space drier, cleaner and warmer.

As a temporary solution, you can apply an all-over treatment, involving coating the roof with three layers of heavy duty bitumen liquid reinforced with glass fibre fabric membrane. This is much cheaper than re-roofing and can extend the roof life for 10 to 15 years. But it is not attractive to look at and eventually re-roofing will be required.

Faulty flashing

Flashings, which may be of metal (usually lead) or cement mortar, waterproof the joints where the roof joins brickwork such as a house wall or chimney stack. Metal flashings corrode and cement flashings crack and pull away from the wall. In both cases, water can trickle down behind the flashing, resulting in damp patches on upstairs ceilings or walls.

Temporary repairs can be made quite easily and cheaply with self-adhesive metal-backed flashing strip. Ideally, new lead flashings should be fitted in the long term.

Rotting wood

Barge boards, fascias and soffits are made of wood and as such, are prone to damage and rotting from the elements. So check regularly that all the timbers round the perimeter of the roof are sound.

They are fairly easy to replace, although highly decorative barge boards can be expensive to recreate using new timber. The job will usually involve erecting scaffolding, which is expensive, or using a platform tower; you cannot carry out the work safely from a ladder.

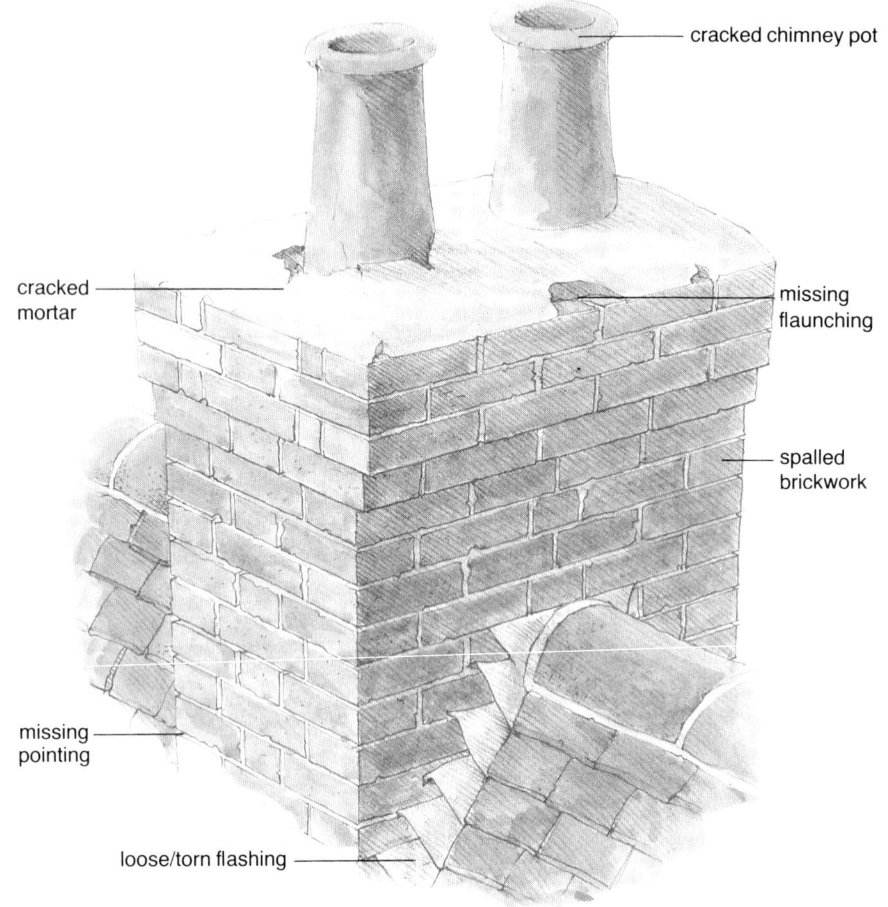

CHIMNEYS AND THEIR PROBLEMS

Chimney stacks are particularly vulnerable to damage, being exposed to the elements and also to attack from the inside by flue gases.

Use binoculars to examine the chimney stack from ground level. If it is leaning and still being used, you will have to have it rebuilt. If it is obsolete, you could have it capped, which would be cheaper. If the mortar joints in the brickwork are crumbling away, these must be repointed. This could be an expensive job if the stack is difficult to reach and a lot of scaffolding is required for safe access.

If chimney pots are cracked, leaning or missing and the flues are still being used, they must be replaced. The mortar (or flaunching) in which they are bedded must also be replaced to ensure that rainwater is thrown clear of the top of the stack.

Chimney pot faults are likely to indicate problems with the stack itself and with the flue lining, which may need to be replaced if the flue is still used. You can fit some types yourself, which will save some expense.

If the flues are unused, fit capping terminals to the chimney pots or remove the pots and fit capping slabs and airbricks to give ventilation to the flues to keep them dry. At the same time, the chimney stack can be reduced in height if it is in poor condition.

■ Chimney stacks are very exposed to the elements and can suffer from a variety of faults (above), including cracked mortar – known as flaunching – round the pots and defective pointing on the stack itself, both of which can allow water to penetrate and cause damp in the stack and rot in the roof timbers.

As the deterioration continues, the stack may start to lean (far left) or to lose any protective rendering it once had (left).

The other major weak spot is the junction between the stack and the roof slope, which is traditionally waterproofed with stepped lead flashings (right). These can be lifted and torn by high winds, or may simply become porous with age. Their failure again allows water penetration.

STRUCTURAL TIMBERS AND THEIR PROBLEMS

All timber in the house must be inspected for wood rot and insect attack. There should be no visible signs of active wood rot in any house, regardless of its age.

In an old property it is common to find evidence of insect attack that has probably long since died out. This will be nothing to worry about if the roof or walls are not sagging, bowing or showing other signs of weakness.

In such houses, the timbers were of sufficient size to allow for a certain amount of insect attack without causing problems – unless, of course, the attack is very severe.

Insect attack

There are several different species of wood-boring insects that can infest structural timbers. They all eat through wood and leave round exit holes in the surface as they emerge.

In many cases attacks will have died out. But active infestation can be spotted by inspecting the timbers (ideally between April and August when the beetles are active) to look for fresh bore dust under and around holes. Clean timber inside the exit holes also indicates they are recently bored.

If there is an active attack, the timber must be treated with woodworm-killing fluid. At the same time affected floorboards, joists and roof timbers should be tested for weakness and any badly weakened timbers should be replaced. This is really a job for wood treatment specialists and, depending on the extent of the damage, it could be expensive work.

Wood rot

Basically, there are two types of wood rot that affect structural timbers – wet and dry. The latter is the more serious.

Wet rot affects timbers in wet, cold environments and turns it dark brown so that it crumbles away when touched or probed. Often cracks form and these will be along the grain.

Dry rot also affects damp timber, especially where ventilation is poor. Once established, the timber can take on a shrunken, dry, cracked appearance, hence the name dry rot. Affected timber develops deep cracks across the grain, while the fungus itself produces grey conductive strands that can even penetrate walls to affect timber a considerable distance from the site of the initial attack.

A distinctive musty smell accompanies a dry rot attack. Under floors, in roof spaces and in cellars you may discover fluffy cotton-wool type growths and pancake-like fruiting bodies with reddish-brown centres.

All affected wood must be removed back to sound timber, brickwork must be treated with dry rot fluid and replacement timber must be treated with wood preservative. Repairs involving ceilings, floors and walls could be extensive – and therefore expensive.

■ Wood-boring insects such as woodworm and the house longhorn beetle can do considerable damage to structural timbers (left), especially if the infestation is not treated. However, the damage is rarely anything like as severe as that caused by dry rot (below left), which can completely destroy timber in time.

0710-G50Y KERCHIEF
1010-G50Y SOFT FERN
2010-G50Y SATYR
ROOF LIGHT DETAILS
Scale: 1:5/1:20
Note:
Installation for Type H flashing is similar,
see page 19
No. 3: 1600mm
No. 2,8: 1400mm
No. 4,5: 1180mm
No. 1,6,7: 980mm
No. 9: 700mm
CHECK MEMBRANE WITH DRAWING A176.
1:20
No. 7,8: 1340mm
No. 4: 1140mm
No. 9,6: 550mm
60-80mm
1:20
1:5
20-40mm
20-40mm
70mm
1:5
can conveniently remove
Lower cover part (pleated apron)
Easy to install
2. Fitting the lower portion of the tile
the high points of the tile
before fitting the lead flashing.
3. Fitting the upper portion. To support
the cut tiles at the top of the window,
a triangular-shaped compensating part
is provided. This is placed on the flat
aluminium portion of the top cover to
support the tile and keep it at the
same angle as the full tiles.
A tile support.
Top/bottom section
Lower cover part with lead flashing
RANGE
741 FH
742 FH Pebble Grey
651 FH Cream

RENOVATING THE EXTERIOR

The obvious place to start work on renovating your house is with the exterior. There is little point in tackling internal improvements if the outer envelope of the house lets in the wind and rain. A top-to-toe overhaul is the solution, working from the roof downwards via the exterior walls, doors and windows, and culminating in a check of the building's resistance to dampness rising from below.

Roofs and Guttering

CHECKING THE ROOF

It is obviously vital to have a sound, well-maintained roof. If it is allowed to deteriorate, it will soon let in rain. This in turn will lead to damp patches on internal walls and ceilings and ruined decorations.

If that is not bad enough, by allowing a leak to go unattended it will not be long before the structure of the roof starts to decay, possibly leading to dry rot in the roof timbers and wall plates. This could spread over a wide area of the fabric of the house, necessitating very expensive remedial work by a specialist contractor to put things right.

The roof could also become a danger to passers-by. Injury to a third party caused by a falling slate or tile may result in legal proceedings, so make sure that the risk is covered by your household insurance. The possible consequences could otherwise be very serious. So it is important to make sure the roof is completely sound before you make any effort to repair and restore the rest of the property.

With roofwork, it is definitely a question of prevention being better than cure. If you can reposition a slate while it is only partially dislodged before it slides out completely – or replace a tile that is only cracked and not completely broken – you will prevent the formation of brown damp patches on ceilings and internal walls that will not only spoil interior decorations but also be difficult to cure.

The main problem with doing your own repairs is the danger of working at a height, which can be off-putting. Safety is a very important consideration. But even if you would not dream of working on the roof, being able to spot potential problems and knowing how they should be repaired will enable you to brief a tradesman thoroughly and not be persuaded to accept substandard work. It is a sad fact of life that many householders are completely ignorant of what work is carried out on their roofs. As a result, roofing contractors include a fair share of 'cowboy' operators.

Knowing how your roof is constructed is the first step to being able to keep it in good condition, whether or not you carry out the repair work yourself. And carrying out regular checks on its condition is a practice you would do well to use. You can do this from ground level using a pair of binoculars.

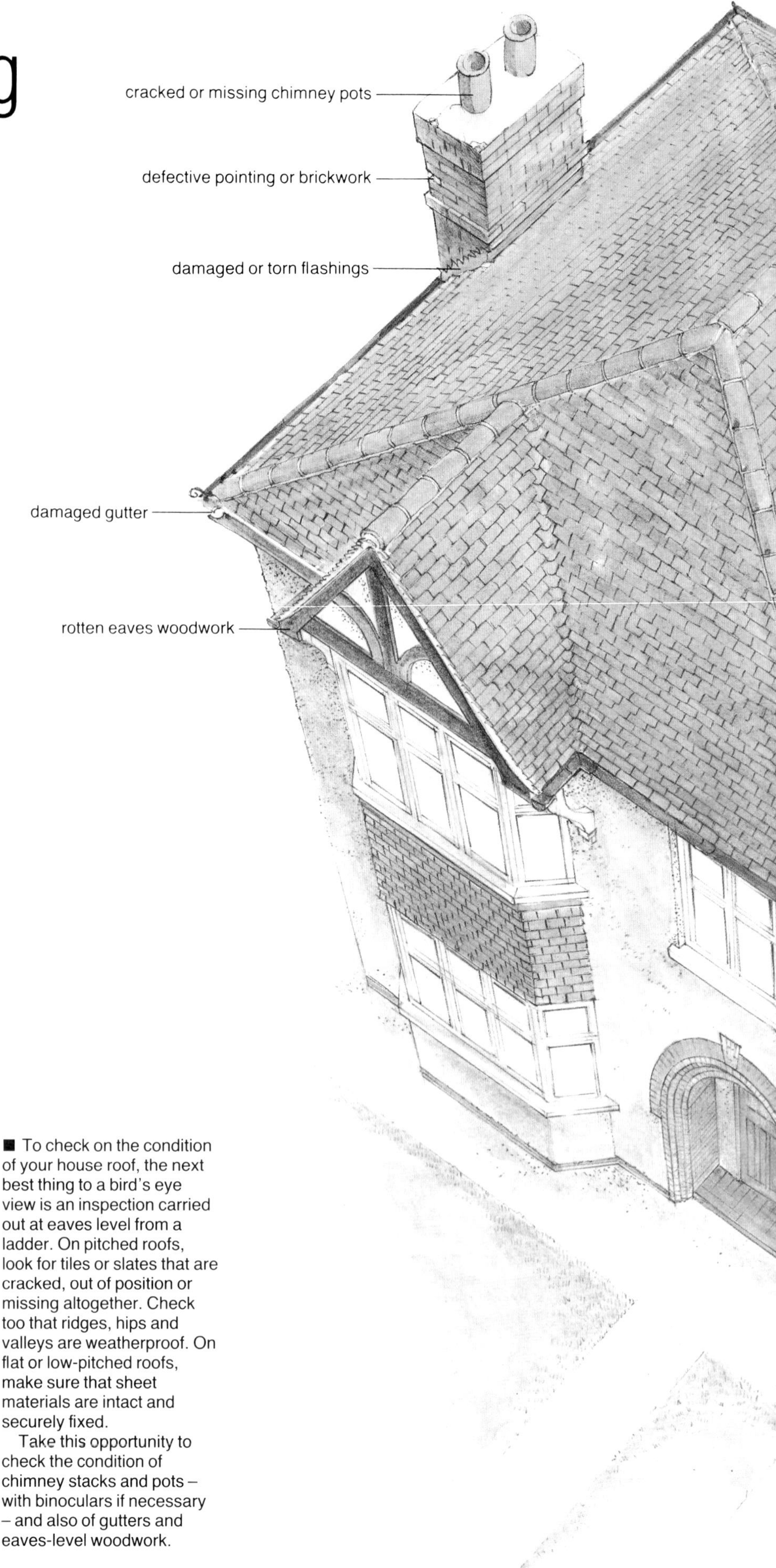

■ To check on the condition of your house roof, the next best thing to a bird's eye view is an inspection carried out at eaves level from a ladder. On pitched roofs, look for tiles or slates that are cracked, out of position or missing altogether. Check too that ridges, hips and valleys are weatherproof. On flat or low-pitched roofs, make sure that sheet materials are intact and securely fixed.

Take this opportunity to check the condition of chimney stacks and pots – with binoculars if necessary – and also of gutters and eaves-level woodwork.

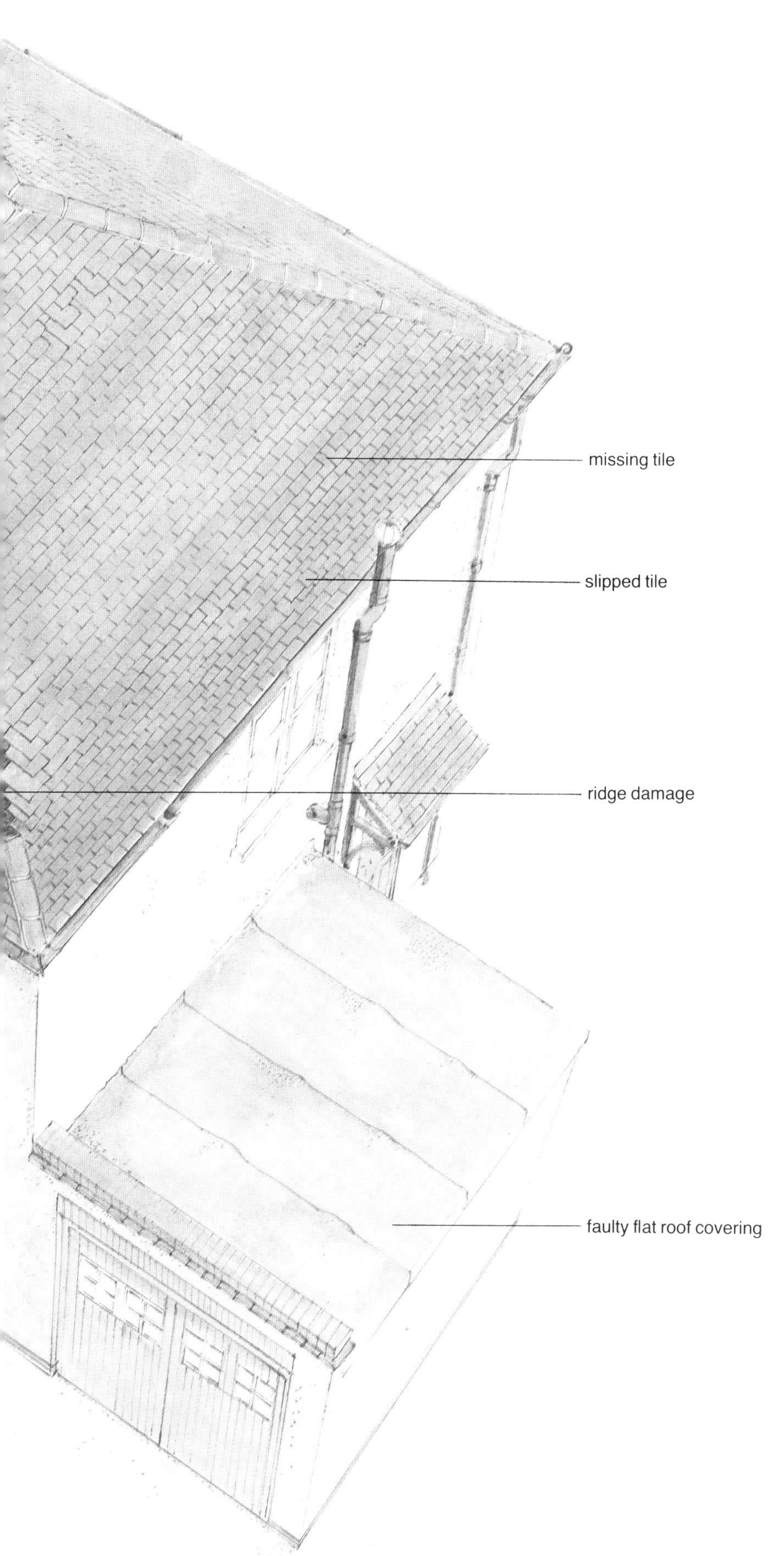

Look for missing and cracked slates and tiles and watch for damaged or crumbling pointing in chimney stacks and parapet walls. Check also for cracked or leaning chimney pots. The flaunching around the pots should also be free of cracks and not obviously loose.

Flashing, which may be of lead or zinc sheet or cement mortar, is used to waterproof the joints where a roof abuts adjacent brickwork – possibly a house wall, parapet wall or chimney stack. This frequently cracks or pulls away from the brickwork, allowing rainwater to trickle down behind it and cause damp patches on internal walls or ceilings.

Check also that your chimney stacks are not leaning. If they are, you will need specialist advice since rebuilding a chimney stack is definitely not a DIY job!

On a wet day, it will pay to go outside and look at the guttering in case there are any leaks. These often occur at outflows and at joints between gutter sections. Water dripping over the edge of a gutter can indicate that it is blocked by debris or that moss or other vegetation is growing there.

Also on a wet day, or shortly after rain, go into the loft space and look for leaks. These will highlight cracked or missing slates and tiles and possibly cracks in flashings and in lead or zinc-lined valley gutters.

As well as knowing enough to be able to tell a tradesman the extent of the trouble, it is helpful to know the names of the various roof components in case you have to brief someone to carry out the repairs.

HOW ROOFS ARE MADE

It is best to start with a knowledge of roof construction so you will understand how your roof is made and therefore will be better able to carry out repairs on it yourself or get someone in to do the work for you.

Roofs basically fall into two types – flat or pitched – and it is quite common to find both on a property. For example, the main house may have a pitched tiled roof and the garage a flat felt-covered roof.

Flat roofs

These are the simplest type and are often found on garages and home extensions and sometimes on house features such as bay windows. In fact they are not completely flat but slope slightly to one side or end to direct rainwater into a gutter at the eaves.

They consist basically of a series of joists which span the walls at each side of the building.

The joists usually rest on a timber wall plate bedded on the inner leaf of the wall, while the spaces in the outer leaf of the wall between the joists are filled with bricks or blocks. The joists are fixed to the wall plate by skew nailing (at an angle) or by means of metal straps screwed to the joists, wall plate and inner leaf.

With an extension, the joists are often notched on to a wall plate bolted to the house wall. Alternatively the joists are supported on that side by joist hangers screwed to the wall. They are covered with boards and waterproofed with two or three layers of roofing felt. Cross ventilation via soffit vents is essential to prevent condensation from causing rot in the roof timbers.

Pitched roofs

This type slopes at varying angles. The simplest is the lean-to, which is widely used on extensions, outhouses and conservatories built on to a house. It is constructed with rafters resting on a wall plate at one side and supported by a wall plate bolted to the house wall or by joist hangers, in a similar fashion to a flat roof, but at a steeper angle.

Pitched roofs may be covered with glass or plastic where it is necessary to let in plenty of light. They can, of course, be felted, battened and tiled or slated in traditional-type construction. The roof slopes at each side from a central ridge. Traditionally, the rafters rest against a central ridge board at the apex, while at the eaves they are notched into a wall plate and tied together with ceiling joists. The rafters are supported with purlins, which are in turn braced with struts. This type of roof is constructed on site and is normally fairly easy to adapt if you decide you would like a loft conversion.

The modern roof is often constructed with prefabricated trussed rafters, in which case there is no ridge board or purlins. Diagonal bracing timbers are nailed to the undersides of the rafters and tiling battens are then nailed to the upper surface of the rafters. This type is often of much lower pitch than the traditional one. Because of this – and its prefabricated method of construction – it is not suitable for conversion into additional loft space.

Three types of covering are commonly used on pitched roofs – slates, plain tiles and interlocking or single-lap tiles.

Because of their age, slate roofs are often unlined, the slates being nailed directly to the roof battens. You will find some lined with timber boards and here the slates are nailed to the boards. If a slate roof has been replaced in the last 20 years or so, it is likely that the roof may have been lined with slater's roofing felt under the battens. This makes the loft space warmer, drier and cleaner. An examination of the loft area will tell you whether felt is present.

■ Roofs come in a wide range of styles. The simplest are the flat roof (1) and the pent roof (2), usually found only on small single-storey buildings. Small extensions and porches may have a lean-to (monopitch) roof (3), which may be hipped at each end to improve its looks (4).

House roofs are most commonly either gabled (5) or hipped (6), but other more elaborate styles are also found. These include the double-pitched mansard roof (7 and 8), the jerkin-head or hipped-gable roof (9) and the gambrel roof (10).

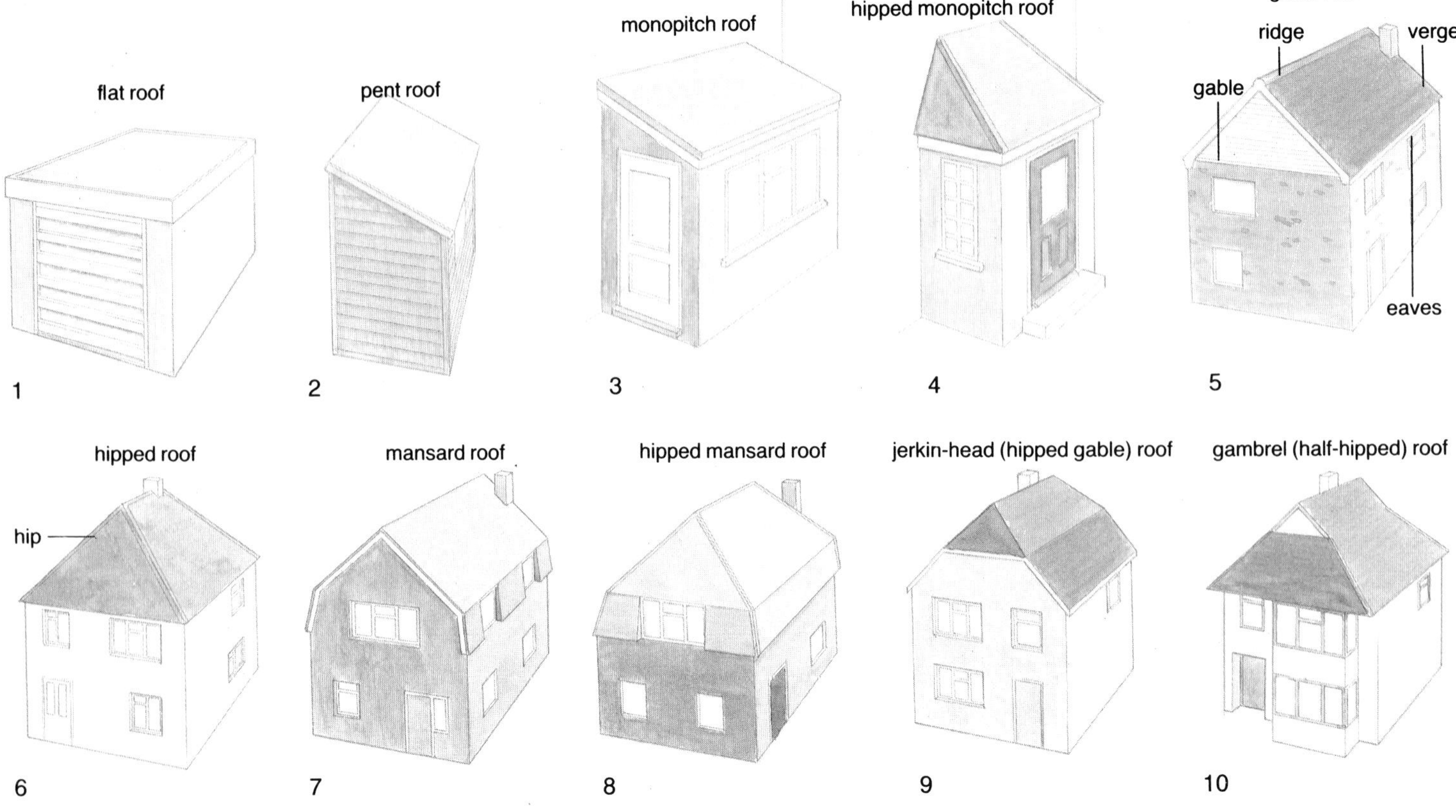

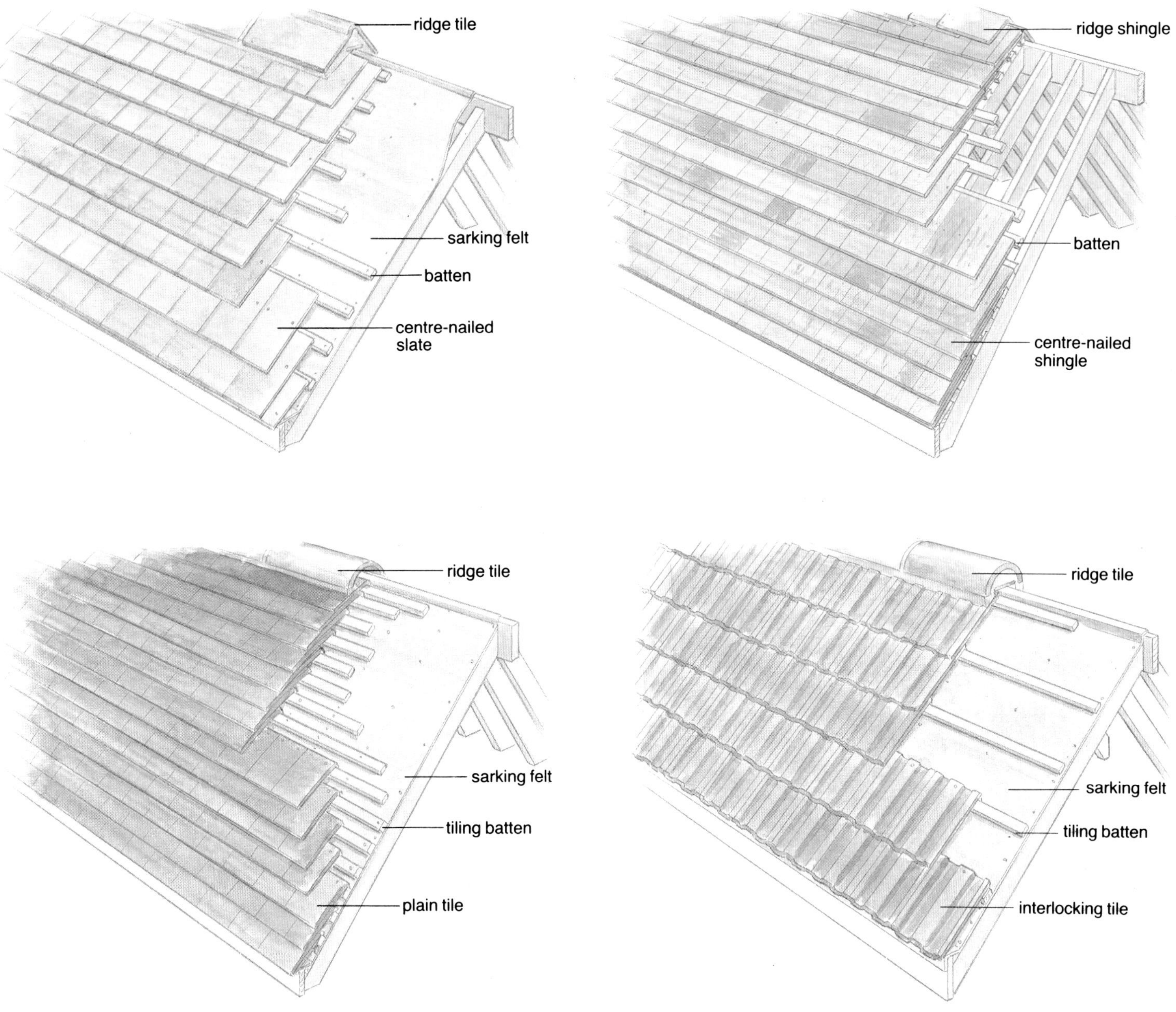

■ Slates are nailed through the head or centre line to battens laid across the rafters. Each overlaps just over half the length of the slate beneath it.

Shingles are sawn or split timber rectangles used like tiles, nailed to battens positioned to match the fixing centres.

Plain tiles have nibs that hook over tiling battens, and are nailed every four or five courses. They may be laid in single-lap or double-lap fashion.

Interlocking tiles also have nibs that hook over the tile battens. Adjacent tile edges also interlock.

To make the roof waterproof, alternate rows of slates are staggered and each row overlaps the one below by about half its length. At any particular point, there are at least two – and perhaps three – thicknesses of slate.

It is also possible for a plain-tiled roof to be unlined, in which case the loft space will be dirty and draughty. You might be lucky and find a roof that is lined under the battens with slater's felt.

With a plain-tiled roof, the tiles have projections at the top edge called nibs, which hook over the battens. In exposed places, every fourth row of tiles may be nailed to the battens for additional security. Plain tiles are hung overlapping, so that at any particular point there is a minimum of two tile thicknesses to ensure that the roof is watertight. Alternate rows are staggered so that the joints between tiles do not line up in consecutive courses.

Interlocking or single-lap tiles are very popular for re-roofing and are often used to replace an old slate roof. Usually made of concrete, but sometimes of clay, they are widely used in modern houses. And because these roofs tend to be newer, they are often lined with felt under the battens.

The tiles have nibs at the top so they hook over the battens. The sides of the tiles, and sometimes the heads, are specially shaped so that the adjacent tiles interlock with one another to form a watertight roof, even though the tiles are laid in a single thickness.

WORKING IN SAFETY

Because undertaking repairs or maintenance inevitably means working at a height, there will always be an element of danger. So make sure you never cut corners on any aspects of safety when working on a roof.

Always use a roof ladder or crawling boards and, if possible, provide access to the roof ladder from a properly erected scaffold tower, rather than an ordinary ladder. The latter may, of course, be sufficient for minor repairs. It is best to put up a scaffold tower if you are working at gutter level – replacing guttering or painting or replacing soffit boards or fascias.

You can buy a scaffold tower. However, since you will need to use it only occasionally, you may prefer to hire one. The platform height should be about 1.5m (5ft) below the eaves if you are working on the guttering or level with the eaves if you are working on the roof.

Most domestic tower frames have a base size of 1.3m (4ft 3in) square and can be used freestanding with a platform height of up to 3.6m (12ft). Above this height they should be fitted with stabiliser legs and should also be securely roped to the building. The best way to do this is to insert expanding ring bolts into the brickwork and secure the ropes to these. Alternatively, tie the tower to a window frame mullion if one is nearby.

Towers are supplied in sections and are quickly and easily erected by slotting together the lightweight frames, diagonal braces, decking boards, handrails and safety toe boards. Adjustable base plates are a must, since these allow you to get the first frames square and level, thus ensuring that the tower is erected truly vertically.

You can use a ladder to gain access to the roof for minor repairs. In this case, there must be at least three rungs above gutter level if you are going to climb on to the roof. It is best to hold the top of the ladder slightly away from the guttering to prevent damaging it. Use a ladder stay, which has rubber feet to prevent the top of the ladder from slipping sideways. With plastic or asbestos cement gutters, the use of a ladder stay is essential.

The top of the ladder must be securely tied to the building. Use rope passed through a large screw eye inserted into the fascia board or, better still, through a large expanding ring bolt inserted into the brickwork.

As already mentioned, a roof ladder or crawling boards are essential for working on the roof itself. Both have small wheels in the top

■ **Right** Always use a special roof ladder for carrying out repairs to pitched roofs. Push the ladder wheeled side down up the roof slope, then turn it over so the hook engages over the ridge. Gain access to the roof ladder from an extension ladder to which the roof ladder should be roped for safety.

For work on chimney stacks, use slot-together platform tower components to construct a safe, sturdy working platform all round the stack.

■ **Left** Extension ladders are the most popular item of access equipment for many outdoor home renovation jobs. When using one, always ensure that there is a four-rung overlap between the sections and that the ladder is set up at the correct angle, with the foot of the ladder 1m or 1ft out from the wall for every 4m or 4ft of ladder height. Use a ladder stay to hold the head of the ladder clear of overhanging eaves and gutters.

For additional safety, tie the head of the ladder to stout masonry anchors in the house walls, or to a baulk of timber inside a window opening. Fit ladder stabilisers for use on flat, solid surfaces, or set the ladder foot on sacking and weight it with a sandbag. On soft surfaces stand the ladder on a board with a batten screwed to it to stop it slipping or sinking.

section so that they can be pushed easily up the roof. When you reach the top, roll the ladder over so that the large hook on the end clips over the ridge and prevents it from sliding back down the roof. It is essential that your roof ladder spans from ridge to eaves. If you do not want to hire a roof ladder, you can get a ladder hook set to convert an ordinary ladder into a roof crawling set.

If you need to carry out minor chimney repairs and the stack is not large, it may be possible to do this from a roof ladder. If extensive work is required or the chimney is large, then you should hire a chimney scaffold set. This will form a safe working platform on all sides of the stack, regardless of the slope of the roof. Reach it via a roof ladder.

FIXING TILES

On the whole, tiles are easy to remove and replace, so it is not worth trying to patch them up with mastic or glass fibre paste if they have cracked or are broken. The only exception is for emergency repairs or if replacement tiles are not readily available.

To make temporary repairs, there is a simple method you can use. First, ease up the tiles in the row above the broken tile using small timber wedges. Cover the crack or missing piece of tile using self-adhesive flashing strip. (This is metal-backed and normally used for flashing repairs.)

If the tiles have a sandy finish, it may be necessary to paint the surface with flashing strip primer. This is supplied with the rolls of flashing strip. Alternatively, you can use waterproof repair tape or trowel-on roofing mastic, which can be reinforced with patches of roofing felt or strips of aluminium cooking foil covered with more mastic.

Replacing a tile

Ease up the tiles in the row above the damaged or missing one, using small timber wedges. With the tip of a large builder's trowel, lift the damaged tile high enough so that the nibs at the top on the underside of the tile clear the tiling batten holding the tile in place.

In most cases plain tiles will simply lift out. Sometimes, however, the tiles are held with nails, particularly in the case of interlocking ones. Here you must prise the tile up to pull the nails out. You may have to hire a slate ripper,

■ To replace a missing or damaged tile, drive timber wedges in to raise the tiles next to the affected area. If the damaged tile cannot be lifted out easily, release it by using a slater's ripper to cut through the nails holding it to the tiling batten. Then slide a replacement tile into place and remove the wedges.

To secure loose ridge tiles, lift the tile off and chip away any old mortar. Then bed the edges of the tile on fresh mortar and point between it and its neighbours.

which can be used to cut through the nails or pull them out.

With the adjacent tiles still wedged up, use the builder's trowel to lift the new tile into place so the nibs hook over the batten. When the tile is correctly positioned, you can remove the wedges so the tiles above drop back into place.

If you have to replace tiles over a fairly large area (see Re-roofing), work up the roof slope, nailing every fourth row as necessary in the case of plain tiles and alternate rows in the case of interlocking tiles.

FIXING SLATES

Slates are held in place with two nails driven into the batten or boarding beneath. In time, these nails corrode (a problem known as nail sickness) and the slates blow away or simply slip out of place.

If this happens over a wide area, it is best to replace the entire roof (see Re-roofing). But if the damage is only in patches, it is worth just replacing the slates.

Where you have to replace several slates together, you can refix the lower ones by nailing them in to the battens as usual, working up the roof. It will, however, be impossible to nail in the final slates. These will have to be held in place with strips of metal, usually lead, called tingles. These are also used to hold isolated slates in place, where these have slipped out.

Nail the tingle to the batten or board that is showing between the two slates below the one being fixed. The tingle should be of sufficient length so that when the slate is pushed back into position, the protruding end of the tingle can be bent up and over the bottom edge of the slate to hold it firmly in place.

When positioning the slate, make sure it is pushed up far enough so that its top edge rests on top of the next batten up. This will prevent the lower edge of the slate from lifting in a gale and working loose.

If a slate has broken, but the top section remains fixed, you will need to use a slate ripper to remove it. Push the blade of the ripper up under the slate you want to remove and move the head of the tool to one side to hook around the fixing nail. Tug the handle of the ripper or hammer it downwards, either to cut through the nail or pull it out of place.

There are many different sizes of slates, so make sure you buy the correct ones. It is a

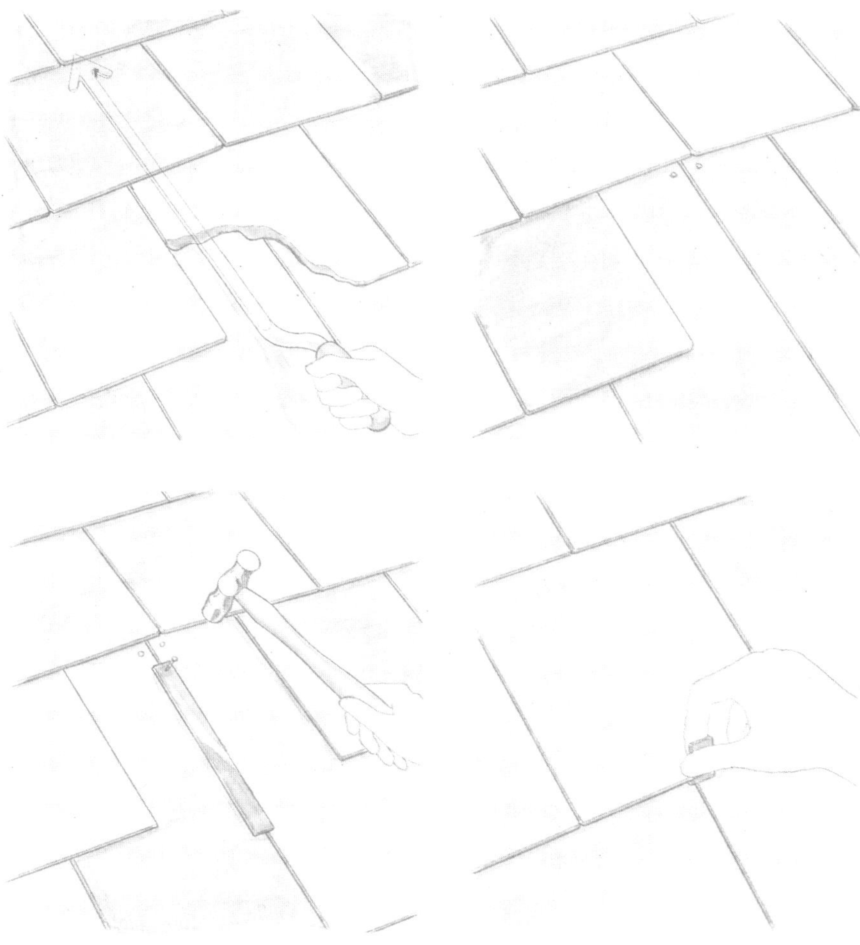

■ To release a damaged slate, cut through the fixing nails using a slater's ripper. Slide out the damaged slate, and nail a strip of lead, zinc or copper to one of the battens between the exposed slates. Slide the new slate into position and secure it in place by folding up the bottom end of the metal strip.

good idea to get secondhand ones, if they are in reasonable condition. If necessary, however, you can trim slates to size with an angle grinder. Fix them with copper nails.

RE-ROOFING

There comes a stage when so much patching up is needed to keep a roof watertight that more extensive repairs are required. The ultimate answer is to re-roof, although one alternative is to cover the surface with a membrane-reinforced bitumen 'skin'.

A membrane treatment can be used on pitched or flat roofs and applying one is well within the scope of the competent amateur. Basically it involves brushing liquid bitumen on to the roof, pressing reinforcing mesh fabric into the wet sealer and then applying more bitumen (see Repairing a flat roof).

This type of treatment is ideal for flat roofs, since it is easy to apply and the end result is not visible from the ground. On pitched roofs, however, being on a slope it is harder to apply and is clearly visible afterwards.

This method can be used on slate roofs, where the effect is reasonably unobtrusive. It also offers the additional advantage of binding the roof together and membranes of this type are commonly seen in areas frequently exposed to wind and rain.

In the case of a flat roof, re-roofing is normally a straightforward, if lengthy, job that you can consider tackling yourself, particularly if the roof involved is on a garage or an extension to the house.

Replacing a pitched roof is another matter altogether. To get the work done quickly and ensure the roof is 'off' for the shortest possible time, most people will opt to have the work done by an approved contractor. In most cases, larger companies will guarantee both the work and the materials for a period of time, which is important. Not only does this ensure the property is protected, but it will also enhance its value.

Although the majority of new roofs are made with interlocking concrete tiles, apart from the expense there is no reason why the original type of roofing tiles or slates cannot be replaced. Sound secondhand peg tiles are still generally available, while in the case of slates you can choose the lighter imitation ones that look quite realistic.

If you are re-roofing your house, you do get the opportunity to check the rafters, replace roofing battens where required and ensure the loft area is draughtproof and watertight. The best way is to line the roof with slater's felt before the new battens are fixed. Related jobs such as repairs to chimneys and flashing can be carried out at the same time.

REPAIRING A FLAT ROOF

By their very nature, flat roofs tend to present more problems than pitched ones. Although they should have been built with a slight fall to enable water to run off, pools of water tend to form on the surface. The wide variation in temperature to which a flat roof is subjected will often separate the covering layers and crack them. Inevitably leaks will occur.

You can reduce any expansion and contraction by topping the roof with a layer of white solar-reflective stone chippings. In time, however, these tend to be washed away.

Where chippings are sparse or missing altogether, coat the roof with bitumen chipping compound and scatter fresh chippings over the surface, pressing them into the bitumen with a light wooden roller. This should give the roof a few years' extra life.

When you are up on the roof, check whether you can find any other existing or imminent

■ To repair small splits and blisters in felted roofs, open up the top layer of the felt with two knife cuts at right angles. Peel back the tongues and spread some bituminous mastic over the repair. Then fix the tongues back down securely with galvanised clout nails and cover the repair with a felt patch, bedded on more mastic and rolled down with a wallpaper seam roller or similar tool.

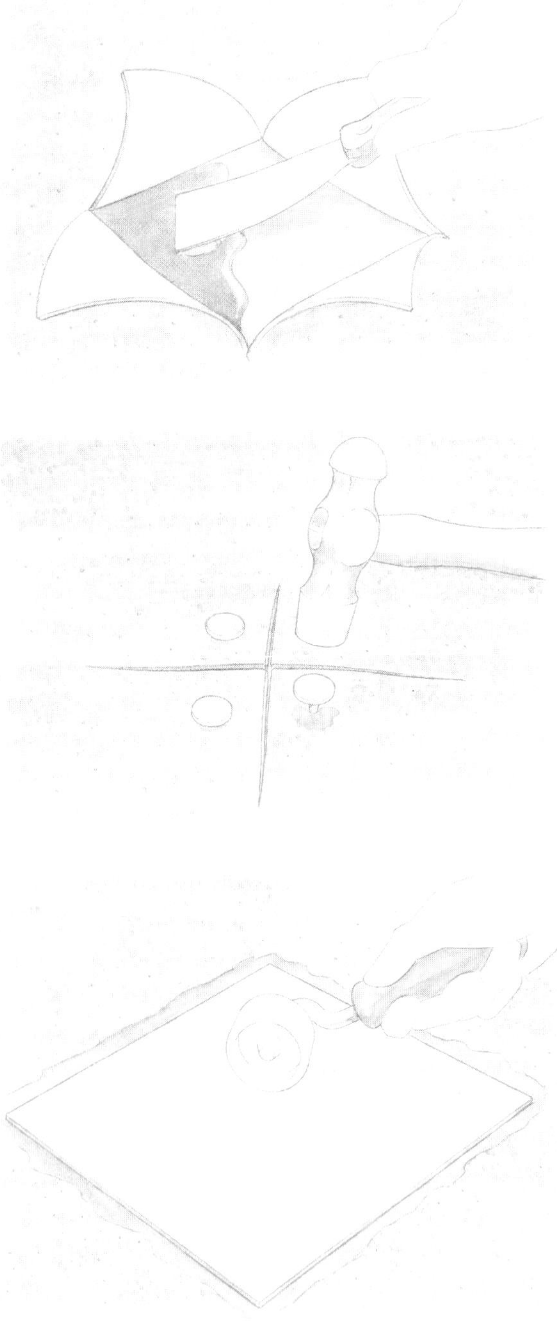

problems. Obviously, if you notice a leak inside, you will not wait for a general inspection before carrying out any necessary repairs.

With a water leak, remember that the point at which you notice the stain inside the roof may be some distance from the problem area. Because it is common for the felt layers to separate, water trickling through the top layer may travel some distance under the felt before appearing on the ceiling below.

When you inspect a flat roof, there are some general signs of potential problems to watch out for. If the top layer of felt has started to wrinkle or looks mottled, these are sure signs that the covering is reaching the end of its useful life. Watch out too for any sign of springiness in the roof decking; this indicates that chipboard decking has begun to break up. Also check the upstands where the roof meets an abutment, like the wall of an adjacent building or a parapet wall. You should also make sure that rainwater outlets, gutters and downpipes are clear of debris and loose chippings, so that any water will run away as quickly as possible.

This initial inspection should give you a good picture of what needs to be done and how to proceed. You will probably have the option of carrying out a patch repair to the damaged area, applying an all-over treatment to the surface or stripping off and replacing the roof.

Patch repairs are obviously the easiest to carry out and are the answer if the area of damage is limited and the majority of the roof is in good condition. If, however, the covering is starting to deteriorate in a number of places and you do not want to go through the expense of replacing the entire covering, you should consider an all-over treatment.

Such a treatment is well within the capabilities of the competent DIY worker who does not mind ruining a set of old clothes; bitumen is a very messy material to handle! And it should give the roof several extra years of life. But it is a warning that you will eventually need a new roof covering. So it is a good time to start saving up for the cost this will necessarily involve when the work has to be done.

If you decide on re-roofing, this is a job for the specialist. It involves applying three layers of roofing felt stuck together with hot bitumen to form a strong durable covering – hence the name 'built-up roofing'. The pour-and-roll technique using hot bitumen is a skilled and potentially dangerous job and not recommended for the amateur.

The only exception, if you are determined to do the work yourself, is to use 'torching' felt, which is backed with bitumen coating. A powerful gas blowlamp is required to heat and melt the bitumen as the felt is unrolled on to the roof surface. It is still not an easy process, but it is safer than working on the roof with buckets of hot bitumen.

If the problem demands only a patch repair over a hole, it is best to use metal-backed self-adhesive flashing strip, although a piece of roofing felt coated with cold bitumen would be a suitable alternative.

Scrape any stones away from the damaged area, then apply the liquid bitumen primer supplied with the flashing strip. When this has dried, peel the backing paper away from the flashing strip, which should be cut large enough to allow plenty of overlap, and press it in place, rolling it down with a wooden wallpaper seam roller. You can use the same material when repairing an upstand.

Your problem may just be blistering on the surface. In this case make a star-shaped cut through the blister using a sharp trimming knife. Then peel back the edges of the blister to expose the underfelt. Coat the area with bitumen roofing compound and fold the flaps back in place, pressing them down with the roller. Finally apply a patch of flashing strip over the repair.

If you decide to apply an all-over surface treatment, there are various materials you can use. The principle is to apply an initial layer of liquid proofing to the roof surface, which you can reinforce with a non-rotting fabric mesh, and then another layer, allowing it to solidify and form a tough, waterproof yet flexible sheet.

First remove the stone chippings and any moss or algae from the surface. It is a good idea to apply a suitable fungicide to kill any remaining traces of growth. Then apply the first coat of liquid proofing, using a soft broom.

If you are using reinforcing mesh, unroll it into the wet waterproofing and stipple it into the surface using a wet brush. Overlap the edges of adjacent strips by about 50mm (2in). When the first coat has dried, apply a second one all over the roof and then a third. You can give this last coat extra protection with a covering of white reflective stone chippings or sharp sand, which you should apply while the final coat of proofing is still slightly tacky.

REPAIRING FLASHINGS

Flashings, which can be of lead or other corrosion-resistant metal or sometimes cement mortar, waterproof the join between the roof and adjacent brickwork, such as a chimney stack or the house wall.

Metal flashings are far superior to the mortar type, but after a time even they can corrode, tear or lift away from the wall, allowing water to trickle down behind them.

If flashing has simply lifted away from the roof, tap it back in place with a piece of wood. If it has pulled away at the top, where it is tucked into a mortar joint along the wall, the job of repairing it will involve more work.

Carefully chip out the mortar joint, then tap the flashing back into place using a scrap of wood. Hold it in position using rolled strips of lead tucked into the joint. Finally, fill the joint with cement mortar (one part cement to five parts soft sand), mixing in a little PVA adhesive to make it more workable.

If metal flashing is corroded or torn, the best solution is to cover it with metal-backed self-

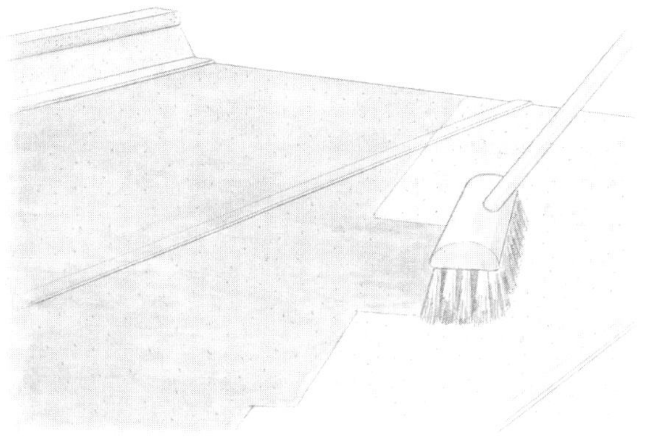

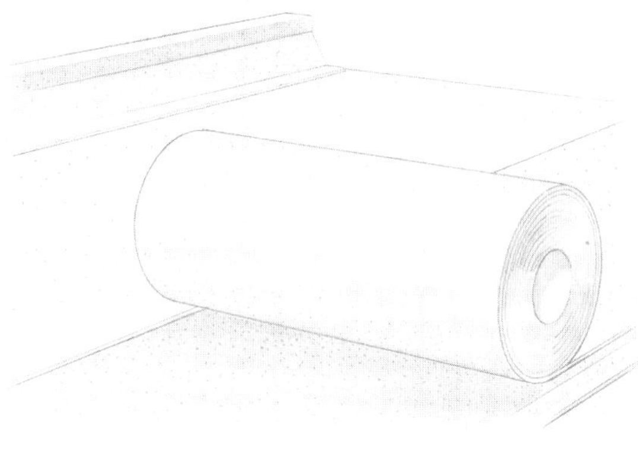

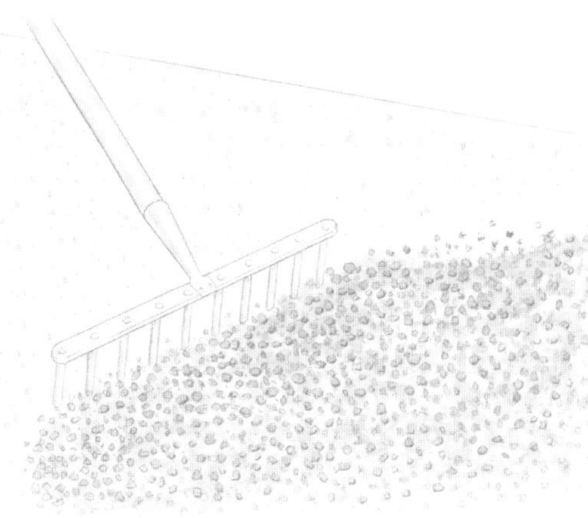

■ Where large-scale pin-holing of a felt or other flat roof appears to be letting in water but the roof is in otherwise reasonably sound condition, brush on a coat of liquid waterproofer and unroll special reinforcing mesh over it. Then brush on a generous second layer of waterproofer, allow it to dry and apply a third coat before covering it with a protective layer of fine stone chippings, raked out while the top coat is still tacky.

■ Where metal flashings have pulled away from a roof/wall junction, rake out the old mortar along the chase into which the flashing fitted. Then reposition the flashing, wedging it into the chase, and repoint with fresh mortar.

If the flashing is porous or is missing altogether, fit a length of self-adhesive flashing tape. Brush on the special primer first and leave it to become tacky. Then cut the flashing tape to length, peel off the release paper and bed the tape in place along the junction. Tamp it down with a block of wood and a hammer to ensure that it forms a good bond.

adhesive flashing strip. Clean the existing flashing with a wire brush, then apply flashing strip primer, which is supplied with the strip, to the affected area and leave it to dry. It will turn from brown to black. Remove the backing paper from the flashing strip and smooth it into place using a soft rag. Press it firmly in place with a small wooden roller.

If the flashing is badly corroded or very loose, you should remove it completely and fit self-adhesive flashing strip in its place.

Apart from the stepped flashing at the sides of the chimney stack and the apron flashing along the front, the flashing at the back of a chimney, which is formed into a back gutter, is also prone to corrosion and water leaks. Here you can make an effective repair with several overlapping strips of flashing material well pressed down.

The same technique can be used to repair the metal-lined valley gutters which you should find between adjoining pitched roof slopes. In such a case, apply the flashing strip from the bottom of the valley upwards, tucking the edges of the flashing under the tiles.

Mortar flashings frequently crack and pull away from the brickwork, allowing water to run down behind. If the flashing is basically sound, fill any cracks by injecting a bead of non-setting mastic into them using the gun applicator supplied.

If the cement flashing is in poor condition, carefully chip it away and replace it with the self-adhesive strip, pressing it down on to the affected surface, which you will first need to clean and treat with primer.

REPAIRING CHIMNEYS

Never attempt any repairs to chimneys unless the stack is small and easy to reach from a roof ladder or you have hired proper chimney scaffolding (see Working in safety).

Because chimney stacks are in a very exposed position, it is common for the pointing between the bricks to crumble away. This can lead to dampness and make the stack unstable. Damaged joints will need to be repointed.

First rake out the old mortar to a depth of about 20mm (¾in) and lightly wet the joints. A garden sprayer is ideal for this. Then press fresh mortar in place and smooth it off at a slight downward angle. The mortar should consist of one part cement to five parts sharp sand, with a little PVA adhesive added to improve its adhesion and workability.

Another vulnerable spot is the mortar (called flaunching) around the chimney pots. If there are cracks but the pots themselves are still held firmly in place, you can fill them by injecting non-setting mastic.

If, however, the flaunching is loose, you will have to chip it away – with care – and replace it with new mortar. Use one part cement to four parts sharp sand, again with a little PVA adhesive. Spread the mortar around the pots, building it up around the base and smoothing it so it slopes down to the edges of the stack. This will allow any rainwater to drain off easily.

Cracked chimney pots can sometimes be repaired with silicone mastic; otherwise they will have to be replaced. If you have an old house, you may be able to get suitable pots from a demolition contractor or architectural salvage yard. To fit the new pot, chip away the old flaunching and replace it with new mortar, as described above.

If the flues are no longer used, you can fit ventilator caps to the pots to prevent rain getting in. Alternatively you can remove the pots and make the flues rainproof by bedding airbricks around the sides at the top and laying paving slabs over the flues to throw rainwater clear of the stack. The airbricks ensure a gentle supply of air to the flues to keep them dry.

Metal flashings and back gutters can also be a

Chimney stack repairs

■ Repair minor cracks in the flaunching securing the pots to the stack using exterior-quality silicone mastic.

■ Rake out any defective pointing on the sides of the stack and remake the joints with fresh mortar, left flush.

■ If stepped flashings are pulling away from their chases, wedge them back in place and repoint the chases with fresh mortar.

■ If the flaunching has deteriorated badly, rope the pot securely to the stack and chop away all the old mortar.

■ Replace the flaunching with fresh mortar, mixed to a stiff consistency and laid about 50mm (2in) thick round the base of the pot.

■ Shape the mortar so it forms a gentle downward slope away from the pot towards the edges of the stack.

source of damp problems around chimney stacks. Work on these is covered under the section on Repairing flashings.

Once repairs to the chimney stack have been completed, it is a good idea to paint the brickwork and the flaunching with silicone water-repellent sealer to prevent rain penetration and help protect against frost damage. The sealer dries colourless and does not affect the appearance of the stack.

REPAIRING GUTTERING

It is important to keep guttering systems in good condition, since leaking or overflowing gutters will cause damp walls, stained interior decorations and possibly rotting of the fascias, soffit boards and rafter ends.

When checking or repairing the guttering, use a ladder fitted with a stay, which will hold the top clear of the gutter. If you are replacing any of the system, you should use a scaffold tower (see Working in safety).

The best time to check gutters and downpipes is when it is raining. Then you can see clearly if there are any leaking joints or whether the system is blocked anywhere and therefore overflowing. Make sure the inside of the guttering is free of debris. Clean the inside of metal gutters with a wire brush and paint the surface with black bituminous paint. Pour a bucket of water into the guttering and check that it drains freely and does not collect in pools. If there are drainage problems, these can only be corrected by realigning the gutters. This is not an easy job and it is better to discard

■ Gutters, especially old cast-iron ones, suffer from a range of common problems. The easiest to cure is the simple blockage, caused by debris washed off the roof surface or blown in by the wind, and resulting in water overflowing and running down the house walls.

Other problems include leaks from faulty joints, from cracks and splits caused by rust or accidental damage, and overflows due to sagging gutter brackets.

Where gutters are in very poor condition, it is often quicker to replace them completely with a new run of guttering, rather than to attempt a series of repairs.

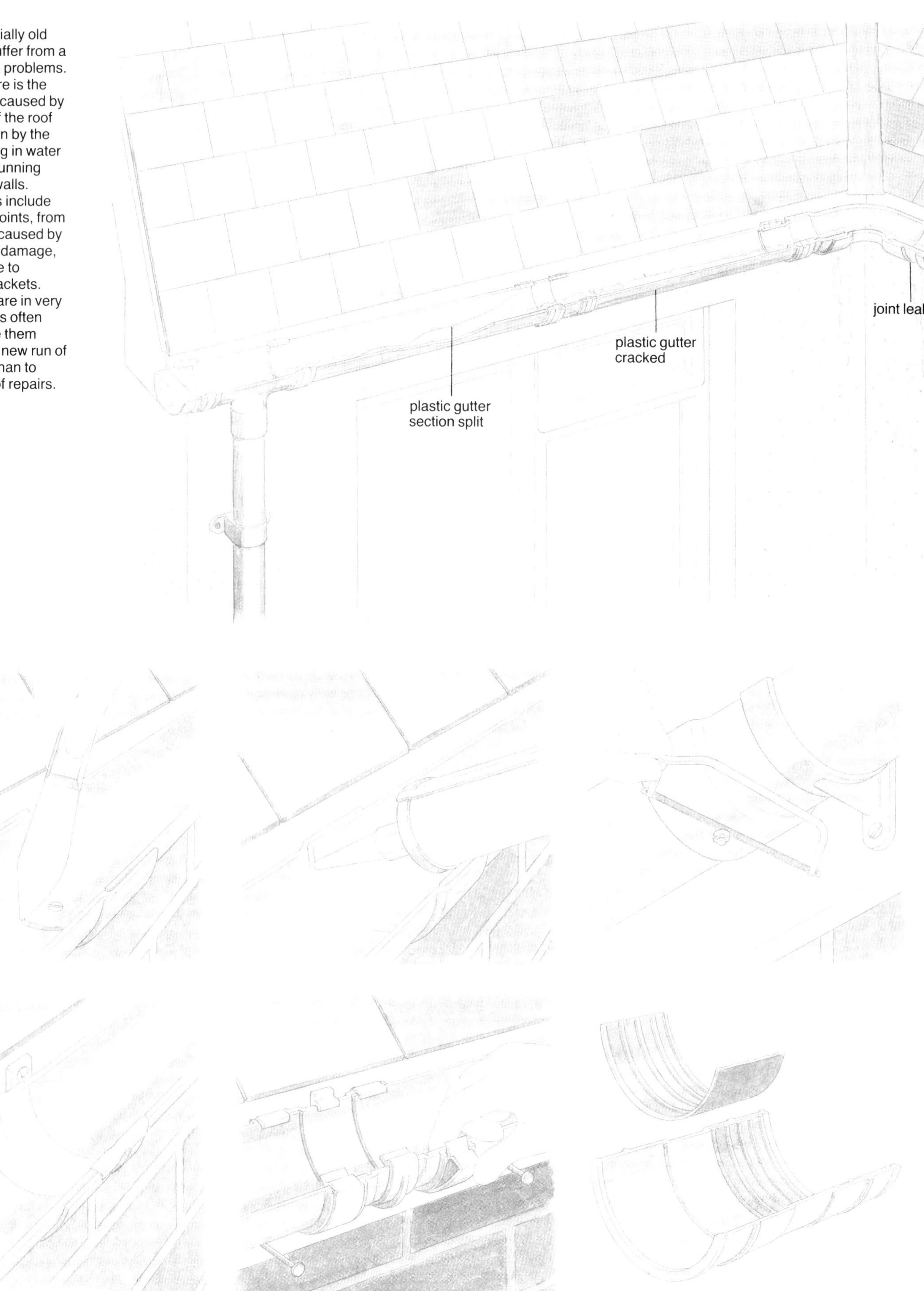

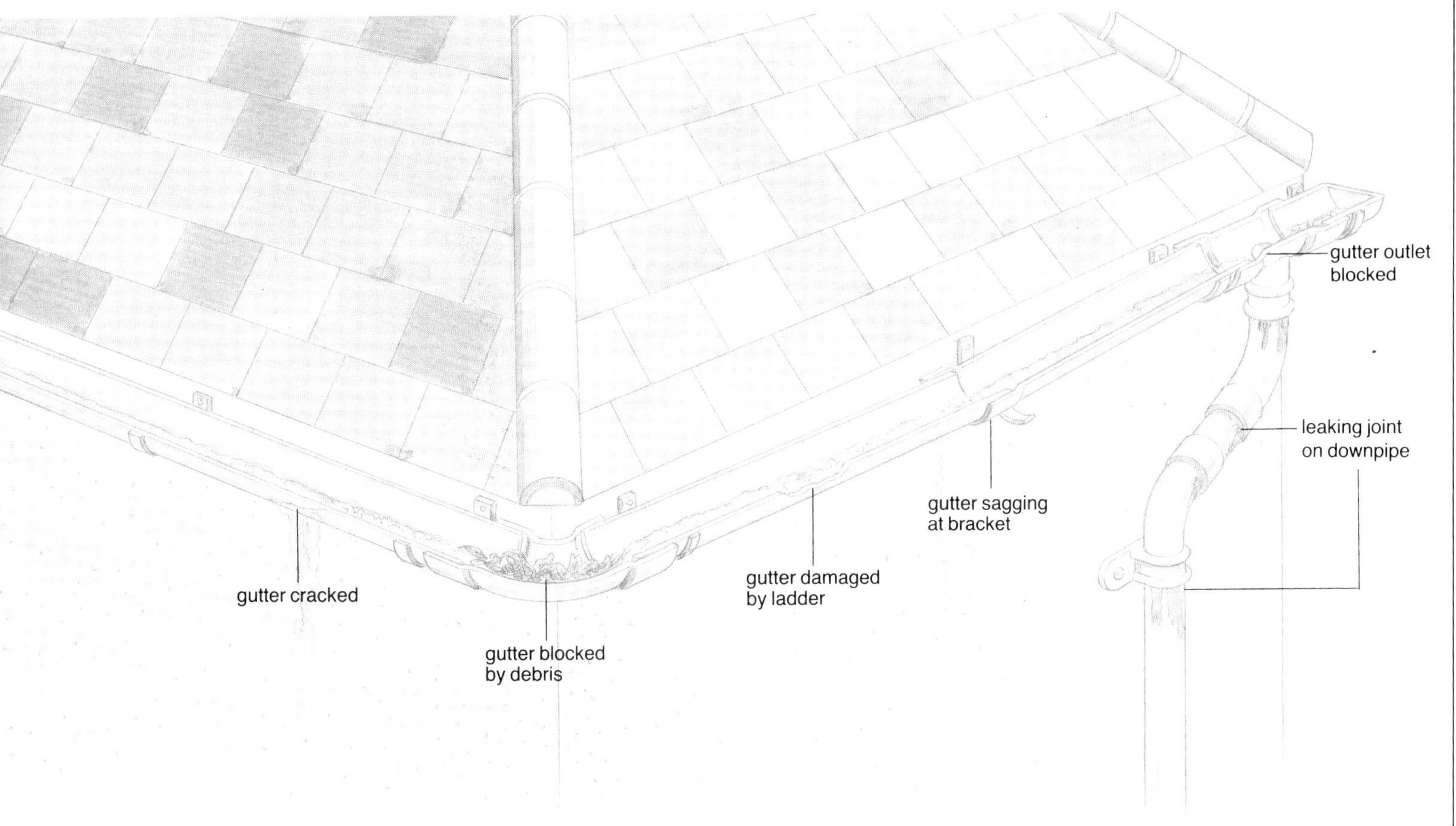

■ **Left** To repair a leaking but otherwise sound joint, scrape out any old sealing compound and re-seal the joint with mastic.

If this fails to work, undo the joint by hacksawing through the nut underneath. Then separate the joint sections, reassemble them on a generous bed of mastic and remake the joint with a new nut and bolt. As a stop-gap measure, try sealing the joint by bedding a piece of self-adhesive flashing tape over it.

If a plastic gutter joint leaks, dismantle the joint by removing the clips and fit a new sealing gasket.

the existing system and fit new plastic guttering (see below), or reproduction cast iron gutters if you are restoring a period house.

If joints in plastic guttering are leaking, the only satisfactory solution is to dismantle them and fit new neoprene gaskets. If you have metal or asbestos cement guttering, the best method is to saw – from the underside – through the bolt and nut holding the sections together to ease the joint apart. Then clean it out, pack it with non-setting mastic and refix it with a new galvanised gutter bolt and nut.

There is an easier repair that may sometimes work. First scrape out the joint on each side. When it is thoroughly dry, inject a bead of non-setting exterior mastic into the crack. Finally, make sure of the repair by sticking a patch of self-adhesive flashing strip inside the gutter to form a complete seal.

Any gutters or downpipes that are cracked or split should be replaced with new sections. However, you can make a temporary repair by covering the affected area with a patch of self-adhesive flashing strip applied over a coating of primer. Metal and asbestos-cement gutters and downpipes can also be repaired with glass fibre paste, as used for car body repairs.

You can also use self-adhesive flashing strip to effect a temporary repair to badly corroded cast-iron and steel gutters and downpipes. However these can be dangerous if they fall off the wall, so it is better to replace them with new cast-iron or steel guttering or with the lightweight plastic type. There are now many styles in grey, white, brown or black plastic and they have the advantage of being easy to fix and maintenance-free.

Guttering is available in different sizes – usually 100 or 112mm (4 or 4½in) gutters, with 68mm (2½in) diameter downpipes. This size will cope with a roof area of up to 1200sq ft.

Plastic gutters are fixed by being clipped into brackets screwed to the fascia board. In theory, they will drain if fixed level. In practice, however, it is best to fit them with a slight fall of about 25mm (1in) in 15m (50ft).

When fitting a downpipe, always work from the outlet. Start by fitting an offset to bring the downpipe back to the face of the wall. Working downwards from the offset bracket, fit the downpipe into the required number of bracket clips to hold it firmly against the wall.

If you are replacing damaged plastic gutter or downpipe sections, note that the various systems are not interchangeable, so it is best to stick to what you have.

External Walls

Houses built in the 1920s and after are almost certainly of cavity wall construction, which can be identified by the formation of the brickwork. Except at corners, only stretchers (lengthwise bricks) show on the surface of the wall. Some late Victorian houses have cavity walls built with snap headers – half-bricks – which could be mistakenly identified as solid walls.

With older houses, cavity walls are about 280mm (11in) thick and consist of a 115mm (4½in) thick facing brick outer wall, a 50mm (2in) wide cavity and an inner wall of 115mm (4½in) thick bricks.

In more recent houses, the inner leaf is likely to be constructed with load-bearing building blocks, probably of lightweight insulating material, and the cavity between the inner and outer leaves may well be filled with insulation. The inner and outer leaves are always linked together with metal ties, of which there are various types. These are built into the mortar joints at regular intervals.

Modern stone-faced houses are also built on the cavity wall principle. The facing blocks may be of natural or reconstituted stones and these are linked by metal ties to an inner leaf of load-bearing blocks.

In most houses built before 1920, the outer walls are usually constructed of solid brick. These can be identified by having headers (brick ends looking like half-bricks) as well as stretchers in the face of the wall. This type of wall is usually 230mm (9in) thick, although 340mm (13½in) brickwork is also found. Check the thickness of the walls at the door and window openings, making allowance for the thickness of any plaster. One significant point to remember about walls in older houses is that they may not include a damp-proof course and footings may be stepped bricks.

Some houses have exterior walls built from regular stone (ashlar) blocks backed with bricks. Often there is a projecting plinth at ground level and such walls may have a damp-proof course.

The latest type of construction is timber-framed, where the inner leaf forms the main structural frame of the house and the outer leaf is used just for decorating and weatherproofing. The inner face is usually of vapour-check or foil-backed plasterboard, which is nailed to a timber frame sheathed on the outside with plywood. The cavity between the plasterboard and plywood is filled with insulation and the plywood sheathing is covered with a building paper vapour barrier.

The exterior brick, stone or block cladding is built on the outside with metal ties screwed to the plywood sheathing to maintain a 50mm (2in) cavity. Where the exterior is tile-hung or weatherboarded, this cladding may be fixed to insulating blocks or direct to the face of the structural timber frame.

■ Natural stone walls often have brickwork at corners and round openings.

■ Fair-faced brickwork is one of the most common exterior wall finishes, and is found in a wide range of colours and textures.

■ Paint is often used to give brickwork a facelift, but is virtually impossible to remove successfully once it has been applied.

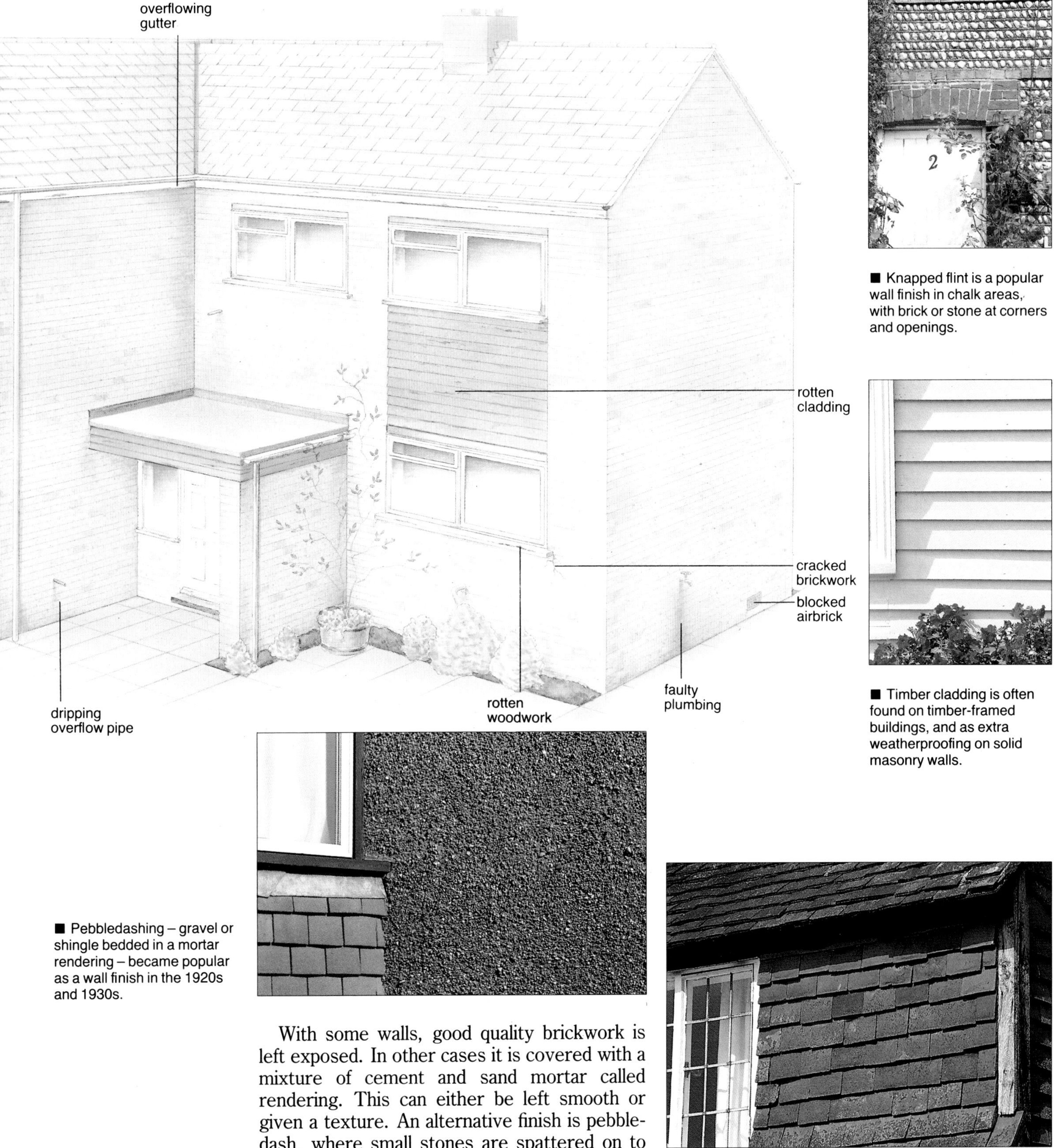

■ Knapped flint is a popular wall finish in chalk areas, with brick or stone at corners and openings.

■ Timber cladding is often found on timber-framed buildings, and as extra weatherproofing on solid masonry walls.

■ Pebbledashing – gravel or shingle bedded in a mortar rendering – became popular as a wall finish in the 1920s and 1930s.

■ Tile hanging is a popular form of weatherproofing for both timber-framed and solid masonry walls.

With some walls, good quality brickwork is left exposed. In other cases it is covered with a mixture of cement and sand mortar called rendering. This can either be left smooth or given a texture. An alternative finish is pebble-dash, where small stones are spattered on to wet rendering. Pebbledash can be left as it is or painted over with a good quality masonry paint.

Another finishing treatment is cladding, which can be applied to the whole of the house or used just as a feature. Using either timber or plastic, cladding may have been part of the original design or added later as a form of weatherproofing – or simply as decoration.

There are plenty of examples of tile-hung walls, where roof tiles have been nailed to horizontal battens. On the whole this treatment, part of the original design, is normally only used as a feature.

In recent years stone tiles, which can be stuck or mechanically fixed over existing wall surfaces as decoration, have been introduced. There are examples where houses have been completely covered with them – and not always to good effect. Normally, however, such tiles are limited to either an upper or lower storey or to the face of a bay.

FINDING FAULTS

Most of the defects that develop in walls are noticeable simply because they make the wall look shabby – mould growth, cracks and so on – or because damp patches form inside, ruining the interior decorations.

Provided that remedial action is taken quickly, most faults are rarely serious. At the other end of the scale, however, you may have major problems that can involve thousands of pounds of professional treatment.

Thankfully faults on this scale are rare and are almost always caused not by neglect but by natural causes. Narrow cracks in walls are usually superficial, even though they can sometimes extend quite a long way. They tend to stay as thin cracks and eventually stop growing. A bad crack will be extensive both in length and depth. It can split bricks in half or cause the wall to bulge. It may also appear inside the house.

You can make a fairly accurate diagnosis of the problem by asking yourself a few basic questions. If the problem proves to be serious, you are going to have to call in a surveyor. But running through a checklist can give you a fair picture of what is going on.

First of all, the crack itself. Have you noticed it getting wider and/or longer over a period of time? A good way to check this is to apply some filler or mortar mix into the gap. If this cracks or falls out after a while, then you know there is still movement.

If you have established that the crack is getting worse, what could have caused this to happen? The weather is the first thing to consider. If there has been an abnormally dry spell, this could have caused the subsoil – especially clay – to shrink. This in turn could have caused movement below the house foundations. In exceptionally dry weather, the ground could have dried out and shrunk, causing the foundations to follow suit.

Are there any large trees close to the affected wall? Roots can create problems by pushing against the foundations or footings. Equally, has a large tree near the house been felled recently? If it has, then it could be that roots extending below the foundations have withered and died. Where previously they 'supported' the foundations, there may now be a hollow and the foundations have sunk into it.

A less likely cause, but still a possibility, is where there has been recent mining or building work close by, which has resulted in the subsoil or foundations moving.

A more obscure reason could be a hidden building failure, such as the roof structure becoming unstable and forcing walls outwards or the wall ties in a cavity wall failing to secure the two leaves of brickwork together.

If the wall is unstable for any reason, the foundations will probably have to be excavated and underpinned (strengthened) and the affected part of the house may have to be rebuilt. Such repair work emphasizes the need to be well insured, since similar structural alterations can cost a lot of money.

■ Various pointing styles are used to finish off the mortar joints between bricks. Flush pointing, as its name implies, is trowelled flush with the face of the bricks, while concave pointing is tooled with a round bar before the mortar hardens. Recessed pointing is raked out to a depth of about 6mm (¼in), while V-jointed pointing is profiled with the tip of the pointing trowel. Weather-struck joints have the face of the pointing angled with the trowel to throw water clear of the wall surface.

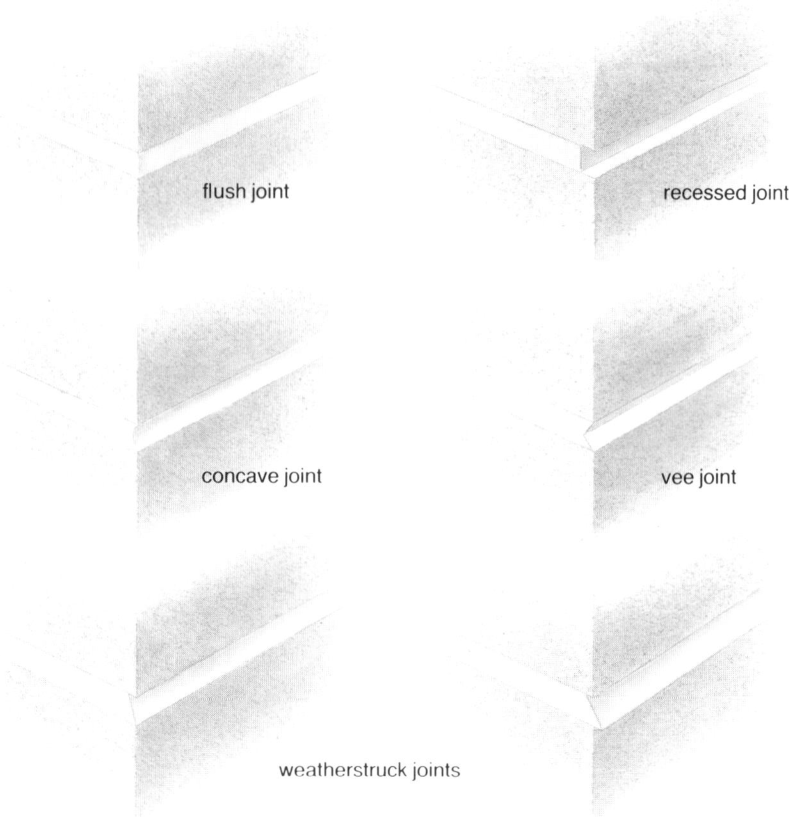

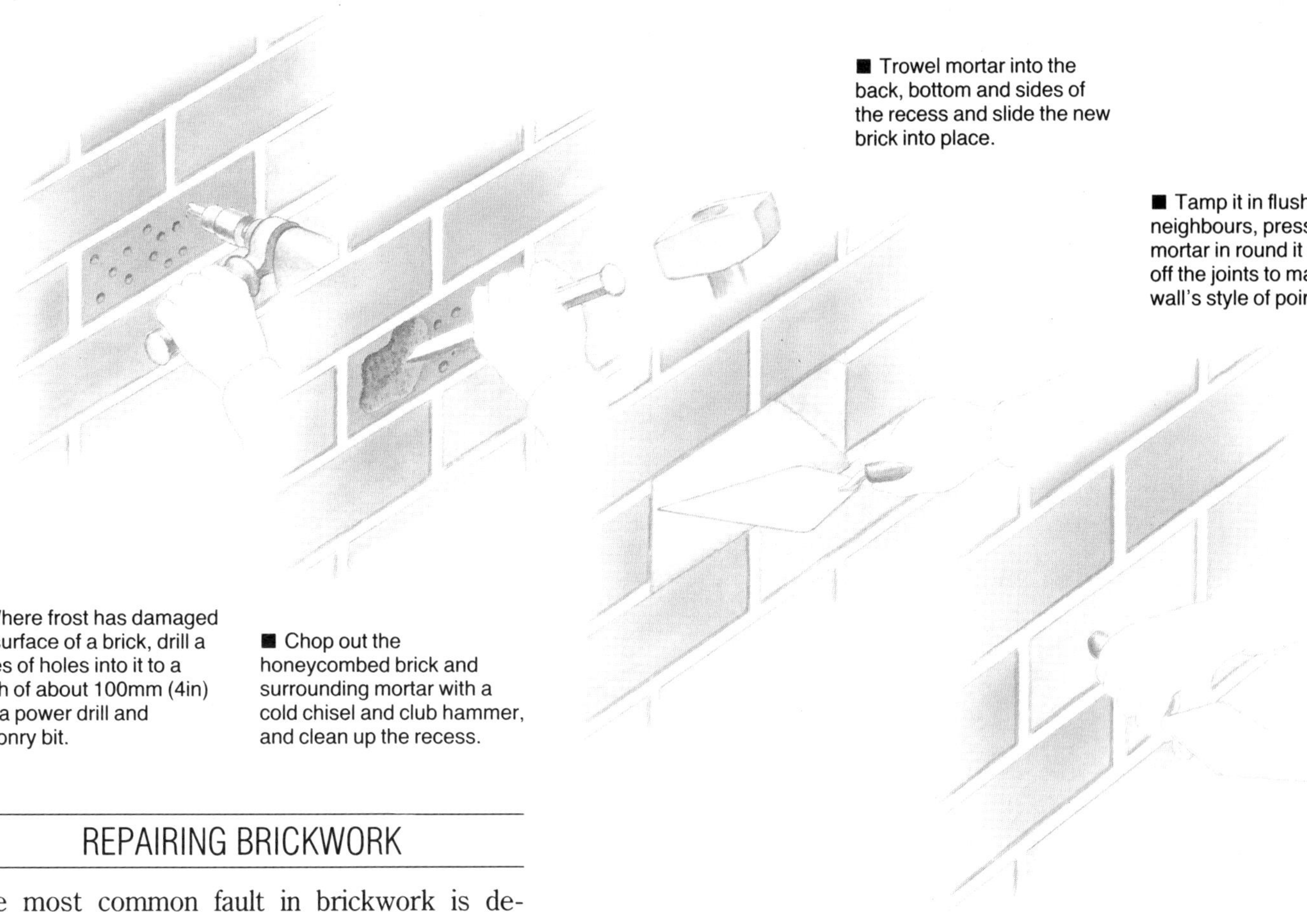

■ Trowel mortar into the back, bottom and sides of the recess and slide the new brick into place.

■ Tamp it in flush with its neighbours, press more mortar in round it and neaten off the joints to match the wall's style of pointing.

■ Where frost has damaged the surface of a brick, drill a series of holes into it to a depth of about 100mm (4in) with a power drill and masonry bit.

■ Chop out the honeycombed brick and surrounding mortar with a cold chisel and club hammer, and clean up the recess.

REPAIRING BRICKWORK

The most common fault in brickwork is deterioration in the mortar joints, when the mortar often flakes, cracks and crumbles. Old age and excessive weathering are common causes, especially if the initial mortar mix used was too weak for the job.

Cracks in the mortar joints allow rainwater to penetrate. In winter this can freeze, causing the crack to widen and the mortar to decay.

Repointing joints

To repoint damaged joints, you must first rake out the old mortar and then insert a new mix. This is normally made up of one part cement, one part hydrated powder lime and six parts soft sand. The lime makes the mix more workable, but you can substitute it with a few drops of a proprietary liquid plasticiser. If you make the mix stronger by increasing the proportion of cement, the mortar is liable to shrink and crack as it dries. It will also impede the drying out of the wall when wet.

If you are only repointing a few joints, then you can buy bags of mortar mix to which you simply add water. Tip out the entire content and mix it thoroughly together, then put back into the bag what you do not need. The ingredients tend to separate and if you only tip out what you need you may well get too much or too little cement.

TREATING OR REPLACING BRICKS

Old age and frost damage can cause brickwork to become porous, eventually allowing damp to pass through to the inside of the house. One solution is to patch up broken or spalled bricks with mortar, colour-matched to the surrounding ones. This is, however, difficult to do well. And if you have any cracks or gaps between the patching mortar and the brick, water can be

■ Weathering, pollution and frost damage can eventually cause serious damage to exposed brickwork and its pointing. Repointing or replacing affected bricks is essential to keep the wall surface weatherproof.

■ To weatherproof exterior brickwork that is porous but otherwise in good condition, brush on a silicone water-repellent sealer.

sucked in by capillary action, causing further spalling problems.

A better solution is to chop out the offending brick and replace it. Apply ready mixed brick-laying mortar, worked to a stiff consistency, to the top of the brick below, and on the sides and frog (the V-shaped indentation) of the new brick. Push it firmly in place, using a stick to compact the mortar inside the joint.

If some bricks are spalling, the rest are probably porous and will need protection. The easiest method is to apply a silicone water-repellent sealer with a brush, spray or roller.

FILLING CRACKED RENDERING

You often find hairline crazing in a rendered wall. Such a superficial situation is easily overcome with a coat of good exterior wall paint. Small cracks must be filled, but any repair will be obvious until the wall is painted.

When treating cracks, you must first under-cut them to ensure the filler is well anchored and will not fall out later. Then dust out the cavity and dampen it with water.

To fill the crack you can use either an exterior grade filler or mortar mix. The former is convenient but only economical for small areas. Dry mortar mix can be obtained in small quantities or you can make your own using one part cement, one part hydrated powder lime and six parts sand. You can of course use a proprietary liquid plasticiser in place of the lime.

■ Cracks often occur in rendering at natural breaks – in line with the corners of door and window frames, for example.

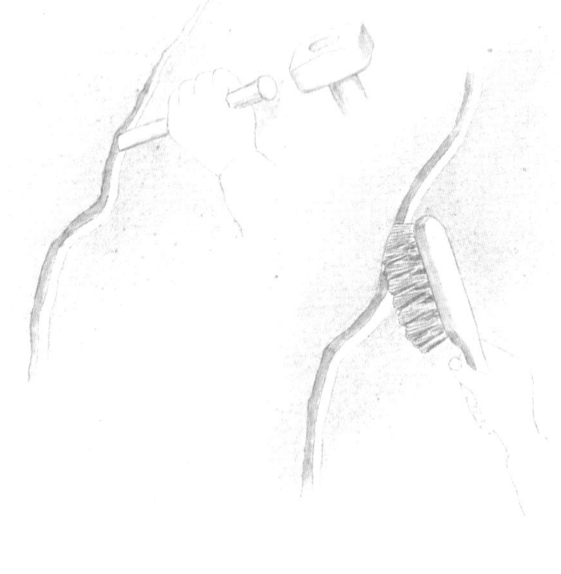

■ To repair cracks in rendering, first chip away all loose material along the line of the crack, under-cutting it to provide a better key for the repair mortar. Brush out all loose material, then spray water along the crack to stop it absorbing moisture too quickly from the repair mortar and causing it to crack. Finally, force mortar into the crack and trowel it off level with the wall surface.

PATCHING RENDERING

If rendering is coming away from the wall, the cause may be dampness, a fault in the rendering mix or defective brickwork joints. This is often evidenced by bulges, where it has 'blown' or, in other words, lost contact with the wall.

Tap suspect areas lightly with a hammer. If there is a fault, the rendering will fall away and you must clean off the affected area with a bolster chisel and club hammer until you reach rendering that adheres firmly to the wall.

A rendering mix consists of one part Portland cement, one part lime and six parts sand. The lime makes the rendering more flexible and easier to use. But it must be applied quickly, since after mixing you only have about 15 or 20 minutes before it becomes too firm to work. Do not add water to a setting mix since this will only weaken it.

If you do not intend painting the rendering later, take care that the ingredients of each batch mixed up are uniform. Any difference will cause the wall to look patchy.

For normal house work, you should apply two coats of rendering. The first should be a thick coat and the second, top coat a skim of about 6mm (¼in) thickness.

Rendering is a skill that requires confidence.

■ Where rendering has broken away from an external corner, repair it in two stages using a batten pinned to the wall as a guide. Pin it in place with masonry nails, repair one side of the corner, then reposition the batten and render the other face of the wall.

■ To patch an area of loose or missing rendering, first cut away all loose material with a cold chisel and club hammer. Then wet the wall surface and trowel on a rough first coat of fresh mortar. Rule off any high spots with a batten drawn upwards in a sawing motion across the repair, fill low spots and rule off again. Finally, use a float to give the repair a smooth finish, and redecorate the wall.

If you try to 'dab' the mix on to the wall, it will just fall off again. The idea is to apply it with a sweeping motion. Always work from the bottom of the patch upwards with the first coat. When that has been applied and is starting to set, scratch it to form a key for the second coat to grip. Allow 24 hours before applying the final coat, starting at the top this time and working from left to right with the same flowing movement. When you have completed the patch, level the new rendering off with the surrounding wall surface. Then leave this till it is almost dry before drawing a steel float, dampened with water, across it to give a smooth, flat finish.

REPAIRING PEBBLEDASH

Although in itself a simple job, the problem with making a repair to an area of pebbledash is that it will be impossible to conceal. Bearing in mind that the existing rendering will probably have been weathering for years, the possibility of recreating a similar colour is most unlikely. You may well have a similar problem obtaining pebbles to match the original material. The only effective way of disguising any repair is to repaint the whole wall afterwards.

To repair pebbledash, you first need to render the wall (see Rendering) in two stages, leaving the first coat short of the wall surface. Mix the second coat to a slightly more buttery consistency so that the pebbles stick well.

Before you start, wash and drain all the pebbles and lay a sheet of polythene below the work area to catch any that fall. You can wash and drain them for re-use afterwards.

Since the pebbles must be applied while the rendering is still wet, work to an area that you can pebbledash in about 15 or 20 minutes. Then render and pebbledash the adjoining area.

Use a small scoop to throw the pebbles at the wall, making sure you cover it evenly. As you complete each area, use a float to press the pebbles lightly but firmly into the rendering.

REPLACING AIRBRICKS

Broken airbricks can cause additional problems, since they will provide access for vermin under the ground floor, where they may multiply and find their way into other parts of the house. You will need to remove the old airbrick and replace it with one of the same style and size.

With a solid wall, it is unlikely that the opening will be lined. In more modern houses, the cavity between the inner and outer skins of the brickwork should be sealed to prevent dissipation of air into the cavity. You can do this with clay ducts or slates.

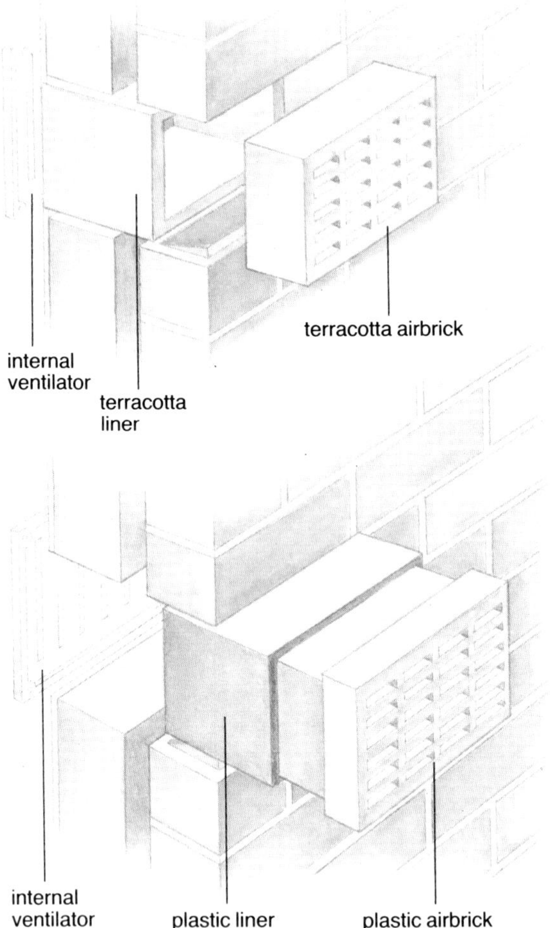

■ Airbricks are essential for providing ventilation to the voids beneath timber floors, and so helping to prevent rot attacking the floor timbers. Terracotta bricks are installed with a matching cavity sleeve, while plastic types slide within a plastic sleeve to cope with a range of wall thicknesses. Both come in a range of sizes.

Replacement airbricks, which are made from clay, cast iron or cast aluminium, must fit flush with the surface of the wall and be bedded in with cement mortar.

Remember to keep airbricks clear. They must never be blocked up, since their purpose is to ventilate timber floors and prevent them from getting damp and being attacked by rot.

REPAIRING CLADDING

Unless timber cladding was properly treated with preservative before being fixed and has been kept well decorated since, it is more than likely to rot. And once this has set in, it can travel quickly from board to board and to the fixing battens behind.

Other problems include boards warping or becoming distorted through inadequate fixings or by having been butted up tightly, leaving no room for natural expansion.

If existing rot is in its infancy, any decayed wood can be dug out and the cavity filled with exterior grade woodfiller. If the damage is more extensive, you should remove the affected

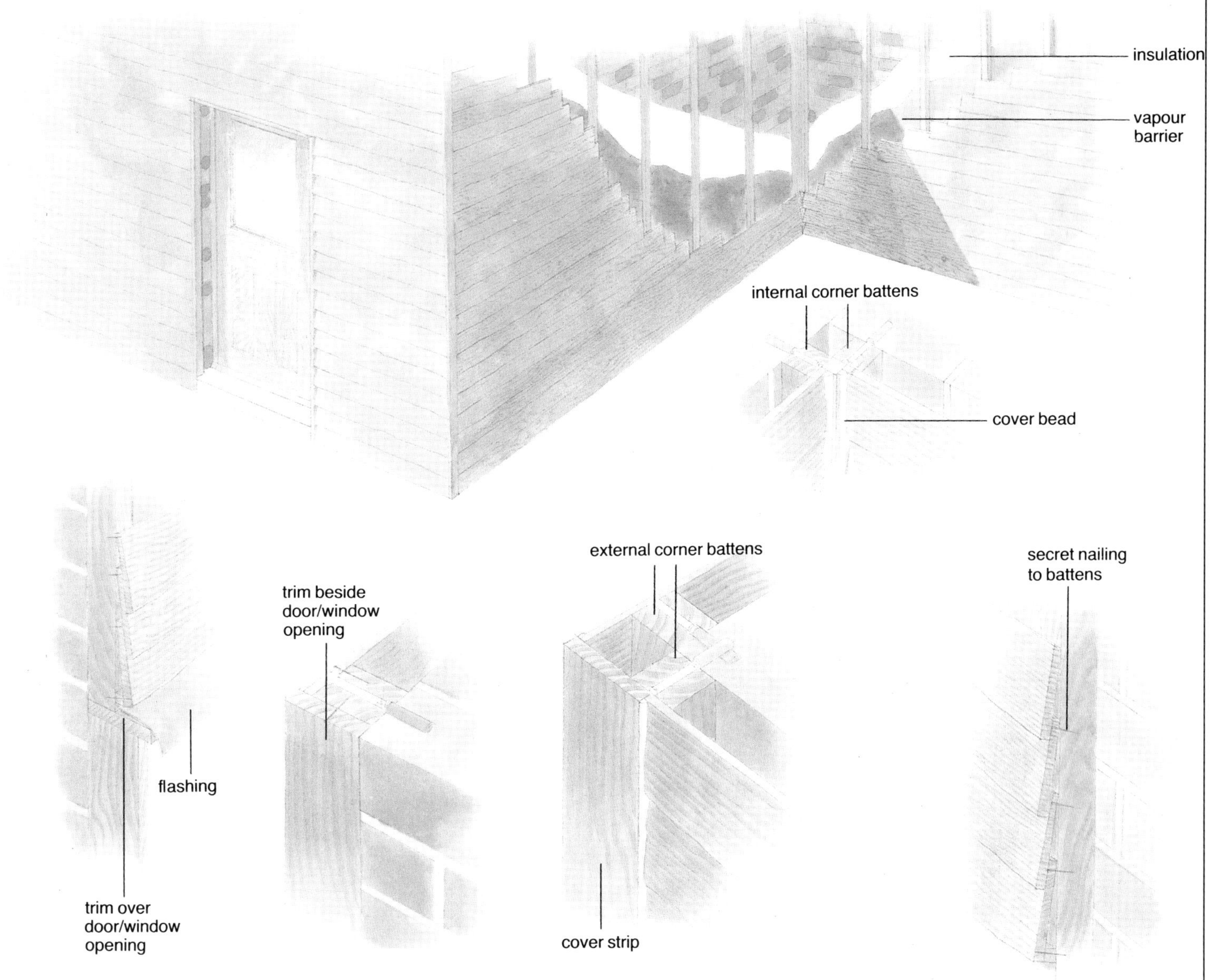

insulation
vapour barrier
internal corner battens
cover bead
external corner battens
secret nailing to battens
trim beside door/window opening
flashing
trim over door/window opening
cover strip

boards and discard them. If the rot is widespread, you may even have to take off all the boards – and the battens, too.

You might get away with refixing one or two boards without tampering with the remainder. But it is probably going to be far easier to refix the boards by working right back to the battens.

Sometimes you can pull warped boards back into place by refixing them to the battens with rustproof screws. If the boards are badly distorted, however, you will have to remove and replace them, again using rustproof screws to fix them firmly in position.

If fitted correctly, plastic cladding should require no more than the occasional cleaning with warm water and detergent. Problems such as cracking, which indicates that the cladding was fixed too tightly in the first place, mean it will have to be replaced.

■ Weatherboarding is fixed direct to the frame members of timber-framed buildings, or to vertical timber battens fixed to the face of solid masonry walls (usually over a waterproof lining of building paper, and often over insulation as well). Extra battens form a neat junction at internal and external corners, and round window and door openings.

Wall Insulation and Damp-proofing

House walls are built in one of two ways – either as a solid wall of bricks or as a cavity wall comprising two walls with a 50mm (2in) gap between them.

Most houses built more than 60 years ago had solid walls although some, of course, used stone as opposed to brick. And it was the thickness of the walling material used that prevented dampness penetrating through to the inside of the house.

In a prolonged rainy spell moisture would seep into the wall, but the bricks would be sufficiently dense to restrict its progress to a minimum. When the rain stopped, the wall would dry out and any damp would disappear. Unfortunately, through the years bricks can age and become more porous, mortar joints decay and the bricks themselves can be spalled or cracked. So the system breaks down. The walls no longer keep out the moisture and very soon you have damp walls, which in turn lead to ruined decorations and possibly mould growth.

The theory behind the cavity wall design is that the wall is bound to remain waterproof since even if moisture seeps through the 115mm (4½in) thickness of the outer skin, it cannot penetrate any further since there is an air space between that and the inner brick skin. So the inside wall stays dry.

By and large the theory works, although occasionally shoddy workmanship at the building stage can cause it to fail. Problems arise when excess mortar is dropped into the cavity, where it lands and sets on the metal wall ties used to hold the two brick walls together. This creates a bridge for the moisture to cross and reach the inner wall.

Dampness caused by moisture forcing itself through a wall is known as penetrating damp. Generally the position of the wet patch inside the house will be directly behind the problem area, so locating the trouble and effecting repairs are relatively straightforward.

Far more serious is rising damp, since this can be fed continuously from moisture in the ground. It can climb right up a wall and eventually soak into structural timbers, setting off a wet or dry rot attack.

To prevent rising damp, most houses have an in-built barrier known as the damp-proof course (dpc). This is a continuous strip of impervious material set into the external brickwork a few courses above ground level, which forms an unbroken barrier against damp.

■ Keeping heat in and damp out have been the main tasks facing the outer envelope of every house through the ages. Modern building techniques still draw on the solutions tried and tested over time, including tile hanging and rendering to improve weatherproofing.

In a modern house with solid concrete ground floors, a damp-proof membrane (dpm) is laid across the floor screed to link up with the dpc. Thus there is a complete blanket across the house. However, with poor building practice or accidental damage, a dpc or dpm can fail.

A house with suspended timber ground floors (that is with floorboards or chipboard sheets laid on joists) does not normally have a damp problem since the floor is raised up from the ground and is continually ventilated through airbricks set around the house walls. These airbricks must be kept clear and never be blocked up or the airflow will be impeded and the wood could eventually rot.

People are often tempted to block up airbricks to cut down on draughts around the floor. Never do this. If you have draught problems, the solution is to seal any gaps in the floor.

COPING WITH PENETRATING DAMP

Where a wall is in good general condition but suffers from damp, there are two ways of keeping it dry. A coat of good quality exterior wall paint will be effective and this can be applied over bricks, rendering or pebbledash.

Should you not want to use paint, but retain the 'natural' look of the wall, the answer is to apply a coat of silicone water-repellent sealer. This is a colourless liquid that you brush on and leave to soak into the wall, thus forming a chemical barrier against moisture penetration.

The liquid does not seal the surface, but rather acts like a micro-porous paint, preventing rainwater penetrating but allowing moisture vapour inside the wall to escape.

Remember to lay polythene sheeting over any path or patio likely to be splashed when you are applying the sealer. Should any fall on these surfaces, you will get a strange patchy effect whenever it rains.

You should apply the sealer only to dry surfaces – never when the wall is wet. And it should not be used before rendering or painting, as it contains silicone resins that prevent good adhesion. Before you apply it, always carry out any essential repair work first, such as replacing damaged pointing and attending to missing or damaged bricks.

COPING WITH RISING DAMP

Inside the house rising damp will show itself in several ways. The most obvious signs will be with the decorations. Paint will blister and flake off; paper will start to peel from the wall; and in the worst cases plaster will begin to crumble.

■ Rising damp can result from a failed damp course (above) or from water splashing above the damp course round blocked gullies (left). The result is damp patches on the inside walls (right), which ruin the decorations and weaken the plaster, and which can also lead to outbreaks of rot in floors and skirting boards (below).

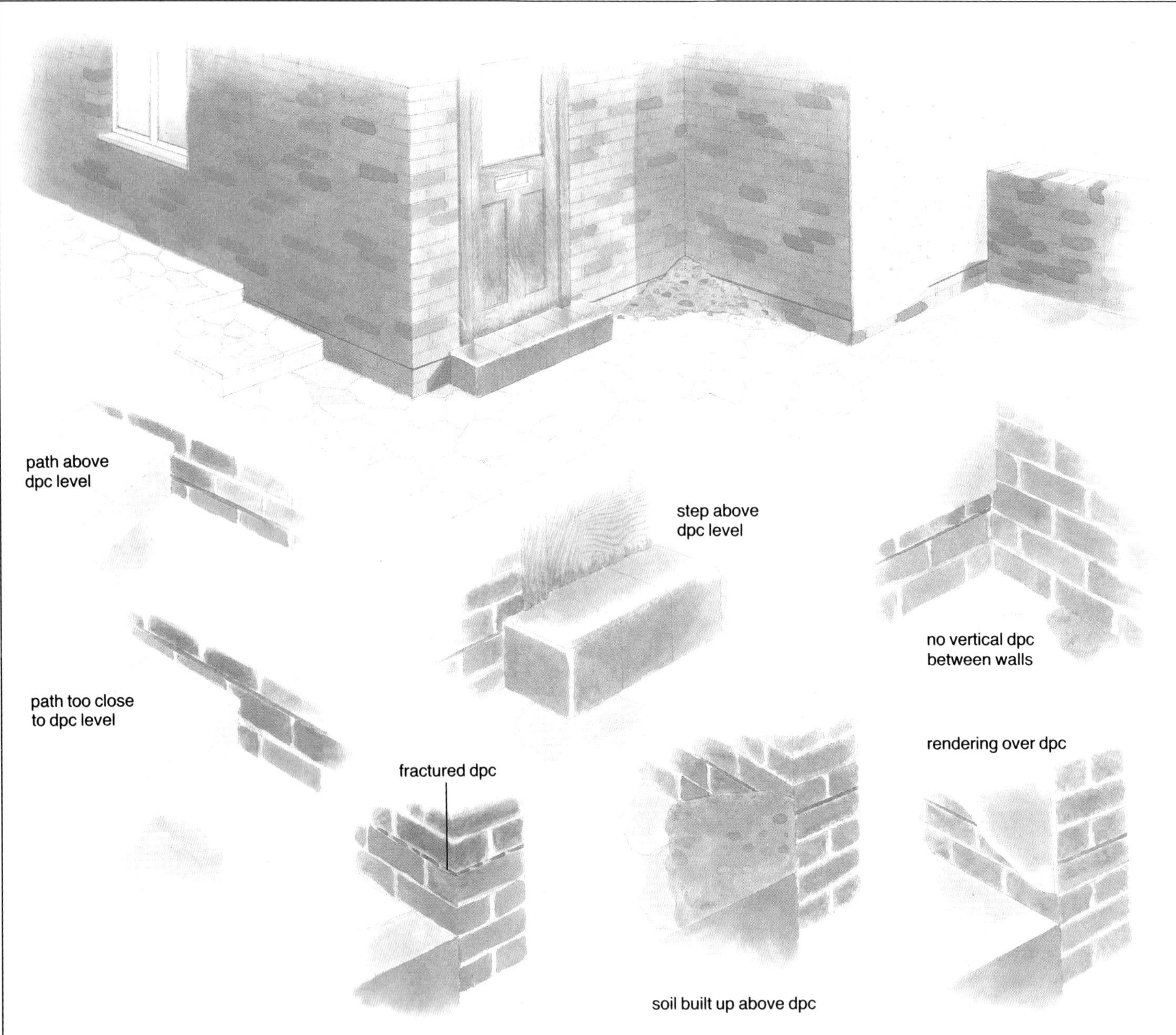

Curing rising damp

Rising damp is caused when moisture from the ground on which the house stands is soaked up into its masonry walls. The dampness can rise to a height of 3ft or so above skirting board level, causing unsightly staining of the plaster and the decorations and also an unpleasant smell in the affected rooms. It can also cause rot in floor timbers, door frames and skirting boards.

The dampness can be caused by a failure in the dampproof course that is built into the walls – a particularly common fault in older properties where slates or engineering bricks were used to form the damp course. It can also result from the damp course being bridged in some way – by an adjoining wall, by garden soil being banked up against the wall, or by steps, paths or other outdoor features being built alongside the wall. The latter need not be above the damp course level to cause rising damp; heavy rain can splash back off these surfaces to soak the wall above. Even a coat of rendering on the exterior wall can suck moisture up above the damp course if it extends down over it.

If you have rising damp, check whether any of the above-mentioned problems are present. Remove any you find and see whether the wall shows signs of drying out. Only if the problem persists should you call in a professional firm of dampproofing specialists for their advice on the best solution to the problem.

■ Common causes of rising damp include cracks in old damp courses, paths and steps built against the wall above (or close to) the level of the damp course, adjoining garden or outbuilding walls built against the house wall without a vertical damp course, rendering covering the damp course or garden soil built up against the house wall above it.

At the highest point of the rising damp there will be an ugly tide-mark. Along this mark a mat of fine, furry salt crystals will form, looking like thin wispy cotton wool. Where the wall is very damp, green and black mould will begin to grow and this will, of course, further affect the interior decorations.

It is not only rising damp, however, that causes these faults. You should also check for such things as leaking gutters and downpipes, internal plumbing leaks, drainage faults and even cracked window and door sills. All can produce the same effect.

Although you can buy a moisture meter to test for damp, you may prefer to call in a specialist to identify and possibly treat the problem. First, however, have a good look round the house to see if something has been done inadvertently to create the condition. A pile of earth or a rockery built against the wall above the dpc level will, for example, serve as a bridge for moisture to rise up within the wall structure unchecked.

The same is true of a path or patio that has been near to dpc level. You should always allow a gap of around 150mm (6in) or two brick courses between the top of a path and the dpc. Internal plaster or external rendering taken down over a dpc would also allow moisture to creep past unchecked. In all these cases, the affected area is usually isolated. Once a repair has been carried out, the wall should dry and remain so.

In the absence of any obvious signs such as those mentioned, a new dpc may well be required. For this you will probably need to call in a professional dampproofing company.

There are several methods available. One is to cut out a course of bricks in sets of three, spaced three bricks apart, and insert engineering or water-resistant bricks in waterproofed mortar. The remaining sets of bricks can be cut out and replaced after the mortar bedding the first sets has hardened.

A special saw can be used to cut through a bed joint and a metal dpc can be inserted in sections, like the bricks. Here the bedding mortar has to be carefully packed in to ensure there is no settlement later.

Alternatively, you can install your own dpc by injecting a chemical into the wall. The method is fairly simple. You drill holes into the wall and force the chemical in through hose nozzles connected to a special machine that pumps the liquid to the hoses.

The pump and injection equipment can be hired and sufficient drums of the chemical injection fluid bought to complete the job. Your supplier will provide details of how to use the pump and how much chemical you will need. The length of the wall and porosity of the bricks are the determining factors.

But even when a damp problem has been cured, it can take several months for walls to dry out. During this time, as moisture finds its way to the surface it carries with it alkaline salts from within the building materials, causing efflorescence. Occurring on both internal and external surfaces, this will cause paint, wall-

■ A battery-powered damp meter will reveal the presence of rising damp in walls, since wet masonry conducts electricity.

■ Once a new damp course has been injected, the old salt-infested plaster has to be hacked off and replaced.

Injecting a dampproof course

The most widely-used method of installing a new dampproof course in a masonry wall is to drill a series of holes into the masonry at regular intervals and then to pump in special waterproofing chemicals under pressure. These soak right through the wall and penetrate up to two courses of brickwork above and below the injection site. The chemical then cures to form a waterproof barrier that prevents moisture from rising up the wall. The injection process can also be used on internal solid partition walls built up off the `house foundations.

As part of the dampproofing treatment, it is usually essential to hack off all interior plastering to a height of about 1m (3ft) on the affected walls, to get rid of mineral salts carried into the plaster by the rising dampness. This is then replaced with specially formulated plaster that will prevent salts in the masonry from being

brought to the wall surface as the wall dries out.

You may prefer to employ a specialist firm to install a new dpc, but this is a highly labour-intensive job and since you can hire the same pressure injection equipment that a specialist uses, there is no reason why you should not do so and inject a new chemical dpc yourself. You buy the special chemicals when you hire the equipment, on a sale-or-return basis.

Exactly how you proceed depends on whether you are dealing with solid or cavity walls. The former are usually about 230mm (9in) thick, while the latter generally measure around 280mm (11in). The injection is carried out in two stages, working wherever possible from outside the house, so the depth of the holes you drill in the masonry depends on the wall thickness. For both types of wall the first hole is drilled about 75mm (3in) deep, and the first stage of the injection is carried out. Then the same holes are drilled deeper – to 150mm (6in) in solid walls, and 200mm (8in) in cavity walls – and the second stage is completed using longer nozzles. It is worth hiring a professional-quality power drill to make the injection holes. This avoids the risk of overloading and burning out your own drill. Check that you have enough chemical – you may need up to 3 litres per metre of wall if the bricks are very porous. Once the new dpc has been injected, you can fill the injection holes with mortar coloured with pigment.

■ Efflorescence (far left) is a powdery surface deposit caused by moisture in the wall carrying soluble mineral salts to the wall surface and evaporating to leave the crystalline salts behind. Brush it off if it occurs; wetting it will redissolve the salts and drive them back into the wall.

paper and other decorations to fall away. The usual practice is not to decorate until offending areas have dried out completely and the salts no longer form on the surface.

Check the drying-out period with the manufacturers of both the chemical fluid and the plaster. Some recommend allowing as much as one month of drying time for every 25mm (1in) of wall thickness.

If you need to complete the work sooner, you can use a special sealer. Several branded products are available. This can be applied to any interior surface where damp has been present, then painted or papered over within a few hours. It does not provide a solution to damp. It just enables you to redecorate after the repair work has been completed.

Of course, sealing the wall from the inside will make rooms habitable but will not solve the problem. If the masonry of the wall is allowed to remain damp, it is possible that mortar joints will eventually crumble, leading to structural damage. So you will need to address this problem as well.

Using frame sealants

Damp patches on the walls around a window frame indicate that rain is seeping through the gap between the frame and the wall. These gaps are sealed when the windows are installed, but often the old caulking material used fails and eventually falls out.

The problem with using a normal cellulose filler or mortar mix to fill these gaps is that both set rigid. Throughout the year the gap opens and closes due to natural seasonal movement of the structure. Since the filling material is rigid, it eventually cracks and falls out.

In this situation you must use a mastic sealant, which will remain flexible. There are sealants available for different situations and you need to buy one specifically for dealing with window frames. They are supplied in a cartridge and used with a special applicator gun, which you have to buy separately. Colours include white, grey and brown and the mastic can be painted over if desired.

First you must prepare the affected area, brushing down the gap and surround to remove dirt and debris. Then apply the sealant as a continuous bead along the length of the gap.

Using expanding foam fillers

Wherever pipes, cables or flues penetrate walls or roofs, there is a potential damp problem lurking. An ideal quick solution for sealing such areas is available with expanding foam fillers. Supplied in an aerosol, these fillers are simply sprayed on, then left to expand and fill any shape of hole. They will stick to virtually any surface and can be cut or shaped with a knife or hacksaw when dry. However, they can be very sticky to the touch, so always wear protective gloves when using them.

Filler foams are ideal for sealing irregular gaps in awkward places, the kind of areas that would otherwise be inadequately plugged or left exposed to allow damp to gain a hold.

Most filler foams need some additional protection, however, when used outdoors. After such fillings have thoroughly dried, you can apply a conventional filler or cement render over the top.

■ Expanding foam fillers are ideal for filling irregular gaps. Trim them to shape once they have hardened, and protect them with a layer of exterior filler or mortar.

■ Mastics are used to seal a wide range of small gaps on house exteriors – round window frames, for example, or on timber cladding. Their surface quickly skins over, allowing them to be painted if necessary, but the body of the mastic bead stays flexible and so copes with any structural movement that may occur.

INSULATING WALLS

Insulating the cavity of modern house walls by pumping in a special insulant is a well-established practice. The insulating material completely fills the cavity and, together with trapped air, serves as a barrier to heat loss through the walls.

You have a basic choice of three materials – mineral wool, polystyrene beads or foam – all of which will remain stable for the life of the building, providing it is not altered structurally. Each material will prevent water passing across the cavity or from below the dpc level. Equally, the fire resistance of the wall is unaffected and rot, fungi and vermin are resisted.

Cavity wall insulation is not, however, a DIY job and you must contact a local specialist company with the right equipment and trained operatives to do the work.

Initially the house will be surveyed to ensure it is structurally sound and suitable for this kind of insulation process. The work involves pumping the material into the cavity through a series of holes drilled in the house walls at strategic positions. When the job is completed, the holes are filled in. Normally such work takes a day – sometimes two.

■ Cavity wall insulation is pumped into the wall cavity via holes drilled in the outer leaf of the wall by trained operatives using specialist equipment; it is not a do-it-yourself job. Once the cavities are filled, the injection holes are plugged with matching mortar.

■ External wall insulation is used to improve the heat retention performance of solid walls where internal insulation is not feasible. The insulation is clipped to the wall surface, covered with special mesh and then rendered over to create a durable exterior wall surface. It is a job for specialist insulation contractors.

Treating solid walls

Normally solid walls are insulated from the inside using one of a variety of methods (see Insulation, page 190). There are, however, ways of doing the job effectively externally.

Certainly exterior insulation is worth considering if the house walls are in a relatively poor state – with patches of missing rendering or damaged bricks, for example. It is also a sound option where fixing internal insulation would cause an undue amount of upheaval.

Any method involving rendering must be left to professional specialists, from whom you should be prepared for a fairly high quote compared to the price of interior work. The alternative is to fix cladding – a job that can be tackled on a DIY basis and should work out much less expensive.

Should you want to have this work done, then you can choose to have a layer – from 25 to 75mm (1–3in) – of polystyrene, polyurethane or foamed glass fixed to the wall, reinforced with metal laths and then covered with a coat of cement rendering.

Alternatively mineral fibre slabs covered with a protective wire lathing or reinforced with fibrous mesh can be used. These are then covered with cladding or rendering.

Finally, expanded polystyrene beads can be incorporated into a cement render and trowelled on to the wall.

Using timber cladding

Cladding all or part of a house serves a dual role of decorating and insulating at the same time. Although it can cover whole walls, it is also popularly used to highlight features such as porches, bay walls, gable ends or dormers. And often just one storey of the house – upper or lower – is clad.

You should remember, however, that cladding is not intended to cover up unsound walls. On the contrary, it can only be fixed to stable rendering or brickwork. Any area chosen for such treatment must also be dry, so existing damp problems have to be solved first. If the timber battens to which the cladding is fixed have started to rot or are prone to do so, the cladding itself will eventually be affected.

Houses have been clad with timber for centuries, with early examples often of expensive oak or elm. In those days, however, the cladding was really part of the house structure, whereas now it is usually decorative.

Today softwood is almost always used because of the prohibitive cost of suitable hard-

■ Timber cladding has a long architectural history, especially in areas where timber-framed construction is commonplace.

Shiplap cladding (below) is an alternative to plain weatherboarding, offering better weatherproofing thanks to the positive overlap of the machined boards. On solid walls it is fixed to a framework of timber battens.

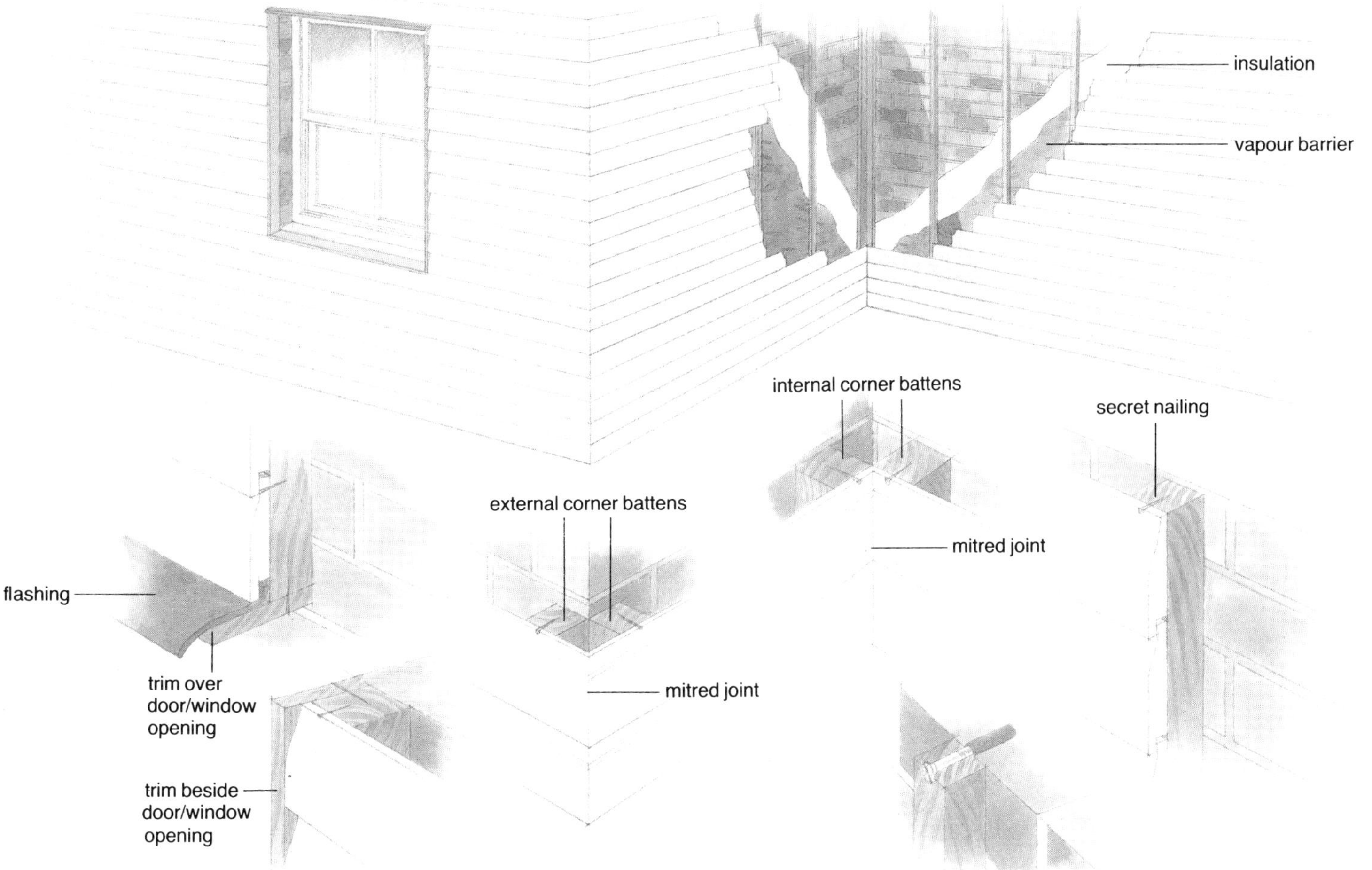

insulation
vapour barrier
internal corner battens
secret nailing
external corner battens
mitred joint
flashing
trim over door/window opening
mitred joint
trim beside door/window opening

woods, quite apart from the environmental considerations involving the destruction of invaluable trees not necessary for such a purpose. And it is widely available in a range of different profiles.

The simplest is feather-edge boarding, wedge-shaped planks similar to those used for fencing. These are fixed horizontally, with their thicker bottom edge overlapping the thinner top edge of the boards below.

Waney-edged boards are usually of uniform thickness, but have irregular-shaped bottom edges (often with the outside bark of the log still attached). These are fixed in the same way.

Both types are, however, prone to warping which can leave open gaps in the cladding. Waney-edged boards are particularly vulnerable because of the way they are sawn. They therefore tend to be used more on garden outbuildings or small feature areas of the house.

Shiplap cladding involves boards with a profiled cross-section with a rebate machined along one edge. These are the most widely used, having a more positive overlap between boards and resulting in a more weatherproof finish.

Tongued-and-grooved boards are also frequently used. Here the tongues of one board interlock with the grooves in the next, so warping is less of a problem and weather resistance is improved. Boards may be fixed vertically or even diagonally with little loss of performance. Additional detailing can be provided if boards with a machined V-joint are used as an alternative to plain boards.

Using plastic cladding

Maintenance problems with timber cladding have been the main reason why unplasticised polyvinyl chloride (upvc) versions have emerged in recent years.

Upvc scores over timber because it does not rot, split or warp, cannot suffer from insect attack and does not need painting. All it requires is an annual clean down with detergent and the occasional, more frequent wash. In all other respects it is like timber, and can be cut and nailed or screwed in much the same way.

It is manufactured in profiles that resemble traditional timber cladding and matching fascias, bargeboards, soffits and window trims are also available. Although mainly used in white, other colours are produced. Lengths are commonly 4 or 5m and widths usually between 100 and 150mm – much as for timber. Special sections are available for joining lengths – edge-on or at corners – and edging strips are used to finish

■ Plastic cladding is the 20th century's alternative to weatherboarding and shiplap cladding. It can be fixed to timber-framed or masonry walls, and an ingenious range of trims and cover strips makes the surface weatherproof and almost maintenance-free.

the top and bottom edges of the cladding.

The material expands more than timber, so extra care should be taken to fix it following the manufacturer's instructions. You must allow enough space for the boards to expand or contract as temperatures fluctuate. Even so, plastic cladding may creak as it expands and contracts with changes in temperature.

Some boards are hollow-backed, while others contain internal stiffening ribs or a solid cellular core. Fixing is to timber wall battens using special clips or by direct nailing.

Where joins between lengths have to be made, these can be randomly spaced and hidden with special clip-on joint covers or aligned and covered with a continuous centre-joint trim.

Plastic cladding can be painted using ordinary gloss. Simply wash down the surface thoroughly to remove dirt and grease, then lightly abrade it with fine wet-and-dry abrasive paper to provide a good key for the paint.

Increasing the insulation value

Although cladding itself provides additional weatherproofing and insulation, you can increase this by incorporating a lining of suitable insulating material between the house wall and the cladding.

The simplest way is to position slabs of rigid polystyrene insulation board between the battens. Alternatively, use mineral wool or glass fibre insulation sheathed in waterproof building paper. This usually has paper edges along each side, which you staple to the battens. This makes fixing the insulation a great deal easier.

Remember to leave a gap at least 12mm (½in) wide between the outer face of the insulation and the inner face of the cladding to allow air to circulate.

■ Tile hanging is a widely used way of improving the weatherproofing of external walls on both timber-frames and solid masonry walls. Decorative inserts can relieve the visual tedium of large areas of plain tiles.

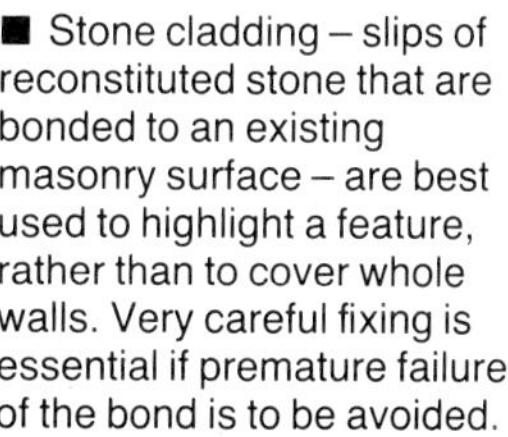

■ Stone cladding – slips of reconstituted stone that are bonded to an existing masonry surface – are best used to highlight a feature, rather than to cover whole walls. Very careful fixing is essential if premature failure of the bond is to be avoided.

Using hanging tiles

Exterior wall tiles are an alternative to cladding for protecting outside walls and enhancing their appearance. They are basically the same as plain tiles used on roofs, and are very durable and quite attractive.

The tiles are fixed on horizontal battens nailed to the wall over a felt or building paper lining. But unlike roof tiles, they are nailed on every row. As well as the plain rectangular tiles, several ornamental patterns are also available for a more decorative effect.

Cladding with stone

Should you wish to make a feature of something like a bay window or porch and you would like a stone effect rather than wood, you can buy stone or brick tiles to use as cladding. These are generally stuck to the wall with a special mortar adhesive.

A variety of types, sizes, shapes and thicknesses is available and you will need to follow the manufacturer's instructions carefully as to the correct fixing methods, especially with the heavier tiles. Some may need additional mechanical support. Most exterior stone cladding is reconstituted, although natural stone such as slate is sometimes also used.

External Doors and Windows

Whatever the type or age of a property, you will need to examine the external doors and windows carefully to see if they need to be repaired – or, at worst, replaced. In the latter case, you have the opportunity of enlarging, moving or adding extra doors and windows and this work is best combined with any plans you may have for repairing or rebuilding walls.

When you fit replacements, you should certainly consider the option of installing double glazing, which will save on energy, reduce heating costs and make the house a more comfortable place to live in.

BASIC TYPES OF DOOR

The chances are that external doors will be made from timber, although you may come across some of aluminium or even plastic. These are usually found in houses where doors have recently been replaced.

Anodised aluminium is widely used for front doors in a modern glass-panelled style. These are usually double-glazed with obscured, toughened safety glass and are supplied ready hung in an aluminium subframe. Normally this is screwed into the existing door frame, although it may be fixed directly to the brick opening. Aluminium is also used for sliding patio doors.

Plastic-framed front doors are sometimes found in similar styles to the aluminum ones and are also usually double-glazed with safety glass. They are often found in houses where the windows, too, have been replaced with plastic-framed versions. Neither type gives rise to any special problems as far as long-term maintenance is concerned.

Timber doors are found in three basic types – panelled, flush or ledged and braced. All external doors should be a minimum of 44mm (1¾in) thick for security purposes.

Panelled doors may be solid or partially or fully glazed. The rails (horizontal members) and stiles (vertical members) are made from solid timber and are mortised and tenoned for strength. A wide middle rail is generally provided for a letterplate.

Doors of this type may be made from softwood (for painting) or hardwood (mainly for staining and varnishing, but sometimes painting). On hardwood doors the four or more panels are usually sculptured (raised and fielded) for an ornamental appearance, while softwood doors normally contain flat plywood panels that may have decorative mouldings fixed around the edges.

Exterior flush doors are naturally stronger in construction than interior ones but are made in

■ Nothing suits a house better than its original front door . . .or a replacement as close as possible to the original in appearance. The choice of door styles is immense, ranging from solid panelled types to glazed versions with plain, patterned or stained glass.

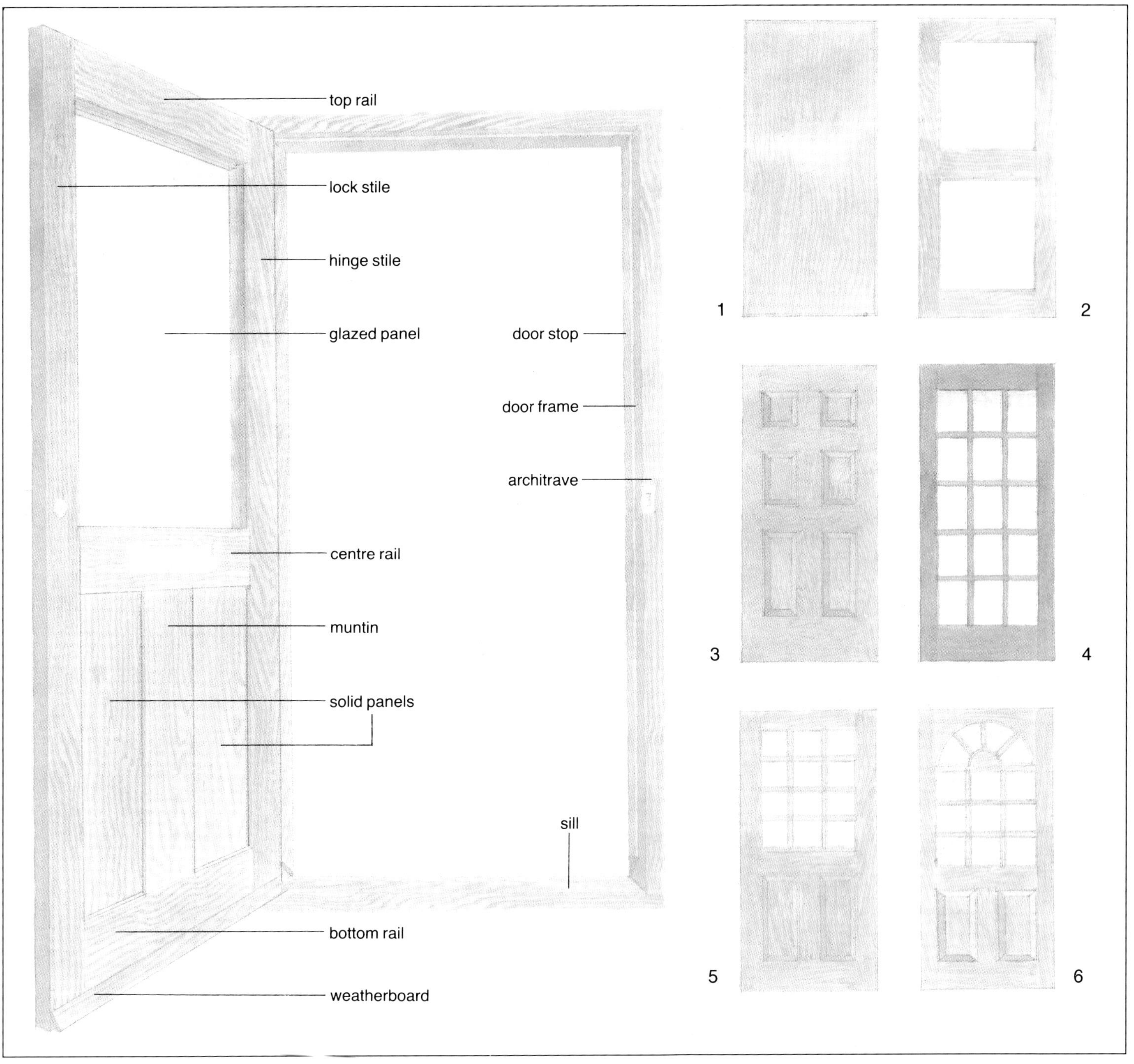

a similar way – from a light timber framework containing a honeycomb of packing material faced with exterior grade hardboard or plywood. Solid-core fire-resistant flush doors are also available.

The surfacing panels are usually flat, although they can be embossed by pressing to give the appearance of a panelled door, particularly after being painted. There is a wooden block set midway along one edge to take a lock and there may also be a centre block to take a letterplate. Usually rubber stamp marks on the edges of a new flush door indicate the precise position of these blocks.

You can buy flush doors with open panels for glazing, although most are available complete.

If you have an older property such as a country cottage, the doors may well be ledged and braced. This type is also often found on outbuildings and as side gates.

They are functional and sturdy, in most cases being made from V-jointed matchboarding nailed to wide horizontal timbers called ledges. To prevent the door from sagging, diagonal braces are fitted and it is most important to check that these run diagonally from low down on the hinge side to high on the lock side.

In superior quality houses you may find

■ Panelled and glazed doors have similar basic frameworks, with vertical stiles and horizontal rails linked by mortise-and-tenon or dowelled joints. Here (top left) a vertical muntin subdivides the lower part of the door into two panels; the upper part is glazed.

Some of the commonest door patterns (above) include the flush door (1); the two-panel door (2); the 15-pane glazed door (3); the six-panelled solid door (4) and half-glazed doors in a range of designs (5 and 6).

■ Doors can suffer from a range of different faults as a result of wear and tear, old age, lack of maintenance or improper hanging. Here are some cures for the most common problems, clockwise from top left.

1 Secure loose door frames by drilling a hole through the frame, then switch to a masonry drill bit and drill on into the masonry behind. Insert a long plastic frame plug, and screw the frame securely to the masonry.

2 Ease doors that bind in their frames at the top by chamfering the top edge slightly with a plane.

3 Tighten up loose corner joints by driving hardwood wedges into the mortise alongside the tenon, or by inserting glued dowels through the tenon.

4 Hinge screw heads that are not driven fully into their recesses will prevent the door from closing. Replace the screws if necessary.

5 Hinges set too deep in their recesses can also stop the door from closing. Fit packing under the hinge leaf to cure the problem.

6 If hinge screws work loose, remove them, drill out the screw holes and tap in a short piece of glued dowel. Make a new pilot hole and replace the screw.

7 If door bottoms bind slightly in solid floors, use abrasive paper to remove a little wood from the bottom edge of the door.

8 Where the door bottom binds seriously, take it off its hinges and plane wood from the bottom edge.

9 Cut out rot in the bottom of exterior door frames and replace it with new wood, scarf-jointed into place for extra strength.

10 Stop the leading edge binding against the door frame by sanding or planing down any high spots.

■ To replace a door frame completely, try to find out how it is assembled and work out the best way to remove it. The sides may be tenoned into a timber sill, or jointed to a solid masonry sill with steel dowels. Saw through the frame at various points so you can prise the sections away, then remove the old fixings.

Brace the new frame square with scrap timber, and cut off the projecting horns at the top unless the old frame had them. Lift the frame into position, check that it stands vertical and square within the opening, and secure it with screws driven into frame plugs.

framed ledged and braced doors. Construction here is more or less the same, except for a mortised-and-tenoned outer frame which considerably strengthens the door and enables you to fit a good mortise lock.

Fitting a replacement door frame

In contrast to internal doors, an external door frame is substantial, with the jambs (side members) and head (top) mortised together and with the sill, which will probably be of hardwood, mortised and tenoned into the jambs.

If the sill is of stone or concrete, there are likely to be galvanised steel dowels in the base of the jambs which are cemented into holes in the sill. The jambs are made from solid pieces of timber and rebated (stepped) to take the door.

If the frame was fixed when the house was built, it is likely to be held by metal ties screwed to the outside face of the frame and bedded into the mortar joints of the walls on either side of the frame. Sometimes frames are fixed by nailing or screwing them to wooden wedges or to plugs set into the horizontal brickwork joints on either side of the frame.

To remove an old frame, you will probably have to chip back the mortar at each side to expose the frame-to-brickwork join. Using a general purpose saw – or a metal-cutting blade in a trimming knife handle – cut through the metal fixings holding the frame to the wall.

At about the mid-point, use the general purpose saw to cut through the jambs at a sloping angle. This will enable you to prise away one part from the wall using a wrecking bar. With one piece out of the way, you will then be able to work round the opening, removing the other pieces of the frame in turn. Finally, with a cold chisel, remove any remaining mortar from around the opening.

If you are working with a cavity wall, check that the vertical dpc between the inner and outer leaves of the wall is undamaged. If not, you must replace it.

Check that the frame fits in the opening, then remove it and bed a strip of dpc on cement mortar at the base of the opening. Reposition the frame, making sure it is central, level and plumb (vertical) – and not twisted.

With a long masonry drill, make holes for special frame-fixing wallplugs and zinc-plated screws at each side of the frame. Make three holes on each side, drilling centrally into whole bricks if possible – and not into mortar joints. If the drill bit is long enough, you can drill straight through the frame into the wall without having to move it.

Countersink the holes in the frame before

inserting the fixings and tightening the screws. Then apply filler over the screw heads and fill the gap between the wall and frame with a bead of non-setting mastic.

Fitting a new door

Saw off the horns of the stiles that protect the corners of the door in transit, then try the door for fit by holding it against the frame. It is certain to need trimming on one or more edges. Get someone to help you hold it in place, if necessary supporting it on wedges.

Working from the frame side, mark round the edge of the frame with a pencil on to the face of the door against the frame, allowing a 2mm gap all round after trimming.

Saw across the bottom of the door and plane along the edges until the door fits correctly in the opening. Pass the plane a couple of extra times along the leading edge of the door to ensure it will clear the frame edge as it closes.

External door frames usually have a metal water bar along the sill. To prevent draughts and water ingress, it is important that the door closes up against this. Therefore you must cut a rebate (or step) along the bottom edge of the door on the face (outer) side. You will need a router and suitable cutter for this. Otherwise use a circular saw to cut the rebate to the correct depth, or form it with a power planer or rebate plane.

If you are fitting the door in an old frame, mark the hinge positions on the back of the door while it is wedged in the opening with the correct clearance all round. Remove the door and transfer the marked hinge positions on to the edge of the door.

Cut the recesses with a chisel, holding it upright and striking it with a mallet to cut the outline of the recess. Then make a series of cuts about 6mm apart across the width of the recess. Turn the chisel so it is flat in the recess and pare out the waste wood.

Get someone to hold the door on wedges in its open position and then, with the hinge flaps positioned in their recesses, initially fit just one screw in each hinge. Close the door to see how it fits in the frame, adjusting the depth of the hinge recesses if it binds. When you are satisfied that it fits correctly, insert the rest of the fixing screws.

If you are fitting the door in a new frame, wedge the door in place and mark the hinge positions on both the door and the frame. Use three hinges for an external door. The highest one should be about 125mm (5in) from the top,

Hanging a new door

■ Hanging a new door can seem a complex operation, especially if the original door was a non-standard size. Buy a door in the next largest available size so it can be cut down to fit.

1 Start by propping the door against the door frame on wedges to give the necessary floor clearance.

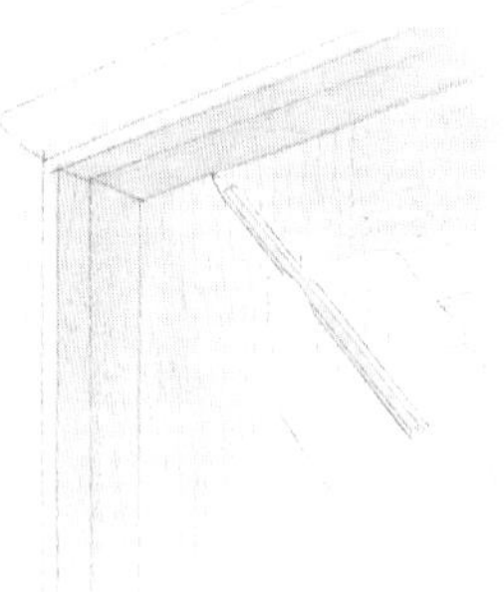

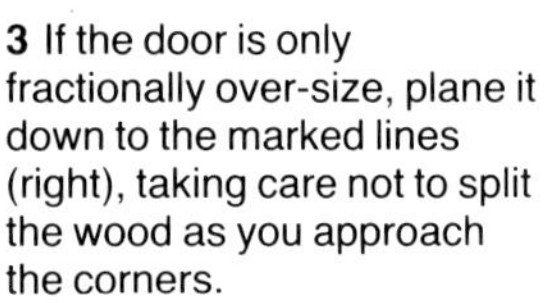

3 If the door is only fractionally over-size, plane it down to the marked lines (right), taking care not to split the wood as you approach the corners.

2 Run a pencil along the door face, first against the top of the frame (above) and then down the sides (right). It helps to have an extra pair of hands available for this stage of the job.

the lowest about 200mm (8in) from the bottom and the third midway between the two.

Remove the door, mark out the hinge recesses on the door edge and frame, then cut the recesses as described above. The width of the recesses should be such that the knuckle (pivoting part) of the hinge protrudes from the edge of the door. Finally screw the hinges in position as before.

Fitting door furniture

A back door needs a good quality mortise lock (ideally with at least five levers) and bolts top and bottom. A front door also needs a deadlocking cylinder rim latch or nightlatch so you can open it easily and quickly. Again, there should be bolts top and bottom and also a door chain and door viewer for complete security.

Locks come with fitting instructions and you must follow these carefully. Mortise locks, for example, are secure because the body of the lock is concealed within the thickness of the door. However, cutting too wide a slot for a lock can weaken the door, so buy the narrowest type available.

To fit this type you will have to mark the outline of the lock on the edge of the door and drill out the mortise slot to the depth of the lock case. Clean up the slot with a chisel and bore the door stile to take the key and spindle holes.

Rim locks screw to the surface of the door and are very easy to fit. The hardest part is drilling a large hole for the cylinder of the lock in the door stile. Use a large-diameter flat wood bit for this or drill a ring of small holes and cut out the waste with a pad saw.

It is a good idea to fit bolts at the top and bottom of all external doors, but rather than fix surface-mounted barrel bolts, go for higher security mortise rack bolts. These comprise a cylindrical bolt enclosed in a barrel which is fitted into a hole drilled in the edge of the door.

By inserting a splined key in the edge of the door, you can wind the bolt in and out. And because it is enclosed, the bolt is difficult to tamper with and therefore provides better security than a surface-mounted bolt.

If you want to fit a door chain or limiter, you simply screw the device to the inside face of the door. This will prevent an intruder barging in should you open the door.

If you have solid doors, you should always combine this type of security with a door viewer to enable you to see who is at the door before you open it. All you have to do is drill a hole of about 13mm (½in) diameter through the door at

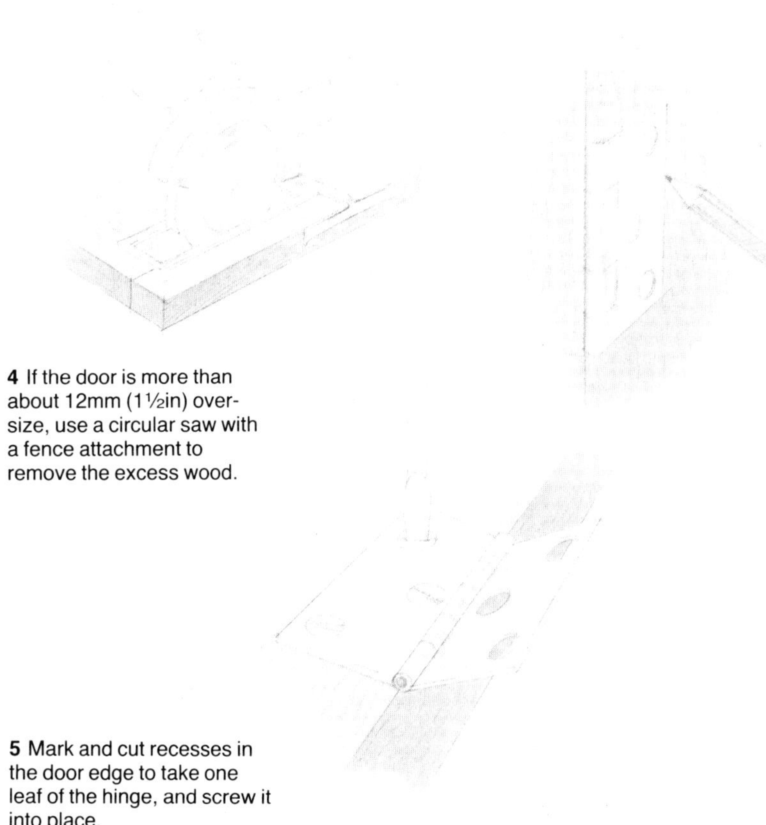

6 Hold the door up within the frame and mark the hinge position on the frame. Cut a matching recess.

4 If the door is more than about 12mm (1½in) oversize, use a circular saw with a fence attachment to remove the excess wood.

5 Mark and cut recesses in the door edge to take one leaf of the hinge, and screw it into place.

7 Screw the hinge to the door frame (left), check that the door closes properly and finish the job by fitting a latch and handle (above).

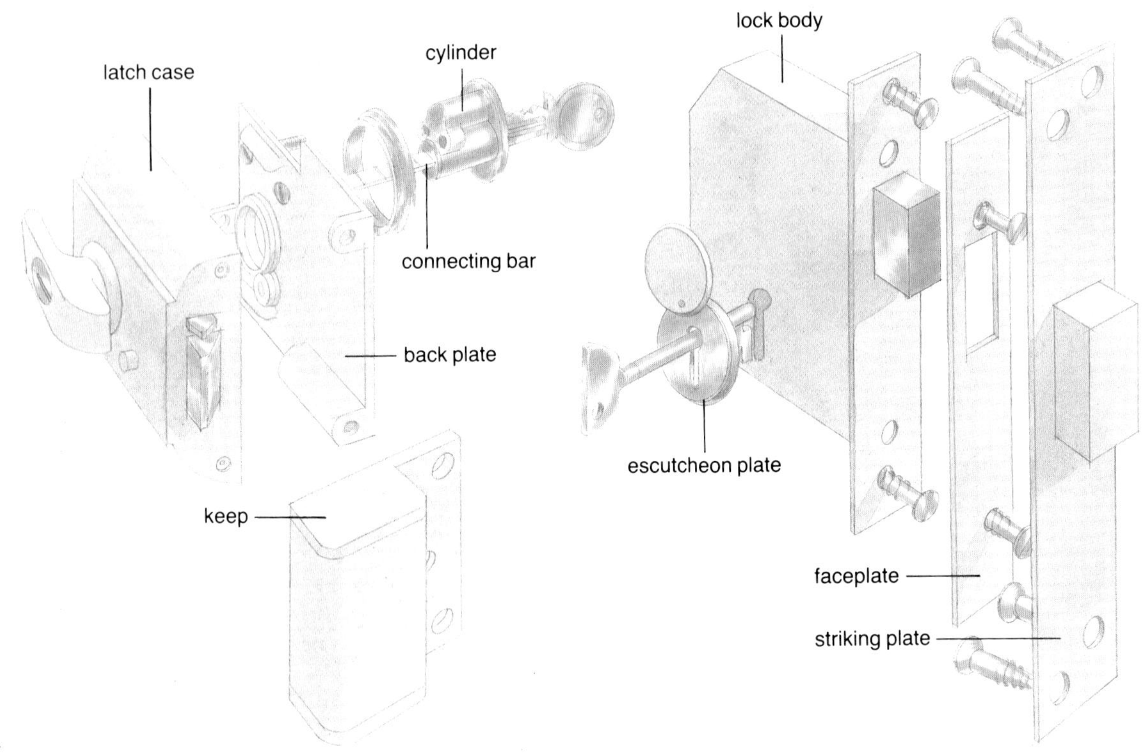

■ A cylinder or rim lock (far left) consists of a latch case that is screwed to the inner face of the door and a lock cylinder that fits in a hole drilled through the door stile. To fit one, use the template provided to mark the cylinder position and drill its hole. Screw the backplate to the door, insert the cylinder so its connecting bar passes into the backplate, and cut this to length with a hacksaw. Insert the connecting screws through the backplate to secure the cylinder, then screw the latch case to the backplate. Finally, fit the keep to the door frame.

■ A mortise lock (left) has a lock body that fits in a mortise cut in the door edge. To fit one, mark the position of the lock body on the door edge, mark out and cut the mortise and chisel out a recess in the door edge for the lock's foreplate. Mark the keyhole position on the door face, drill and cut the keyholes, then fit the lock into its mortise and check the key operation. Finally fit the striking plate to the frame.

eye level and screw the two halves of the viewer together in it.

To fit a door knocker or door pull you simply drill a hole (or holes) centrally for the fixing bolt. You fit the knocker or pull in place from the outside and then hold it secure with a fixing nut or screw on the inside.

Fitting a letterplate is more tricky. Mark out a rectangular opening on the centre of the door slightly larger than the plate flap. Drill a hole at each corner big enough for a power jigsaw blade or pad saw blade to pass through. Cut out the rectangle of wood and clean up the sides of the opening with a large chisel.

One refinement is to slope the top and bottom edges of the cut-out downwards so that letters do not lodge in the opening. Finally drill a hole at each end of the opening to take the fixing bolts and screw the letterplate in place.

BASIC TYPES OF WINDOW

Apart from the variety of styles, the first thing you will notice about windows is the range of materials from which they are made. What sort you have in your home will have a dramatic effect on the maintenance required and the problems encountered.

In the majority of cases, the windows will be made of timber. Here the type used will have a significant influence on their likely lifespan.

Many Victorian and Edwardian houses still have their original softwood windows, providing they were properly installed and have been regularly maintained since. Softwood windows on newer houses, however, are often made from European redwood and are much less durable. Even if they are correctly maintained, they are unlikely to last more than 30 or 40 years. On the other hand, you may be fortunate enough to have a house with hardwood windows. With regular maintenance these should last 60 years or more.

There are advantages of having timber windows – durability, as long as they are properly maintained; cheapness; a well-insulated frame; and a wide choice of finishes, using paint or preservative wood stains.

The disadvantages include the need for regular maintenance every few years; the rapid deterioration that takes place if the windows are not painted regularly; the lack of built-in weatherstrips to prevent draughts; and the variable quality of timber used.

The other common material used in older houses is steel. Such windows are poor insulators and condensation on the frames and glass is a frequent problem. This condensation often leads to rusting, especially on earlier frames which were not galvanised.

This type is often draughty, can look out of keeping with traditional-style properties and needs frequent painting. On the plus side, galvanised frames tend to be unaffected by damp, can be painted any colour and are not expensive to replace if required.

In houses where replacements have been fitted, you may find aluminium windows and, as likely as not, these will be double-glazed. Although they may not be aesthetically suited to an older property, they do present few problems. Bear in mind, however, that the timber subframes into which they are fitted will need frequent decoration.

Aluminium frames are unaffected by damp and are usually weather-stripped to prevent draughts. But sometimes they can suffer from condensation since older types were not fitted with a thermal break.

Anodised finishes and acrylic coatings should last 50 years or more if they are washed down regularly, although their life may be considerably shortened by pollution in industrial areas.

Plastic is a comparative newcomer to the replacement window scene, although the material has been used for years on the Continent. With such material you can expect a life of at least 30 to 40 years.

One advantage is provided by the 'chunky' look, enabling such windows to make good replacements for timber ones in older style properties. They offer good insulation and, because they are self-coloured, they generally need no decoration. You may, however, have to freshen them up with a coat of paint after 10 or 15 years.

FITTING A REPLACEMENT WINDOW

If a window has deteriorated to such an extent that repair becomes impossible, then it will be best to replace it with a new frame.

Although you will have the choice of a wide range of designs, do bear in mind the style of the house and that of the windows in neighbouring properties when selecting new ones to ensure they are sympathetic to the house's architectural style.

Removing the old frame

Always start by removing the opening frames, unscrewing them at the hinges. If the screw slots are clogged with paint, clear them by striking the handle of the screwdriver lightly with a hammer.

Next remove the fixed panes. Wearing safety spectacles and thick gloves, chip away the putty and prise out the securing brads (nails) if you

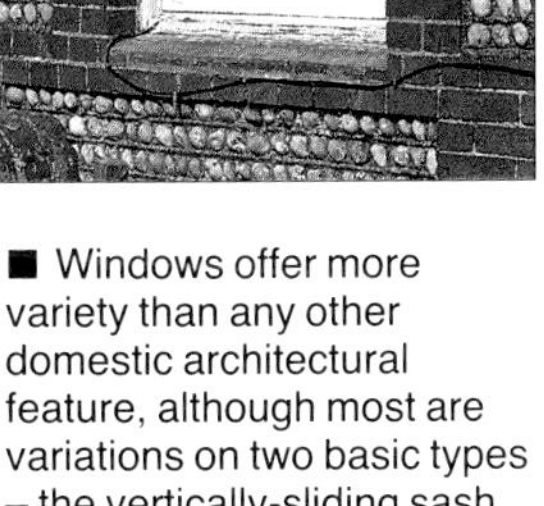

■ Windows offer more variety than any other domestic architectural feature, although most are variations on two basic types – the vertically-sliding sash window and the horizontal hinged casement. One of the biggest sins committed by home renovators is to replace old windows with new ones in a style that is inappropriate to the house – large picture windows in a Victorian terrace, for example. Careful restoration is always preferable if this is possible; otherwise having a faithful replica made is the best option.

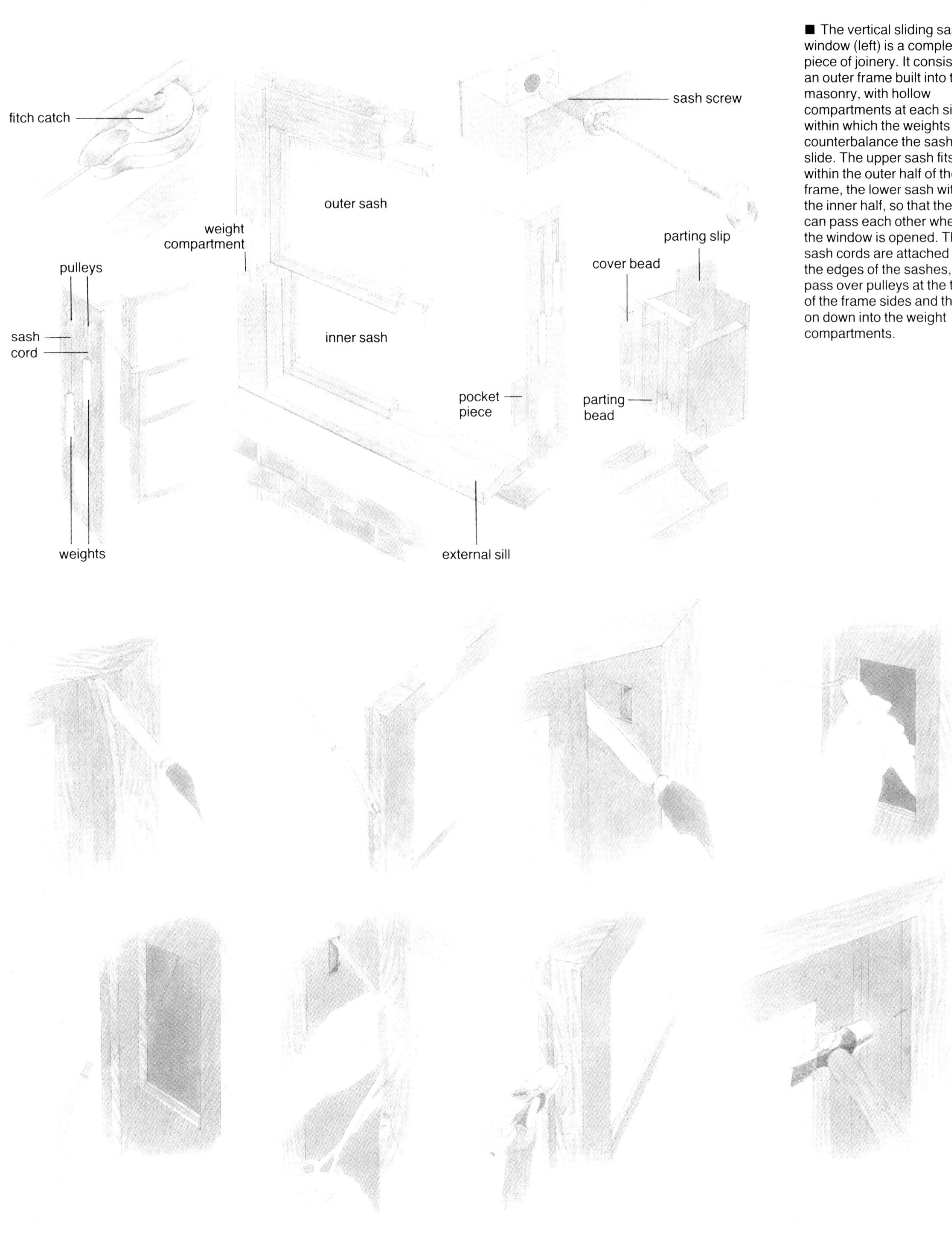

■ The vertical sliding sash window (left) is a complex piece of joinery. It consists of an outer frame built into the masonry, with hollow compartments at each side within which the weights that counterbalance the sashes slide. The upper sash fits within the outer half of the frame, the lower sash within the inner half, so that the two can pass each other when the window is opened. The sash cords are attached to the edges of the sashes, and pass over pulleys at the tops of the frame sides and then on down into the weight compartments.

■ The casement window (right) is simpler in construction than the sash window, consisting of a main outer frame into which fixed glass and hinged casements and top lights are fitted. The frame may simply be screwed to the sides of the masonry opening, or may be secured with fixing lugs or with cavity closers with built-in wall ties.

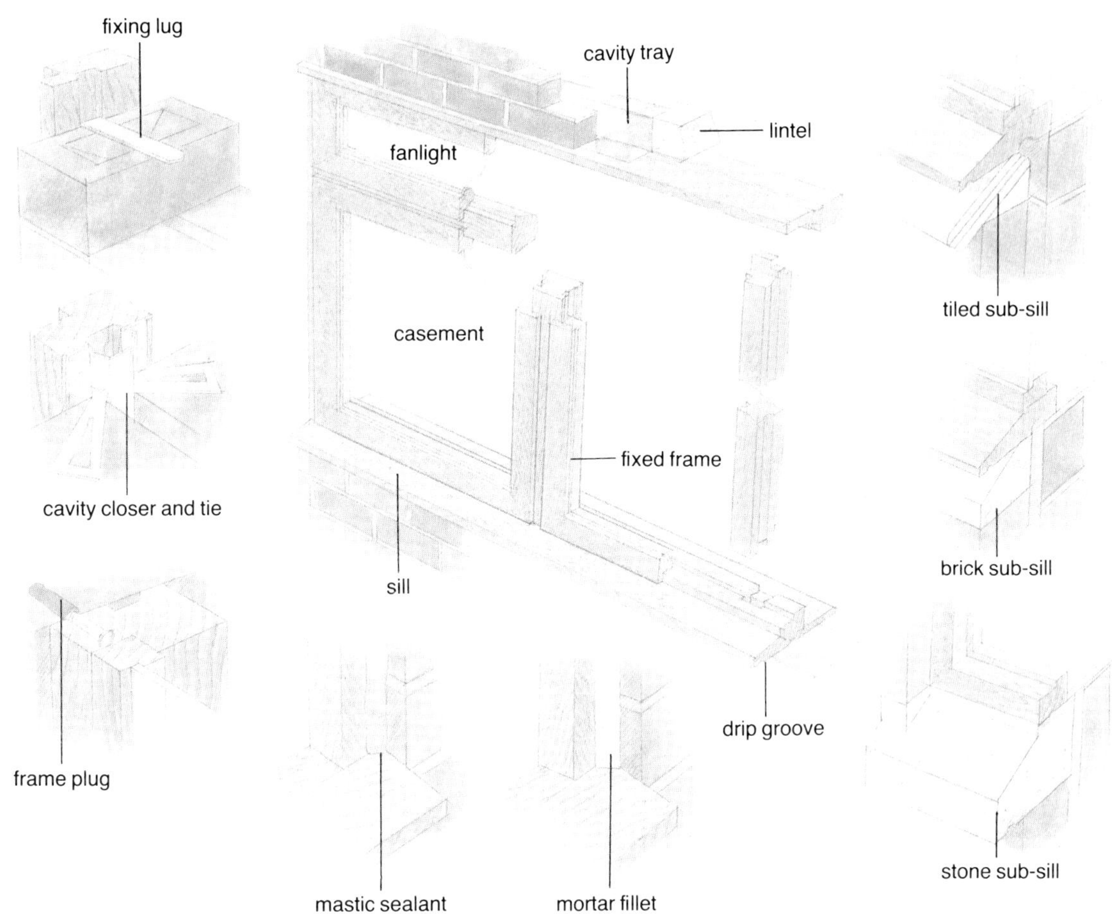

■ **Left** To replace a broken cord, start by prising off the parting bead at each side so you can lift out the inner sash. Tie string to its cords, and cut them from the sash. Remove the parting beads and repeat the procedure to free the outer sash. Then lever out the pocket pieces, lift out the weights and pull the cords out so they draw the strings over the pulleys.

Remove the old cords and tie the pulled-through string to the new cords. Draw them over their pulleys, tie on the weights and trim the other end of the cord roughly to length. Get a helper to offer up each sash in turn, and nail the new cords to the sash sides. Finally, replace the parting bead and then the sash bead.

want to save the glass. Otherwise carefully break out the old glass. If the window being replaced is itself a recent replacement, it may be possible to unscrew it and lift it out of the sub-frame in one piece.

To remove the sub-frame from the opening, use an old saw to cut through the side members. The reason for using an old saw is simply that it will not matter if the teeth hit fragments of glass, brickwork or hidden metal frame fixings.

Lever the side pieces away from the wall and then prise away the head of the frame and the sill. With a hammer and bolster chisel, clean away old mortar and frame fixings from around the window frame opening. In the case of a newer building with cavity walls, take care not to damage the dpc that separates the two leaves of the cavity wall around the opening.

If you are considering altering the size of the opening, this is the time to do it. A large opening can be partially bricked up to make it smaller, while a small opening can be made deeper by removing bricks below the sill. To make the opening wider, however, you will have to fit a new, longer lintel (supporting beam) at the top of the opening.

Fitting the new frame

If your replacement frame is a conventional timber one, this will be supplied as a ready-made unit that is fixed in place and then glazed on site. If it is of plastic, aluminium or galvanised steel, this will usually be fitted into a subframe that must first be fixed into the wall opening. The new unit may well be supplied ready-glazed.

In the case of a conventional timber frame, it will probably be possible to keep the original internal window frame ledge and fit the new frame against it.

The new frame will probably be supplied with horns (corner projections) for protection in transit. Cut these off and give the exterior surfaces of the frame an extra coat of wood primer or preservative stain, depending on the final finish you require.

Lift the frame into position and check it is square – that is, with equal diagonals. Wedge it in place so that it is level and plumb (vertical), making sure it is not under strain or twisted. If the frame is slightly too small for the opening, you can tack packing pieces on to the edge to build it out.

When it is correctly fitted, mark the positions

of the wedges and the fixing screws. Most window frames need three or four screws on each side and these should be positioned so they go into the middle of bricks, rather than into the mortar joints.

Remove the wedges and the frame and drill holes in the frame to take the fixing screws. Special zinc-plated, frame-fixing screws complete with wall plugs are available for this job.

Spread a layer of mortar at the bottom of the opening for the frame to rest on and then replace the frame and the wedges, checking that everything is square and plumb.

Use a long masonry drill bit to make holes through the frame into the wall. Countersink these holes, then position the frame-fixing screws and plugs (there is no need to remove the frame to position the plugs) and tighten the screws so the heads lie flush with the surface of the wood. A little wood filler will cover up the screw heads.

Press mortar into any wide gaps between the frame and the wall and use plaster to make good the wall on the inside of the frame. Fill any narrow gaps between the frame and the wall with mastic injected into the gap, using a trigger-operated applicator gun.

If installing a ready-glazed replacement win-

■ The commonest problems with casement windows are casements that bind in their frames, and sagging joints. Use a plane to shave the binding edges, then stain or paint the bare wood. Repair sagging joints temporarily with metal repair plates. For a more permanent repair to a mortised-and-tenoned frame, either knock the corner joints apart and re-glue them, or drive in slim hardwood wedges alongside the tenons.

■ To replace a window frame, unscrew any opening casements or top lights, and carefully break out fixed panes of glass. Then saw through the frame at each corner and prise the sections away. Clean up the opening with a club hammer and cold chisel or brick bolster.

If no dampproof course (dpc) is present beneath the old window, lay a new dpc strip across the sill and set the new frame in position. Check that it is level, then drill holes through the sides and into the masonry so the frame can be secured with wood screws and frame plugs at each side.

■ To reglaze a window, lift out the broken pieces of glass and chip out the old putty. Then press some fresh putty round the rebate and press the new pane into place to compress it to a thickness of about 3mm (¼in). Secure the pane with glazing sprigs, press in the facing putty and finish it to a neat 45° angle all round. Finally, trim off excess bedding putty.

dow, you will probably have to install a new hardwood sub-frame. You fit this in exactly the same way as a conventional window frame.

After fitting the sub-frame, apply a bead of mastic to the gap between the edge of the sub-frame and the brickwork. Also apply a bead of mastic to the face of the frame around the window opening.

You will certainly need someone to help you lift the window into place and press it back against the sub-frame on to the previously applied mastic. Then you can fix it in position from the inside by screwing through the pre-drilled holes in the window frame into the sub-frame. There is often a covering bead which you simply snap into place to hide the fixing screws.

Glazing a window

Before glazing a window, you must first treat the frame with a suitable primer paint and allow this to dry.

Select your putty according to the type of frame – conventional or brown for timber frames and universal or metal putty for metal frames. Modern double-glazed windows have gaskets to hold the glass in position. If they are not already glazed, fitting instructions will be supplied with the frames.

Work the putty in the hands to soften it before applying a 3–4mm thick band into the rebate of the frame. Press it out between the thumb and forefinger. If the putty is too sticky to handle easily, wrap it in newspaper for 24 hours to dry out the oil a little.

Now lift the glass into place in the rebate and carefully press it (edges only) back on to the putty. Hold the glass in place by inserting glazing sprigs (small wedge-shaped nails) about 200mm (8in) apart round the perimeter in front of the glass. Tap in the sprigs carefully with the edge of the glazing knife or large chisel held flat over the face of the glass.

Apply a second layer of putty to the outside of the glass and smooth it off to a bevel of about 45 degrees with a putty knife. If the knife sticks, moisten it with water.

Remove excess putty from the inside and outside of the pane with the knife and allow the putty to harden for about two weeks before priming and painting it.

INSULATING WINDOWS

Of the total heat lost from the average house, about 15 per cent will go through ordinary single-glazed windows, two-thirds of which can be cut by fitting double glazing. Secondary benefits from this will include a reduction in draughts and noise from outside as well as a considerable interior heat gain on sunny days, even in winter.

So you should, when replacing windows, seriously consider the advantages to be gained from installing one of the systems available (see Insulation, page 190). Although the initial costs will be increased, the long-term savings can be considerable. A major consideration here is that you will be removing your old window anyway, so the actual installation costs of a sealed unit will be the same.

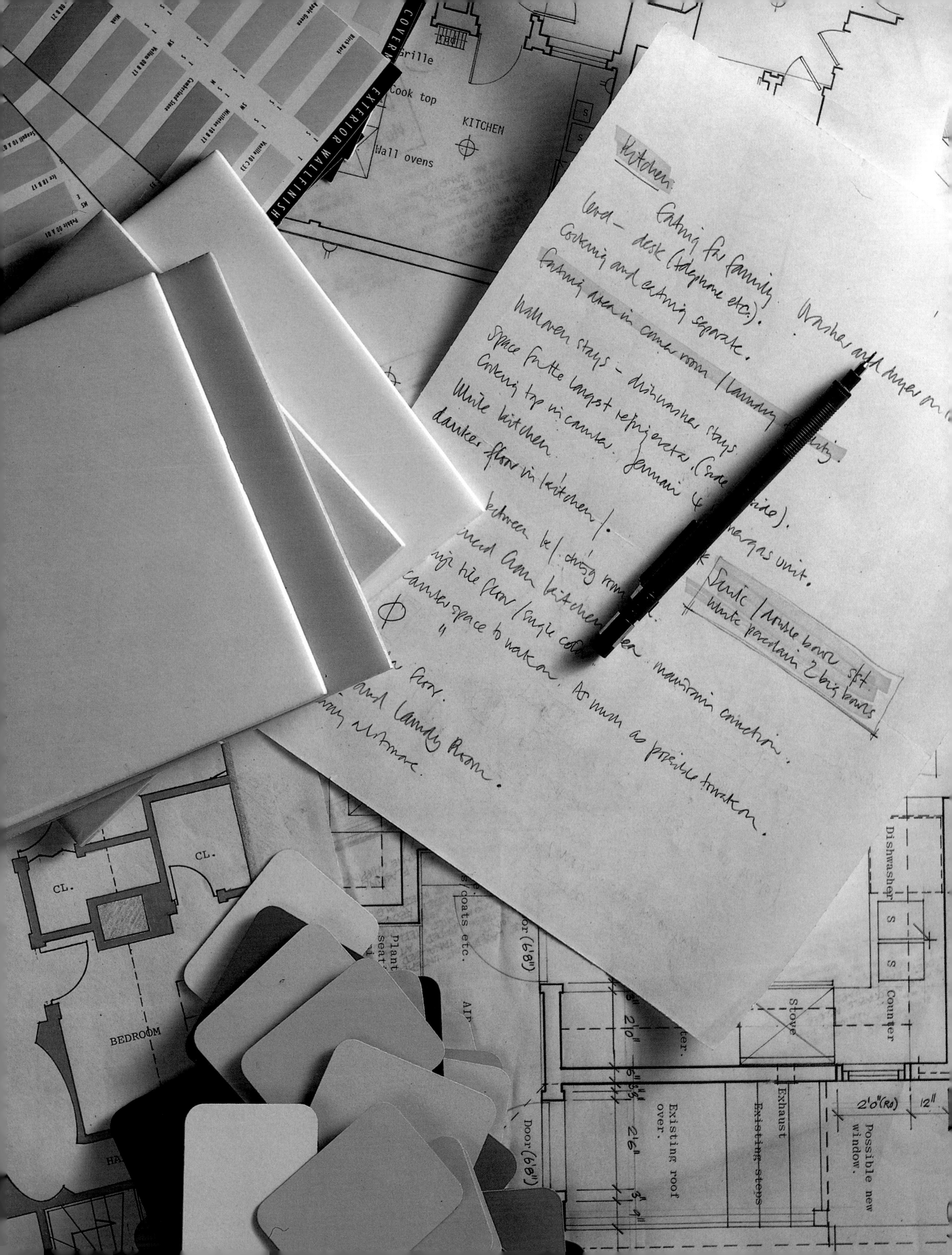
EXTERIOR WALLFINISH
Grille
Cook top
KITCHEN
Wall ovens
CL.
CL.
BEDROOM
Dishwasher
S
S
Counter
Stove
Exhaust
Existing steps
Existing roof over.
Possible new window.
Door (6'8")
Kitchen

RENOVATING THE INTERIOR

The inside of your home offers you even greater opportunities for restoration and renovation than does the exterior. Not only do you have a greater variety of features and materials to work with indoors; you also have the opportunity to ensure that both the looks and the performance of the interior suit the needs of your family and match your lifestyle.

Floors and Staircases

TYPES OF FLOOR

Two kinds of floor are to be found in houses – either a suspended timber construction or a directly laid solid concrete slab.

Suspended timber ground floors are found mostly in older houses – those built before the Second World War. You may, however, also find them in modern houses where on-site problems have made it impractical to lay a solid floor – for example, on acutely sloping ground. Upper floors are always suspended.

The term 'suspended' means that the floor hangs from the house walls. Timber joists span the exterior walls and are supported either on wall plates (ledges jutting out from the brick-work) or let into gaps in the walls. Recently constructed floors may be supported on metal joist hangers. The joists are spaced between 400 and 600mm (16–24in) apart.

Ground floors are further supported on small 'sleeper' walls. Upper floor joists are sometimes given intermediate support by internal walls (hence the term 'supporting wall') if they have to bridge particularly long spans.

The joists are covered by floorboards, which are nailed in position. These boards can either be square-edged or tongued-and-grooved. Square-edged boards generally develop gaps between them which allow dust to pass through. In the last 50 years these have largely been superseded by interlocking tongued-and-grooved boards. If you pass a blade down between the boards, you can establish which type is fitted.

In the most modern houses, it has become commonplace to dispense with floorboards and nail large sheets of flooring grade chipboard or plywood to the joists. The sheets are either 19 or 22mm (¾ or ⅞in) thick and can be either 2440 × 1220mm (8 x 4ft) or 2440 × 600mm (8 × 2ft) panels. Like floorboards, their edges can be square or tongued-and-grooved.

Timber floors have to be kept clear of the ground and be well ventilated to prevent wood rot developing as a consequence of the timber

■ **Below left** Suspended ground floors consist of timber joists resting on wall plates at each end; on long spans they may also be supported at intervals on walls of honeycombed brickwork built up off the oversite concrete. The joists are nailed to the wallplates and are then topped with floorboards or panels of flooring-grade chipboard.

■ **Below** Upper floors are similar in construction to ground floors, with joists resting on supporting walls and on metal joist hangers. Floor-boards or chipboard again form the floor surface above, while the ceiling surface below is formed with plasterboard in newer homes or lath-and-plaster in older ones. Blocking or strutting is sometimes fitted between the joists to prevent them from bowing.

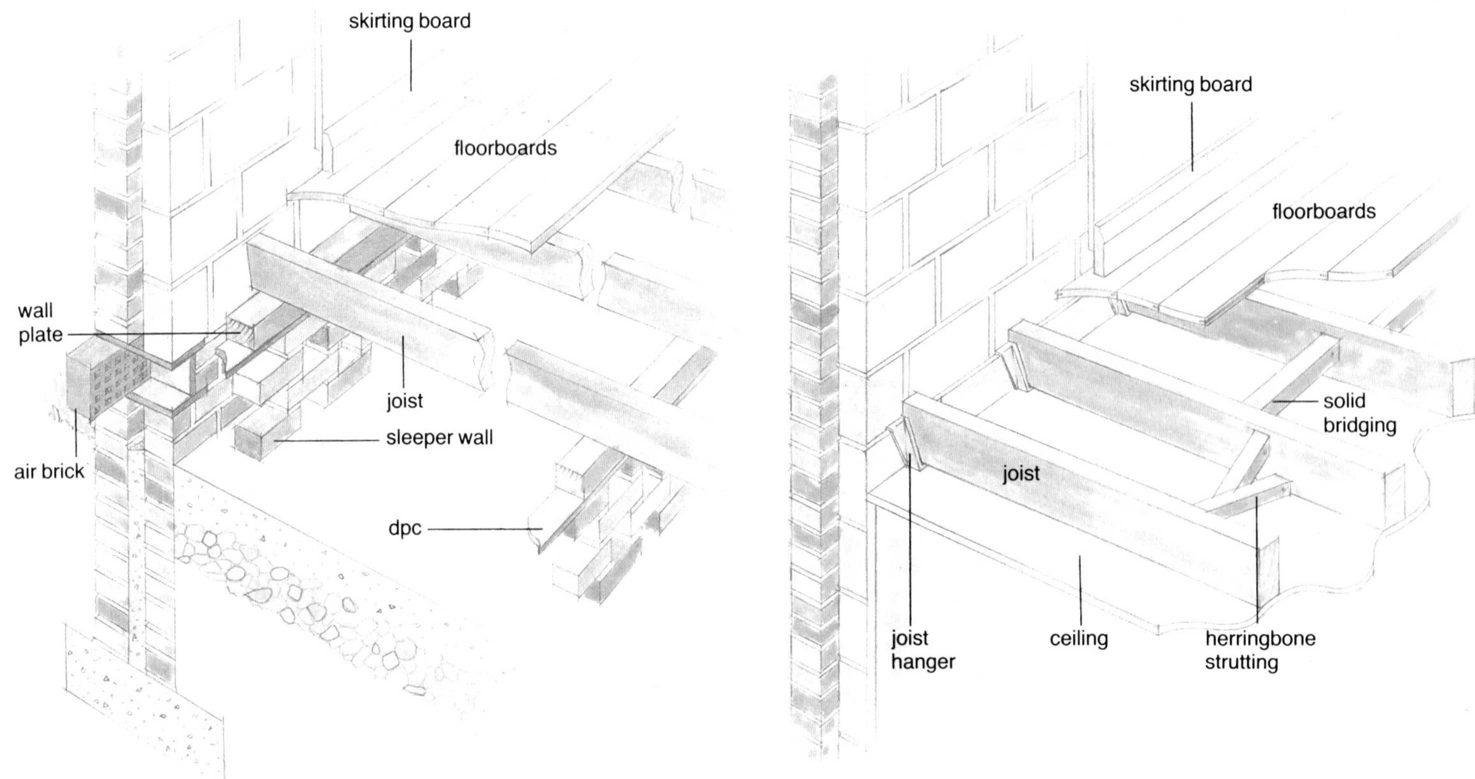

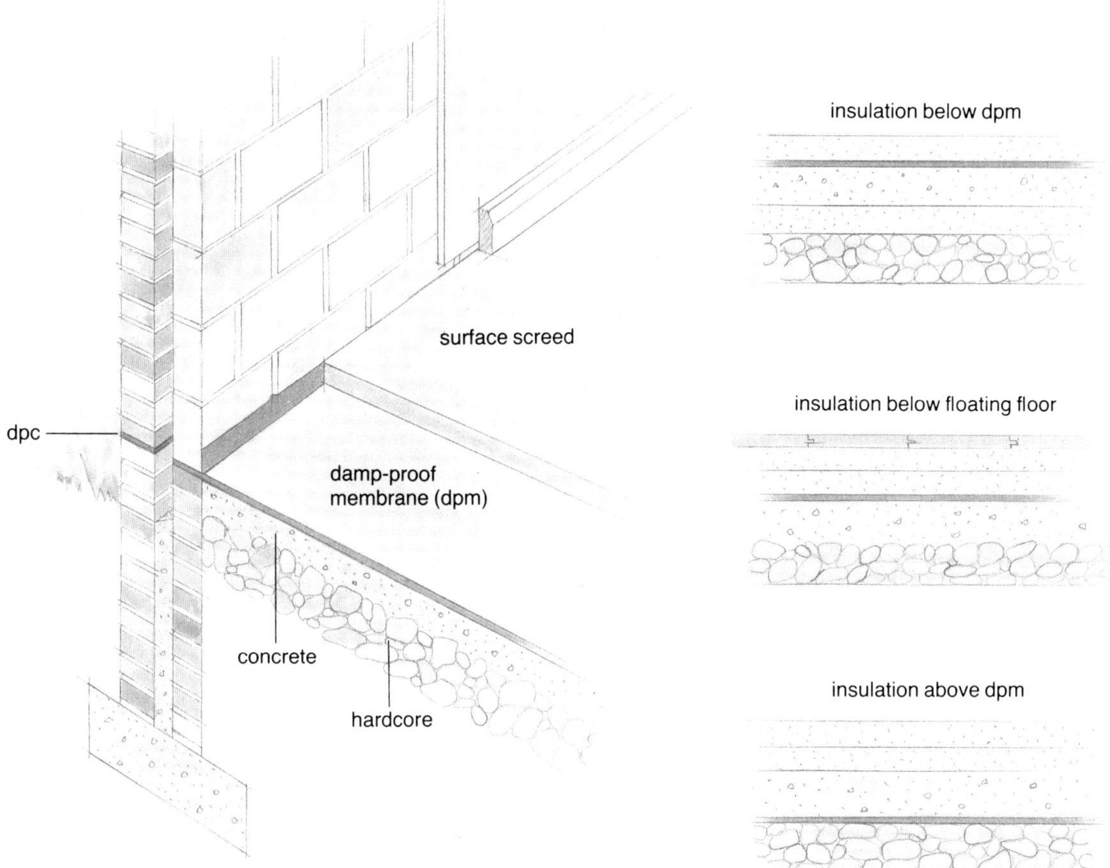

■ Solid floors are concrete slabs laid on top of the over-site concrete, topped with a continuous dampproof membrane (dpm) that is linked to the horizontal damp course in the house walls. The dpm is then covered with a thin screed of fine concrete which forms the finished floor surface.

Solid floors benefit from the inclusion of insulation; this can be added to an existing floor underneath a new floating floor surface or new floor screed (far right) or, if the floor is being completely re-laid, it can be placed beneath the level of the new dpm.

becoming damp. Ventilation is provided through airbricks situated in house walls.

Solid ground floors are found both in old houses and in most post-war houses. There was a period in between when the timber was cheap and plentiful and the suspended construction was particularly popular.

Older solid floors can be the source of damp problems simply because there is no damp-proofing layer built into them. This is not normally the case with their modern counterparts, although they too can suffer through poor workmanship or faulty materials.

Nowadays a solid floor consists of a layer of 100 to 150mm (4 to 6in) of hardcore topped by a blinding layer of ash, sand or weak concrete. This provides a solid firm foundation and a smooth base on which to lay a damp-proof membrane. This cannot be laid directly on to hardcore since it is often comprised of a sheet of 1000-gauge polythene, which could otherwise be damaged by sharp stones or bricks. The alternatives to polythene are bitumen, asphalt or an epoxy pitch compound.

The concrete floor, which should be 100 to 150mm (4 to 6in) thick, can be reinforced with mesh for extra strength and may have a fine concrete screed laid on top.

Insulation can be built into the floor by incorporating sheets of 50mm (2in) thick expanded polystyrene between the floor slab and the top screed.

Should damp become a problem in a solid floor, it can be treated by brushing on a membrane. This can be a moisture-cured plastic sealer, a black pitch epoxy type or a bitumen product. These are all available from builders' merchants.

Normally the membrane has to be taken up the surrounding walls to link with the dpc. You must follow the manufacturer's specific instructions for each product regarding drying time, the number of coats and so on.

Lifting floorboards

The type of floorboard determines the way each board can be lifted. If you do not know what kind you have, look for a board that has been screwed down and remove it. Alternatively stick a knife blade between several boards. If it goes right down, the boards are square-edged. If it cannot be inserted, the boards are tongued-and-grooved.

To lift a square-edged board, you can sometimes insert a bolster chisel near one end and lever the nails free from the joists below. Insert another bolster or lever on the opposite side and work them along until the nails at each joist

■ Old boarded floors suffer from a variety of faults. Board ends may warp and lift, especially if they have been prised up before for maintenance work on services run beneath the floor surface. Shrinkage can lead to gaps between boards or along skirting boards, while physical damage can cause splits and cracks. Boards may also bow upwards along their length, pulling up their fixings and causing the boards to creak when stepped on.

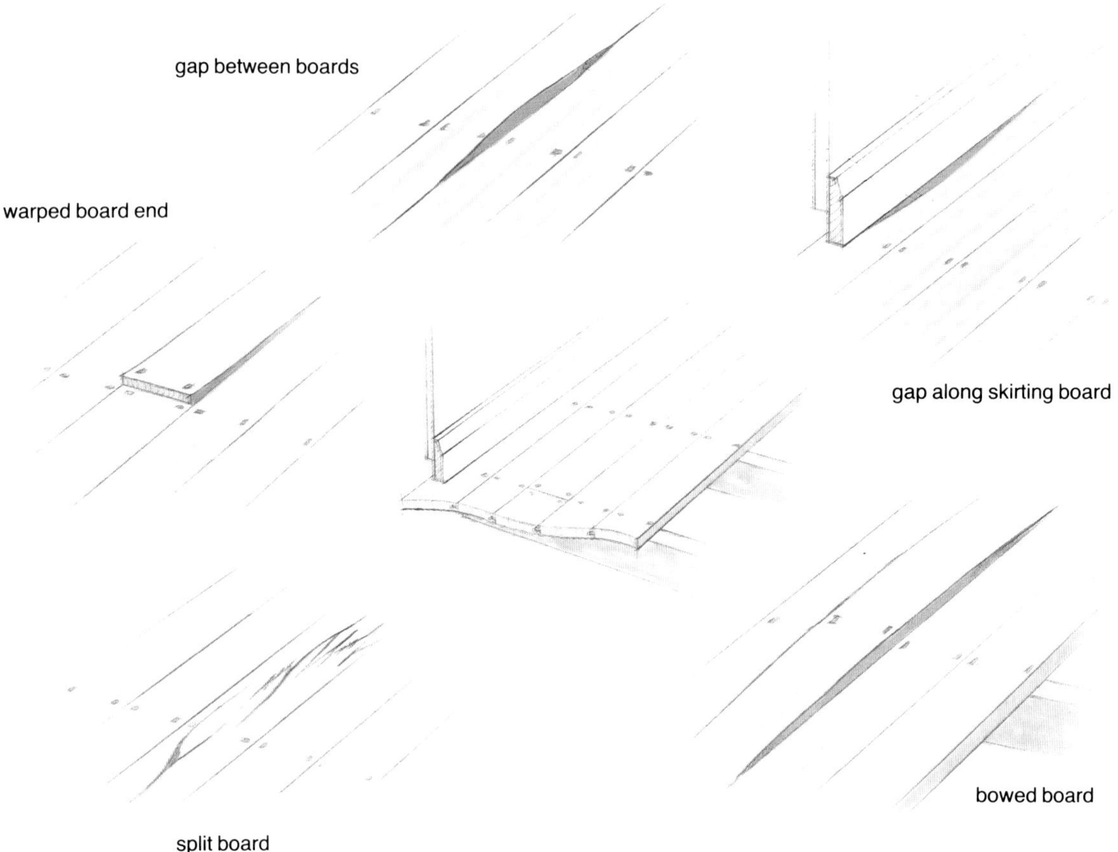

■ **Below** Lay square-edged chipboard flooring with the long sheet edges running parallel to the joists and butt-jointed along the joist centres. Add noggings between the joists to support the short board edges, positioning them so both boards can be nailed to each individual nogging.

■ **Right** Lay tongued-and-grooved sheets with their long edges at right angles to the joist direction, with butt joints between the short board edges centred over a joist. Nail the boards to every joist. Stagger the joints in alternate rows of boards.

tongued-and-grooved boards

square-edged boards

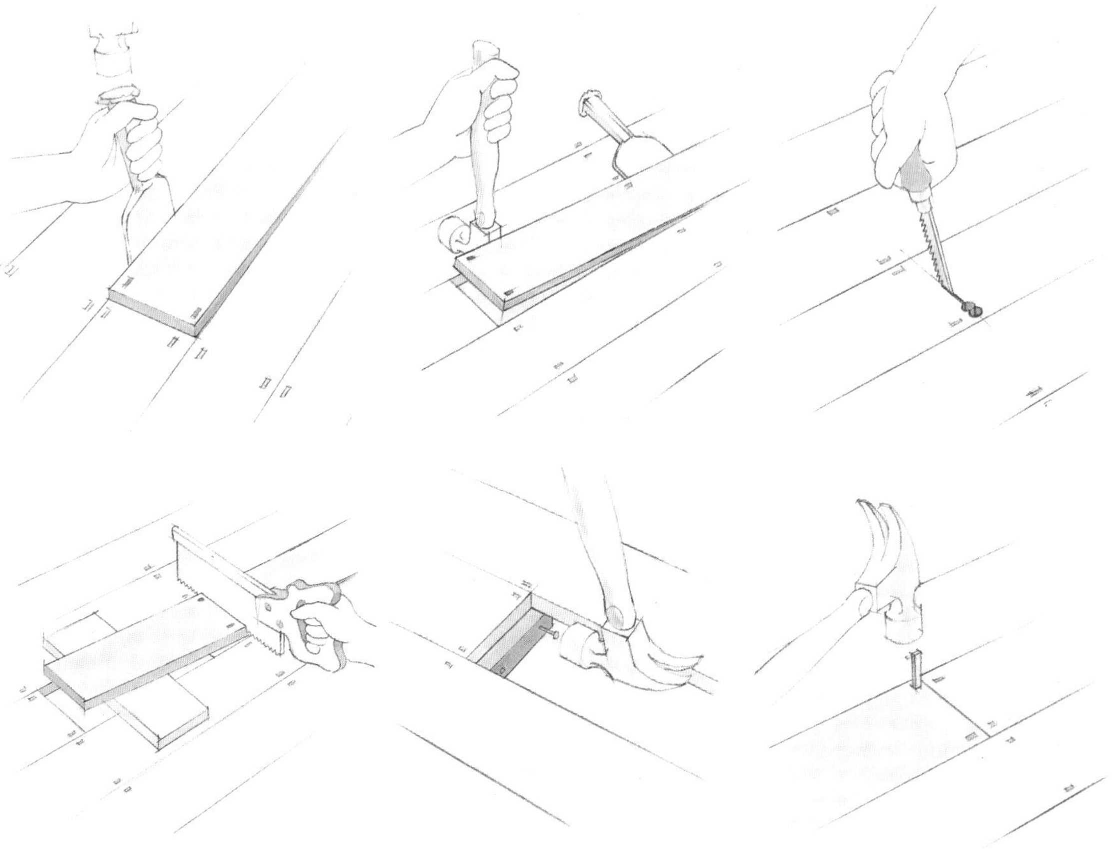

■ To lift old floorboards for repair or replacement, or to gain access to services run beneath them, prise up a board end with a bolster and then lever it up along its length. If the boards are tongued-and-grooved, saw through the tongues along each side of the board first with a circular saw set to a cutting depth of about 12mm (½in). To lift just a section of board, drill a starter hole through it beside a joist and cut across the board with a padsaw. Wedge up the cut end and saw through the board at the next joist position. Fix battens to the joist sides to support the ends of the new length of board, and nail it into place.

have been released and the board is free. Alternatively slide a metal bar or piece of wood under the board and press down on the end to 'spring' the nails free.

If you can't get a bolster below the board, drill a 10mm diameter hole near to a joist end. The nail positions will guide you. Then cut through the board at a right-angle using a jig saw or a pad saw, taking care not to cut any cables below. You can now raise the board as described earlier.

Removing the first tongued-and-grooved board is more tricky. After that, the others are easy. First you will have to cut through the tongue along the length of the board using a circular saw or a floorboard saw. The circular saw should be set to cut to a depth of only about 12mm (½in).

Lifting chipboard flooring

To take up a damaged area of a chipboard floor you need a circular saw set to cut to a depth of either 19 or 22mm (¾ or ⅞in) depending on the thickness of the board. Do not go any deeper than necessary or you may cut through the joists. Make a cut along the joint between adjacent boards and lever up the board with a bolster chisel.

Measure up carefully for the replacement piece of board (of the correct thickness) and refix it, if necessary on to 50 × 25mm (2 × 1in) cross timbers screwed between the joists. If there are gaps at the edges, fill them with mastic or wood filler.

Treating warped boards

If boards are warped, but the trouble is only slight, you can use an electric industrial floor sander to smooth off the surface. Remove any carpet tacks and punch all nails below the surface using a nail punch and hammer so they do not tear the abrasive belt fitted to the sander.

A floor sander can be obtained from a tool hire shop. Apart from levelling boards, it can also be used where you want to resurface the boards before varnishing them. Because sanding is very dusty work, make sure you seal off the room, cover any furniture left in and wear a dust mask.

The sander will be supplied with sheets of abrasive, which you fit to the large revolving drum of the machine. Assuming that the boards are in an average state, then start sanding with a medium-grade abrasive and end with a fine grade to get a smoother finish. Only on a very

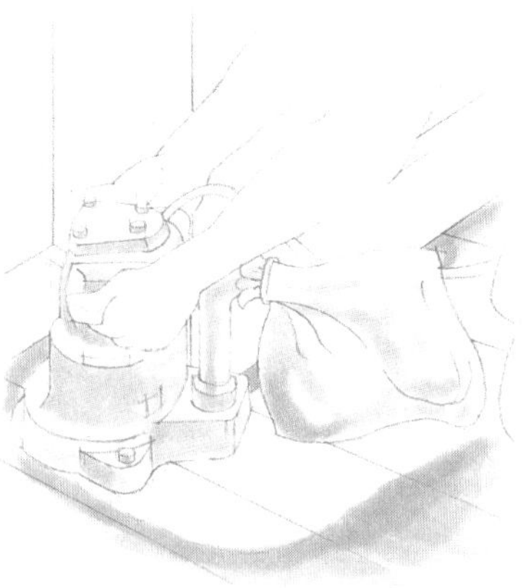

■ To restore floorboards that are sound but very dirty or marked, hire a powered floor sander. Use coarse abrasive initially and sand at 45° to the board direction. Then sand along the board direction, first with medium-grade abrasive and then with a finer grade. Finish off the edges of the room with a smaller disc or belt sander.

uneven surface or where there is a thick coating of wax polish, paint or varnish should you need a coarse abrasive. Since a large floor sander will not reach into the edges, you will also need a belt sander to finish off at the skirtings.

Normally you sand a floor in the direction of the boards. If, however, they are in a poor condition, make the first pass at a 45 degree angle to the boards. Finish off working parallel with them. Never work at right-angles to the boards, since this will tear the surface.

Tilt the sander off the floor before switching it on. Then lower it on to the boards and work it slowly backwards and forwards over a few feet. Then move to the next section of board and repeat the process, overlapping the previous sanded area by about 75mm (3in). The machine is powerful enough to take off about 3mm (⅛in) of wood fairly quickly.

If you switch on with the sander flat on the floor or work too slowly, you can make indents in the floor surface. Before applying any final treatment such as varnish, you will have to vacuum the floor thoroughly to remove dust.

Where floors are generally uneven, nail or screw the boards down firmly and then lay sheets of hardboard over them.

Filling gaps between boards

An odd gap between boards can be filled with mastic sealant. With a wider gap, glue a suitably sized wedge-shaped piece of wood and tap it into the gap. Then level it off with a plane.

Where there are lots of gaps, the quickest repair is to lay hardboard. You would normally do this anyway if you were laying a floorcovering on top.

Where you want to leave the boards exposed so they can be varnished and rugs or a carpet square laid in strategic areas, you will have to relay them. This gives you the opportunity to refix the boards upside down to provide a fresh, clean surface, although you are likely to have to do some localised sanding to remove the joist marks from the boards.

Treating sunken boards

If any of the floorboards have dropped, take them up and insert packing pieces of hardboard or plywood where they are fixed to the joists. If they have warped downwards slightly, refix them upside down and sand them smooth. If either problem cannot be cured using these methods, then fit a replacement board of the required thickness.

■ **Right** If all the boards have shrunk to leave wide gaps, it is best to lift them all and re-lay them to close up the gaps. Loose-lay four or five boards, then nail another board to the joists about 50mm (2in) away and use a floorboard cramp or a pair of wedges as shown to tighten up the first group of boards. Nail them down, remove the odd board and lay the next group in the same way. At the far side of the room, lay the last board tight against the wall and fit a cut-down strip of board in the gap.

■ **Below** Before laying any new floorcovering, check that the heads of all the nails securing the boards to the joists are well punched down. Fill occasional gaps with narrow strips of timber, glued and hammered into place and planed down flush with the floor surface. Cover uneven floorboards with sheets of hardboard before putting down thin sheet floorcoverings, with narrow strips laid over pipe or cable runs for easy access.

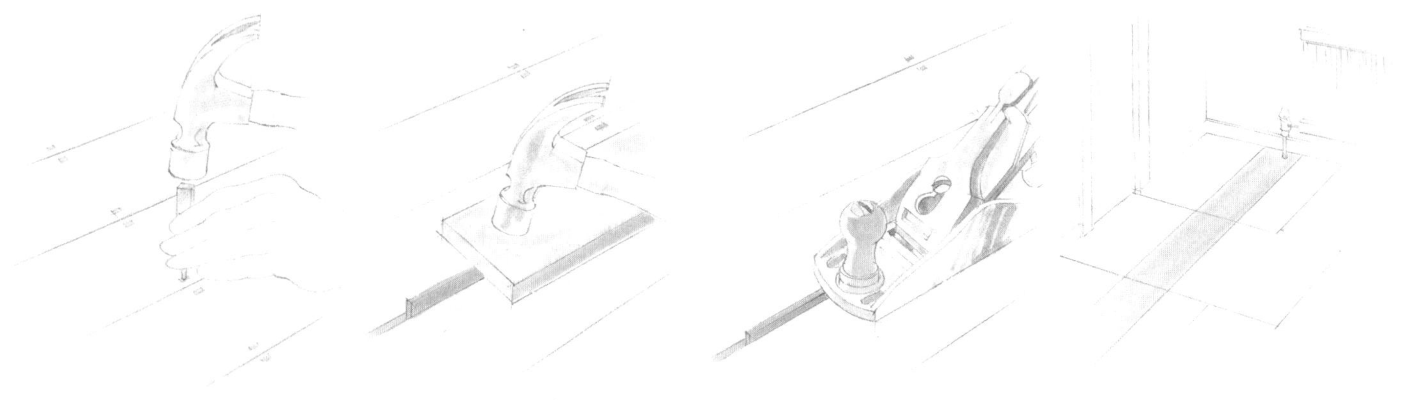

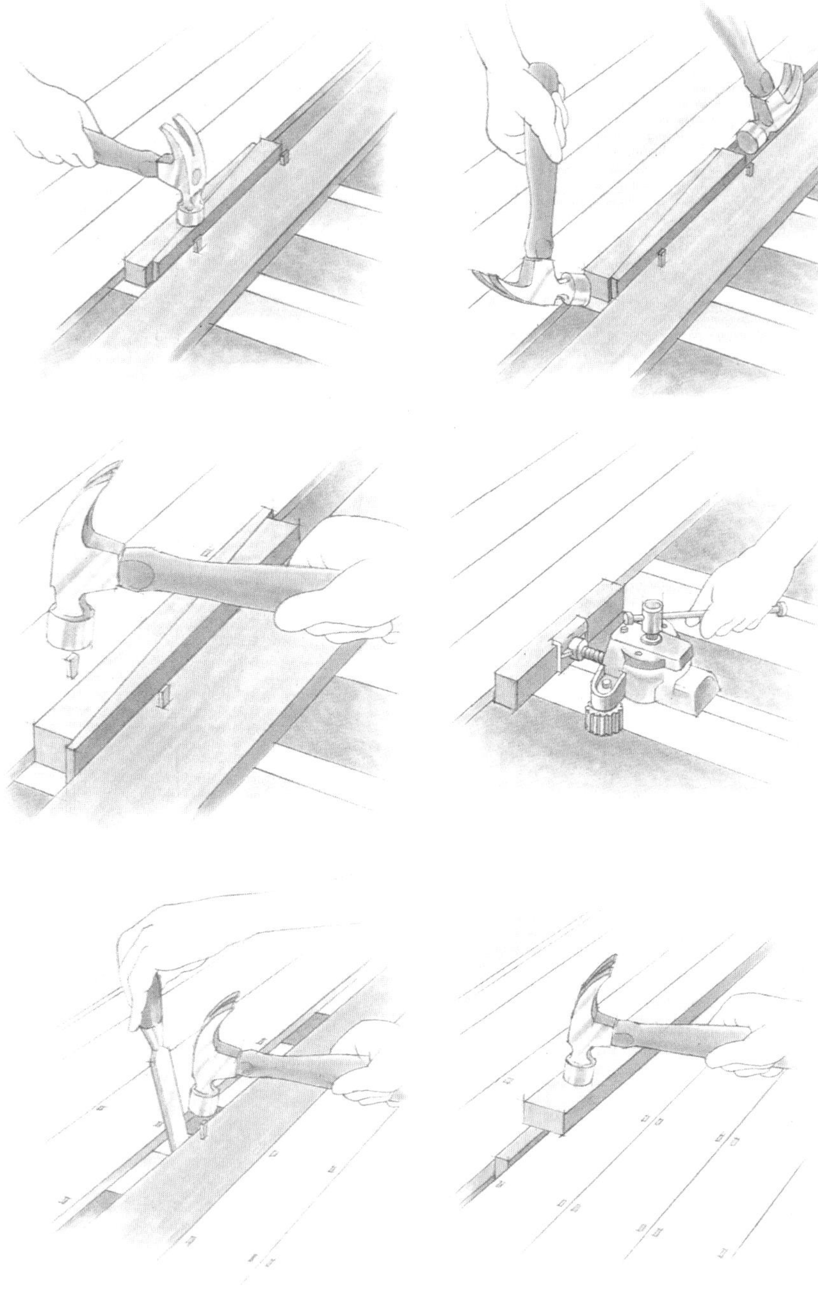

REPLACING FLOORS

Replacing a complete floor either of a suspended or solid construction is a rare requirement. Normally you will find any work involved should be a matter of straightforward repairs.

If joists are badly affected, new ones will have to be laid. This is not skilled work since all you have to do is replace the old joists with wood of the same dimensions that has been treated with preservative. You also have to renew the dpc on which the wall plates rest. However, you may prefer to leave this job to a builder.

If you do it yourself, make sure the joists are properly secured and levelled before nailing down the floorboards. These must be tightly fitting and should be butt-jointed to meet neatly at joist centres.

Relaying boards

If you are replacing boards, lay four or five in position on the joists, butting up their edges closely. Next nail a length of 100 × 25mm (4 × 1in) timber to the joists about 75 or 100mm (3 x 4in) away. Cut two tapered wedges and hammer them into the gap between the piece of wood and the boards. This will force the boards tightly together so that they can be nailed correctly in place. Then remove the wedges.

Repeat this with the next group of boards and carry on with this procedure until the floor is complete. You will probably have to cut a narrow strip of board to finish off at the skirting when you reach the far side of the room.

LEVELLING SOLID FLOORS

You can fill irregularities on a solid floor with cement mortar and then smooth it over, up to about 3mm (⅛in) deep, with a self-smoothing screed. This is mixed with water to form a creamy paste, which you pour on to the floor and roughly spread out with a steel float. The screed will automatically smooth out any trowel marks before it hardens. This takes up to 12 hours to harden completely, but can be walked on after about 4 hours.

With irregularities up to about 9mm (⅜in) deep, you can apply a ready-mixed screed to fill in and level the surface.

Indentations up to 50mm (2in) deep can be filled by resurfacing the floor with a conventional cement mortar screed consisting of three parts sharp sand to one part cement. Before applying the screed, paint the floor surface with pva bonding agent to improve adhesion.

■ Use self-smoothing compound to level an uneven solid floor. Pour it on . . .

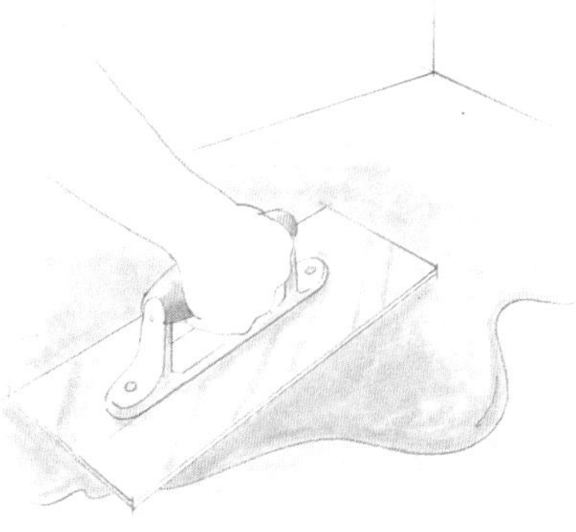

. . . then trowel it out evenly and leave it to find its own level and harden.

■ You can treat woodworm infestation yourself, using hired spraying equipment and protective clothing, but the chemicals needed are unpleasant and potentially dangerous to inhale. So, for all but small-scale attacks it is preferable to call in a professional firm who will treat the attack thoroughly and also issue a guarantee against fresh attacks.

LOOKING OUT FOR WOODWORM AND ROT

Timber floors in a house have two natural enemies – woodworm and rot. Both will attack where the right conditions exist. It is a classical case of prevention being better than cure, since the upheaval and cost of remedying either can by considerable.

You are more likely to recognise the signs of woodworm than the beetle itself, since the surface of attacked timber is punctured by tiny holes about 2mm (1/16in) in diameter. One beetle species differs in that it leaves irregular oval slits up to 9mm (3/8in) wide on the surface.

Curing woodworm

Under the floorboards the timber will probably be covered with dust and dirt. This must be removed to enable you to carry out a thorough inspection and treatment. Where there is severe damage to the joists, you will have to have them strengthened or replaced, so expert advice could be essential.

When it comes to treating affected areas, insecticide is available in cans, which you can either spray or brush on. With some cans and aerosols a special plastic nozzle is supplied to enable you to inject the fluid more easily into the flight holes – for example, in furniture.

Although it is possible to brush on the insecticide, you will find it easier, quicker and more efficient to use a sprayer. Most pneumatic garden sprayers with one-gallon capacity that can be adjusted to give a moderately coarse spray are suitable.

The spray pressure is important. If it is too fine, then the timber will not be sufficiently drenched. If it is too coarse, the timber will be over-soaked and the treatment will prove more costly as a result.

Most fluids should be applied at the rate of about 200sq ft per gallon. Spray all timber surfaces thoroughly and flood areas where the beetles are likely to lay their eggs, such as in crevices, end grain and open joints.

Although the treatment can be carried out at any time of the year, the best period is in the summer when windows and doors can be left open. Woodworm fluid leaves a pungent odour which is very strong for the first couple of days and will still be evident several weeks later.

You should wear old clothes and shoes to tackle the job or, ideally, some overalls and boots. A light fume mask and goggles are also essential precautions. Make sure you put on strong leather gloves and rub barrier cream on to any exposed parts of your skin.

Fire is a potential hazard, so ensure there are no naked flames near the work area. Isolate any electrical circuits nearby and, if light is needed, use a portable flameproof handlamp connected to a socket outside the treatment area. Never smoke while spraying or in the area you have treated for 24 hours afterwards.

When tackling floor joists, take up every third or fourth board and use a sprayer with a hand-lance extension to reach under the fixed

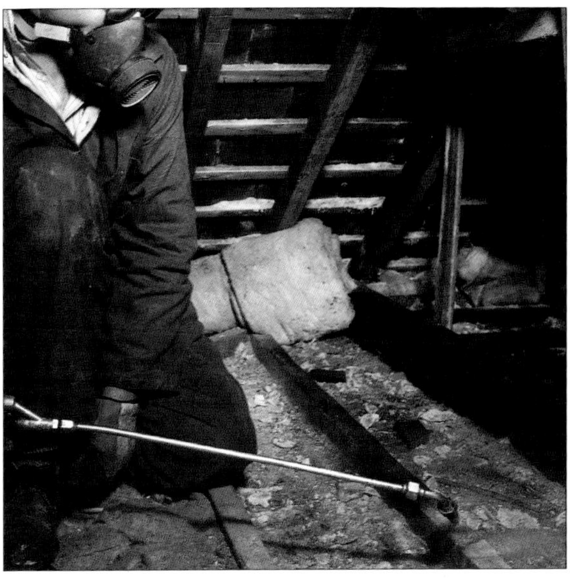

■ Infestation can spread to roof timbers too, and here spraying is the only effective way of tackling the problem. Since ventilation is generally poor in loft areas, it is vital that special masks are worn; again it is best to leave the work to professionals.

boards and on to both sides of hidden joists. The ends of joists resting in brickwork cannot be reached by a spray. Here you should trowel on a special thick mastic preservative paste and leave it to soak in.

Replace boards loosely as you work to prevent the possibility of stepping back either into a hole or on to a nail protruding from an upturned board. To be absolutely safe, it is wise to remove all nails from the boards as each one is taken up. Check the manufacturer's instructions as to how long you should leave the treatment before replacing floorcoverings.

With skirtings and panelling, you can usually get away with spraying just the exposed surfaces. However, in severe cases of attack, you will have to remove facing timbers to gain access to the rear surfaces and also to any unpainted studding timbers.

ROTTING WOOD

Wood rot is usually categorised as either 'wet' or 'dry', which is confusing since dampness causes them both. They are both fungi and there are various species of each type. Wet rot confines itself to damp wood, whereas dry rot can spread itself from wet to dry material. So obviously the best way to discourage rot is to guard against damp penetration.

Recognising wet rot

Wet rot is the name given to the cellar fungus *Coniophora cerebella*. This is found in floors and also causes decay on fence posts, wooden sheds, window sills and other outdoor timbers.

It occurs much more frequently than dry rot and requires substantially wetter conditions in which to flourish. Mercifully it does not produce well-developed conducting strands, so it will not penetrate brick walls. Bathrooms, kitchens and cellars are typical places to find it. Once cured an attack of wet rot is unlikely to start again, provided the damp is eliminated.

Cellar fungus is evident where timber is stained dark brown or black and starts to soften. Yellow or brown streaks or patches can also be found in decayed timber. There may in addition be cracks along the grain and fine cracks across the grain.

Attack is often internal, showing little or no sign on the surface. Where surface growth is present, this consists of thin dark brown – almost black – strands.

Curing wet rot

First locate the source of the damp and cure it. Then allow the wood to dry out, since this will make the fungus inactive. Cut back infected timber to sound material and replace it with new timber. Smaller areas can be repaired with a wood filler. Finally treat new timber and all surrounding areas of wood with preservative.

Recognising dry rot

The dry rot fungus *Merulius lacrymans* flourishes under conditions of bad ventilation and high humidity. It is more efficient at destroying wood than any other fungus and, once established, can even spread to wood that would normally be too dry to be attacked.

Early on, dry rot is a fluffy white growth, which soon resembles thick cotton wool. The wood later appears to be coated with grey matted strands, behind which the fungus forms thicker strands capable of transporting moisture from one part of the timber to another. This creates the ideal conditions for the spread of the fungus to new sites.

Dry rot fungus is extremely dangerous, since its strands will pass through brickwork in search of new timber to attack. Even if the strands are cut off from the fungus and isolated from the timber, they can remain for three of four years and then attack any new timber nearby that is inadequately seasoned and dry. Then the whole process starts all over again.

Once it has matured, the fungus produces what are called fruit bodies. These have brick-red centres with white edges tinged with lilac. They are sometimes several feet square and can give off as much as 2,000 spores a minute from each square foot for several days.

A damp, musty, 'mushroom' smell, which at times becomes quite offensive, indicates dry rot. So investigate further. The surface of the timber can take on a warped appearance and paint may start to flake off. Unpainted timber splits both along its length and across the grain into large cubes up to 50mm (2in) wide.

Since attacks usually start at ground level and may work their way up the building, lift floorboards and look behind skirtings for signs of the strands. You may even first notice the condition by the 'cotton wool' material seeping out under skirting boards.

Where only a fruit body is visible, remember that a great deal of wood must already have been consumed before that stage of the plant's growth is reached.

If you are not confident of being able to eradicate the problem completely yourself, you must call in a specialist company. But make sure they are prepared to give you a reasonable guarantee against further outbreaks. Long guarantees from unknown or newly formed companies may be of questionable value.

Curing dry rot

Remove all affected timber and burn it immediately. Examine any surrounding plaster to determine the full extent of the attack and make sure you cut back the problem area to about 1m (3ft) beyond the farthest sign of trouble. Use a blowlamp to kill surface spores and strands on brickwork and the subfloor.

Having sterilised all surfaces, paint the brickwork, subfloor and all timber within about 2m (6ft) of the attack with dry rot fluid. Apply the recommended number of coats.

To eradicate completely the fungus that may be within the wall, drill into the bricks at several points using a large diameter drill bit, then drench inside the holes with an acidic fungicidal chemical applied by a pressure sprayer.

To be on the safe side, also treat any built-in furniture close to the area – or destroy it, if the rot has spread to it.

Pay particular attention to electrical socket outlets, too. Dry rot can infest even these and it has a detrimental effect on pvc-sheathed cables. Rcplace all electrical accessories and cables in the danger zone.

Make sure you locate and cure the cause of the dampness that enables the fungi to flourish and ensure that, when the floors are hollow,

■ Dry rot not only looks and smells disgusting: it can also wreak havoc with concealed timbers if the attack is not caught in time, leaving affected wood dried out and so brittle it can simply crumble away.

■ Treating a serious outbreak of dry rot can involve major structural work. All infected timber must first of all be cut away, as must any plaster behind which the fungus strands may have travelled.

■ Once all the infected timber and plaster has been removed, all neighbouring timber and masonry must then be treated with special chemicals, before new timber is fitted and the walls are replastered.

there is adequate ventilation. Clear airbricks and ventilators and check that sleeper walls are honeycombed to allow a through passage of air which will keep the floor timbers dry.

Any new wood to be fitted must be well seasoned. Treat it with a wood preservative (according to the manufacturer's instructions) before fixing it in place. Similarly treat any fresh surfaces you have exposed as a result of cutting or drilling the wood.

Since the ends of ground floor joists in a wall are prone to dampness, it is better to stop the joists just short of the wall and support the ends on a new sleeper wall with a bituminous dpc.

Where this is not possible, it helps just to coat the joists ends with a bituminous waterproofing compound. An alternative is to locate the joist ends in galvanised steel joist hangers.

■ Staircases are more than just a means of access to upper storeys. They are a focal point of both the entrance hall and the landing, and their design and decoration are often a major feature of the home.

TYPES OF STAIRCASE

Staircases come in a variety of styles, depending on the age of the property and the amount of space available. But the straight flight is the most common.

Where space is restricted, the staircase may have either a quarter (90 degrees) or half-turn (180 degrees). At each turn, there may be a small landing. To save even more space, the staircase may have been built with tapering treads, called winders, rather than landings. Spiral stairs may have been installed where space was really restricted.

A traditional staircase incorporates what are known as closed-riser stairs, with vertically fitted boards between the treads. Open-riser stairs have spaces between the treads, thus letting plenty of light through.

Either type of timber staircase may have closed or cut (also called open) strings. These are the sloping timbers at each side of the staircase that support the treads and risers. Most stairs are made with closed strings, which have straight parallel edges with both the treads and risers fixed into grooves in the inside faces of the strings.

Cut strings are formed into a series of steps and the treads are supported on the flat tops of them. Being weaker, these strings are made from thicker timber than the closed type.

REPAIRING STAIRCASES

If you attend to minor defects promptly, staircases will generally give little trouble during their long life, unless they are affected by any movement of the house.

You do not need either planning permission or Building Regulations approval to make minor repairs to staircases. However, any change affecting the size or angle of the staircase itself may be subject to Building Regulations control and needs the approval of the local authority's building inspector.

If, for example, you want to replace a traditional staircase with an open-plan one or a spiral design, you must get approval since it may impose added stress that the building structure is unable to cope with.

If there is a cupboard under a staircase, the access it provides to the underside of the steps will make any repair work that much easier. A plastered or boarded underside, on the other hand, will make life more difficult since these should not be disturbed unless absolutely essential. Repairs should therefore be made to the staircase by working from above.

Replacing balusters

Balusters on cut-string staircases fit into mortises or slots in the ends of the treads. On a closed-string staircase, they rest in a groove in the string capping and have short lengths of timbers set between them as spacers. Their top ends are either skew-nailed to the handrail or set in a groove in its underside.

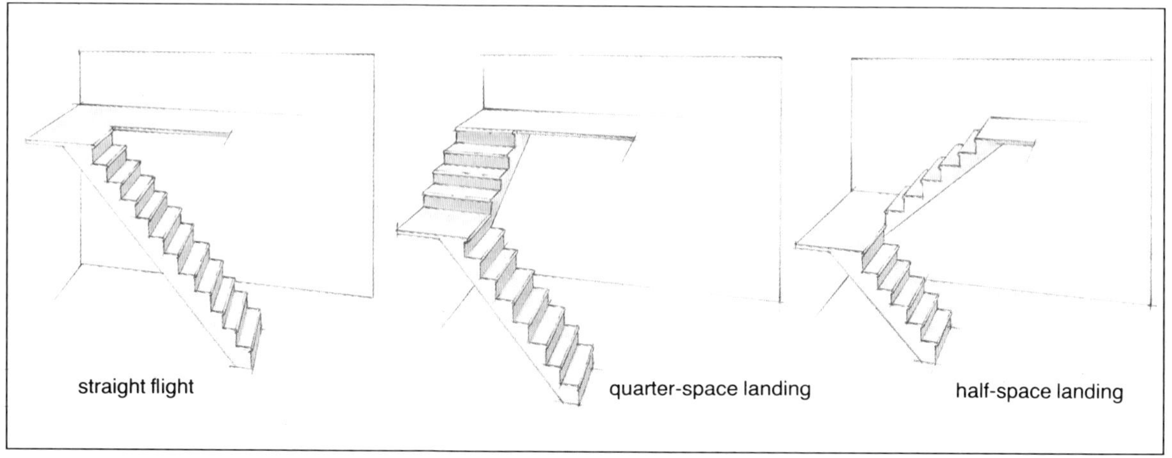

■ Domestic stairs usually come in three common configurations – straight flights, flights that turn through 90° via a quarter-space landing and flights turning through 180° via a half-space landing.

■ The staircase is one of the most complex wooden structures in the home. Two parallel boards called strings fixed to the newel posts link the upper and lower floors. The treads and risers are housed into the strings or, in the case of an open or cut outer string, are fixed to cut-outs in the upper edge of the string. A handrail links the newel posts, and balusters are fitted between it and the string to guard the flight.

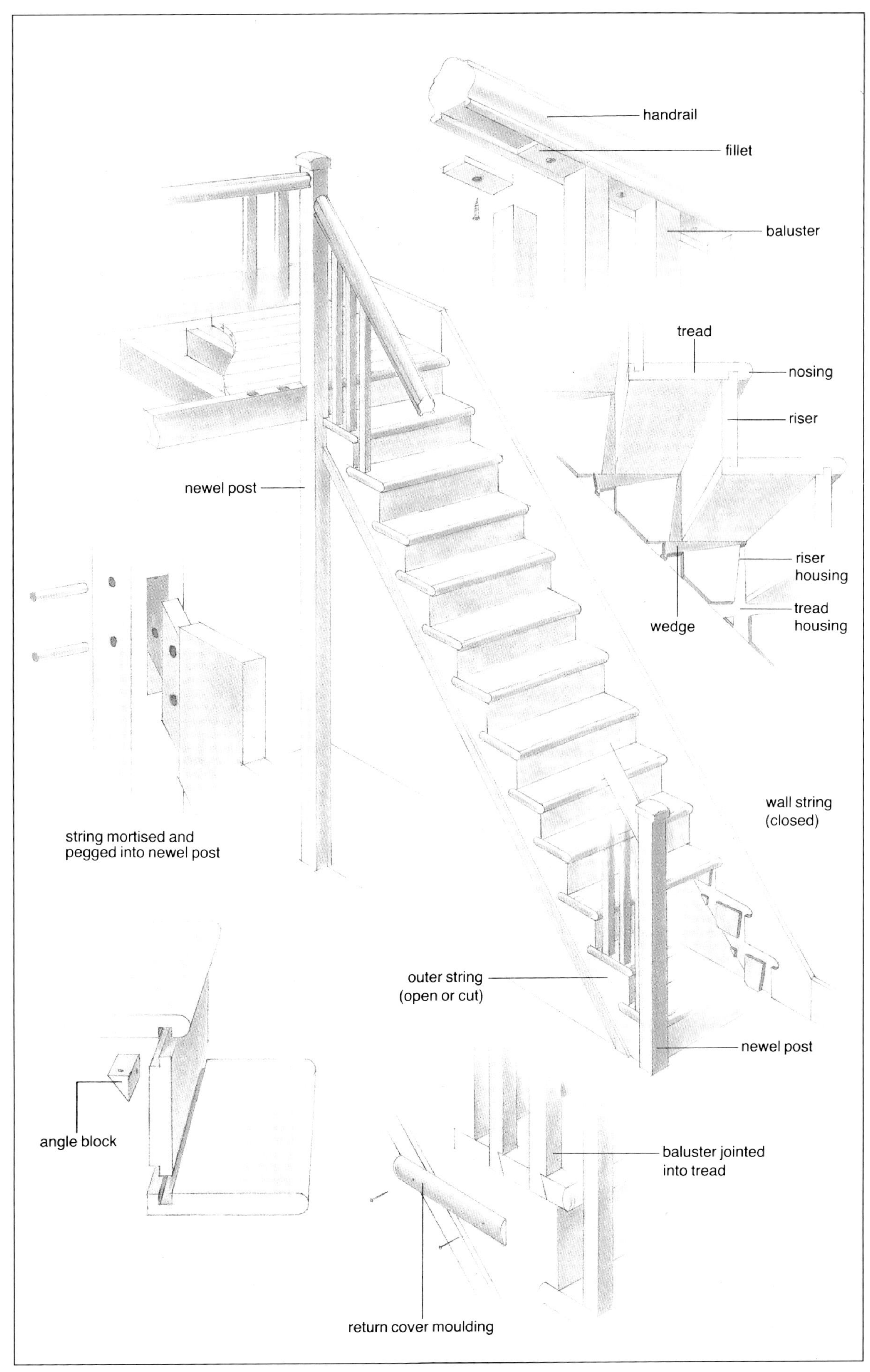

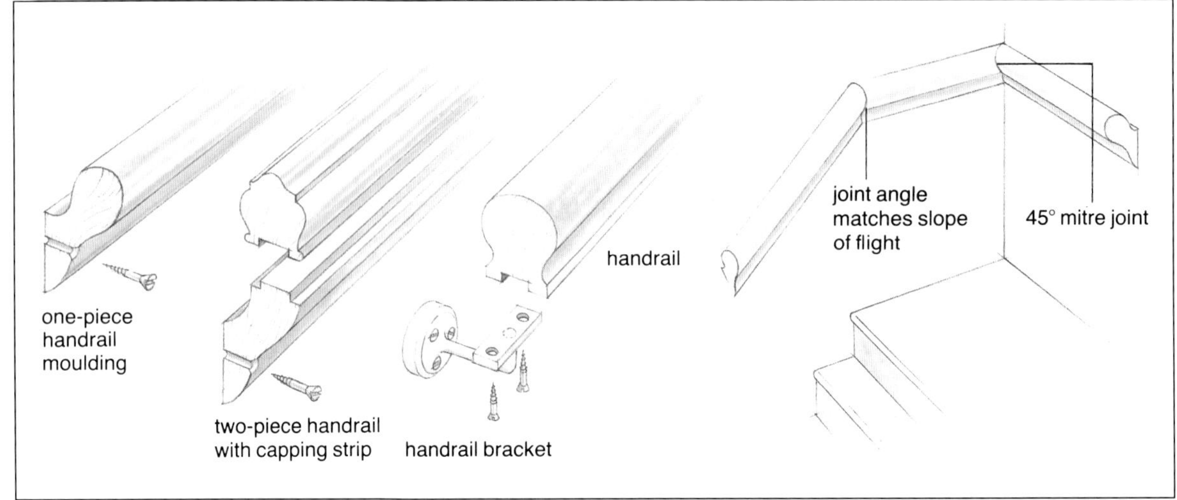

■ An inner handrail may be secured directly to the wall beside the flight, or may be mounted clear of the wall on handrail brackets. The rail follows any change of slope or direction taken by the flight itself.

Replacing a missing baluster normally means having to dismantle the balustrade. However, it is possible to replace the odd one by splicing a new baluster into two at an angle in a convenient position, fitting new top and bottom pieces into the rail and string and then carefully remarrying the mating halves with glue and countersunk screws.

If you have to replace several balusters, then make sure that identical ones are available before completely dismantling the staircase. Square-section balusters are easy to match; but turned balusters may have to be specially made. If you give an undamaged baluster to a skilled woodturner, he will be able to make replicas but it will be expensive.

If the balusters on a cut-string staircase have worked loose, drive small glue-soaked timber wedges into any gaps in the tread mortise. Then, to secure them completely, drive in two nails or fine screws at an angle to lock the end of the baluster to the tread. With closed-string flights, skew-nail the baluster to the string.

With either type, do the same at the point where the baluster meets the handrail. Finish off by concealing the repair using wood filler.

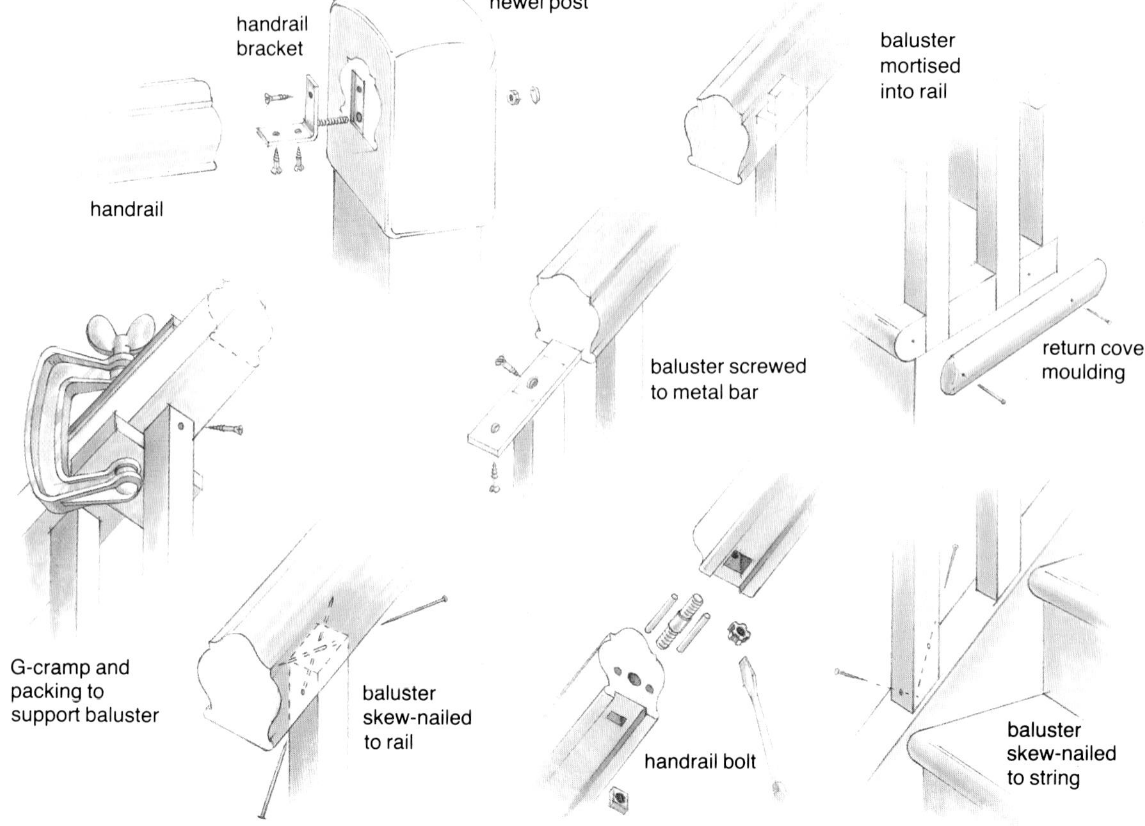

■ A variety of carpentry techniques and specialist fittings are used to assemble the balustrade. The handrail itself may be secured to the newel post with brackets, and lengths of rail are often joined with concealed handrail bolts. The balusters may be simply skew-nailed into place, or may be set in mortises in the handrail and housings in the treads.

Repairing handrails

Handrails with balusters usually have their ends tenoned into the newel posts. If an end becomes loose, simply secure it by driving a screw or dowel peg in through the side of the newel post into the handrail tenon.

Where a handrail is damaged, cut out the offending section and replace it with a new matching piece, if available. Saw at a sloping angle to the line of the rail to give a greater contact area for the new piece to form a scarf-joint. Glue and screw the piece into place. On the underside of the rail, screw on a metal plate as reinforcement. Then refix the baluster tops, as previously described.

If a matching section of handrail is not available, then you can either have a piece specially machined or else replace the complete rail with a different one.

Refixing a wall-mounted handrail

Wider staircases and those having a wall either side should have a handrail fixed to a wall to provide any necessary support for those who need it while using the stairs.

The only fault likely here is if the screw fixings become loose. Sometimes the handrail is supported on brackets which are screwed to the wall. Depending on its type, you might be able to detach a single bracket for refixing or, possibly, you will have to remove the complete handrail to remake the fixings.

Either way, you need to refix the screws after plugging the old holes with filler and drilling new ones. Insert wall plugs and screws the same size as the old ones to make the bracket secure.

If the rail is screwed directly to the wall, it may be possible to replace the existing (loose) screw with a thicker one – even though this may mean drilling a new hole through the rail. If this does not work, then take the rail down completely and make a similar repair to that previously described.

To ensure all the screw holes line up again, replace the rail while you mark off the position of the new hole. Remove the rail, drill and plug the hole and then replace and refix the rail. This is the only way you can be sure the holes will line up. Where you are fitting a new handrail or replacing an old one, the important thing to remember is that it must run parallel with the string throughout its length. If it does not, it will prove very awkward and disorientating for anyone using it.

Mark the position for the rail on the wall at the top of the stairs, then screw it to the wall. Repeat this at the bottom. When you are satisfied with its position, mark the intermediate holes and then remove the rail while you drill and plug the wall. If you are using brackets, fix these to the rail first before screwing the whole assembly to the wall.

Curing creaking treads

The problem of creaking treads is caused by staircase timbers shrinking, which allows adjacent parts to rub together when someone uses the stairs. The situation has tended to be increasingly common where central heating has been introduced.

If the underside of the staircase is accessible via a cupboard, the first things to look for are the wedges securing the ends of the treads and risers into their grooves in the strings.

If these are loose, tap them in firmly with a mallet. If they will not tap in then remove them, coat them with woodworking adhesive and hammer them back into place. It is rare to find one missing, but if you do it is very easy to cut and fit a replacement.

If that does not cure the problem, fix the back of each creaky tread to the bottom of the riser above it using two screws, placed one-third and two-thirds of the way across. The screws will need to be 50mm (2in) long. To avoid splitting the wood, first drill pilot holes up through the

■ If the staircase creaks and the underside of the flight is accessible, check that all the wedges holding the treads and risers in their housings are secure. Then glue and screw wooden blocks into the internal angles between treads and risers, and drive screws through the rear edge of each riser into the tread to lock the two components together.

If there is no access beneath the staircase, use recessed repair brackets to secure the rear edges of the treads to the risers, and drive screws down through the fronts of the treads into the top edges of the risers beneath them.

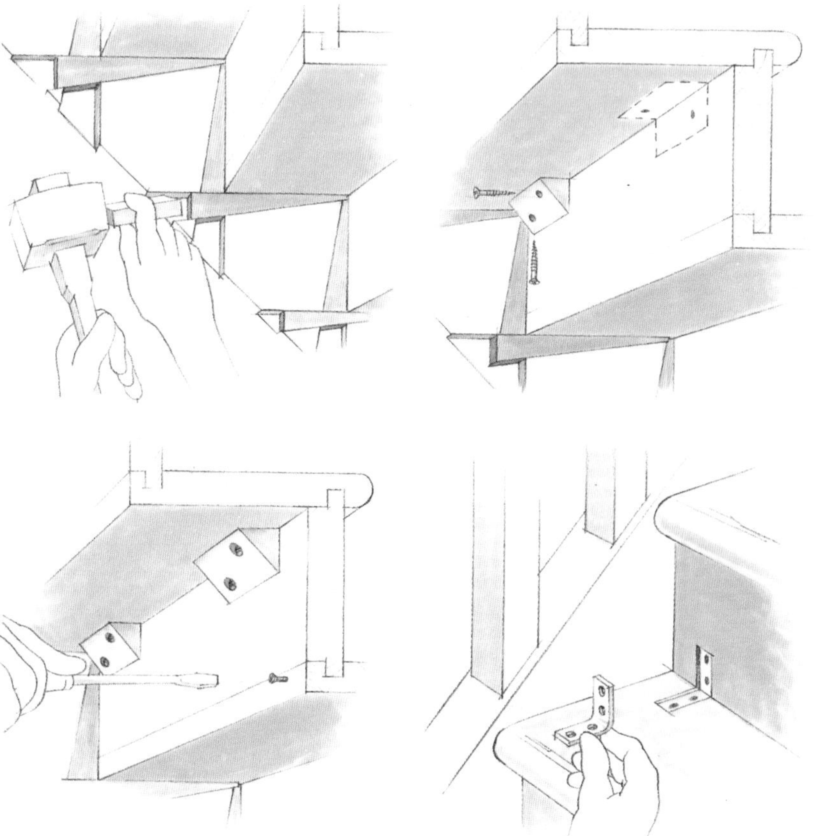

rear edge of the tread into the centre of the riser. Countersink the screw heads.

Finally, secure the joint between the front of each creaky tread and the top edge of the riser beneath it by gluing and screwing wooden blocks into the angle between them. Use two blocks to each tread.

If there is no access, tackle the problem from above. Screw the front of each creaky tread to the top edge of the riser beneath by driving screws down through the tread nosing. Use two screws and countersink the heads neatly so that they will not snag the carpet underlay or backing when this is replaced.

At the rear of each tread, prise open the joint between the tread and the riser above, using a chisel, and squirt in pva woodworking adhesive right along the gap. If possible, do the job last thing at night, when the stairs are less likely to be used until the adhesive has set.

Treating worn treads

The tread nosings can wear and in time split. Such splits can also be caused by resting heavy furniture on the tread edge during removals.

Using a chisel, coping saw or jig saw, cut back the split or damaged nosing flush with the face of the riser beneath and plane the exposed edged flat. Round off the edge of a piece of timber that matches the tread thickness, saw it to the required width and glue and screw it to the front edge of the tread. Fix the screws about 3in (75mm) apart. Plane the strip as necessary to fit.

■ To repair damaged tread nosings, first cut away the wood flush with the face of the riser beneath. Then cut a new nosing to match the tread thickness and width, and plane its edge to a semi-circular profile. Check its fit, then glue and screw it into position. If the damage is small in scale, saw and chisel it out and fit a smaller patch instead.

If, particularly in older houses, you find the treads and risers have parted from the strings, the cause may be wall movement. In newer houses, it may be the result of wall ties disintegrating and allowing the inner leaf to move. Sometimes it is evidence of a general deterioration in the staircase's condition.

If it is simply settlement, which has finally come to rest, and the movement has wrenched the string no more than 19mm (¾in) from the treads and risers, you can effect a do-it-yourself repair. But make sure that all movement has stopped first.

Make some wedges sufficient to hold the string away from the wall. These can be of 25 × 12mm (1 × ½in) timber and roughly 300mm (1ft) long. Hack off the wall plaster above the string and drive the wedges as far as possible between the string and the wall. Saw off any protruding wood.

Make sure that the treads and risers are securely locked back into the string. Doubly secure the wedges by screws through the string, then countersink and conceal with filler and paint. You can then replaster the wall and pin a moulding in place to conceal the gap. If this gap widens again, get professional advice.

Fitting new treads and risers

If a tread or riser is cracked or rotten or has pulled away from a string, it may be possible to replace it. Balusters that slot into the treads will have to be removed. You will also need to ascertain whether the treads are tongued and grooved to the risers or are simply nailed or screwed in place.

Making a new riser or tread should not be a problem provided you take the necessary measurements carefully and accurately. Any replacements can be fixed with small wedges and glue or by using screws.

Any balusters you have temporarily eased out of the way to enable you to remove the old riser and tread can be slid into a prepared slot in the new ones and covered with a moulding.

REFURBISHING A STAIRCASE

If the staircase itself is in good condition, you can give it a complete facelift by replacing both handrail and balusters. Alternatively, you can leave the handrail in position and just fit new balusters between handrail and string.

■ Kits of replacement stair parts are now widely available, allowing the complete balustrade to be replaced. Strip out the old handrail and balusters, cut off the newel posts at string level and join on the new posts. Then fit the new handrail, and secure the new balusters in place with spacer fillets between them.

All the components you need for a new balustrade are available from timber merchants and DIY superstores. When calculating the number of balusters to buy, remember that they must be set with a maximum gap of 100mm (4in) between them.

Remove the old balusters or other infilling. With wooden balusters, the simplest method is to saw through them and prise each end away from the tread or string and the handrail. It is then simply a question of cutting each new baluster to length, using a sliding bevel to give the correct angle at its upper end (and at the lower end on closed-string flights).

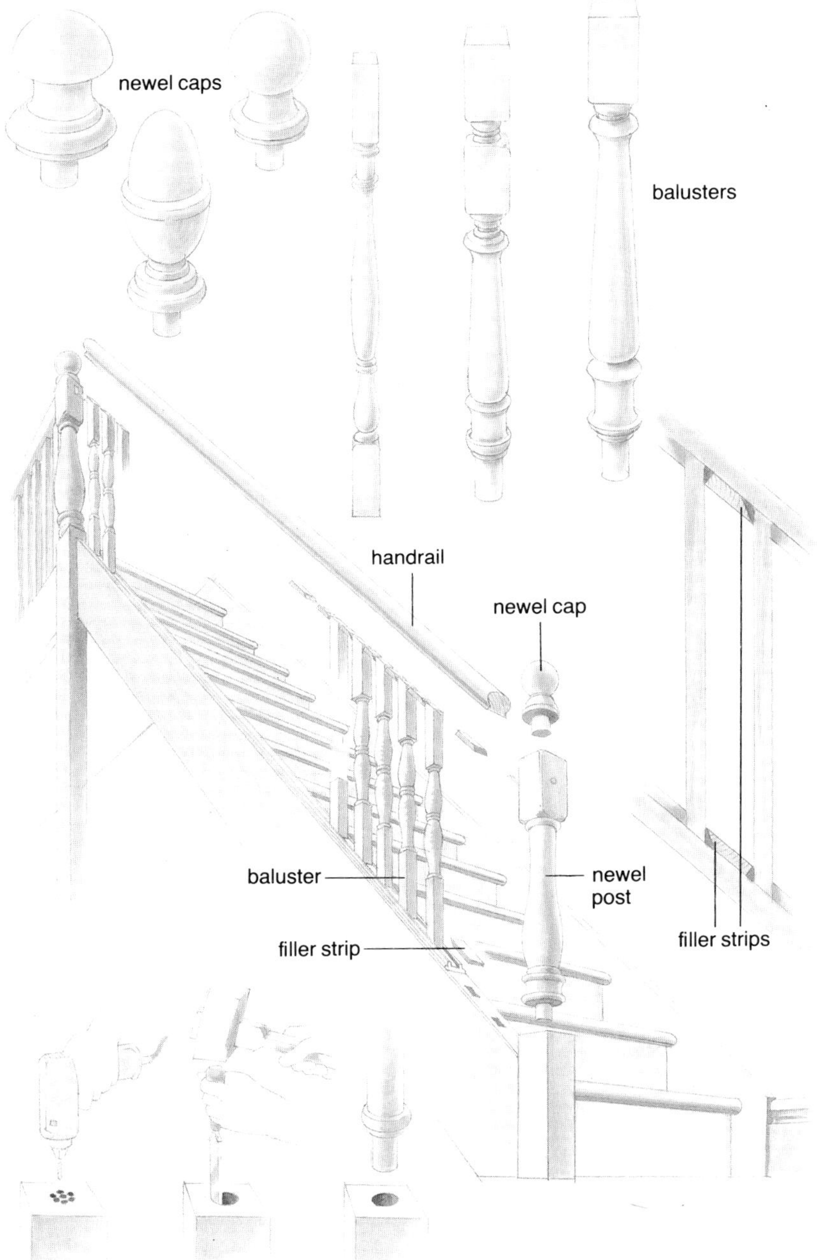

Set the first baluster in position, check that it is vertical and skew-nail it to the string or tread and handrail. Then fit spacers top and bottom before offering up the next baluster. Continue working along the flight in this way until the new balustrade is completed.

If you want to replace the handrail and newel posts for a complete refurbishment, then you can buy kits of parts that bolt together.

If you want to refurbish an old staircase to give it a new look, then you can infill the balustrade with wrought ironwork or laminated or toughened glass. Tailor-made wrought iron panels can be ordered from specialist fabricators in a wide range of designs. The panels are positioned in the frame formed by newels, string and handrail and screwed into place through pre-drilled holes in the panel edges.

Glass must be the toughened variety. Ordinary float glass can be highly dangerous if accidentally broken, and wired glass is also unacceptable. Your local glass merchant will cut laminated glass to size for you. But he will have to order toughened glass in the panel shapes you want, since it cannot be cut once toughened. Make a paper or card template of each panel to ensure an accurate fit.

First create a rebate using slim wooden battens glued and pinned to the staircase woodwork. Then position the glass panel in the rebate and add further battens or beading to hold it securely in place. It is a good idea to bed the glass in putty, mastic or proprietary bedding tape to prevent it from rattling through vibration as people walk up and down the stairs.

FITTING A NEW STAIRCASE

It is rare to have to replace a staircase completely, but you might need to install one to provide access to a new loft room, for example. Prefabricated standard staircases or spiral kits are available and, if they are suitable, will be much less expensive than having one tailor-made by a carpenter – which, incidentally, is not a task for an amateur. Skilled joinery is required to calculate, cut and fit the staircase components together exactly, and to ensure that its treads and risers conform to the requirements of the Building Regulations. If you are planning to have a new staircase, submit drawings to your local authority for approval before you start installing it.

It is worth remembering that if you like the idea of a spiral staircase, it is not always easy for older people and children to negotiate. It is also very awkward to move larger items of furniture up or down this type of staircase.

Working on the Walls

Interior walls obviously have an important part to play in the building of your home and you should therefore understand their purpose and construction before attempting to repair, modify, remove or build them.

By referring to your plan of proposed alterations, you can identify which walls if any need to be removed or repaired. But before starting work, you must know how they are built and what type they are. That way there will be no danger of the wall – and perhaps the floors above or even the roof – crumbling around you.

IDENTIFYING TYPES OF WALL

Some walls are structural or loadbearing, while others are non-loadbearing partitions, and it is essential to know the difference between the two before attempting to alter or modify them in any way. Basically a structural wall is holding your house up and a partition wall is acting just as a divider.

In many rooms, one or two walls will be the inside face of external ones, which are of course always loadbearing. The remaining walls of the room could be either structural or partition.

A non-loadbearing wall acts merely as a divider between rooms and supports no load from the structure itself. The wall may be one single room height or it could extend upwards from the ground floor to bedroom ceiling level. The crucial point is that it supports only its own weight, not the house structure.

You can identify a non-loadbearing wall by looking at the floor and ceiling joists. These run parallel to the wall and the ends of the joists will not be built into it. Upstairs you can tell which way the ceiling joists run by looking in the loft. You can see which way floor joists run by looking at the floorboards, which will be at right angles to the joists.

Non-loadbearing walls are usually built of lighter materials than loadbearing ones and they are frequently constructed on top of floorboards with no special foundations.

Loadbearing walls support part of the structure of the house – usually floor and ceiling joists or roof timbers, which rest on the wall or are built into it. The floor and ceiling joists will be at right angles to the wall and the floorboards

■ **Right** Internal walls may be loadbearing – supporting parts of the house structure higher up the building – or non-loadbearing. You can remove the latter without affecting the house structure, but the former must be replaced by loadbearing beams.

It is generally possible to identify the type of wall involved by examining the direction of the floor joists in the room above.

The first dividing wall (top right) carries no load and stops at ceiling level, so can safely be removed.

The second also stops at ceiling level, but this time supports the joists of the floor above, so a beam must be provided if it is removed.

The third wall is not supporting any floor joists, but the ground-floor section supports its continuation upstairs, and this may in turn support the roof structure, so again a beam is needed.

The fourth wall is clearly loadbearing in all respects.

■ Knocking two rooms into one is a very popular home renovation project. Before tackling the job, however, it is essential to identify exactly what function the dividing wall has as far as supporting the house structure is concerned.

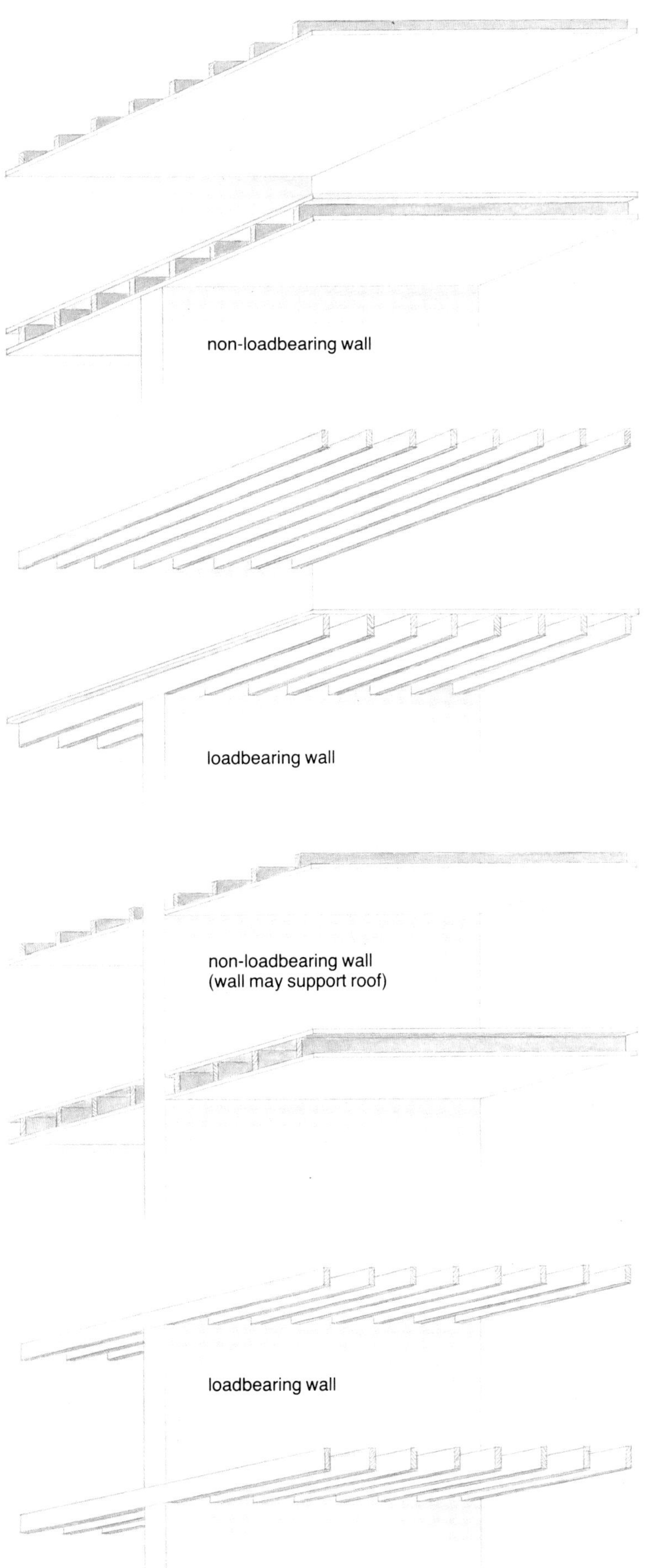

will run parallel with the wall. This type of wall has proper foundations and is usually built of brick or loadbearing concrete blocks.

The real significance of knowing whether a wall is loadbearing or not comes when you are considering making a hole in it, perhaps for a window or door, or you are considering removing it to knock two rooms into one.

The wall above any opening must be supported with a special beam called a lintel, which is fitted into the wall before the opening is made. How the wall is supported while this is done and the size of the lintel required will depend on whether or not the wall is a loadbearing one.

Cutting a hole up to about 1m (39in) wide in a non-loadbearing wall should present no real problems. Even if it is made of brick, as long as this is sound no lintel should be required.

If you are dealing with a loadbearing wall, however, or making larger holes or a hole close to the corner of a building or close to a floor supported by the wall, then it will be necessary to get advice. So check with a building surveyor before you decide whether to continue with the job and equally whether to tackle it yourself. You may prefer at that stage to call in an experienced builder.

In either case, remember that you will need Building Regulations approval for the work from the local authority.

Using lintels

Before deciding what type of lintel to fit above a proposed opening in a wall, you need to know what load it will have to support. This is a job for an expert, so take advice from a building surveyor, experienced builder or the building control officer at your local authority.

Lintels have to rest on the wall at each side of the opening and it is important that there is sufficient brickwork or 'bearing' to support the ends. For openings up to 1.5m (5ft) wide, the bearing should be about 125mm (5in) deep. For wider spans, the bearing should be 200mm (8in) deep. For heavy loads, bed the ends of the lintel on pre-cast concrete or hard stone slabs to help spread the load.

Lightweight, galvanised pressed steel lintels are widely used nowadays, although heavyweight RSJs (rolled steel joists) are normally used for wide spans, such as when two rooms are knocked into one.

Reinforced concrete lintels are not so widely used now because they are very heavy to lift into place. Stone, wood and brick lintels are found in older properties, but equally are rarely used today.

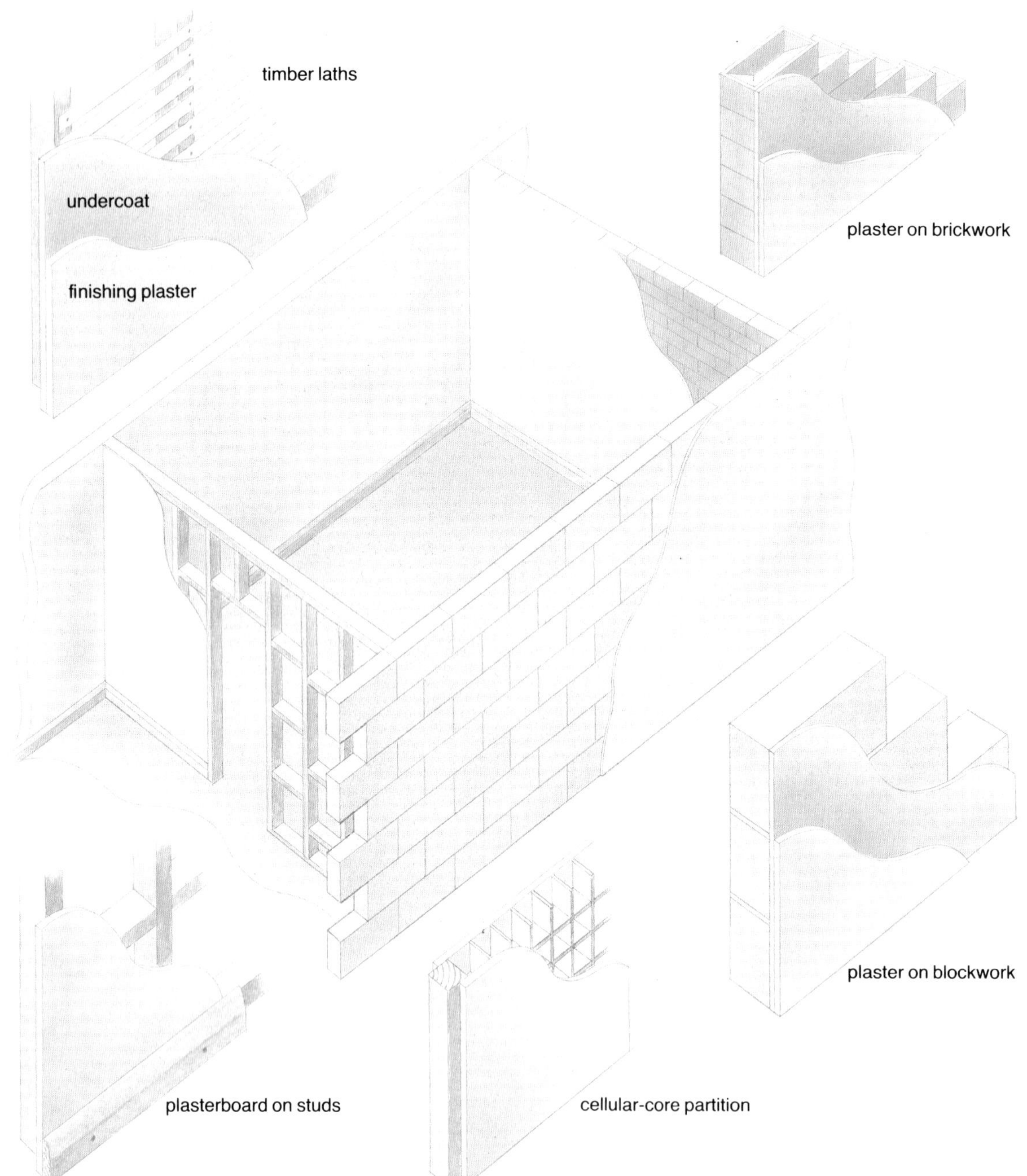

■ Internal walls may be of solid brick or blockwork, plastered on each face with a two-coat layer of plaster. Alternatively, they may be built up as timber frame partitions clad on each side with lath-and-plaster (older homes) or plasterboard (newer homes). Cellular-core partitions are another possibility in newly-built or recently-renovated buildings.

TYPES OF INTERNAL WALL

Depending on the type and age of the property, there are five basic types of internal wall construction you are likely to come across. Recognising each type of construction may in some cases help you determine whether the wall is loadbearing or not.

Plaster-covered building blocks

Building blocks are commonly used for internal walls in modern houses. Non-loadbearing walls may be made from lightweight concrete blocks, insulation blocks or breeze blocks surfaced with plaster or plasterboard. Loadbearing walls may be made from concrete or other loadbearing blocks, also covered with plaster or plasterboard. These walls sound solid when tapped and often produce a greyish dust when drilled.

Plaster-covered single brick

Bricks are often used to make partition walls in older houses. These may be loadbearing or non-loadbearing. They sound solid when tapped and usually produce a reddish dust when drilled.

Stud partitions

Stud partition walls are made with a timber framework covered with plasterboard. Normally they are non-loadbearing, but can be structural. In this case, diagonal braces are fitted between the studs – or timber uprights.

With a loadbearing stud partition, the main timbers are 100 x 50mm (4 × 2in), while with a non-loadbearing stud partition they are usually 75 × 50mm (3 × 2in). This type of wall is lightweight and easy to build and makes an ideal new partition.

Lath and plaster stud partition

This type of wall is often found in older houses. The timber framework is as for a modern stud partition, but the wall has a lath and plaster finish. In the same way, it can be either non-loadbearing or structural (with diagonal braces).

You will often find that the plaster is loose and in poor condition. Although messy, it is an easy job to hack off the old plaster and laths and nail up sheets of plasterboard in their place.

Cellular-core wallboard partition

These walls form non-loadbearing partitions. They are made from plasterboard partitioning panels that have a hollow cellular cardboard core. Adjoining panels are linked with timber studs wedged into the core.

Such walls are thin – only about 60mm (2½in) thick. Although they are obviously hollow, as you will discover when drilling them, they will not necessarily sound so when tapped.

PROBLEMS WITH INTERNAL WALLS

Internal walls can be prone to a number of problems, depending on the type of construction and their overall condition. In some cases, these can be local to the wall itself or caused through another source, which you must first trace and cure.

Damp patches

It is important to ascertain whether any dampness you find is due to penetrating or rising damp in the wall, indicating a structural fault, or whether the problem is condensation caused by a build-up of moisture-laden air in the room.

A simple test to distinguish between penetrating (or interstitial) dampness and condensation can be carried out using cooking foil. Dry out the damp patch with a heater and stick a sheet of foil over the area, sealing the edges with adhesive tape. Then leave it for a few days. If moisture droplets accumulate on the surface of the foil, the problem is due to condensation and steps should be taken to reduce the amount of moisture in the air. If the underside of the foil becomes damp or the damp patch reappears on the wall under the foil, then the problem is due to dampness coming through the wall from the outside.

Damp patches on internal walls usually indicate problems elsewhere. If the damp is on the inside of an external wall, look for faults on the outside. Damp patches on a chimney breast wall can often be traced to water penetrating the flue at or above roof level.

If the damp patch is on a partition wall, it may be caused by rising damp due to a faulty dpc, if the wall is loadbearing with conventional foundations. In this case, a new dpc may be required, which can be installed as for an external wall.

If the wall is simply an internal partition one, it is likely that the damp patch will have been caused by a problem in the plumbing. This could be a leaking water pipe within the wall or possibly a leaking waste pipe nearby. Equally a poor seal around a bath, shower tray or washbasin could be the culprit, if the damp patch is within the vicinity of these fittings or in a room that backs on to them.

If the problem is condensation, the cure is to reduce the amount of water vapour released into the air and to increase ventilation and heating levels. Fit extractor fans in kitchens and bathrooms, where most water vapour is generated. Depending on the circumstances, other action to be considered includes making sure tumble driers are fitted with vent kits, installing a cooker hood, buying a portable dehumidifier to remove excess moisture, and improving the insulation of walls and windows.

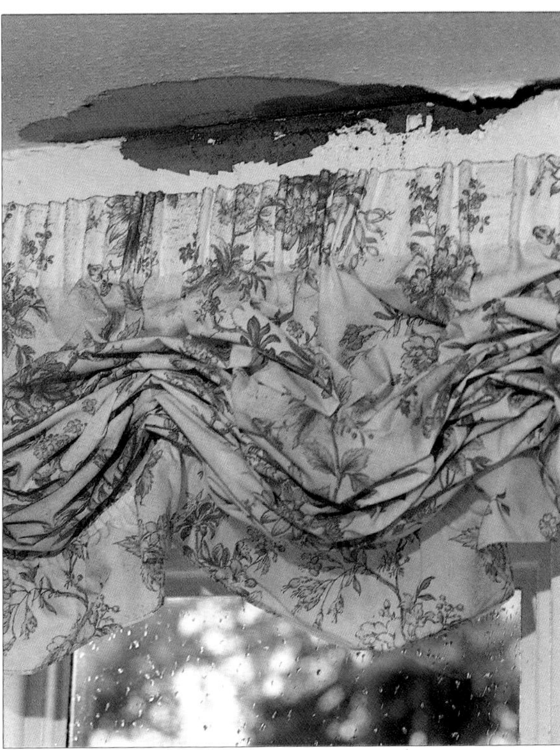

■ Penetrating damp often shows up around window and door openings, or at the edges of ceilings next to external walls. Tracing how the water is getting in can be a difficult task.

Mould growth

Black mould spots on internal walls form as a result of damp or condensation problems. So if you cure these faults, the mould should not return. After curing the fault, remove the black mould by scrubbing the wall with a strong fungicide solution as used in the preparation for exterior painting.

Small cracks and holes

Small cracks and holes in the surface of internal walls are the result of such things as natural movement, knocks, drying plaster, passing traffic and slamming doors.

Use the edge of a filling knife to enlarge the crack or hole and remove all loose plaster. Brush or blow out the dust, then fill the space with a ready-mixed filler or a powder filler to which you add water. Draw the blade of the knife over the top of the repair to leave a smooth surface.

If the crack or hole is quite deep, apply the filler in two parts, allowing the first application to dry before putting on the second.

Cracks between skirting boards and walls tend to reopen if conventional fillers are used. In this situation use a flexible mastic-type filler, which can be applied using a mastic gun and smoothed off with a damp finger. Mastic fillers are available in white, brown and various other colours such as grey and cream.

Large cracks and holes

These can be repaired using proprietary fillers, building them up in layers as described above. For particularly large cracks and holes, however, these will prove expensive to use.

On solid walls, a cheaper option is to use conventional plaster. Chip away all loose material and brush out the dust. Then with an old brush or hand-held sprayer, wet the area and apply an undercoat or browning plaster to fill the patch to within about 2–3mm (1⁄16–1⁄8in) of the existing wall surface.

As soon as the undercoat has set, apply the top coat of finishing plaster, which you smooth on using a steel float (also called a plasterer's trowel). Allow this to become firm, then spray the surface with water and polish it flat and smooth using the steel float.

If the hole is in a lath and plaster wall, cut the plaster away to expose the laths. If these are broken, fold a piece of expanded metal mesh over the sound laths at the top and bottom of the hole and then replaster as described above.

Where the holes in plasterboard walls are

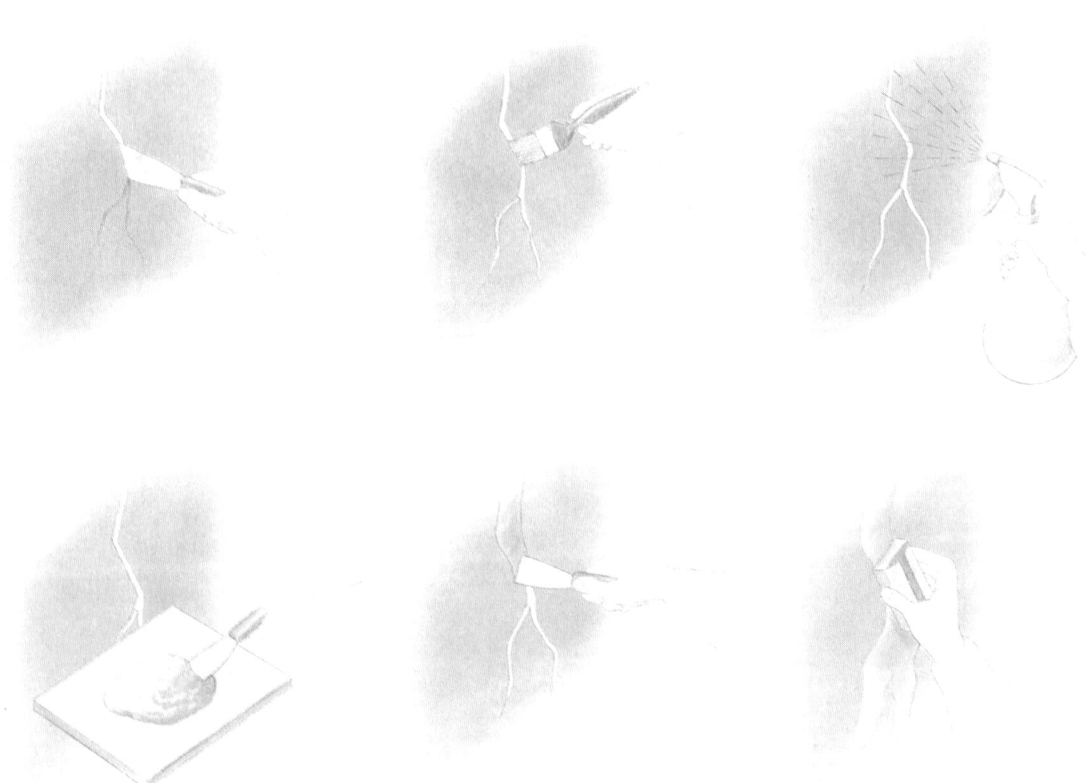

■ To repair cracks in wall plaster, first strip off any old wallcoverings. Then use a filling knife to rake out the crack along its length, undercutting the crack edges slightly so the filler can bond well. Brush out all loose material, and spray water along the crack to cut down the absorbency of the surrounding plaster; if the filler dries out too quickly it may crack.

Mix up some plaster filler to a firm consistency and fill the crack slightly proud of the surrounding plaster. When it has hardened, sand it down flush with the surface for an almost invisible repair.

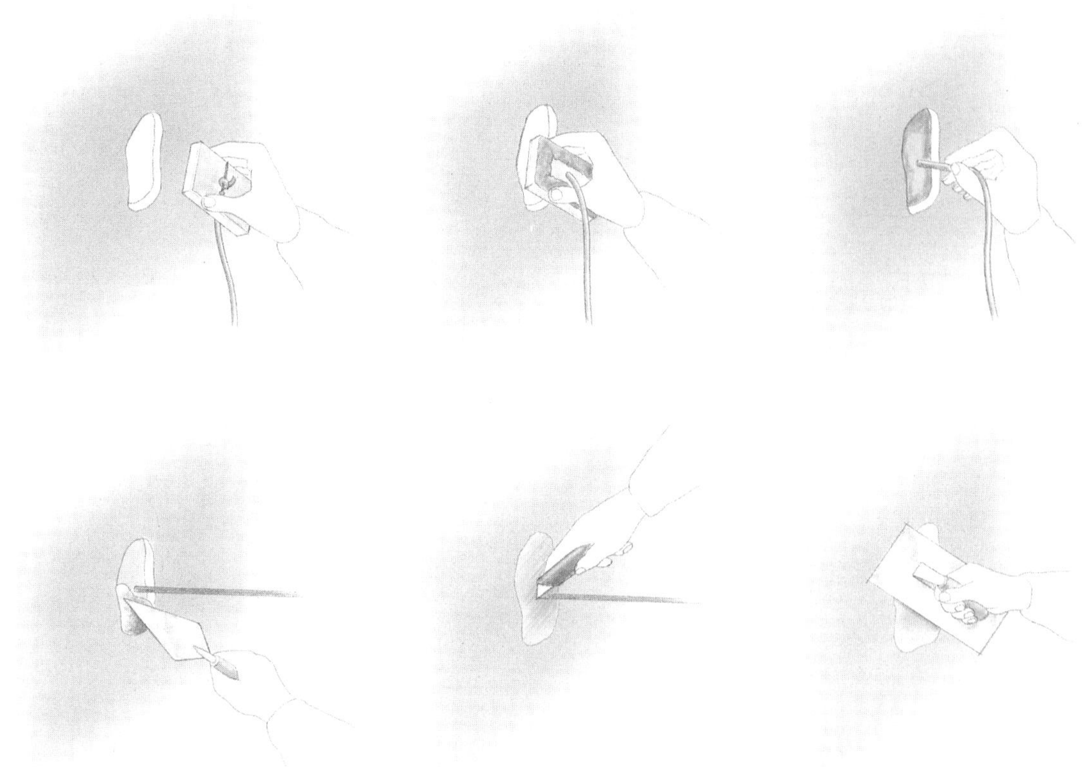

■ To repair small holes in plasterboard, take a small offcut a little taller and narrower than the hole and thread some knotted string through it. Butter some filler onto each end of the patch, insert it through the hole and use the string to pull it against the inner face of the plasterboard. Fill the hole with more filler, then cut off the string. When the filler has hardened, skim over the repair with a little more filler for a flush finish.

small, the use of an ordinary filler should do the job. But larger holes will have to be patched. Use a trimming knife to cut back the damaged board to leave a clean outline. Then prepare an offcut of plasterboard slightly wider than the hole and use this to fill behind the hole.

To help you position this offcut, make two holes in it and feed some string through them, leaving the two end lengths hanging so you can use them to hold the offcut while you position it.

Apply some fresh plaster or filler around the edges on the face of the offcut. Then, keeping hold of the string, pass the offcut through the hole and pull it up behind. Leave it like this until the plaster has set. Pull out the string or cut it off, then fill the hole in the normal way.

In the case of a large hole, it may be better to fill the majority of it with a scrap of plasterboard over the previously fixed offcut using wet plaster. When dry, you simply have to fill the remaining cracks around the edge of the repair and possibly finish off with a skim coat of plaster over the whole surface.

If the hole is very large – more than 200mm (8in) across – then it will be better to cut out a rectangle of plasterboard to expose the timber studs at each side of the damaged area. You can then fix a new section of plasterboard to the studs on each side with galvanised plasterboard nails. Use joint filler to repair the crack around the patch and reinforce the joint with scrim or paper jointing tape, which can be concealed with a skim coat of plaster applied to the surface.

Blown plaster

If a plastered wall sounds hollow when you tap it – and often there will be a surface bulge as well – the plaster is said to have 'blown', which means it has come away from the undersurface. This is a common problem in older houses, especially on lath and plaster walls.

With lath and plaster, the first stage is to hack off the blown plaster to uncover the extent of the damage. Once one area is affected, it is likely that much of the wall will be in a similar condition. This is because the nibs that hook over the laths drop off with age and the plaster then becomes loose.

If this has happened over more than half the wall surface, then it will be best to hack off all the old plaster and the laths as well. You can then nail new plasterboard sheets on to the now-exposed timber studs.

This will provide a good opportunity to uprate lighting and power circuits or heating pipework and enable you to install wall insulation within the timber studwork.

If you decide to replaster patches of lath and

■ **Right** To patch larger holes in lath-and-plaster, cut back the plaster and the broken laths to the adjacent studs or joists. Do the same round a large hole in plasterboard. Then nail or screw supporting battens into place as shown, nail in a matching plasterboard patch and skim over the repair with plaster or filler.

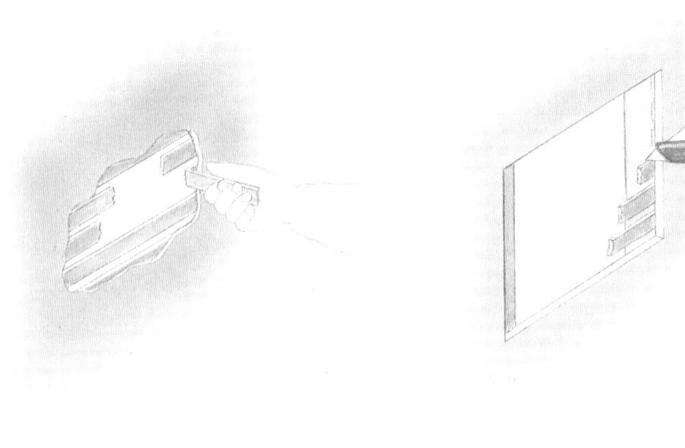

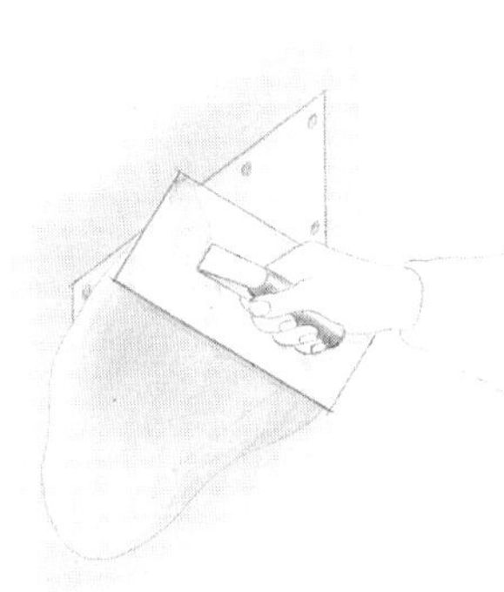

■ **Below** To patch areas of loose plaster, cut back the area until sound plaster is reached. Then apply new plaster with a float, rule it off with a batten flush with the surrounding wall surface, and polish it off with the float.

plaster wall, first remove any damaged laths and nail new ones to the studs. Brush the edges of the adjacent plaster to remove dust and debris, then dampen these edges and brush down the laths with a wet brush.

With a steel float, apply a coat of lightweight bonding plaster or metal lathing plaster, using a fairly firm pressure to ensure the plaster pushes through the laths at the back. Allow this coat to harden, then apply a second coat to within about 3mm (⅛in) of the surface. Check this is smooth and level by drawing the edge of a long length of straight timber across the area. Lightly scratch the surface of the second coat to give a good key and, when hard, apply a coat of finishing plaster.

If you find blown plaster on a solid wall, again you will have to cut back all the loose material until you reach sound plaster. Extensive re-plastering could be required. If half the wall or more is affected and you do not feel particularly confident about plastering, a sensible solution would be to hack off all the plaster and 'dry-line' the wall with plasterboard.

To replaster a large area, brush down the brick or blockwork to remove any remaining dust or debris, then dampen the wall. Use a lightweight browning plaster as the undercoat

■ To replaster corners and reveals, hack off all the old plaster. Then nail a timber batten to one face of the corner, projecting beyond it by the required plaster thickness, and plaster that face of the corner. When the plaster has hardened, remove the batten carefully and reposition it on the other side of the corner. Plaster the second face, remove the batten and round off the corner with fine abrasive paper when it has set.

and mix this with water to make it smooth and easy to apply.

Starting at the bottom of the wall, load the steel float and apply the plaster firmly to the wall with an upward stroke. Continue this way, building up the thickness to just below the surface level of the sound surrounding plaster.

As already mentioned, use a long length of straight timber held on edge to pull over the replastered area to check there are no high spots. The surface of this undercoat should be 2–3mm (1/16–1/8in) below the finished surface level required.

As soon as the undercoat has hardened, you can apply the finishing coat, again using the trowel. Pull a straight-edge over the surface to ensure no high spots. Smooth the surface with a steel float and, as soon as the plaster has hardened, dampen the surface with water from a small hand spray. Then polish it smooth and flat with the float.

Pitted plaster

Small indentations and gouges over a wide area of the surface of a plastered wall are easily rectified by applying a skim coat of finishing plaster over the whole wall.

Lightly dampen the wall surface and, with a steel float, apply the plaster in as thin a layer as possible. As soon as the plaster begins to harden, lightly spray over it with water and polish the plaster smooth with a steel float. If you cannot get the surface flat, it will help if you draw a timber straight-edge over it while the plaster is still wet.

Corner cracks

You will find two types of corner in a room. Internal (inside) corners are created where two walls join at right angles. External (outside) ones are formed where the corner projects into the room, such as on the outside of a chimney breast or in a door opening.

Internal corners usually give very few problems and you can normally repair any cracks you find with wall filler. Sometimes cracks tend to reopen after they have been repaired. If this occurs, you should be able to prevent it from happening again by raking out the crack, applying filler and running plasterboard joint tape into the wet filler. You then have to apply more filler on the joint tape and feather it out with a wide filling knife. Finally wipe it over with a damp sponge to leave a smooth finish.

You can also use filler to repair a slightly damaged external corner. With more extensive damage, you will have to build up the corner with one-coat or two-coat (undercoat and finishing) plaster.

Repair the corner one side at a time. Using masonry nails, fix a batten to one side of the corner so that the edge of the batten is level with the plaster surface on the other side. Apply undercoat plaster to this side, using the batten to give you an edge to work against.

Allow this side to set, then move the batten to cover the repaired section and fill the other side of the corner in the same way. When that plaster has set, again remove the batten and, if necessary, rub the corner smooth.

If the area is particularly prone to damage, such as with a doorway, it is best to reinforce the corner at its susceptible point using a strip of metal corner beading.

Trim back the plaster to accommodate the beading, then apply blobs of undercoat plaster to the wall. Press the beading in place on the wet plaster, checking with a spirit level that it is vertical and that the rounded edge of the beading is level with the wall surface on each side of the corner. Allow the plaster to dry, then apply more undercoat and a skim coat of finishing plaster to complete the repair.

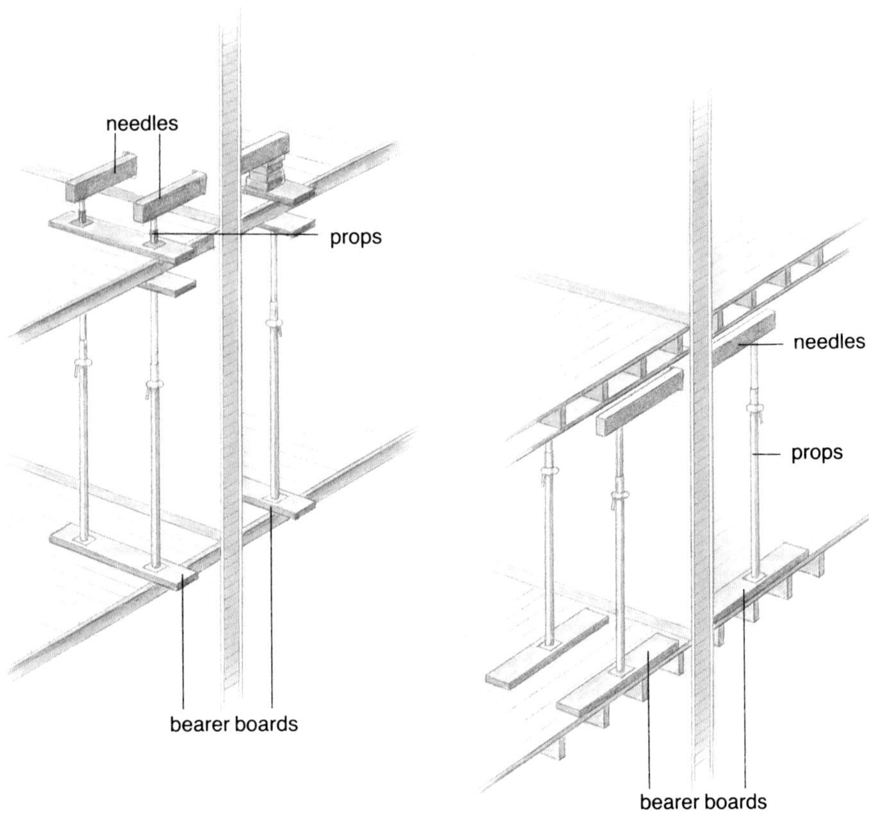

■ Before starting to remove part of a loadbearing wall so a supporting beam can be inserted, take the weight of the wall above on timber needles and adjustable props. If the wall is to be removed right up to ceiling level, pass the needles through the wall at first-floor level, supporting them on two sets of props as shown (above left). If the beam will be installed below ceiling level, the needles can be passed through lower down (above right).

REMOVING A WALL

If you want to gain extra space, it may be possible to remove a dividing wall and so knock two rooms into one. Remember that you must obtain local authority approval before doing this. You will have to supply structural calculations to show that the lintel you must install above the opening will support the load.

If the wall is non-loadbearing, it will only have to support the weight of the wall above the opening. If it is loadbearing, a substantial lintel will be required to support the other parts of the building above it.

Basically the job involves cutting holes in the wall above the proposed lintel position so that the wall can be temporarily supported on timber beams, known as needles, held up with adjustable steel props, which you can hire. With a loadbearing wall, two sets of props will be needed. One set supports the wall as described above, while the other set is placed under the ceiling to support the upper floor joists, which run at right angles to the wall.

If the room has a high ceiling, the holes for the needles can be knocked through the wall just under the ceiling above the planned position of the lintel.

If the room has a low ceiling, some floorboards will have to be removed in the room above the opening to allow the props to pass through and support the needles, which are positioned to support the wall in the upstairs room. This allows the lintel to be positioned immediately below the floor joists to give maximum headroom.

With the wall and floor well supported, the wall can be demolished and brick piers built up at each side of the room to support the lintel. The blocks on each side that will bear the lintel must be very carefully levelled. When set, the lintel can be lifted into place on them.

The next stage is to make good the wall above the lintel by bricking up around the needles. When the new brickwork has set, the needles are removed and the holes bricked up. Finally, the whole area is plastered.

BUILDING A PARTITION WALL

If you want to divide a large room, the easiest way is to build a stud partition wall. This involves making a framework of 75 x 50mm (3 × 2in) timber studs, clad on both sides with sheets of plasterboard.

Thc first stage is to screw a length of timber called the sole plate to the floor at the wall position. Mark plumb lines up the side walls to ascertain the corresponding position on the ceiling and then fix another length of timber (the

■ A stud partition wall consists of a head and sole plate with evenly-spaced vertical studs nailed in place between them. The studs themselves are braced and prevented from bowing by short noggings nailed between adjacent studs. If the head plate runs parallel to and between the joists above, fit noggings between the joists to which the head plate can be secured. Screw side studs to the side walls, and add extra studs at corners as shown. Finish door and top light openings with linings. Run in any services such as wiring and plumbing before completing the fixing of the other layer of plasterboard cladding.

head plate) to the ceiling. The screws holding the head plate should go into the ceiling joists, which you can find by probing with a thin screwdriver.

Next screw the end studs (vertical timbers) to the side walls between the head and sole plates. Decide on the door position, remove a section of the sole plate and fix studs at each side, using rebated housing joints in the head plate for a secure fixing. Allow for the thickness of the timber lining that will frame the door.

Fix further studs at 400mm (16in) centres by skew-nailing them to the head and sole plates. Three studs should support each 1200mm (4ft) wide plasterboard sheet.

Next nail the noggins (horizontal timbers) between the studs at about 1200mm (4ft) centres. In tall rooms extra noggins may be needed to coincide with the top edge of the plasterboard sheets where single lengths will not reach the ceiling. You will need a noggin at the top of the door frame and you can fix additional noggins as required to form windows in the wall. This may be necessary, for example, to allow 'borrowed' light into one room from the adjoining one.

At this stage you should run any services, such as plumbing pipes or electrical cables, within the framework of the wall. Then cover the wall with sheets of tapered-edge plasterboard, fixing them with plasterboard nails at 150mm (6in) intervals. After putting up the plasterboard on one side, you can fit insulation into the cavity before you clad the other side to reduce sound transmission.

Cover up all nail head depressions and joints with filler. While this is still wet, press joint tape into the filler and smooth off. Apply further filler as a wide band over the tape and feather off the edges using a damp sponge.

BLOCKING A DOORWAY

Remove the door and lining or frame by sawing through and prising off the lengths of timber. With a stud partition wall, the best way to block the opening is to fix an additional timber frame in the gap and clad both sides with plasterboard, fixing the board grey side outwards. You can then skim over the plasterboard with finishing plaster to bring the surface level with the adjacent walls.

With a brick or block wall, you can use the same method, but it is better to block the opening with a similar material to that used for the wall construction. In this case there will be

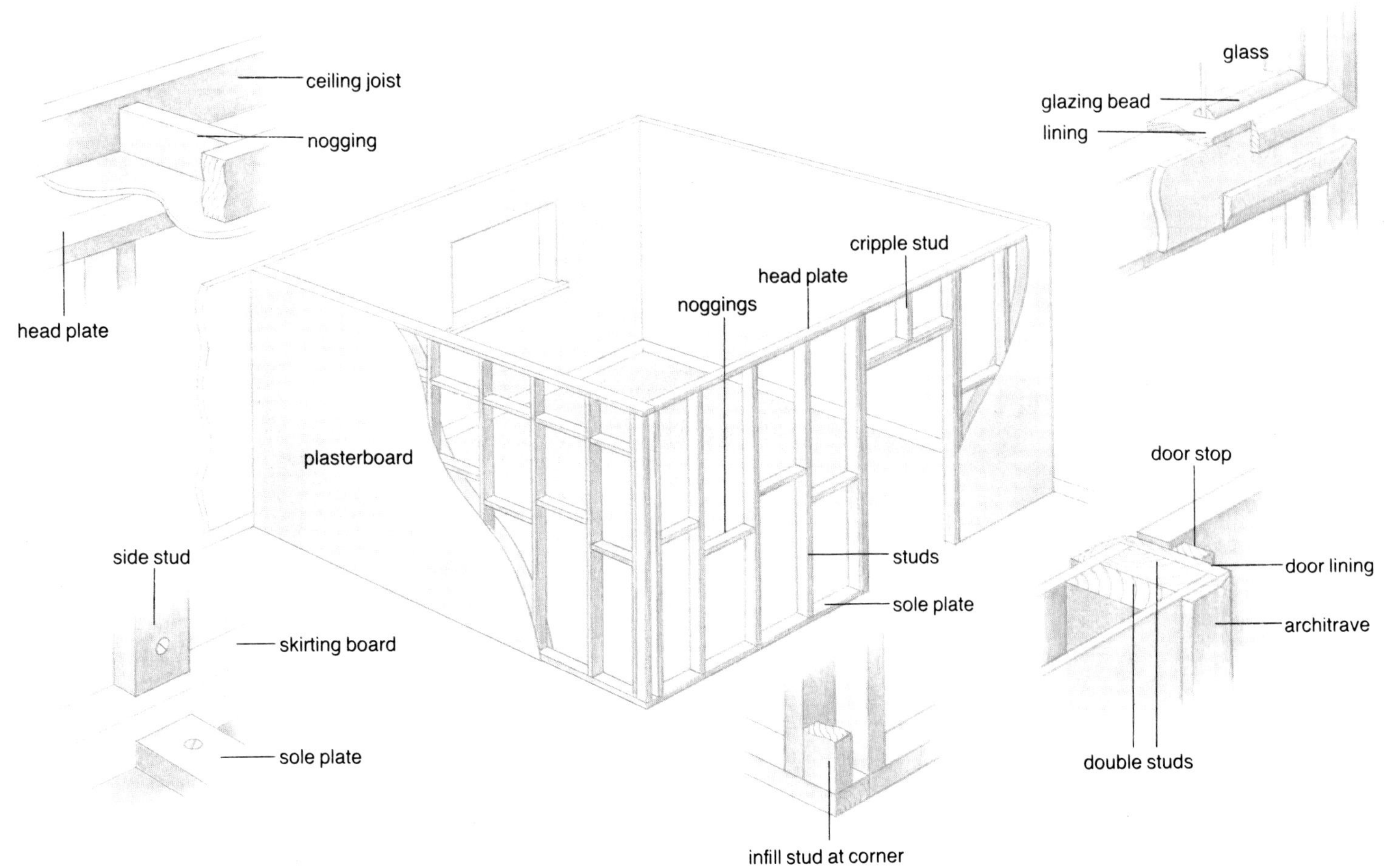

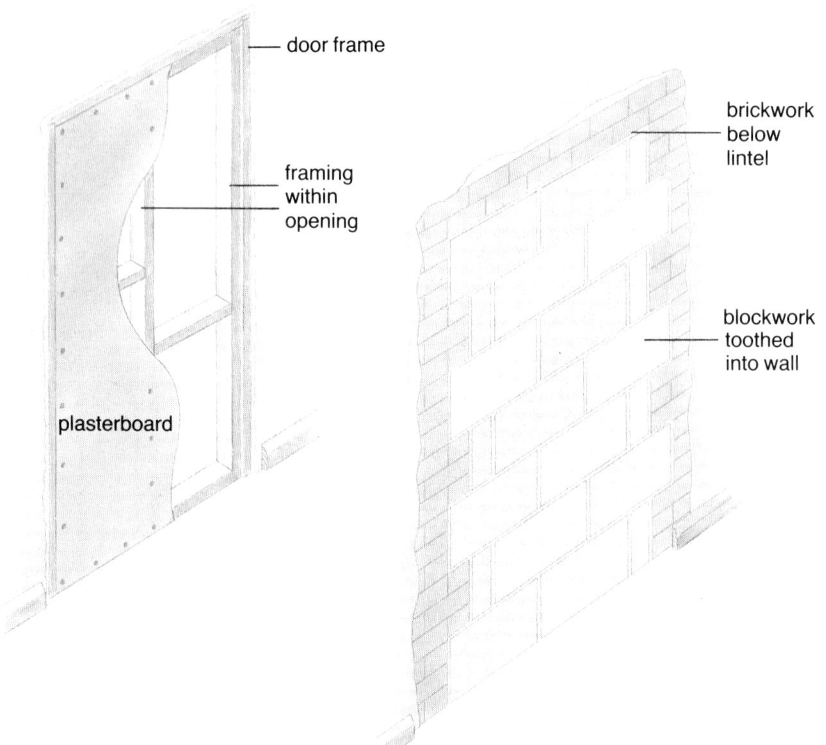

■ Block off an unwanted doorway with a timber framework fixed to the door frame and covered on both sides with plasterboard, or remove the frame and fill the opening with blockwork.

less chance of differential movement causing cracking that would later highlight the presence of the infill.

Remove the door frame and chop out half bricks or blocks at approximately 300mm (12in) intervals so that the bricks or blocks being used to fill the opening will key into the walls at either side. When you have bricked up the opening and the mortar has set, apply an undercoat of browning plaster and then skim over with finishing plaster, levelling if off flush with the original walls on either side.

WORKING ON THE CEILINGS

While ceilings may not suffer a lot of wear and tear, things can go wrong with them. So it pays to check them over from time to time. It is surprising how long a crack or stain can otherwise go undetected!

In upstairs rooms look out for damp patches caused by roof problems and also for signs of stress – possibly through too much bric-a-brac being stored in the loft.

If an old lath-and-plaster ceiling is badly cracked and sagging, carefully probe it and pull away the loose parts. You may find that the plaster has come away from its backing. In this case you will have the messy job of pulling away all the old laths too so that a new plasterboard one can be fixed in its place.

To get to the ceiling in safety and comfort for small localised repairs, a pair of steps will provide suitable access. Ideally this should have a platform and handrail for safety. For larger repair work you should work from the base section of a wheeled scaffold tower or stand on a builders' scaffold board supported between two pairs of stepladders.

You should be able to stand upright with your head about 75mm (3in) below the ceiling to avoid undue neck strain. Remember to wear safety spectacles if you are drilling, scraping out cracks or cleaning off old finishes.

Some ceiling alterations can have a noticeable effect on the appearance of a room and significantly reduce the heating costs. A lowered ceiling, for example, will reduce the volume of air in the room and thus create a smaller space to be heated. Cladding the ceiling in wood or fixing insulating plasterboard in place of the standard type will significantly cut down on the amount of heat lost through it, and will also reduce condensation.

■ Older ceilings are formed by nailing slim timber laths across the joists at about 10mm (3/8in) spacings, and then plastering their undersides. Plaster is forced up between the laths and forms a key that holds the plaster surface in place. If the key fails, areas of plaster may collapse.

More modern homes have ceilings of plasterboard, which is nailed directly to the underside of the joists.

Sometimes ceilings are formed with plain-edged or tongued-and-grooved softwood or hardwood boards, either nailed directly to the joists or fixed beneath an existing ceiling.

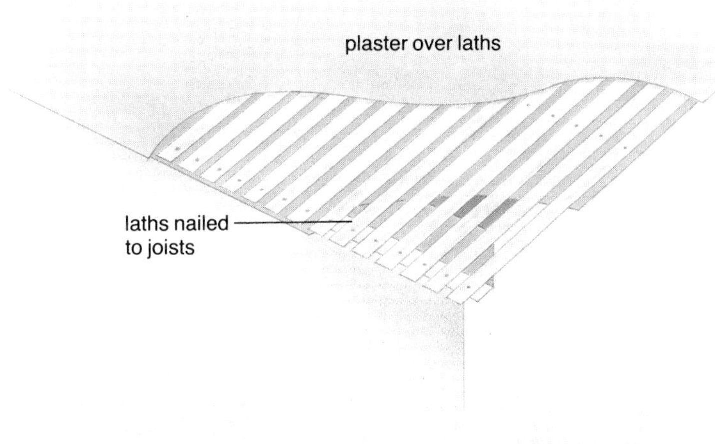

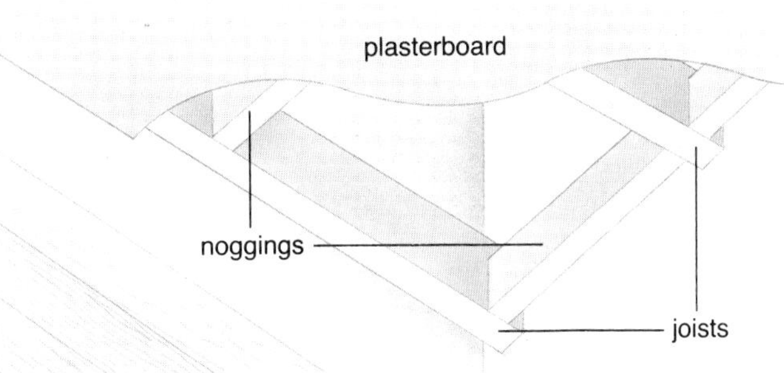

tongued-and-grooved cladding

noggings

joists

■ Ceilings are often ornamented with decorative plaster coving and centre pieces, both of which may need as much renovation as the ceiling itself.

Replacing a ceiling or fixing a lowered one also gives you the opportunity to improve the standard of lighting in a room. You could, for example, fix downlights, spotlights or track lighting instead of the single pendant light.

TYPES OF CEILING CONSTRUCTION

There are four basic types of ceiling construction, depending on the style and age of the property. Check which one is used in your house since it can affect the type of problem the ceiling has and therefore the repair work that might be required.

Plasterboard ceilings

Plasterboard is widely used to dry-line ceilings in modern houses and may be found in older houses where original lath-and-plaster ceilings have been replaced.

The plasterboard is nailed directly to the ceiling joists and is either finished with a skim coat of plaster or the joints are sealed with filler and paper joint tape.

Lath and plaster ceilings

Lath and plaster is the traditional way of finishing ceilings. Timber laths are nailed to the ceiling joists with narrow gaps between them.

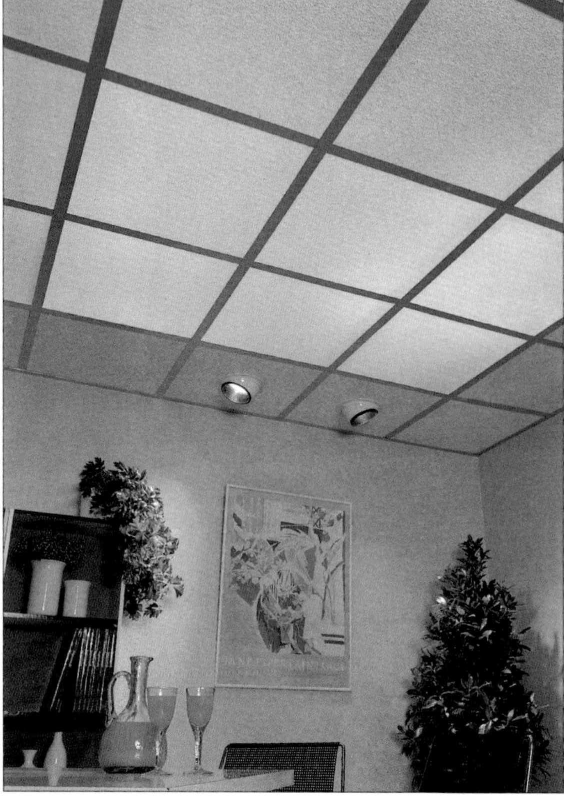

■ Suspended ceilings are a perfect cover-up for old plaster ceilings in poor condition. They may be tailor-made from timber (above), or bought as a kit in a form that can also permit concealed lighting effects to be used (right).

These are then covered with two or three layers of rough browning plaster and a skim coat of finishing plaster to achieve a flat surface.

Timber or boarded ceilings

Where this type of ceiling exists, often it was put up to replace an earlier plastered ceiling. Matching tongued-and-grooved timber boards can look attractive when stained or varnished, and form a well-insulated ceiling too.

Ceilings of fibreboard, fire-resistant building board and plywood sheets, with timber battens pinned to the surface to hide the joins between boards, have a utility appearance reminiscent of immediate post-war repairs.

Suspended ceilings

These ceilings can be conventionally constructed, fitted to a timber framework to lower the height. In many cases, however, proprietary suspended ceilings comprise a light metal framework forming a grid, which is hung from the original ceiling by wires. Translucent plastic or fibreboard panels are fitted into the grid framework and often there is a lighting arrangement above the ceiling to create a concealed illumination effect.

FITTING A PLASTERBOARD CEILING

A new plasterboard ceiling can be fitted directly under the existing one. But you will probably have to screw the new sheets in place. By hammering in nails, you could well shake down the original material. It is much better to pull down the old ceiling and replace it with new sheets of plasterboard nailed directly to the ceiling joists.

Pulling down an old ceiling is messy, but not difficult. Wear old clothes, a hat, dust mask and safety spectacles. Open all the windows in the room and tape round the door to prevent dust from drifting to other parts of the house.

Take down the old ceiling using a hammer and cold chisel or a wrecking bar, which is a small crowbar. This usually has a nail-puller at one end and this is ideal for removing nails from the joists. If this proves difficult, drive the nails into the timber instead.

If you are replacing the ceiling using plasterboard nailed to the undersides of the joists, use tapered-edge board in the smallest sizes available. Plasterboard is heavy and awkward to lift.

Start in one corner and fix the first sheet so its length is at right angles to the direction of the joists. It will probably be necessary to trim the board so its end falls midway across a joist. Fix it in place with galvanised large-head

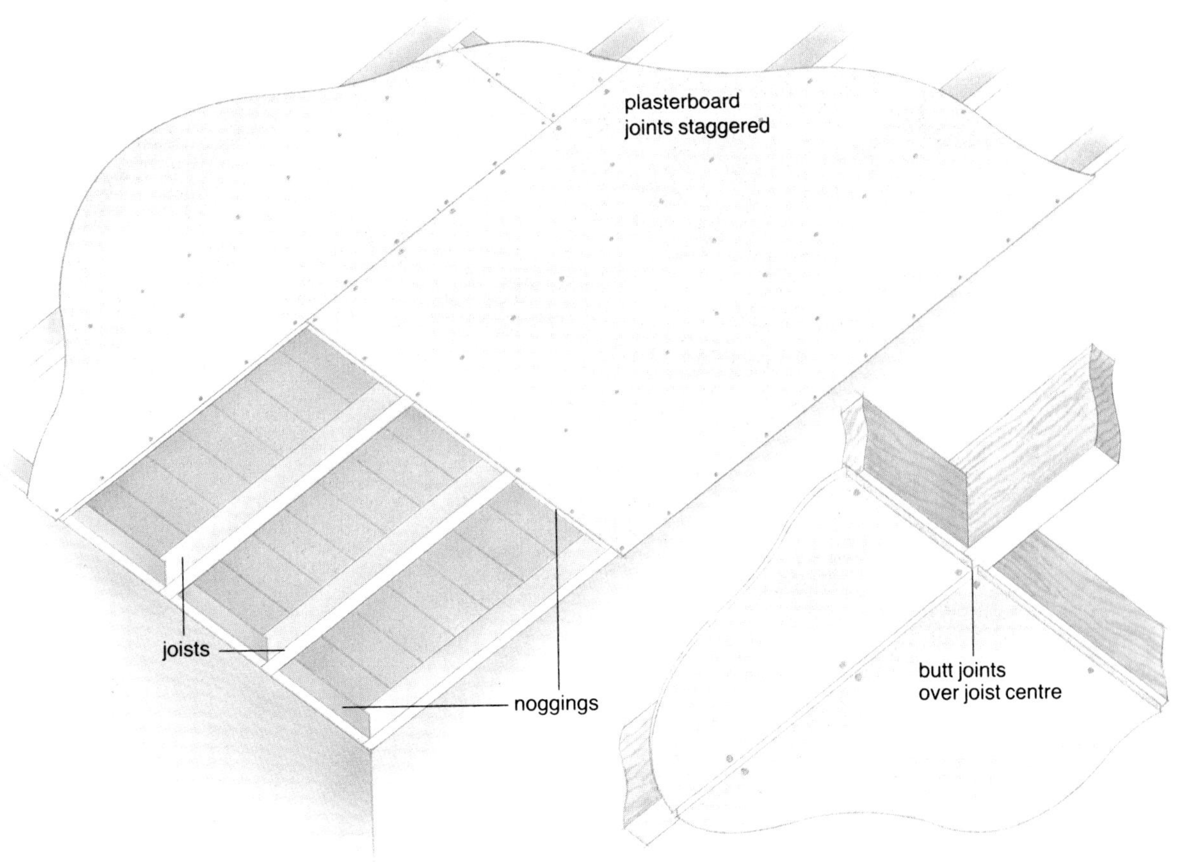

■ Plasterboard sheets are nailed directly to the undersides of the joists with galvanised nails. Adjacent boards are butt-jointed along the centre line of each joist, and board positions are staggered in adjacent rows. The joints are taped over before the ceiling is given a skim of finishing plaster.

■ Cast plaster ceiling centrepieces are a common feature in older homes. If they cannot be restored, modern replicas can be used to replace them.

plasterboard nails with the cream-coloured face of the board downwards. Insert the nails 150mm (6in) apart and drive them in so their head just dimples the surface of the board but does not tear it.

Cut subsequent sheets so that the joints between the ends of the sheets do not line up. You should butt the long paper-covered edges together, but keep the short cut edges at the ends about 3mm (1/8in) apart. Fill nail heads and finish the joints with filler and paper joint tape.

FITTING A CENTREPIECE

If an ornate centrepiece is damaged, it may be possible to repair it. You can try using a rubber moulding, which is normally sold in craft shops, to copy a section of the undamaged moulding. This forms a mould into which you pour plaster of Paris. When the new piece is set, you glue it into the missing section using pva adhesive. Some trimming of the new piece of plaster may be necessary to get it to fit exactly.

Modern ceiling centres, made from rigid polyurethane or fibrous plaster, are easy to fit. Turn off the lighting circuit at the mains, disconnect the wiring and fit the centre direct to the ceiling, remembering to thread through the wiring first. Spread adhesive filler over the back of the centre and press it into position on the ceiling. Prop it with springy battens until the adhesive sets. Then reconnect the light fitting and restore the power.

Heavy ceiling centres should be further fixed with zinc-plated screws driven into the ceiling joist; the heads can then be covered with filler.

FITTING COVING

Plaster or rigid plastic coving round the wall and ceiling join provides a neat finish to the room as well as sealing off those awkward and unsightly cracks that always appear.

First pencil a guide line, the width of the coving, around the top of the walls and the perimeter of the ceiling. Cut lengths of coving as required to fit, mitring the corners at 45 degrees to ensure a neat, snug fit. Use a mitre box for this or the template that is sometimes supplied. All types of coving can be cut with a fine tooth saw. Remove burrs from rough edges with abrasive paper.

Spread coving adhesive on the fixing edges and press the coving in place so it is aligned with the pencil guide lines. The adhesive should hold the coving. If, however, the wall is uneven, you can temporarily hold it in place with masonry pins until the adhesive has set. These can be pulled out later and the holes filled.

Remove excess adhesive with a damp cloth while it is still wet. You can also use the adhesive for making good any gaps between the coving and the walls or ceiling and between adjacent lengths. If using expanded polystyrene coving, you can smooth over the surface using a fine surface filler, which should be rubbed down lightly when dry.

LOWERING A CEILING

This alters the proportions of a room and makes any with a high ceiling much more economical to heat. The lowered section can be all over or just part of the ceiling.

It is best to make up a sturdy timber framework and cover it on the underside with plasterboard. Screw 50 × 50mm (2 × 2in) timbers around the room at the desired new height. Across the shortest width, span these with 75 × 50mm (3 × 2in) timbers fixed 400mm (16in) apart to form the framework. If the span is more than 2.75m (9ft) wide, fix hangers of 50 × 50mm (2 × 2in) timber centrally between the framework and the joists above. Cover the underside of the framework with sheets of plasterboard fixed as described earlier.

■ To fit new coving, cut a mitre joint on one end of the first length, butter adhesive onto its rear surfaces and press it into place in one corner of the room. Fit a second length at the other end of this wall, then fit square-ended lengths (cut to size if necessary) in between. Work along the other walls in the same way, mitring any external corners as shown. Finally wipe off any excess adhesive along the lengths and at joints.

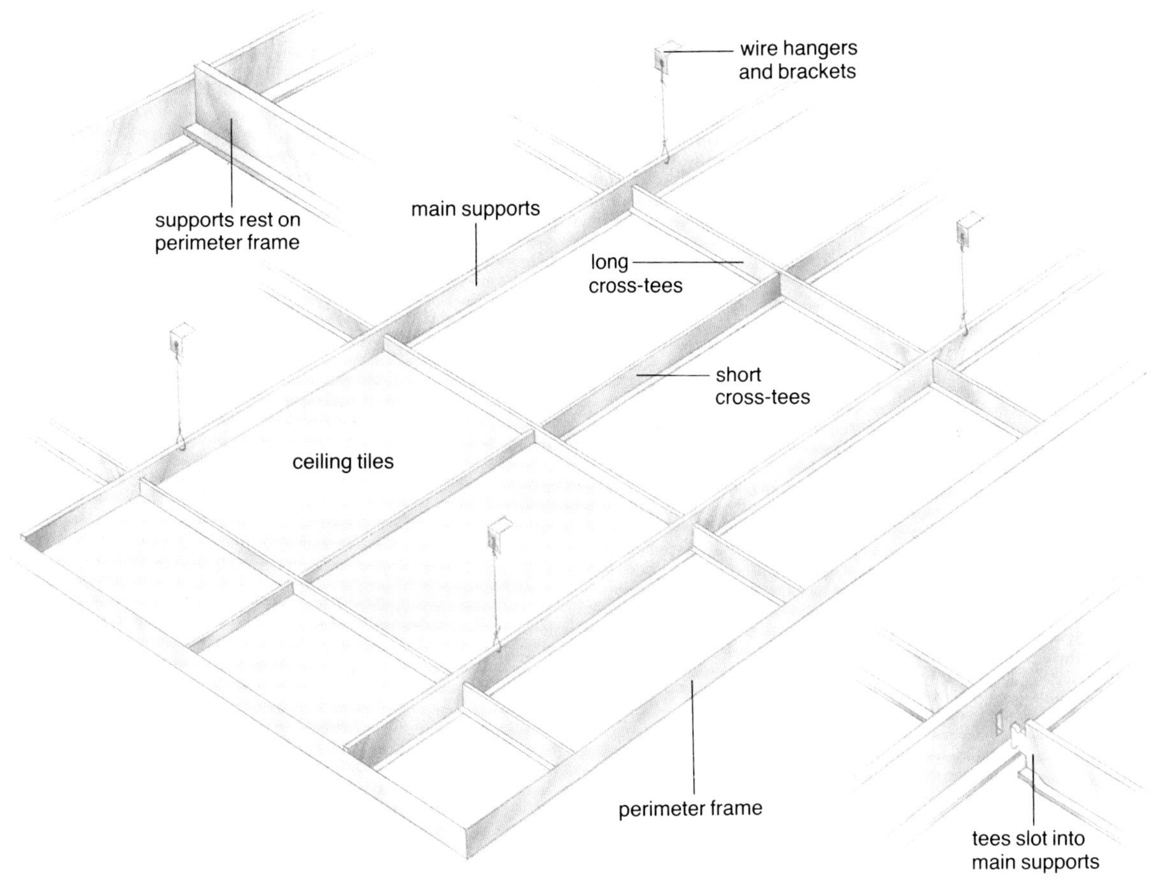

■ Suspended ceilings come in kit form. They consist of a series of bearers and cross-pieces that interlock to form a grid into which the ceiling tiles fit. The grid perimeter is fixed to the walls all round the room, and the centre is suspended from wires attached to the ceiling to prevent it from sagging.

FITTING A SUSPENDED CEILING

A proprietary lightweight suspended ceiling provides an attractive surface, while at the same time hiding unsightly pipework, cracks, sags and stains in a ceiling. By incorporating lighting above translucent panels, it is also easy to create an illuminated ceiling.

Decide on the height of ceiling required and, with a spirit level, mark a line around the perimeter of the room for the support channel. Screw and plug the lightweight aluminium channel to the wall, mitring it at the corners for a neat join. Next, calculate the size of the border tiles so that they will create a balanced appearance all round the room. Then fit main bearers along the length of the room, so they rest on the wall channel at each end and are supported every 1.2m (4ft) with wires fixed between hooks in the ceiling and the bearers. Form a grid into which the ceiling tiles rest by cutting the cross pieces to fit between the main transverse bearers.

Fit whole ceiling tiles by placing them into the grid from above and finally cut the border tiles to size and fit them into the perimeter of the grid all round the new ceiling. Most can be cut easily with a sharp handyman's knife.

FITTING A TIMBER-BOARDED CEILING

A good way to hide a cracked ceiling is to fit tongued-and-grooved timber boards. You can either pin the boards to battens screwed to the ceiling surface or remove the ceiling and fit the boards direct to the ceiling joists.

Allow the boards to 'condition', which will reduce shrinkage, by storing them in the room for a few days before fixing. Also, if possible, prime or varnish them before you put them up.

By probing or using an electronic joist and stud detector, locate the joist positions and mark these on the ceiling. They are usually at 400mm (16in) centres. Nail 50 × 25mm (2 × 1in) battens to the surface of the ceiling, fixing them about 600mm (24in) apart and at right angles to the run of the joists.

Starting at one side of the room, fix the boards to the battens using special metal fixing clips or by secret nailing through the tongues into the battens. If the boards will not span the room width in one length, cut them so that butt joints will coincide with the batten positions.

Around the edges of the ceiling, leave a small gap to allow for natural expansion of the timbers and cover this gap with scotia or quadrant timber beading to create a neat finish.

Fireplaces and Chimneys

Although central heating is regarded as a necessity for modern living, many people still want a 'real' fire as a focal point in their living rooms, even when this is gas-burning with a log or coal effect. As a result, probably more fireplaces are being opened up than sealed, as was at one time fashionable.

When you come to plan your rooms, possibly to make alterations or additions, it is most important to give consideration to the position and use of any existing fireplace, whether you are going to retain or replace it or maybe seal it up. And if you do not have a fireplace but would like to install one, you must decide where it can go, bearing in mind the practical requirements of siting a new chimney.

RESTORING OLD FIREPLACES

If you are lucky, you may have one or two original fireplaces in the house which are worth restoring. It is amazing how many 'improvements' in the past involved daubing a thick layer of paint over what was once a perfectly respectable fire surround or even covering it up with a layer of hardboard.

In the first instance, therefore, it is worth looking behind such treatments to see exactly what kind of fire surrounds you have, so that a decision can be made on whether to restore or replace them.

If the covering is of hardboard or a similar material, remove this carefully to cause as little damage as possible to the surround and wall plaster. You may find fixing screws and be able to remove these. Otherwise you will have to prise the cover away from the wall. Use a wrecking bar for this and take care not to pull away chunks of plaster.

■ Surrounds may be of timber, masonry or metal and may be highly ornamented, requiring considerable skill and patience to restore them to their former glory.

■ Period fire surrounds are one of the most desirable features of old houses, and are almost always worthy of careful restoration.

Old layers of paint, whether on timber, metal or ceramic tiled parts, can be removed with paint stripper. The paste type is especially useful here since it will remove several thick layers of paint at one time.

If on examination you decide the surround is not worth keeping, you will have to remove it and fit a new one. If the surround looks interesting and can be restored, the result should be a good-looking fire in keeping with the age of the house.

Some timber surrounds were intended to be painted and here a white satin sheen finish looks good. But if the surround has been stripped and the timber is knot-free, then all you need do to restore it is to fill in any cracks and then stain and polish it. Alternatively, you can use a varnish finish.

Cast iron is often used for fire surrounds. A wash with a wall and floor cleaner in hot water should take off most of the grime. You can get rid of difficult spots of tar or soot with car bodywork tar remover, white spirit or methylated spirit. Apply this with fine wire wool to speed up the cleaning. Fireplace and wood stove shops sell proprietary black lead for restoring the shiny finish once so popular with cast iron surrounds.

Ceramic tiled surrounds are also very common and you may come across some fine Victorian tile inserts. These must not be treated with any abrasive cleaner or they could be scratched. A wash with sugar soap or detergent in hot water should be sufficient.

If you find any loose tiles, remove and refix them with heat-resistant ceramic tile cement. White or coloured tile grout can be used to fill the gaps between the tiles (see Repairing a fireplace for more details).

Brick surrounds are difficult to clean. A stiff brush may be sufficient, but where they are heavily soiled you may have to use a proprietary brick, stone and concrete cleaner, which is available from builders' merchants. This type is very caustic, so wear protective clothing and rubber gloves and make sure the room is well-ventilated as you work.

Stone surrounds are also difficult to clean. Since there are many different types of un-

■ A popular alternative inset style features panels of decorative stone such as marble, with the opening framed in brass.

■ The fireback and grate is often a cast iron insert set within the fireplace opening, and may be surrounded by panels of decorative tiles.

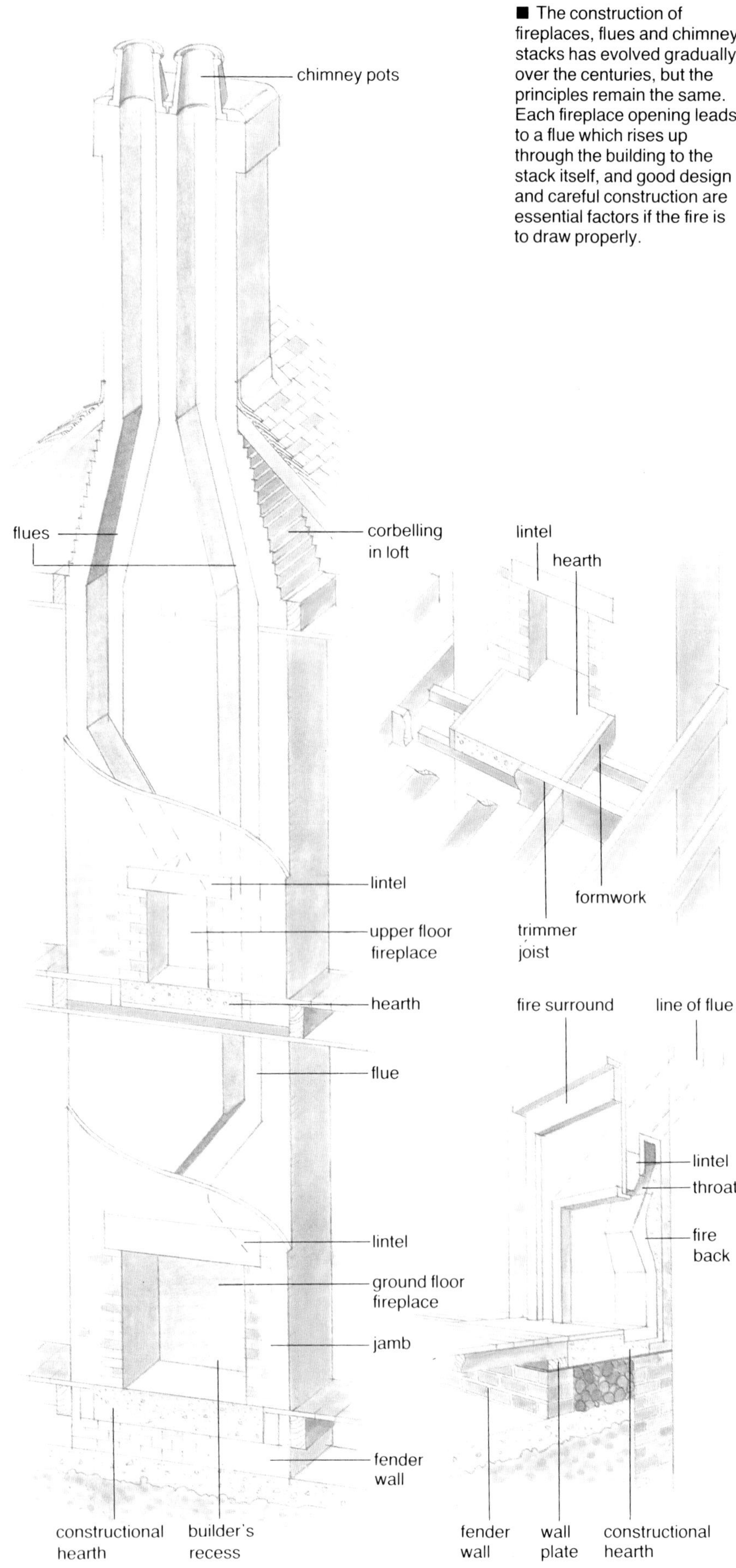

■ The construction of fireplaces, flues and chimney stacks has evolved gradually over the centuries, but the principles remain the same. Each fireplace opening leads to a flue which rises up through the building to the stack itself, and good design and careful construction are essential factors if the fire is to draw properly.

polished stone used – granite, slate, Yorkstone and Kentish rag are just a few examples – it is impossible to make blanket recommendations.

Start by cleaning with a stiff brush. If this does not work, a wash with detergent in hot water may be successful. Only use a caustic brick and stone cleaner as a last resort.

Polished stones such as marble, slate and granite should be washed with soapy water, then leathered off. The polished surface can be maintained with a good quality wax polish.

Repairing a fireplace

If you are going to keep a fireplace, you may find you have to make certain repairs. There are a number of different problems you are likely to encounter.

Loose tiles Concrete fire surrounds are often covered with ceramic tiles and over the years it is quite common for these to work loose or become cracked or chipped.

Loose tiles should be carefully eased out so as not to disturb adjacent ones, unless these are also loose and therefore need removing. With a small, sharp cold chisel, carefully remove traces of the old tile adhesive or mortar from where the tile came away from the concrete background. Never attempt to chip old adhesive off the back of the tile, since this would probably crack it. Soak it in water instead.

Clean off the debris then spread heat-resistant tile adhesive with a notched spreader on to the back of the tile. If only one or two tiles are being replaced and they are fairly well away from the heat source, you can use ordinary tile adhesive, to which a little pva adhesive or bonding agent should be added.

Press the tile into place so it is level with adjacent ones and wipe away any surplus adhesive. You can grout the tile once the adhesive has set. You will probably need a cement-based grout to match the existing one.

Cracked and chipped tiles In an old fireplace the tiles may well be valuable. In this case it is certainly worth keeping the original ones, whether or not they are crazed, cracked or chipped. To attempt to replace them would ruin the value of the fireplace.

Damaged tiles in an attractive, but not particularly valuable, fire surround can be replaced. You will be very lucky to find a good match for the old ones. So rather than attempt to find an exact replacement, it may be better to go for harmonising, but entirely different, tiles.

You must remove the damaged tiles bit by bit using a small cold chisel and hammer. Start in the middle of the tile and work outwards to the edges, taking care not to damage adjacent ones.

■ Removing an unsuitable fireplace is generally quite straightforward. Once the fixing lugs at each side have been located and freed, the surround and then the hearth can be prised away. Both components are likely to be very heavy, so make sure help is available to support, lift and remove them.

■ Re-bed ceramic tiles on hearths and in tiled surrounds with heat-resistant tile adhesive, making sure that the replacement tile sits flush with its neighbours.

■ Lay replacement quarry tiles on a bed of cement mortar, taking care not to smear it onto the faces of the tiles. Then seal the surface of the new tile to match its neighbours.

Once the tile is out of the way, proceed as described for loose tiles.

If a number of tiles are damaged, you should consider retiling the entire surround using heat-resistant ceramic tiles. The new ones can be stuck directly on to the existing tiles, if these are firmly fixed. Where tiles are missing, you can fill the gaps with new tiles, using a heat-resistant ceramic tile adhesive.

Cracked hearth If a crack in the hearth is due to settlement, do not disturb it. Simply fill it with wall filler. If the sections of the hearth either side of the crack are at different levels, brush the lower section with pva bonding agent or adhesive and build up the surface with filler, cement mortar or self-smoothing screed. When the repair is complete, you can retile the hearth as necessary.

Damaged marble If cleaning does not remove stains on marble, you can try using a proprietary marble cleaning kit, available from specialist fireplace shops. There are various types you can buy. A popular cleaner includes a paste which you spread over the stained area and leave for 24 hours to absorb the stain. A special abrasive polish for marble is available to complete the repair.

If a marble surround is chipped and you still have the broken piece, use a two-part epoxy resin adhesive to glue the chip back in place. If the broken part is missing, make a marble-coloured filler by mixing some kaolin powder (china clay) with epoxy resin adhesive, if necessary colouring it with a dye. Rub it down with a carborundum stone or wet-and-dry abrasive paper when the filler has set and finish with a clear varnish or lacquer.

Damaged fireback If a fireback is cracked or chipped, it can be repaired with fire cement. Let the fireback cool, if you have been using the fire, and rake out the cracks with the edge of a wallpaper scraper or the tip of a builder's trowel. Ideally you should undercut (widen at the back) the crack so that the fire cement will hold better after hardening. Remove all soot with a wire brush and clean away any dust and debris from the area.

Spray the whole area, particularly inside the cracks, with water then press the fire cement into the cracks and holes, making sure the surface is smooth. The cement, incidentally, is supplied in tins ready for use. Leave it to dry for as long as possible before lighting the fire again.

Loose, damaged or missing firebricks If you are going to use the fireplace, even with a gas-burning unit, you will need to repair or replace the fireback. In most cases it will be moulded in fire clay from one or two pieces. In older fireplaces, however, the fireback may be formed from several specially shaped sections.

Modern firebacks are made in one or two pieces and in standard sizes to suit modern openings. So if you have a Victorian cast-iron or other old fireplace, it will be worth keeping the old firebricks even if they are badly cracked. They can be patched up with fire cement.

If they are very badly damaged or there are missing pieces, new firebricks can be formed in situ with mouldable firebrick. This is a very stiff fire cement supplied ready to use. After cleaning and dampening the opening, you simply tap balls of the fire cement into place with a hammer and mould them to the shape required for the firebrick.

Remove any loose firebricks and carefully brush them clean – as well as the backing to which they are to be refixed. Damp this area and the back of the firebricks, trowel fire cement on to the backing and then press the firebricks in place, tapping them into position using the wooden handle of a hammer. Do not hit these bricks too hard or you will crack them.

If you have a standard – 400mm (16in) or 450mm (18in) – opening (measured across its mouth), it will probably be best to fit a new fireback. In many cases you can do this without removing the fire surround. But if the surround has to be moved anyway, do this first before you install the new surround to make fitting the fireback easier.

Removing a fireback is a messy job, so empty the room as far as possible and cover any remaining items with dust sheets. Wear old clothes and a dust mask and lay extra dust sheets over the hearth and the floor around the fireplace. Take away any separate parts of the fire such as the grate and then remove the fireback in pieces, using a cold chisel and hammer to break it up.

There may be a fire-resistant rope between the fireback and the back of the surround. It will probably be asbestos-based and should be left in place if it is in good condition. If the rope is crumbling, however, you will have to remove it – but very carefully.

Wearing a dust mask and gloves, first lay plastic sheets in the opening, then spray the rope with water to dampen it. Place it in a plastic bag for disposal by the local authority. The plastic sheets should also be disposed of in a similar way.

Behind the fireback will be loose cement and rubble. If this is in sound condition, it can be left. If, however, the heat has made it crumble badly, you should shovel it up and clear the cavity, which is known as the builder's opening. This is, incidentally, a good stage of the job at which to have the chimney flue swept.

The fireback may be supplied in one or two pieces. A one-piece fireback will be cast with a central horizontal cutting line. If you tap the back gently along this line with a bolster chisel and hammer, the two halves will separate.

Put the bottom half of the fireback in position so that it lightly compresses the fire-resistant rope at the back of the surround. If this has been removed, put a straight piece of wood across the opening to be sure that the front face of the fireback will be just behind the inside edge of the surround when it is fitted.

Mark the outline of the fireback on the hearth, remove the fireback, dampen the hearth and spread a layer of fire cement on it.

■ If the existing fireback is badly cracked, the best solution is to replace it. Check the measurements across the front of the fireplace opening, and buy a matching replacement. Then break out the old fireback, remove it and clear out any rubble that was packed between it and the walls of the fireplace recess.

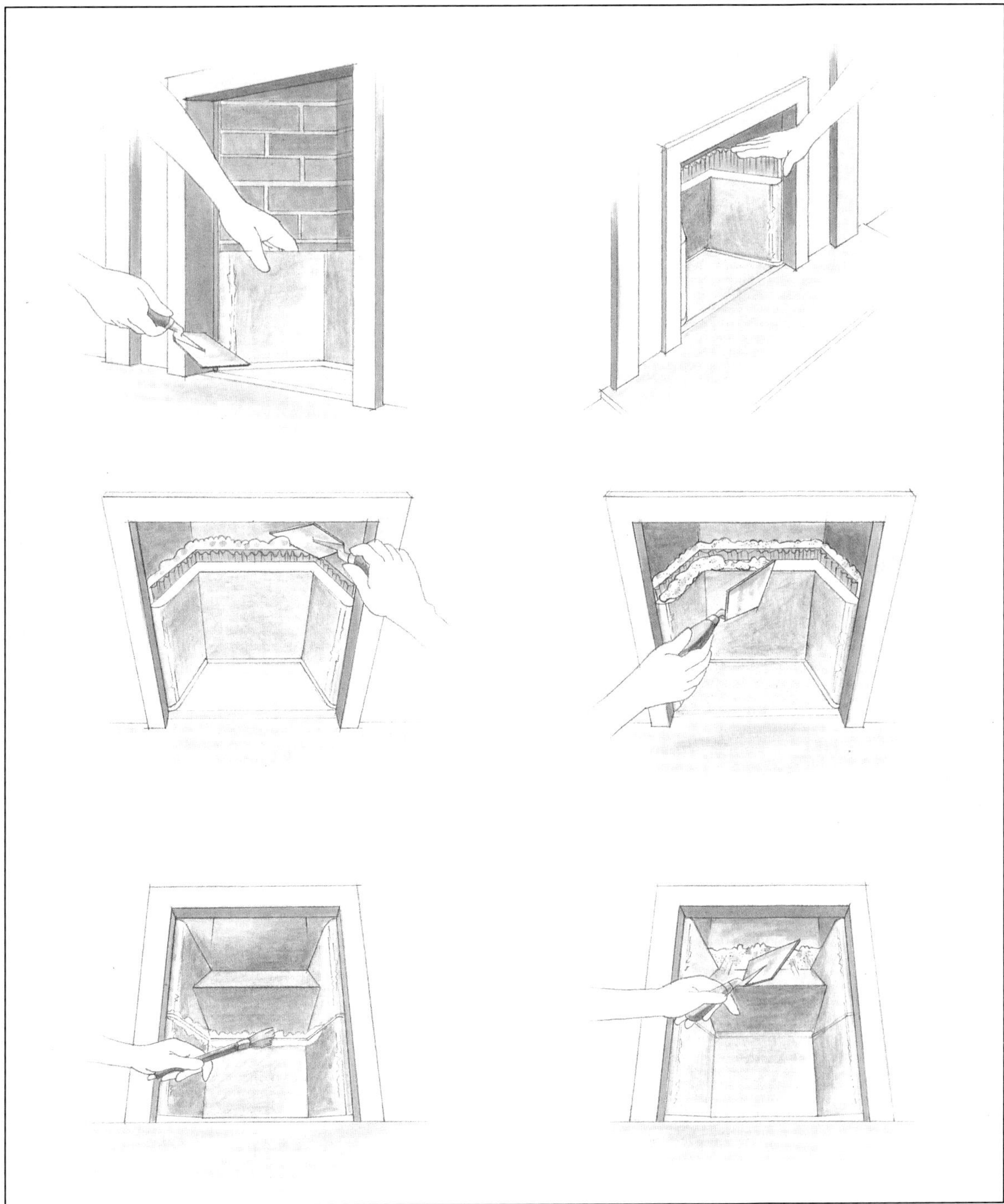

■ Position the lower fireback section within the opening on fire cement. Then place some corrugated paper behind the fireback to form an expansion gap, and fill the void behind the fireback with clean rubble and weak mortar. Next, trowel more fire cement along the top edge of the lower fireback section, position the upper section on it and neaten the fire cement joint. Finally, use more fire cement to seal the joint between the fireback and the throat leading to the flue.

Lift the fireback into place and tap it down until it is correctly positioned and level.

Now place two thicknesses of corrugated cardboard behind the fireback to provide an expansion gap between that and the infilling that has to be put into the builder's opening.

Fill in behind the fireback with vermiculite mortar – made from one part hydrated lime or cement and four parts vermiculite (as used for loft insulation). Alternatively, make up a mix of one part lime, two parts soft sand and four parts broken brick. These soft insulated fillings will allow the fireback to expand under heat without cracking. They will also absorb heat to protect the builder's opening.

Lay a bed of fire cement on the top edge of the lower section of the fireback, lift the top section into place and tap it down. Again, put two layers of corrugated cardboard behind the fireback and fill in with weak insulating mortar. Tamp down the filling with a stick and, at the top, smooth it off at an angle of about 45 degrees to form a smooth 'throat' into the flue. Sloping mortar may also be needed at the sides to prevent the formation of any ledges, where soot could otherwise collect.

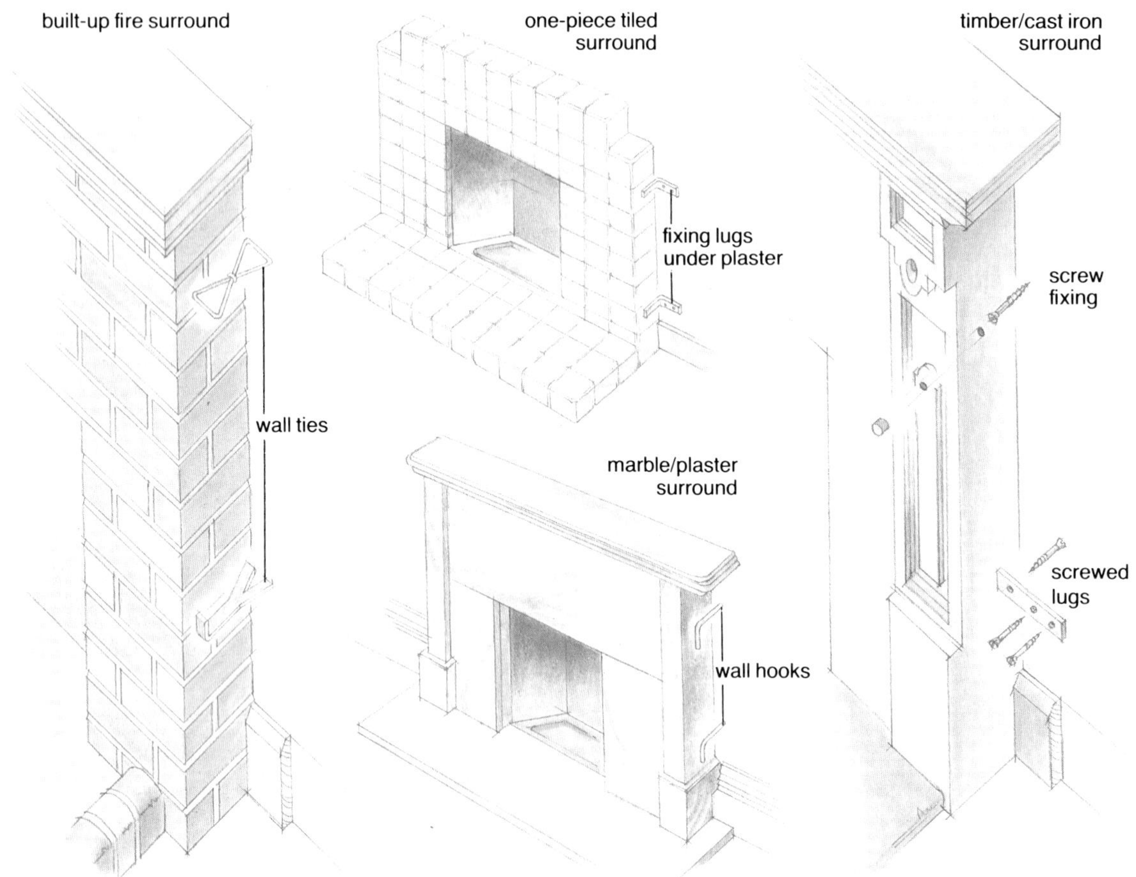

■ Fire surrounds may be secured to the wall in a variety of ways – by wall ties, lugs, dowels or screws and plugs. The fixings are generally at either side of the fire surround, concealed beneath the wall plaster.

For most modern fires, the throat should be about 300mm (12in) wide and 100mm (4in) deep. In older houses the throat may be much larger than this and it will be a good idea to fit an adjustable throat restrictor into the flue at this stage of the renovation.

If the flue is old and has not been used for some time, it may have deteriorated to the point where it leaks fumes and does not draw properly. It would be sensible to have it tested by a chimney specialist. If a new flue lining is required, this can be fitted at this stage (see Lining a chimney).

Removing a fireplace

If you have fireplaces in the house and decide to remove any or all of them, you will have to take away the surround and seal up the opening. This is not a particularly difficult job to carry out, but it may involve a considerable amount of work and mess.

Fire surrounds are usually screwed or nailed to the wall through metal lugs or wire loops attached to the surround on each side, close to the top. The lugs will have been plastered over, so the first job will be to chip away the plaster to expose them.

When you have located the fixings, you may be able to saw the heads off the securing screws. It is most unlikely that you will be able to undo the screws; however, it may be possible to cut them off with a sharp cold chisel and a club hammer.

With someone to help steady the surround, which will be very heavy, the hearth can be prised from the floor. A garden spade is ideal for this. Have some timber wedges handy to slip under it to enable you to get a handhold underneath. As you drag the hearth out of the way, you will find the concrete constructional hearth, which should be retained. Chip off any bedding cement remaining on the surface.

Timber fire surrounds could be valuable, so think twice before removing them. They could also be in keeping with the style of the property and perhaps be worth more than the fireplace you are thinking of installing.

A timber surround may have a tiled or cast-iron insert. The timber itself will be a hollow box section fixed to battens nailed or screwed to the wall. The surround will probably be fixed to the battens by screws which go through the box sections at the side. It may, however, be difficult to find these screws since the heads will be covered with filler. A metal cable and pipe detector may help locate them.

■ To decommission an unwanted fireplace, remove the fireback and lift the superimposed hearth to reveal the constructional hearth beneath. Cover this with sections of new boarding. Block off the fireplace opening either by fixing a timber framework within it and cladding this with plasterboard, or by bricking it up. In either case, include a small ventilator near floor level to allow some air to flow up the flue and help to prevent condensation from forming.

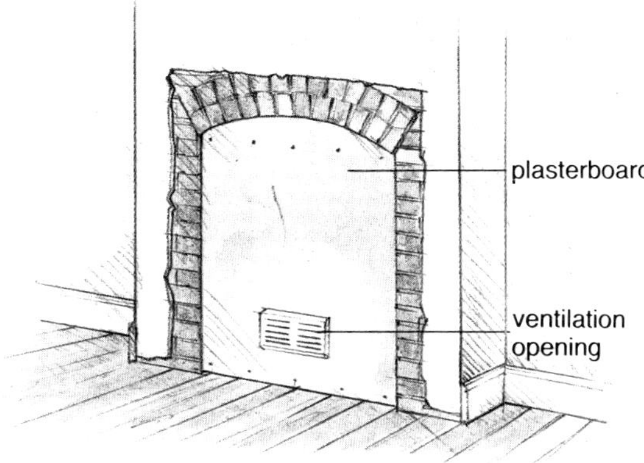

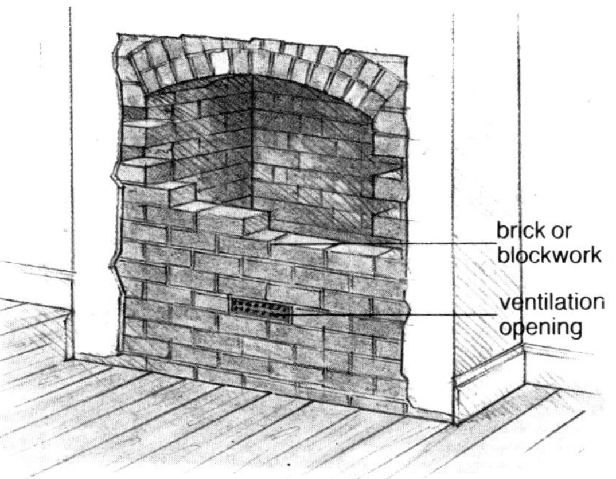

Carefully chip away the filler, enabling you to remove the screws. Keep the surround in good condition, either to be refitted elsewhere in the house or for maximum resale value.

The tiled or cast-iron insert will probably be held by lugs fitted at the top and sides. These will be visible when the outer timber surround is removed.

Cast-iron fire surrounds are definitely valuable – and fragile. So take great care when removing them. They will be held by metal lugs set in the wall plaster at each side of the surround, close to the top and just under the mantelshelf. Because the lugs can crack off, drill through the fixing screw heads to remove them. There may also be lugs along the top edge of the mantelshelf.

Sealing a fireplace opening

There are basically two ways to seal a fireplace opening – by fitting plasterboard over a timber frame or by building a brick or block wall and plastering over it in the normal way. In both cases it is important to leave an opening for ventilation. By providing a gentle flow of air through the flue, you will prevent the chimney from becoming damp. Before starting any work, make sure you have the chimney swept.

The timber frame method is best if you are likely to want to open up the fireplace at a later date or if you are sealing the opening for use with a gas fire. In this case, the cover should be of asbestos-free insulation board, rather than ordinary plasterboard.

Bricking-up produces a solid wall that is unlikely to crack. Of course, you could always remove the bricks later on, but they will not prove as easy to dislodge as a plasterboard infill on a timber frame.

In most cases the constructional concrete hearth can be left in place. Skimming it with a self-smoothing cement screed will bring the surface up to floorboard level. When the floorcovering is laid, the hearth will not be seen.

The only reason for removing a constructional hearth would be if the floorboards are to be left exposed. Here you will have to remove the hearth and lay new joists and floorboards to match the existing floor.

If you decide to seal the opening with bricks or blocks, it is a good idea to fit stainless steel brick-jointing channel to the inside edges of the wall at each side of the opening. This way you will avoid having to chip out half-bricks to bond the new bricks into the wall at each side.

Make sure you fit an airbrick into the new wall three or four courses up from the floor to provide ventilation into the flue. Providing the airbrick is set this high, it will not get blocked if debris subsequently falls down the flue.

To make a frame for the opening on which to fix the plasterboard or insulation board, use 75 × 50mm (3 × 2in) sawn timber. Cut the head (top) and sill (bottom) frame members first so they wedge into place. Then cut the side (upright) members so they wedge in place between them.

Set the timbers so that the face of the board when fixed will either be level with the surrounding brickwork, if the wall is to be plastered in the normal way, or so the plasterboard will be level with the surface of the surrounding plaster for direct decoration.

When the timber framework is correctly positioned, fix the uprights to the side walls with screws and wall plugs, then skew-nail the head and sill members to the uprights. Nail the plasterboard in place with galvanised plasterboard nails, fixing the board with the grey side facing outwards for plastering or the cream side outwards for direct decoration.

With a pad saw, cut a 225 × 75mm (9 × 3in) section out of the plasterboard and glue a plastic or metal ventilator plate over this hole.

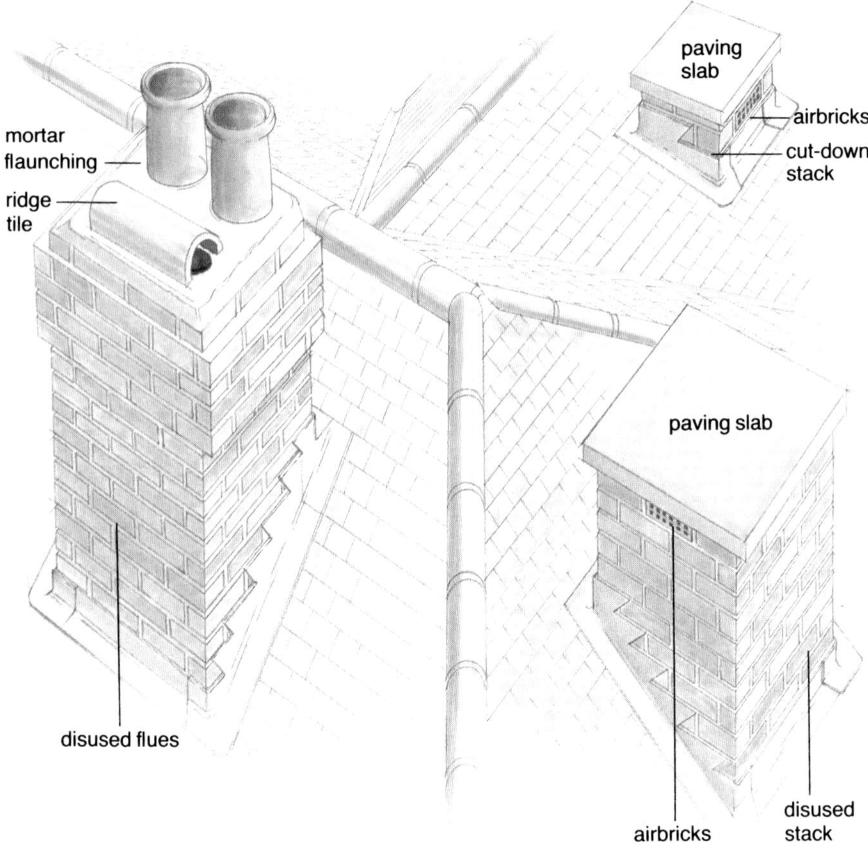

RESTORING AN OLD CHIMNEY

Before you attempt to repair or renew a chimney, you must understand how it works. Basically, it is a vertical tube running between the fireplace and the chimney stack. As wind blows over the stack, it should create a suction which draws the harmful combustion gases from the heating appliance up the flue and out of the chimney. Most chimneys are built with a bend in them to prevent rain from falling straight down the flue and on to the fire.

Building Regulations specify how high above the roof the chimney should terminate and the dimensions of the flue. Many old flues are too wide for modern heating appliances and such flues can be made narrower by using a chimney liner, which will also protect the brickwork in the chimney from damage caused by corrosive combustion by-products.

Capping a chimney

The simplest way to cap a chimney is to fit a capping cowl into the chimney pot. This will seal the flue from rain penetration while at the same time allowing a gentle airflow to keep the flue dry. Alternatively you can remove the pots and flaunching and bed a roof ridge tile in cement mortar over the flue.

Another method is to replace a couple of bricks at the top of the chimney stack with airbricks (to give an airflow) and then bed a paving slab in mortar at the top of the stack. Remember to allow for an air vent at the base of the flue if the fireplace is being sealed.

Lining a chimney

A flue lining serves several useful functions. It cures any problems of a faulty flue, protects the brickwork against further tarry deposits and keeps the chimney warmer, thus improving the draw of combustion gases.

There are several ways to line a flue and the type to use will depend on the fuel to be burned. Some you can install yourself if you want to save money. Others will involve employing the services of a specialist.

An example of a professional installation is the pumped type of lining, which is suitable for solid fuel and includes wood, gas and oil-fired heating appliances. Here an inflatable 'sausage' is inserted in the chimney and a free-flowing lightweight insulating aggregate concrete is pumped into the damaged flue around it.

The concrete flows into any cracks and holes in the chimney, seals them and at the same time reinforces the chimney. Once the concrete has set, the 'sausage' is deflated and withdrawn to leave an 'inner' chimney with a perfectly smooth internal surface. This needs several days to harden before the flue is used.

■ It is best not to leave the top of a disused flue exposed to the elements. If just one or two flues in a stack are no longer used, remove the old pot(s) and cover the flue(s) with a ridge tile bedded in mortar. If all the flues are disused, remove the pots and the flaunching and fit a paving slab on the top of the stack. Before doing so, remove a brick from two opposite faces of the stack and fit airbricks in their place to provide some ventilation through the flue. If the stack itself is in poor condition, cut it down to near roof level before capping it off.

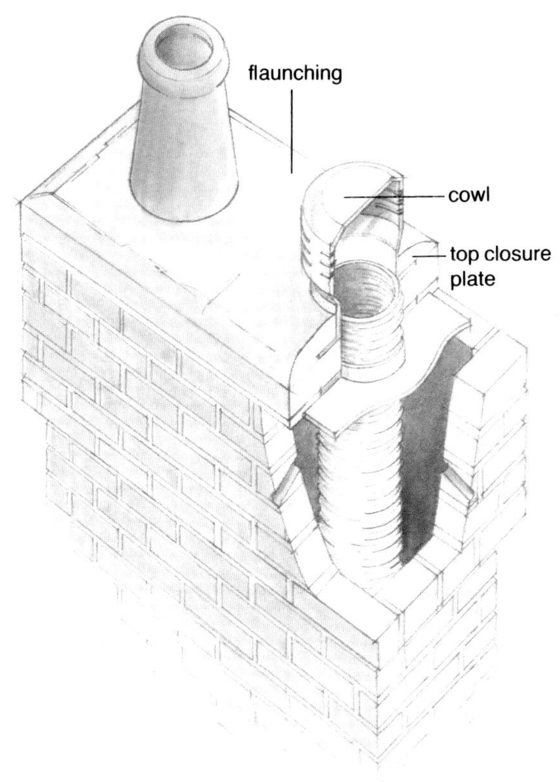

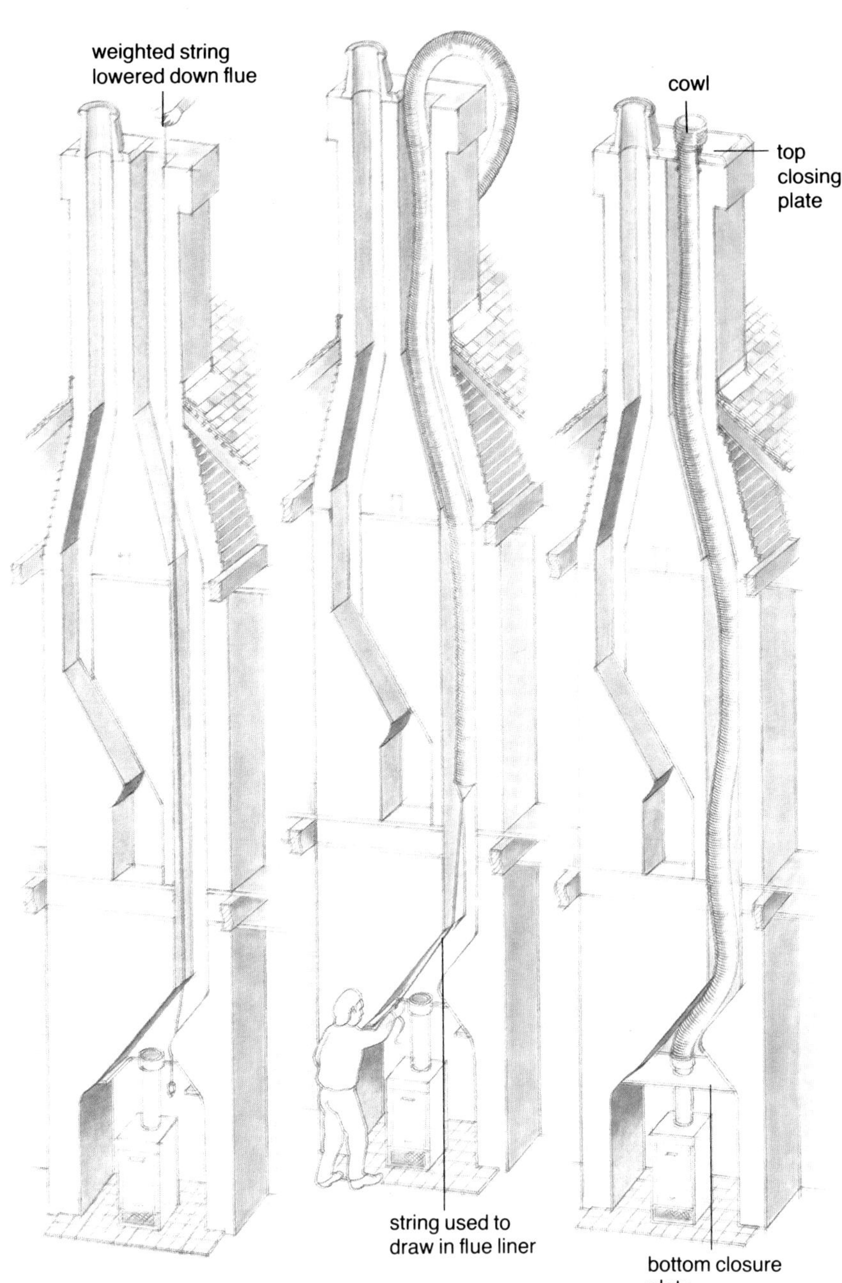

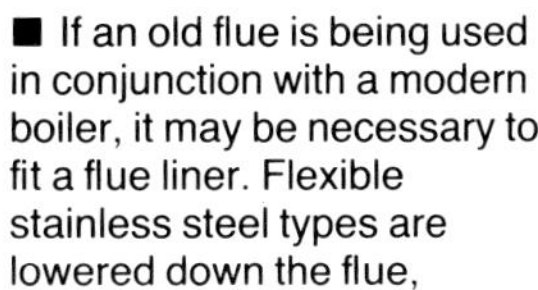
■ If an old flue is being used in conjunction with a modern boiler, it may be necessary to fit a flue liner. Flexible stainless steel types are lowered down the flue, guided by a weighted string, and are then clamped at top and bottom, ready for a flue cap to be fitted and the final connection of the liner to the boiler to be made.

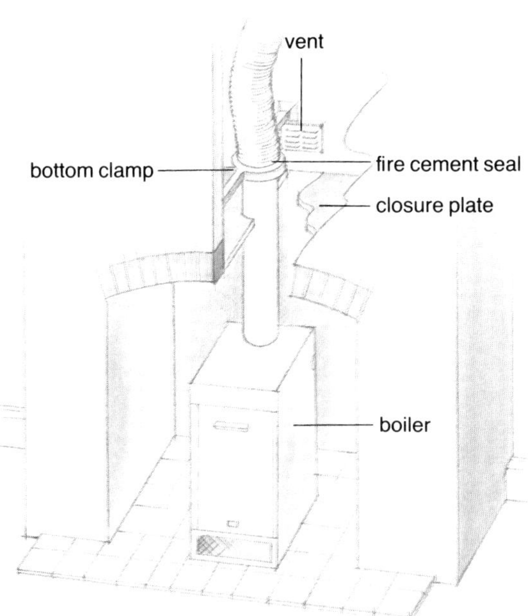

The easiest liners to install are the flexible, single-skin corrugated stainless steel ones. Most of these are suitable for gas and oil-burning appliances only, although some are suitable for wood and coal. To install one, you need scaffolding for safe access to the roof and the chimney stack.

Having swept the chimney and removed the chimney pot, you feed the liner into the flue from the top. A length of string is attached to the conical end piece, which allows someone inside the house to pull the liner down the flue. When you have fed the liner through, you simply cut it to length and connect it to closure plates at the top and bottom of the flue. You then fit a cowl and new flaunching at the top.

The third type is the lightweight sectional

insulation flue liner, which is suitable for solid fuel and woodburning appliances. The lowest section is installed on a steel plate at the base of the flue and subsequent sections are lowered down the chimney by rope and interlock with each other. Where there are bends, it will be necessary to break into the chimney. While this may not matter in the loft space, it can prove particularly disruptive if it has to be carried out elsewhere in the house.

After the liner is fitted, a free-flowing insulating mortar is poured into the chimney to seal round the lining.

FITTING A NEW FIREPLACE

Before you fit a new fireplace, make sure you have the chimney swept. Then install a new fireback (see above). Now you are ready to fit the new fire surround.

Although there are many styles of surround, there are only three basic types. These are traditional wood, plaster or marble with a cast-iron, marble or composition insert; the raised hearth type; and the brick or stone-built fireplace, which you can make from a kit or to your own design.

For the traditionalist, there are some wonderfully ornate and fashionable Victorian and Edwardian fireplaces available from architectural salvage yards and antique shops. These can be expensive, so it may be better to opt for a ready-made fireplace. New ones are available from specialist fireplace suppliers in an enormous variety of styles – from reproduction Regency to ultra-modern.

To fit a traditional-style fireplace, first make sure you have a solid constructional hearth at least 150mm (6in) wider than the fireplace and extending at least 300mm (12in) into the room. If this has been cut away and filled with floorboards, you must remove these and the joists supporting them and build up the hearth with concrete so it is level and flush with the surrounding floor.

The first stage is to fit the decorative hearth on a thin bed of weak mortar, comprising one part cement to seven parts sand. Tap down the hearth pieces so they are completely level. If necessary, make the back hearth level with the top of the decorative hearth.

Then fit the insert to the face of the opening. It will probably have protruding fixing lugs to enable you to screw it in place to the wall.

■ The commonest types of replacement fireplace surrounds are formed with machined timber mouldings (below left), often with a decorative insert, or are built up in brick or stonework (below right).

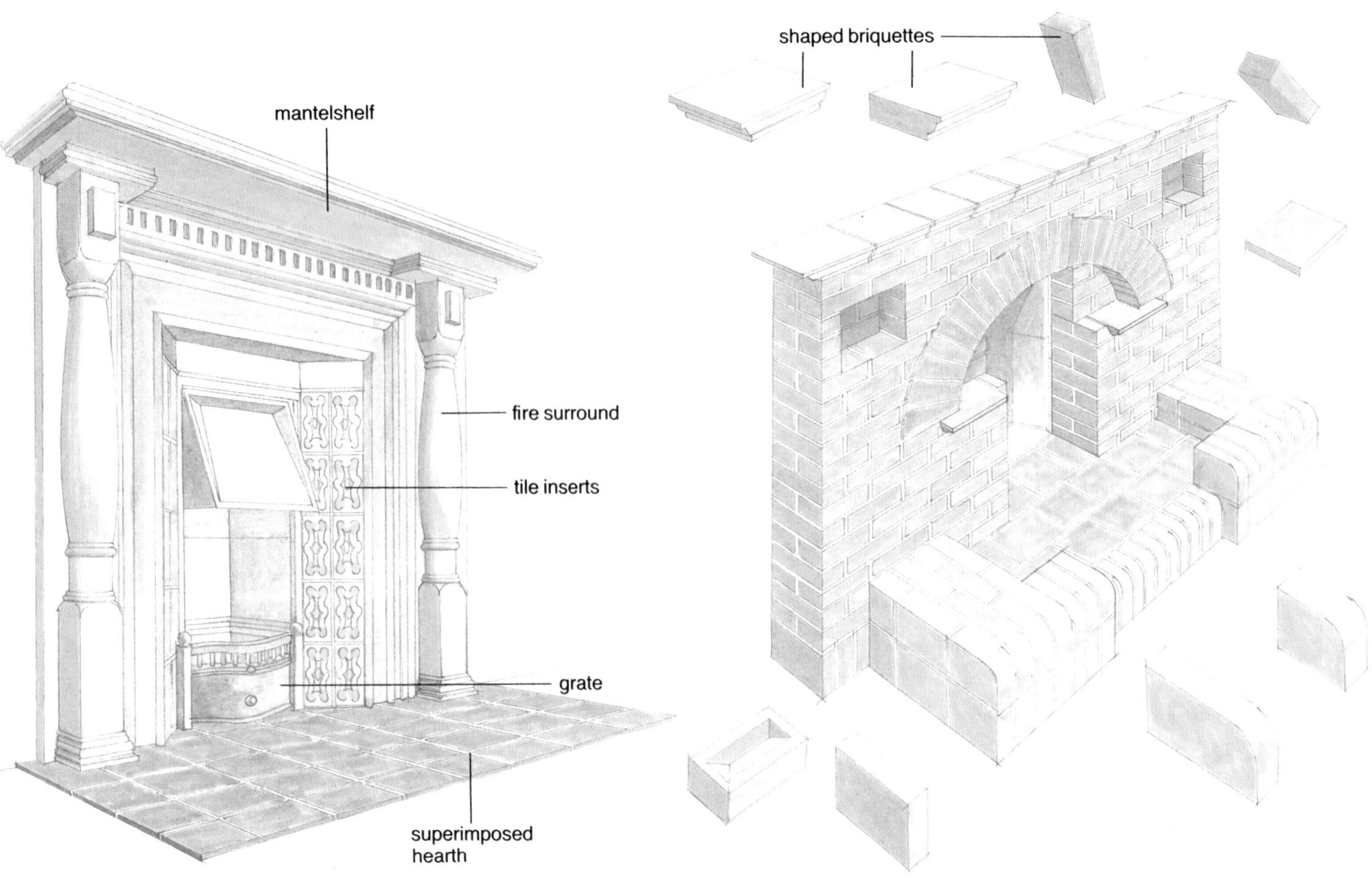

Fire-resistant rope is used as a flexible seal between the front edge of the fireback and the rear of the fireplace insert.

The fire surround stands in front of the insert and is fixed to the wall either by screwing through protruding lugs at the sides of the surround or by screwing through its sides into battens, which you will have to fix to the wall. To complete the job, make good any damaged plaster around the edges of the surround.

With a raised hearth fire, you will probably have to brick up the bottom of the fireplace opening about three courses high and cast a reinforced concrete hearth in situ at this level. If you are installing a prefabricated type, you will have to fix a pre-cast hearth at this level. In this case, follow the manufacturer's fixing instructions to the letter.

To cast a raised hearth, first fill in with brick rubble at the base of the bricked-up opening. Next make up a smooth tray for moulding the hearth using plastic-faced chipboard. Build up a reinforcing mesh by wiring together 9mm (3⁄8in) steel rods, which should be inserted into holes bored into the brickwork at the back and sides of the opening. Pour the concrete into the mould, press it down and smooth it off. When it has set, remove the mould. You can then tile the hearth surfaces.

With brick or block-built fire surrounds, you must lay the decorative hearth first and then construct the fireplace as if building a wall against the chimney breast. Screw brick ties into the wall at regular intervals to ensure the fire surround is properly secured.

Take care not to get mortar on the face of the bricks or blocks and make sure there is either a stone or metal lintel above the fire opening to support the surround at this point.

If you want to install a timber mantelshelf, bed this in mortar on the surround and hold it against the wall using mirror plates screwed to the back of the shelf, buried in the wall plaster and covered over with filler.

INSTALLING A NEW CHIMNEY

A balanced flue heating appliance, whether gas or oil-fired, can be fitted on any outside wall. But if you want to install an open fire or a woodburning stove, you must build a chimney. This is not, however, as difficult as it sounds, since chimneys are available in kit form and can be installed internally or externally. You will need to apply for Building Regulations approval before you install one.

First you must lay a concrete constructional hearth where you want the fireplace. The next stage is to install a builder's opening or fire chamber, which is available pre-cast from lightweight concrete sections.

Then you need to build up prefabricated flue sections from the top of the fire chamber. Use 230mm (9in) sections for an open fire and 150mm (6in) sections for a room heater. The 230mm flue is suitable for either type of fire and allows you to keep options open should you want to change to a different type of heating appliance at a later date.

The flue sections can be taken up through the house to the roof or fed outside and then up. If kept inside, the flue can be boxed in with timber and plasterboard to form a chimney breast. If taken outside, it can be left in its natural state or clad with bricks or stone to blend in with the walls of the house itself.

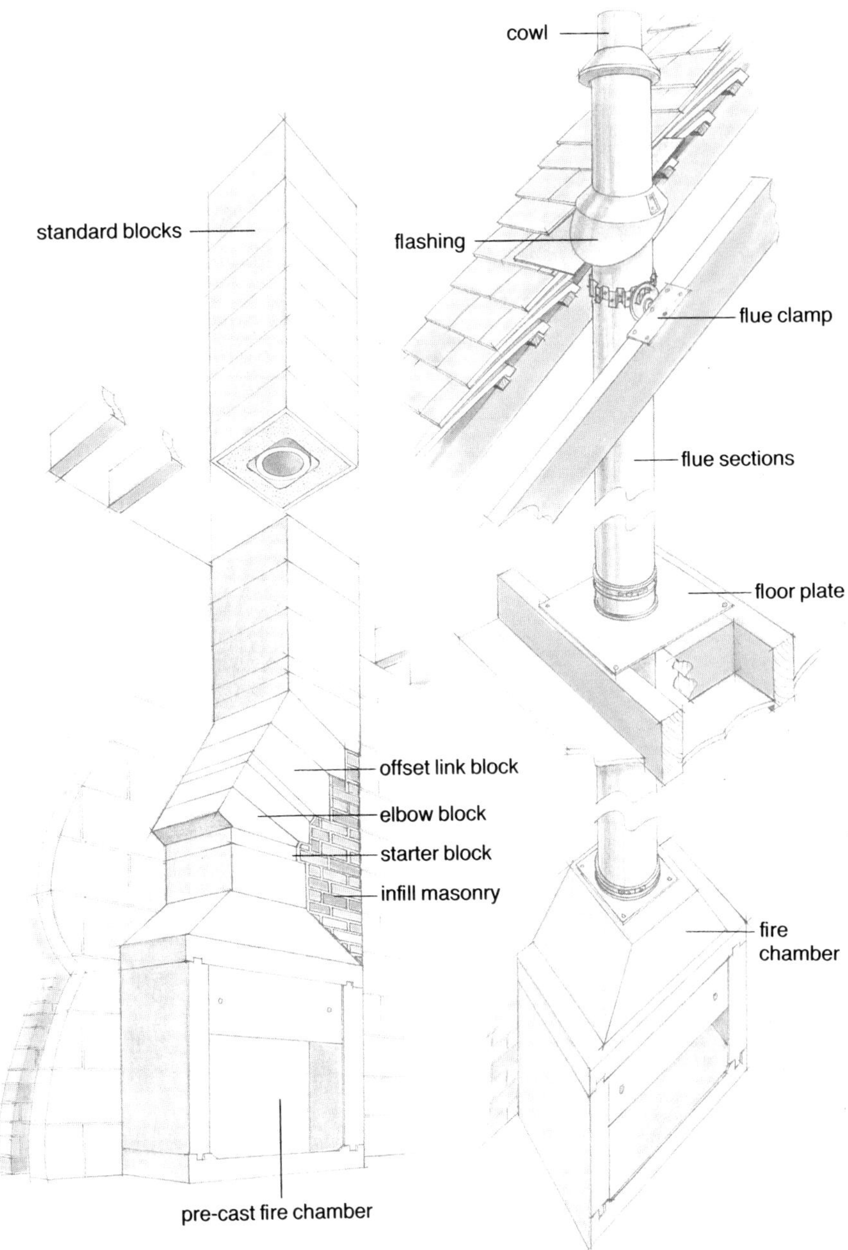

■ Several types of prefabricated chimney are available for domestic installation, and are far quicker to construct than a conventional chimney. The new flue can be taken up within the house or built against an outside wall.

Organising the Kitchen

The size and shape of an existing kitchen will depend on the age and style of the property. In an older house, designers were usually more generous about space and the kitchen was normally a reasonably large, workable area which could accommodate a table and chairs for eating, as well as the regular facilities.

In more modern homes there has often been a desire to economise on space and therefore kitchens have tended to become more compact space-saving areas. In some cases the kitchen and dining room are combined. This arrangement, of course, requires considerably more thought in terms of planning and layout to make it as practical and functional as possible.

Before planning your kitchen, you must decide what size budget you are prepared to allocate to it, since there is a wide range of price options available.

If you are prepared to spend a reasonable amount of money on the kitchen, there are plenty of specialist designers who will be only too pleased to give a quotation for redesigning the whole kitchen lock, stock and barrel. They will take on the job of installing the entire room, right down to the last fitting, electrical appliance and light switch.

If your budget is more limited, most of the large DIY chain stores offer a kitchen design service of varying quality. Normally this is a free service and is well worth investigating. If you do not like the plan – or the price – at least you have the benefit of some basic ideas to use in your own design.

Whichever route you decide to take, you must ensure that the new design incorporates

■ Kitchen design is very much a matter of personal taste. The choice between modern and traditional styles is less important than practical things like having an efficient layout and providing adequate services and storage facilities.

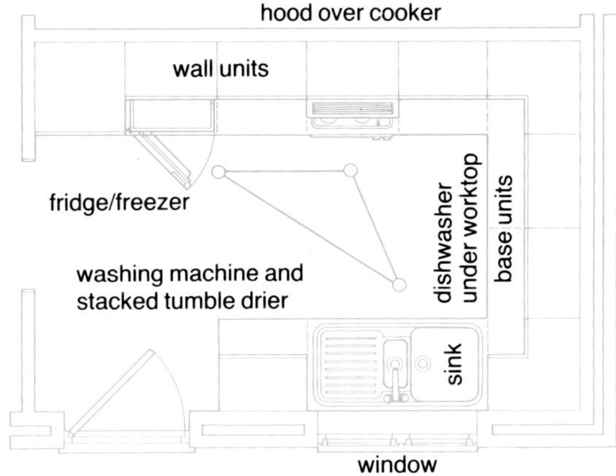

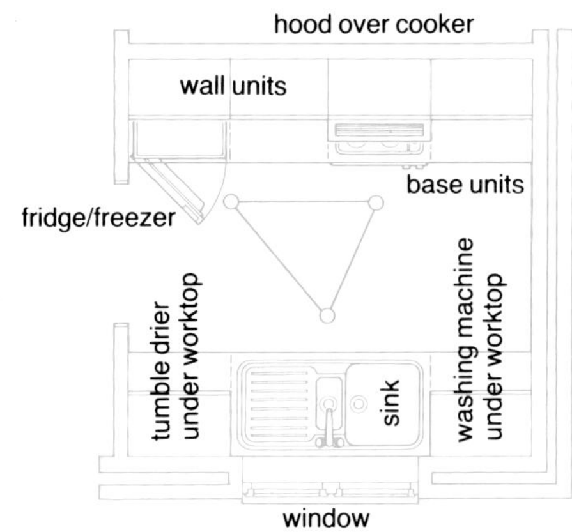

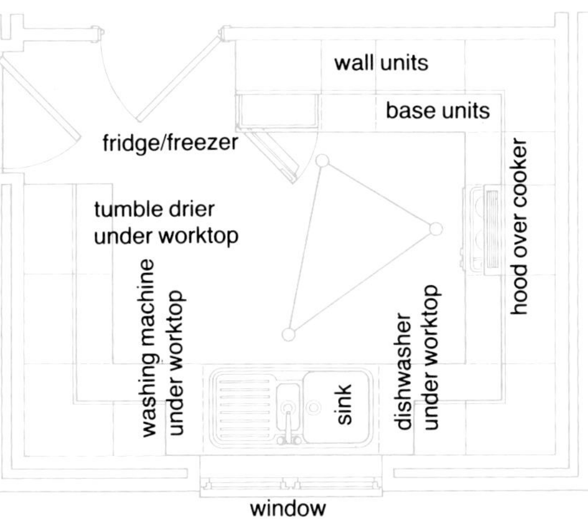

wall units
base units
fridge/freezer
hood over cooker
washing machine
and stacked
tumble drier
dishwasher
below worktop
sink
window

■ The key to an efficient kitchen lies in keeping the 'work triangle' as small as possible. This represents the route taken between the food preparation area, the cooker and the sink; in a badly-designed kitchen the cook can spend unnecessary time and effort walking constantly from one end of the room to the other. The layouts shown here give an idea of how to arrange efficient layouts for four different floor plans.

all the basic requirements of this room. These obviously include a sink, cooking facilities, fridge, food and utensil storage space, a waste disposal system and adequate working surfaces. To this list, most cooks would nowadays normally add a washing machine, a dishwasher and a freezer.

LAYING OUT THE KITCHEN

The first determining factor for any layout is normally the location of the sink waste pipe. While it is fairly straightforward to run water pipes and electrical cables behind units, the run of the waste pipe to the outlet should be kept as short as possible with the minimum number of bends along the route.

One important aspect to remember is that there must also be a continuous slight drop in the pipe from the sink to the soil stack. If you need a run of more than 1.5m, you should seek the advice of a qualified plumber.

Before you establish the position of the sink, bear in mind that about 75 per cent of the working time in the kitchen is spent here. So the surroundings should be as pleasant as possible. This normally means placing the sink by a window.

With the location of the sink decided, the next items to consider are the washing machine and dishwasher. One of the most common problems encountered with a dishwasher is where to put it, since there is often not enough space in the kitchen for both that and a washing machine. There is no doubt, however, that a dishwasher is a great timesaver and also cleans more efficiently than a manual operation since it uses stronger detergents and much hotter water. This gives it priority as far as finding space is concerned.

Traditionally the washing machine has been situated in the kitchen, mainly because of easy access to hot and cold water and waste facilities. But there is no reason why it has to be there. While not every house has a utility room, there may well be a space elsewhere in the house near the soil stack where a washing machine could be installed.

A further point to remember is that the cold water supply to washing machines and dishwashers must be fitted with a double check valve to prevent the possibility of back siphonage of contaminated water into the mains supply should its pressure drop.

The next items to be located are the cooking facilities. These should be near the sink but not so close that an electrical switch or component can be touched while your other hand is in the sink. This also applies to power points.

The fridge should also be situated in the vicinity of the sink to minimise the amount of walking while preparing food. With regard to working surfaces and storage space, these are normally determined by the position and number of cabinets and cupboards.

Although it is obviously impossible to have all your requirements located within the same area, you should try to plan or rearrange your kitchen so that it 'works' in the most convenient way, but safely.

CHOOSING SINKS

There are many types of sink available nowadays in a range of styles and materials – and, of course, price. So your choice will be determined not only by what you like but also by what you can afford.

Sinks made of stainless steel, which contains chromium and nickel, are impervious to all household chemicals and heat. They cannot be cracked or broken, but can and will get scratched. The finishes available range from polished high gloss to satin matt.

A sink made from polycarbonate, a very tough plastic which is coloured right through, is also resistant to household chemicals and heat. Scratches can be polished out, although textured finishes are available that do not even show such marks.

Asterite is a new material made up from natural minerals polymerised with resin. It is heat-resistant up to 180°C and resists all normal household chemicals. It is very hard and will not crack or chip under normal usage. It can be cleaned using standard household detergents. Other similar versions of this type of material are available.

The latest flexible enamelled sinks are very much better than the old enamelled ones. They do not chip or crack and can be easily cleaned.

With the exception of stainless steel, all these types of sink come in a variety of colours to suit the colour scheme you have chosen for your kitchen.

With regard to shape, there are countless combinations. The traditional style of one rectangular bowl with either a single or double draining board is still available. One of the more recent trends is for multiple bowl sinks, where the bowls may be of standard size or what are known as half bowls, which are much smaller. These are, among other things, very useful for jobs such as vegetable preparation and soaking.

■ Double and triple-bowl sinks (left and right) are the most popular style in modern kitchens, allowing different tasks to be carried out at the sink simultaneously. The smaller bowl is often fitted with a waste disposal unit, while the larger bowl can have removable baskets and drainers. A swivel mixer tap serves whichever bowl needs filling, and can be pushed out of the way if necessary.

Circular and other unusual shapes are also available to suit all tastes.

Most sinks sold nowadays are the inset type, which means they are fitted into a specially shaped hole cut into the work surface. There are also special purpose shapes, including one that fits round a corner. This can be particularly useful in a kitchen where space is limited. The other practical aspect of this shape is that it utilises a space that is otherwise awkward for things like cupboard storage, so releasing the more useful straight runs of work surface.

The supply of water to the sink has been given considerable thought by tap manufacturers over the years. The days of twin taps have almost gone, although sinks with two tap holes are still available. Most modern sinks have monobloc mixer taps, which are fitted to a single hole in the sink.

There are many different designs to suit all tastes and budgets. Many now use the modern ceramic disc valve, which eliminates the washer replacement problem.

One point to check when buying a mixer tap is that the hot and cold supplies have separate channels right up to the tap nozzle. This is a requirement of the water supply bye-laws.

On many sinks a pop-up waste system is either fitted or available as an extra. This solves the problem of where to put the plug and avoids the unsightly and unhygienic chain.

Most of the multiple bowl sinks come complete with their own waste and overflow fittings, but normally you will have to supply the trap – or U bend – for the waste outlet.

ORGANISING WASTE DISPOSAL

Most of the waste in the kitchen is generated at the sink. It makes sense, therefore, to arrange for its safe disposal here. One of the most common methods is with a bin on the inside of the door of the cabinet under the sink. Most manufacturers of cabinets supply a bin of this type to suit their units. Although it is a very convenient system, its one limitation is normally the small size of the bin itself.

Some of the more modern sinks incorporate a removeable flap through which the waste can be dropped into a larger bin below. The only snag here is that the extra space encourages less frequent emptying. The obvious problem is that any waste left too long will start to smell and this will permeate the kitchen and even drift into other rooms in the house.

For large families and homes where a lot of waste is generated, a kitchen sink waste disposer may be the answer. This is an

■ A waste disposal unit beneath the sink can dramatically reduce the volume of waste food and preparation leftovers that would otherwise end up in the dustbin.

electrically operated grinder which is fitted to the waste outlet.

There is a removeable perforated disc fitted into the drain hole during normal sink use to prevent cutlery and other smaller items slipping down into the waste disposer. When you want to dispose of waste, you remove the disc, turn on the cold tap and switch on the disposer. As you drop the waste down the hole into the disposer, it is ground up and runs away with the water. However, waste disposers are not suitable for houses which rely on cesspools or septic tanks instead of mains drainage.

These disposers can be used for all vegetable waste (apart from very fibrous matter), bones, fruit pips, fat, grease, tea leaves and coffee grounds. With every disposer comes a full set of instructions and the necessary wrench to release any blockages.

ARRANGING COOKING FACILITIES

There is a very extensive range of cookers available, which is constantly being added to. Most models nowadays use either gas or electricity although you may prefer the traditional Aga-style cooker that can be run off oil or solid fuel and combines covered hotplates on top and two ovens below.

The choice between gas and electricity is one that usually comes down to personal preference. It is normally claimed that electricity is cleaner, while gas is more easily and instantly controllable. Both of these arguments are hotly contested by the respective national fuel authorities.

Gas cookers are mostly used with nationally supplied natural gas. For areas that do not have piped supplies, bottled gas is available at a slightly higher price. The cooker will require some modification to use this fuel.

The traditional all-in-one cooker is still widely used and available with an eye-level or lower level grill. It is supplied as a slot-in cooker that fits tightly between two cupboards units with the hob at the same height as the worktop.

The cooker can, however, be made up of as many as three separate components. The hob itself fits into a pre-cut hole in the worktop, the oven can be fitted into a special unit at a number of different heights and the grill positioned on the wall at a suitable spot anywhere in the kitchen. Generally speaking, it is more expensive to install separate units. But it does allow for more versatility to suit individual requirements and tastes.

As far as the grill is concerned, it is normally true to say that a gas grill is quicker than an electric one. However larger areas can be heated with an electric grill within an oven.

Ovens come in both standard and fan-assisted versions. All gas appliances supplied nowadays have automatic ignition, which may need an electricity supply, and all ovens have a flame failure device which turns the gas off if the flame is somehow extinguished. Some of the more modern hobs and grills are also offering this safety feature now.

■ The cooker is the heart of the kitchen, and should be sited so that other kitchen facilities can be placed conveniently round it. It may be free-standing or built in. Gas and electricity are the most popular fuels, but solid fuel cookers still have many devotees.

Many gas appliances are now available with automatic controls which enable you to present the time you want to turn your cooker on – or off, for that matter – if you are out of the house.

All gas appliances must be installed by a registered fitter. Another point to bear in mind is that the hobs with combined gas and electric burners are not generally popular with the gas or electricity boards, who may refuse to service them due to a conflict of interest.

Electric cookers are available in the same basic configurations as gas ones. They need a very high current supply and have to be connected to a special power point and circuit.

Various types of hobs are available, including those with a single flat surface which is very easy to clean. One point to bear in mind, however, is that some electric rings remain very hot long after they are switched off. This could be a danger to inquisitive young children or elderly people.

Electric ovens come in a variety of forms. One of the most popular is that which gives four different cooking methods. These include the traditional method with the heat from the bottom of the oven; fan-assisted with a uniform oven temperature coming from a fan at the rear of the oven; variable grilling using a large grill in the top of the oven, which can be thermostatically controlled; and a fan-assisted grilling with heat coming from the grill and the fan.

■ A cooker hood is essential for getting rid of steam and cooking smells. The concept of a lower-than-usual hob makes it easier for the cook to keep an eye on things.

Microwave cookers have proved very popular in recent years and modern developments mean you can do as much with them now as with the standard cooker. They are of course ideal for quick preparation. They can be purchased with heating elements fitted that can assist in the cooking process.

Although you can buy fitted models, it is probably true to say that most microwave cookers are still free-standing and can therefore be situated anywhere in the kitchen.

CHOOSING COOKER HOODS

You can fit a hood over the cooker or hob to help reduce the problem of fumes and steam. Most models also have a light fitted to illuminate the cooking area. They come in two basic types – circulators and extractors.

The simplest one to install is fixed to the wall at the recommended height above the hob and is connected to a 13amp socket outlet. This type has a built-in fan with two or three speeds. The fumes are drawn up into the hood, where they pass through an activated charcoal filter. The cleaned air is then passed back into the kitchen above the hood. The filters are very effective, but will need changing from time to time to maintain their efficiency.

The second type is fitted in a similar manner but the fan has a duct connected to it that allows it to blow the fumes outside the house. Although harder to install, it is more effective.

Cooker hoods are ideal where you do a lot of cooking and want to keep the air in the kitchen as clean and fresh as possible without having to rush to open the windows all the time. And it is really essential if you are using the frying pan.

CHOOSING FRIDGES AND FREEZERS

Now regarded as a basic necessity, the fridge is available in many shapes and sizes to suit any kitchen requirement. If you get one that fits below the working surface, it allows more space for other functions such as preparing food.

Wherever you site it, you must leave plenty of room around it to allow free circulation of the air needed to cool the heat exchanger at the back. Failure to do this will result in much higher power consumption, poor temperature control and a short life for the fridge.

Some manufacturers make special versions of their standard cupboard units that contain a fridge. This means it can blend in unobtrusively with the rest of your kitchen units.

Fridge freezers are a useful compromise for a couple or a single person but cannot really do the job of the individual freezer in coping with the demands of a family. So do not be tempted to put more unfrozen food in than the freezer can comfortably handle.

Freezers come in two basic types – upright and chest. The upright version is easier to keep tidy and easier for you to keep a check on what you have inside. But the chest freezer holds more frozen food per cubic foot. One other snag with the upright freezer is that when the door is opened more of the cold air is lost. Manufacturers have gone to great lengths to prevent this, but some loss is inevitable.

■ Appliances such as fridges and upright freezers can be concealed within built-in cupboards to give the kitchen a streamlined look.

The same precautions should be taken with the siting of freezers as with fridges to make sure that enough air can circulate around the heat exchanger. Another point worth remembering is that nothing else should be plugged into the same socket outlet. This should ensure that the freezer is not turned off by mistake, with the possible complete loss of its valuable contents.

CHOOSING WASHING APPLIANCES

The majority of washing machines sold today are front-loading automatics, which are all around 600mm (2ft) in width and fit below a standard work surface.

A recent innovation is the washer drier, which has a tumble drying sequence available. This means that the machine can wash and fully dry clothes in a continuous operation. The drying function takes considerably longer and handles smaller loads than a full-size tumble drier. But it is obviously very useful and its compactness is a major advantage.

There are two types of washer drier – one that discharges the damp air into the kitchen or out through a vent and the condenser drier that discharges the moisture out through the drain hose. With the former, make sure you site the machine to allow for the dissipation of damp air. The latter can be sited anywhere.

Full-size tumble driers take up a lot of valuable space and need special arrangements for discharging the damp air. This can be through a permanently installed wall vent or a large tube hung out of a convenient window while the drier is in use. Some driers are designed to be stood on top of the washing machine, which obviously saves floor space if the latter is not installed under a work surface.

Dishwashers normally take up similar space to washing machines and have the same plumbing and electrical requirements. As the doors open downwards, they must be positioned in a suitable area that allows for this. There are slimline models available that take up less space, but of course handle smaller loads, and ones you can sit on a worktop.

FITTING WASHING APPLIANCES

As previously mentioned, there is some argument as to whether the washing machine should displace the dishwasher in the kitchen. The main problem with finding another location is that it normally needs both hot and cold water, an electrical supply and a suitable connection to the house drainage system.

■ Where space is at a premium, washing machines and tumble driers can be stacked one above the other. Dishwashers can be fitted neatly underneath sink draining boards.

While the first three requirements should not pose any major difficulty, drainage can be a different matter altogether. Other possible sites, therefore, are in or near the bathroom or downstairs toilet or against an outside wall near to a gully drain. A conveniently situated garage may be suitable, but you must make sure it is completely weather- and frost-proof.

Plumbing in a washing machine is quite a simple operation. The water supply comes from

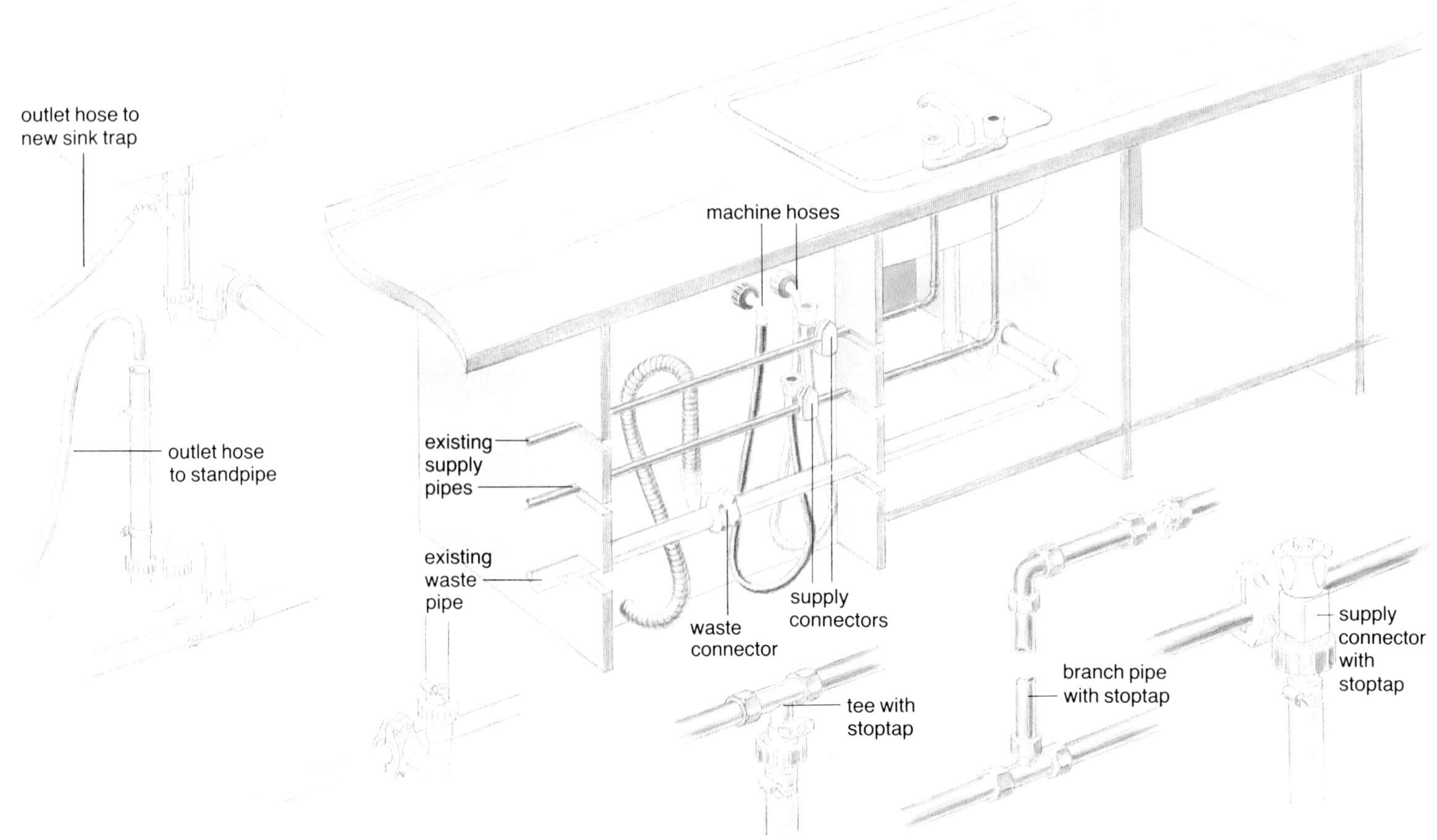

■ A washing machine needs a water supply – sometimes cold only, or more commonly both hot and cold – and also some means of discharging its contents into the waste water system. It is best to site the machine close to existing water and waste pipes in order to make the connections easier. Water supplies to the machine can then be connected up via a conventional tee and branch pipe with a stop tap on it, or by means of special connectors. The machine's outlet hose can be taken to an open-ended standpipe, or can be connected directly either to a special sink trap or to the sink waste pipe using a special connector.

the rising main for cold water and from the nearest hot water supply pipe.

The easiest way to break into an existing pipe is to use a self-cutting valve. You should fit this in a suitable position around the appropriate pipe, which you should first clean with wet and dry abrasive paper. You then tighten the screws holding the two halves of the valve together so that the clamp firmly grips the pipe. By screwing the body of the valve tightly and quickly home, you will cut through the pipe and thus release water to flow through the valve.

By using this method, you not only make it easy to break into the supply system but also create an emergency shut-off valve should you ever need to stop the water supply to the washing machine. You then run your pipework from these valves to a convenient position at the rear of the washing machine.

When installing the cold water supply from the rising main, you must fit a double-check valve before the shut-off valve to prevent back-siphonage unless the machine itself incorporates one. You then screw the hoses from the washing machine tightly by hand on to the threaded ends of the valves.

The drain hose from the machine can be hooked into a vertical piece of drainpipe with a trap fitted at the bottom. This pipe should be a minimum 600mm (2ft) in length. Finally connect an outlet pipe from the trap through the exterior wall either directly into the drainage stack or to discharge into a convenient gully.

It is important to leave an air gap around the top of the vertical pipe and the hose from the machine. If there is no gap, the water could be siphoned out of the machine.

You can also connect washing machine and dishwasher hoses direct to special traps fitted beneath the kitchen sink waste outlet.

FITTING WORKTOPS

Apart from the very expensive versions, worktops come in three basic forms, two widths and two thicknesses. They are all made from laminate-faced chipboard. The widths are 500 and 600mm (20 and 24in) to suit standard cupboard and unit sizes. The front edge can be square, postformed (rounded) or with a moulded beading fixed in position. Thicknesses are generally either 30 or 40mm (1¼ or 1⅝in).

Worktops can be cut to length and shape, but care should be taken since laminate will chip very easily. It is best to score the surface with a sharp knife along the line of the cut first. It is not possible to cut a postformed profile around a corner and any mitred ends should normally be covered with a strip of laminate, which is usually supplied with the worktop. Holes for a sink, hob unit and similar fittings are best cut with a jig saw.

Worktops are normally screwed on the underside to light brackets fixed to the wall and then up through the tops of the units. It is this fixing that usually gives such kitchen furniture its rigidity. For special applications you can get custom-made worktops. However, these can be very expensive.

CHOOSING STORAGE UNITS

There are many suppliers of kitchen units and cupboards who offer a vast choice of styles, colours and individual shapes. Care is needed if you decide to mix units from different suppliers, since they are not all interchangeable.

The material used for these units is chipboard, with special fixings supplied. The quality of the chipboard does vary, with the higher priced units generally being made with better grades of material.

Most of the drawers operate on steel runners, which are finished in a variety of ways to achieve smooth, silent operation. Doors are normally hung with special hinges that can be adjusted in three directions to ensure the doors align accurately and shut neatly. These hinges also incorporate a spring return to hold the doors shut, thus eliminating the need for catches that often failed to engage and were a constant source of trouble and annoyance.

■ Kitchen base and wall units meet every possible storage need, and many have special internal fittings for particular storage requirements (below). Installation is quite straightforward and adjustments are easily made to line up cupboard and drawer fronts (above).

The way in which the doors are finished is one of the main features affecting the choice of unit or system. The cheaper models normally have basic melamine-covered chipboard doors. As the price increases, the finish improves. Top of the range are solid wooden doors. These incorporate attractive moulded contours, which can take different forms – from basic panelling to cathedral or gothic styles.

How these units are supplied again depends on the price you pay. The less expensive ones normally come as flat-packs, which means they can be easily carried home. But assembly is down to you from the instructions supplied. Although the quality of these instructions has improved considerably over the years, there are still some manufacturers who leave much to be desired in this respect. As the price increases, the units are normally delivered pre-assembled and very carefully packed.

The height of the base units that fit beneath worktops varies between manufacturers – from 870 to 890mm (34 to 35in). Most units are designed with a depth to suit 600mm (24in) wide worktops, although some are available for the smaller size of 500mm (20in).

Units can be bought in standard widths from all suppliers, although not all lengths are available in all styles. The commonest sizes are 300, 400, 500, 600, 800, 1000 and 1200mm (12, 16, 20, 24, 32, 40 and 48in).

To take up the odd spare space, manufacturers produce a range of ingenious devices such as towel rails and ironing boards that slide away underneath the work surface when not in use.

You can also choose from a range of taller units to house ovens, fridges or for use as food storage areas. These are normally 600mm (24in) wide. The side panels can normally be obtained in white or coloured melamine to suit.

To provide added storage, wall cupboards are available in matching styles and colours. These are normally about 720mm (29in) high and 280mm (11in) deep and come in a similar range of lengths to the base units, with various shelf and door configurations.

You can also get bridging units, which are about 280mm high and come in a limited range of lengths. They are intended to be fitted high on the wall between two deep cupboards, thus allowing you to work comfortably and safely on the surface beneath them.

FITTING UP THE KITCHEN

Once you have finalised plans for your kitchen, obtained all the units you need and assembled them, it is now time to fix them in place. But first you must empty the kitchen as far as possible and clean off the walls. If the floor is uneven, this must be levelled to ensure the base units sit squarely.

You must also make sure all the necessary services are in place, particularly those running along the kitchen walls. Incidentally, units are designed with a space at the back to allow for pipe and cable runs. You will obviously not be able to finalize, for example, the plumbing for the sink until the unit is in place. But you can fit the main pipe runs to the approximate final position, and extend them later.

You should also install any electrical socket outlets or cooker points. In some cases you may have to cut a hole in the back of a unit to accommodate an outlet where the two coincide. Ideally, however, you will have planned beforehand the position of these to avoid such a problem. For example, socket outlets should preferably be sited above the worktop and below the wall units.

With regard to any gas supply, you will not be able to fit this yourself. So you should leave sufficient access to the nearest gas tapping for a later connection.

The first units to be fitted should be those in any corner. Normally this will involve screwing to the floor and wall as appropriate using special brackets. Make sure the top of the unit is absolutely level. You can then fix the adjoining units, using the screw holes drilled for that purpose to lock each one together.

You are almost certain to find that the wall is not square or straight – particularly at the

■ Storage units are now available to fit every usable space in the kitchen, from awkward corners (above) to the wall above the sink (left). Tall larder units (above right) take care of food storage, while slim shelves beneath wall units (right) keep smaller items conveniently to hand.

corners. The important thing to remember is that the front of the units need to be joined accurately together for a straight, flush finish. This is the part that is visible. But you do not have to worry if there is the occasional gap at the back, since the worktop will cover this. Continue fitting the units you have completed the planned run round the kitchen.

The next stage is to fit the worktops. These can be bought in 3m lengths and joined where necessary end to end using the special joining strips available. If you have to make a right-angled join using preformed worktops, you can buy special jointing strips that enable you to make a neat and hygienic joint.

You will have to cut the required holes to accommodate a sink or cooker hob in the worktop. Normally manufacturers supply a template for this purpose or the exact dimensions for the hole. Mark this out accurately on to masking tape stuck on to the worktop. This will ensure you do not accidentally erase the mark before you have finished cutting.

Drill a 6mm (¼in) diameter hole in the waste material near to the edge and insert the blade of a jig saw through it. Make sure you fit the small plastic anti-chip guard to the jig saw and carefully cut out the required shape. It is best to take care to cut out the exact shape with your saw, since it is a very slow process to clean up the edges afterwards.

Before installing the sink, apply a fillet of bath caulk to the underside edge before screwing up the special clamps that locate it. This helps to ensure a watertight seal. You can now complete the plumbing for the sink.

To fix the taps, you may find it easier to use tap connector pipes, since these overcome the problem of bending pipes accurately. Then connect up the waste. All sinks should take 40mm (1½in) connections and the waste needs to be connected to a suitable trap. The pipe must then fall at a slight gradient – roughly 1.5 degrees from the trap.

You are almost certain to find that the back edges of the worktop do not fit snugly to the wall. It is more than likely you will want to fit tiles above, so a gap of about 6mm (¼in) is acceptable without posing any problems. If the gap is larger than this, you will have to scribe the rear edge of the worktop to shape to fit the contours of the wall behind.

To achieve a really neat, watertight finish between the worktop and the wall or tiles, you can use one of the many sealing strips available. These are very easy to fit and separate corner and joining pieces are available to cope with these awkward areas.

Bathrooms and Showers

The bathroom is often called the 'smallest room' and unfortunately in many modern homes this is all too often true. Glossy magazines frequently carry pictures of luxurious bathrooms occupying a space two or three times the size of the average. For many, the reality is very different.

Whatever the size of your bathroom, there are general problems that arise in any event and these must be tackled to ensure the efficiency of this vital area and your enjoyment of it.

One point you should bear in mind is that as far as this room is concerned, small definitely can be beautiful and with careful planning there is much you can do even in the most confined spaces, thanks to the wonders of modern designed fittings.

SOLVING PROBLEMS IN THE BATHROOM

It is often said that there are no permanent solutions to bathroom problems. Fortunately nowadays many products are available that at least keep problems at bay for longer periods. The range is extensive and forever changing, so you should keep a check on what is available. Some work well, others offer reasonable benefits and inevitably there will be the occasional gimmick. So beware before you buy.

Dripping or leaking taps have already been dealt with in the section on kitchens. One problem sometimes inherited when moving into a house is staining below the bath taps where they have been allowed to drip continuously.

In the case of a cast-iron or steel bath, the stain may respond to one of the more aggressive bath cleaners. Another way of dealing with such stains is with special bath paint. If properly applied, this can be quite effective, but you must follow the manufacturers' instructions carefully to get good results.

Another problem is a blocked bath trap, where the usual culprit is hair. To gain access to the trap normally means removing the panel at the side of the bath. Where this is of wood or hardboard, it is usually held in place by screws, sometimes mirror screws with chrome-plated dome-shaped heads that unscrew out of the main screw. Plastic panels tend to be clipped in

■ **Right** Rewashering a dripping tap is one of the commonest plumbing maintenance jobs. It involves removing the tap handle by releasing its retaining screw, unscrewing the tap mechanism and then fitting a new washer to the jumper which closes down onto the tap seat to shut off the water flow through the tap.

■ Bathroom design revolves around fitting three or four basic ingredients – a bath, a basin, a WC and often a bidet too – into what is often not an over-generous amount of floor space.

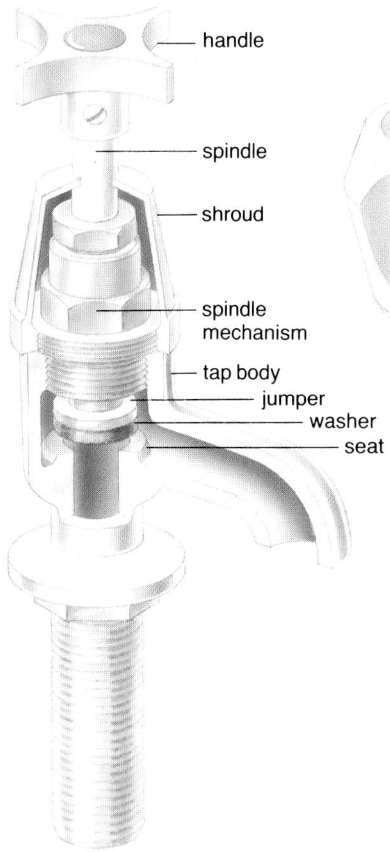

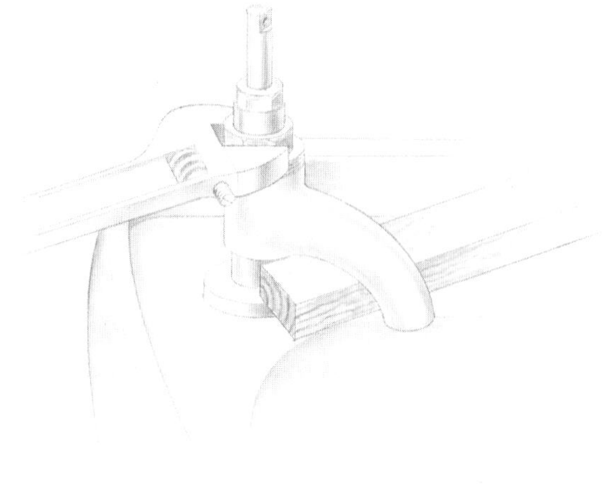

handle
spindle
shroud
spindle mechanism
tap body
jumper
washer
seat

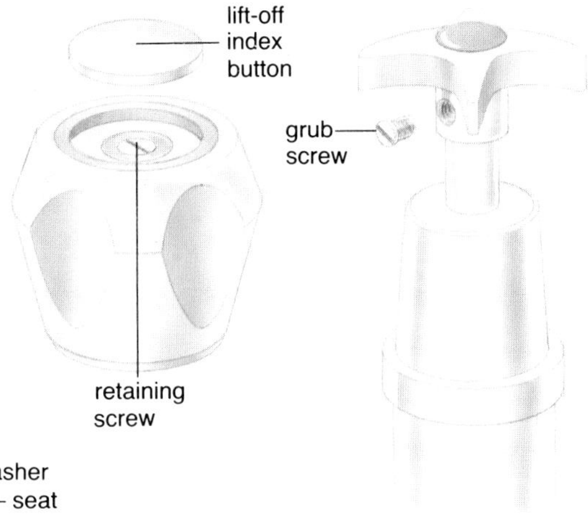

lift-off index button
retaining screw
grub screw

place neatly underneath the rim of the bath.

Of the other common problems in the working of the bathroom fittings, the main ones affect the wc – either water running from the warning or overflow pipe or the flush not operating correctly. With the former, the trouble lies in the cistern valve and should be dealt with as soon as possible, especially in winter since the outside pipe could freeze up and this might lead to indoor flooding.

Repairing the cistern valve

First take off the top of the cistern and look at the valve. It will be either a piston-operated type (the Portsmouth valve) or a diaphragm type (the Garston valve). In either case, the first thing to do is turn off the water supply. This may mean turning off the main stopcock, although you might find a gate valve below the cold water storage tank in the loft or even one on the supply pipe feeding the cistern.

One frequent piece of advice is to bend down the rod or arm connected to the float. While this may provide a temporary cure, it does not remedy the basic trouble in the valve, which will eventually have to be sorted out.

To repair a Portsmouth valve, first remove the split pin holding the arm in place using a pair of pliers. Take off the arm and shake the float. If it sounds as though there is water inside, replace the float.

Unscrew the knurled cap at the innermost end of the valve with a pair of pliers and take out the valve itself, using a screwdriver in the slot where the arm is fitted. Look inside the body at the valve seat, which should be a continuous ring with no scratches or grooves in it. If it is damaged, the whole valve must be replaced – ideally with the more modern Garston valve.

Now look at the end of the piston that fits against the valve seat. In this there is a small rubber disc (or washer), which presses against the seat, and this is where the problem is most likely to be. If the disc is damaged, replace it. The end of the piston screws off the body, but the joint is often impossible to see. The easiest way to unscrew it is to hold the end with a self-grip wrench and insert a stout screwdriver in the slot.

Once you have taken the end off, remove the old rubber disc, clean out the piston and insert a new disc. Do not be tempted just to turn it over and use the other side, since this will soon wear down and the problem will recur. Smear some petroleum jelly on the thread and replace the end of the piston. Clean up the outside of the

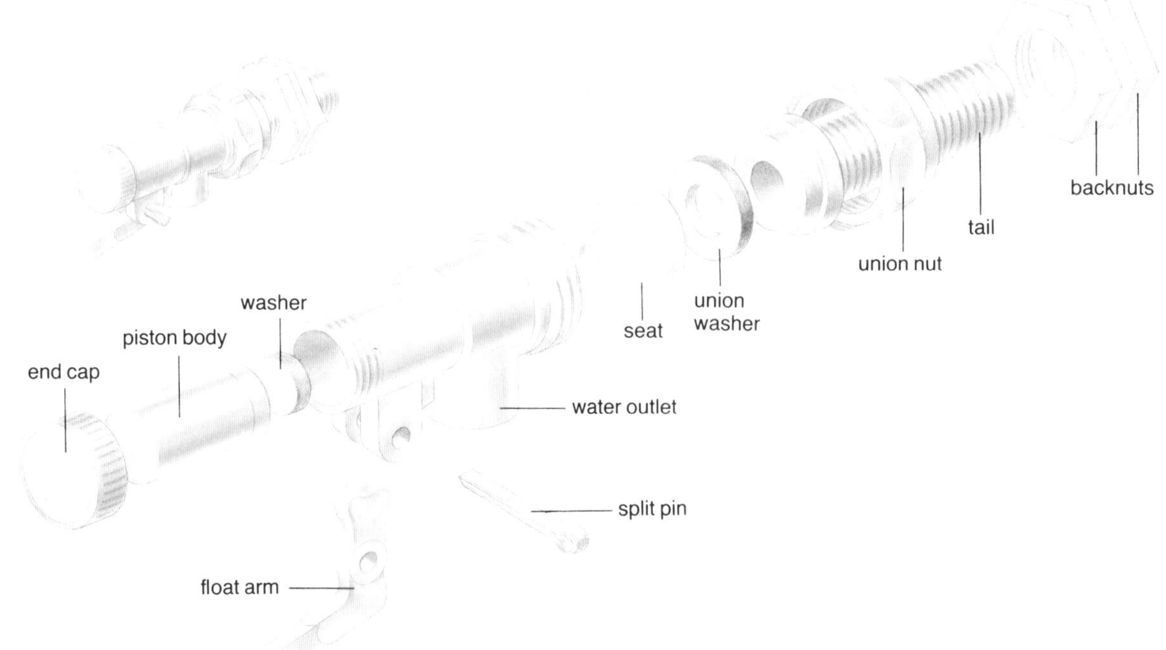

■ Old brass ballvalves have a piston which is operated by the float arm. As the water level in the cistern falls, the float drops and the lever moves the piston and its washer away from the seat, allowing water to flow through the valve. Debris within the valve can prevent the washer from closing on the seat, allowing the valve to drip; so can a worn washer. In both cases, turn off the water supply to the valve and dismantle it so it can be cleaned out and a new washer can be fitted.

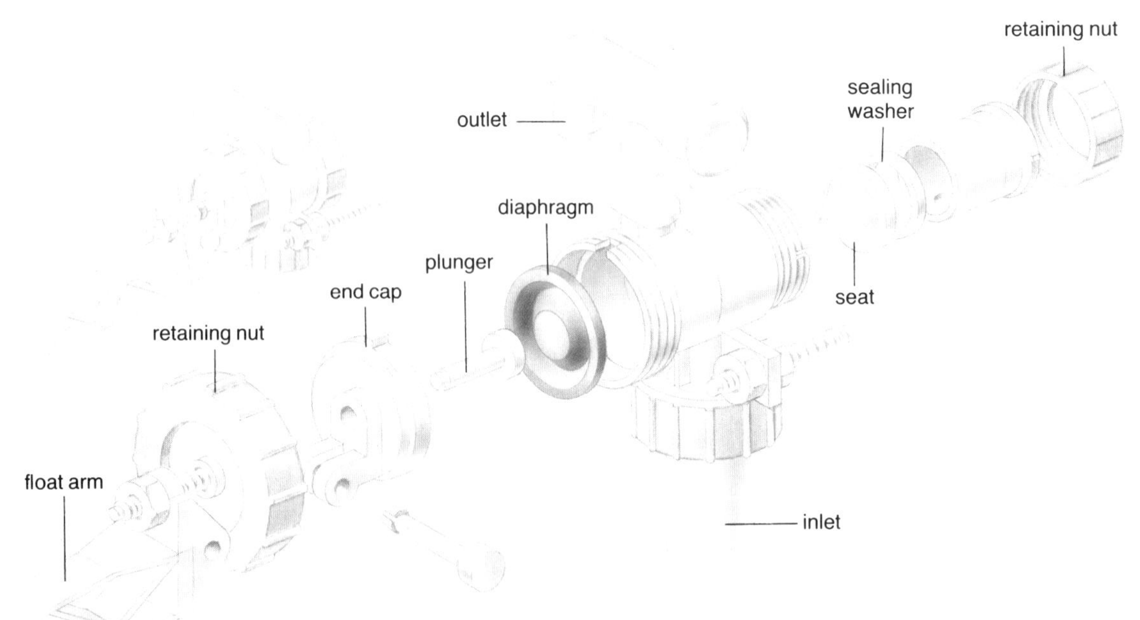

■ More modern valves generally have plastic bodies, and contain a diaphragm which is pressed against the inlet valve by the float arm, instead of a piston and washer. If they give trouble, it is usually the diaphragm which needs replacing. To do this, dismantle the valve after turning off the water supply.

piston, removing any wrench marks with fine wet and dry abrasive paper.

Refit the arm and float using the old split pin – or replace it with a new brass one. Refit the cap to the end and turn on the water. The valve should cut off the water at the correct level, which is marked on the inside of the cistern. This should be at least 25mm (1in) below the warning pipe. If the level is not correct, carefully bend the arm up to raise it or down to lower it. Support the arm when bending it so there is no strain on the valve.

Some of these valves have a silencer tube which runs down into the water. These are now banned by the water authorities, since back siphonage of water can take place. You should remove this tube if you have one by unscrewing it from the body of the valve.

The more up-to-date Garston valve is fitted either through the side of the cistern or, with more modern versions, at the top of the plastic tower that rises from the bottom of the cistern. The water is discharged from above the valve to prevent any possibility of back siphonage. Although there are some slight variations of this valve now on the market, the same basic instructions apply as far as maintenance and repair work is concerned.

■ **Right** The commonest problem with WC cisterns is a failure of the siphon mechanism, usually due to a worn or split diaphragm. With a close-coupled cistern, disconnect the supply and overflow pipes, undo the fixings to the pan and lift the cistern away so you can undo the siphon backnut. With a separate cistern, disconnect the flush pipe and take this opportunity to check that this pipe is clear by pulling some rag through it with a weighted string.

Next, uncouple the lever mechansim, lift out the siphon unit, pull out the lift rod, remove the washers and slide off the old diaphragm. Fit a replacement and reverse the dismantling sequence to reassemble everything.

To gain access to the valve, you must undo the large serrated plastic nut nearest the float. This nut unfortunately sometimes locks on to the body. If so, pour boiling water over it to try and release it. If this does not work, you may have to use a self-grip wrench on the nut and another wrench on the body. Turn it anticlockwise, looking from the float end.

You can now remove the diaphragm to inspect it and, if punctured or damaged in any way, replace it. Check the plastic seat it presses against, which should be smooth, clean and without any scratches or grooves. If the seat is faulty, you can remove it by unscrewing the other large nut on the body. Make sure the new seat you fit has a hole the same size. Before reassembling the valve, lubricate the threads with petroleum jelly. Use only hand pressure (no wrenches) when replacing the nuts so you do not damage the threads.

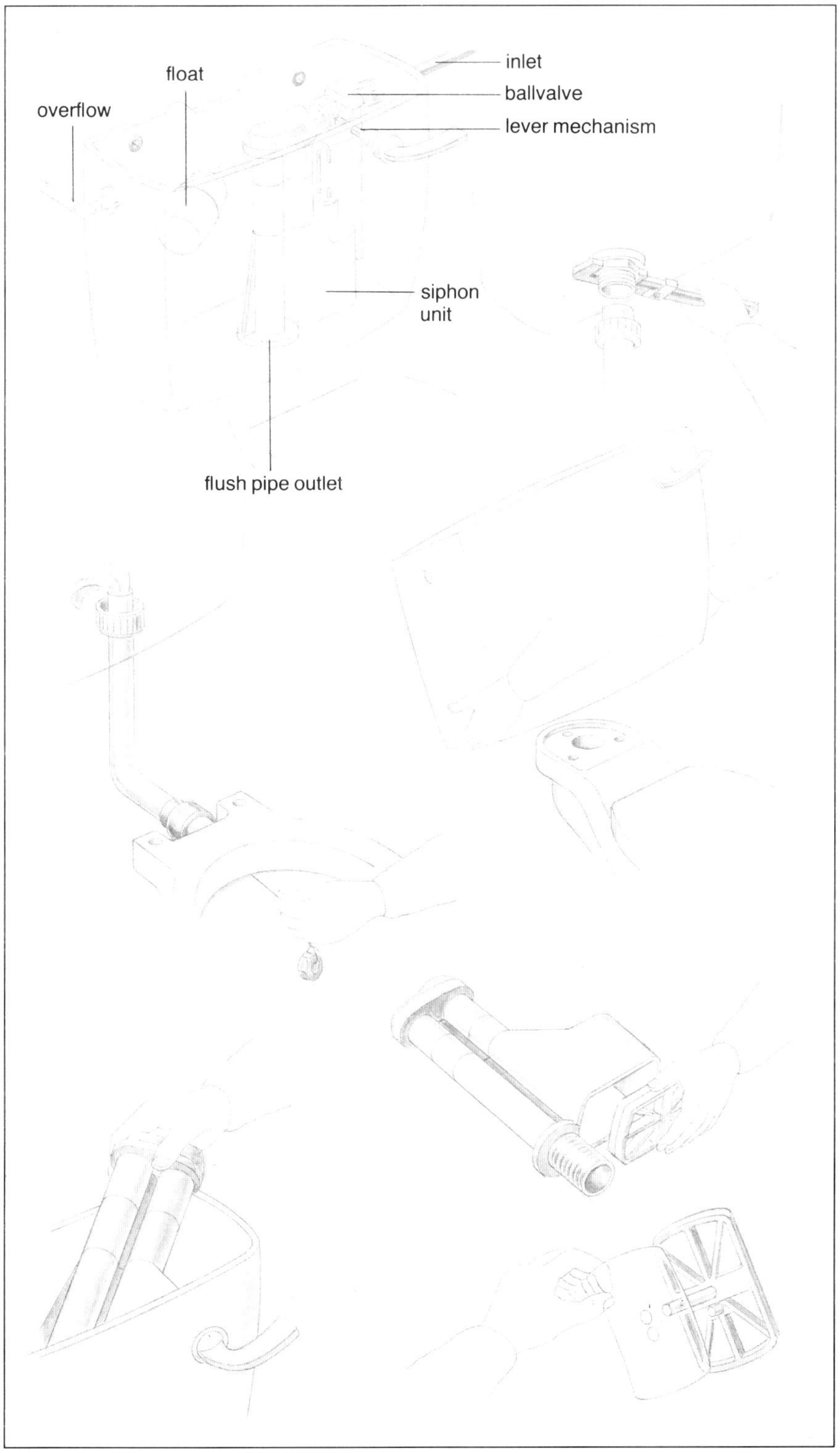

To adjust the water level, never try to bend the float arm. If you have a tower valve, first check that the support screw at the opposite side to the float arm is resting lightly but firmly against the side of the cistern. This is to stop the tower bending with the pressure from the float. If it is not touching the side, loosen the locknut and turn the screw by hand until it is in firm contact with the side of the cistern. Then tighten up the locknut.

You will see that the float arm is fixed to a pivot bracket with a locknut on either side. To alter the level, slacken one locknut and tighten the other, thus moving the float arm through the bracket. To lower the level move the arm towards the valve and in the opposite direction to raise it.

Replacing a diaphragm

This is necessary when the flush handle does not work properly and you have to pump it to get the wc to flush.

There are two basic cistern arrangements – wall-mounted with a short flush pipe connecting to the bowl, or close-coupled, where the cistern sits on an extension of the top of the wc. With the wall-mounted type, it is not necessary to remove the cistern. For the close-coupled type, however, it has to be removed. The following instructions apply to a close-coupled cistern. Once the cistern is removed, the method is the same for both types.

First check that the water level is correct. If not, adjust it as already described and try again. If it still does not work properly, turn off the water supply and flush the cistern fully. Then empty out all the remaining water with a jug, mopping up any left in the bottom with an old towel or cloth.

You must now disconnect the water supply and warning pipes and then undo and remove the wing nuts below the cistern. Check that the cistern is not screwed on to the wall and lift it off. Do not lose the rubber gasket.

Disconnect the operating linkage from the handle and undo and remove the large backnut beneath the cistern that holds the siphon assembly in place. Lift out the siphon and you will see the old diaphragm on the plunger in the siphon tube. This will either be split or torn, so remove it.

Fit the new diaphragm, carefully trimming it to size as necessary with a sharp pair of scissors. It should fit well to the sides of the tube without dragging. Use the plunger as a guide. Then refit the plunger to the siphon, clean out any debris and use a non-setting mastic to assemble the siphon to the cistern. Screw the backnut up tight.

When reassembling the cistern to the wc, do not forget the rubber gasket. Reconnect the water and warning pipes and the flush linkage and finally turn the water back on. Make sure that none of the joints leak. The cistern should now flush correctly.

Changing the flush

All modern cisterns have a means of changing from single flushing, where all the water inside is used when the handle is held, to double flushing, where if the handle is released only part of the water is used. The advantage of double flushing is that you can save unnecessary waste of water.

Depending on the manufacturer, methods to effect this do vary. Some use a plug on top of the siphon, which can be hollow or solid. Others use a hole elsewhere, which may be plugged. Instructions are normally printed on a label inside the cistern.

Coping with condensation

Condensation occurs whenever warm, moist air meets a cold surface, which obviously happens frequently in a bathroom. It can play havoc with paintwork and any wooden fittings such as window frames and, in severe cases, can cause problems with the carpet or flooring when it runs down the walls.

■ Whether a bathroom is small and simple (above) or large and well furnished (below), it needs to be warm and also well-ventilated. Radiators and towel rails provide the heat, while an extractor fan quickly gets rid of steam and smells.

It is also responsible for the black mould that forms on ceilings and at the top of walls. If left, this can be very difficult to remove. Aggressive cleaners can sometimes solve the problem. There is also a product you can paint on the walls and ceilings which will prevent the growth of this mould. It is transparent and effective for quite long periods.

The ideal solution is to overcome or reduce condensation in the bathroom and one way of doing this is to cut down the amount of cold surfaces. These include ceramic tiles – a particular favourite in this type of environment – and you would be well advised to avoid the temptation of using these on all your walls. Obviously the area around the bath, washbasin and shower is best tiled this way. But warmer surfaces like cork tiles or tongued and grooved knotty pine, which is sealed with polyurethane varnish, or vinyl wallpaper can happily be used on other wall surfaces and all help reduce the level of condensation.

An unheated bathroom merely aggravates the problem, since any tiled surfaces will naturally be that much colder. Various forms of heating can be installed, the most economical and practical being a heated towel rail. You can buy an electric version, which must be permanently wired in, or install one that runs off

■ Baths and basins can be boxed in neatly to give the room a streamlined look and also to provide much-needed storage space for toiletries and cleaning materials.

the central heating system. The latter should be plumbed into the same circuit that heats the domestic hot water, so that the rail remains warm for relatively long periods and keeps the chill off the bathroom.

Other heaters commonly used in the bathroom include an infra-red radiant heater. Since this type is only switched on when the bathroom is occupied, however, it has a limited affect on condensation.

Never be tempted to use a standard electric heater in the bathroom, since this is a potential killer. Electricity and water form a lethal combination. In any case, it is illegal to install an exposed socket outlet in the bathroom and any electrical appliance must be specially wired and switched, using a pull cord.

The other method of reducing condensation is to reduce the amount of moist air. This can be done by fitting an extractor fan, but its position is important. The window is a popular place to fit one, mainly because it is easy and cheap. But this is often not the best location. You should position the fan where it is likely to remove the air that is most moist. Over a bath or shower is the ideal position and you may be able to do this by fitting the fan so that it can exhaust through an exterior wall. There are a number of models available that come complete with the necessary fittings for this type of installation.

When installing central heating, it is recommended that the calculations allow for three complete changes of air per hour in a bathroom. When the room is not in use, ventilation naturally diminishes. So it is quite in order to exceed this figure when taking a bath or shower. When you buy an extractor fan, the manufacturer always quotes the amount of air that it will extract per hour. A simple calculation will enable you to select a fan with sufficient capacity for your bathroom.

You should bear in mind, however, that any air removed has to be replaced from somewhere. If you shut the bathroom door and keep the window closed, the fan will not be able to 'extract' any air. You can, of course, gain 'new' air by leaving the window open. While this may be acceptable in the summer, it will not help your condensation problem on a cold, damp, winter morning. The best arrangement is to allow air to enter the bathroom from inside the house. You can do this by deliberately leaving a small gap underneath or at the top of the door. About 6mm (¼in) should be sufficient.

Another advantage from fitting an extractor fan is that it will help to get rid of the inevitable smells from the wc quickly. There is a special device to overcome this problem, which extracts the fumes from the wc by sucking them up the flush pipe and blowing them out of the cistern warning pipe. But this will not help solve any major condensation problems.

Giving tiles a facelift

After a number of years the grouting between ceramic tiles will become discoloured and spoil the overall effect of what was once a clean, shining surface. By freshening up the tile joints, you can give these areas a real facelift so they look like new again.

If the grouting is in poor condition, rake it out with a suitably thin sharp tool, such as an old hacksaw blade. This can be a tedious operation. Then replace it with new waterproof grouting. Mix this according to the manufacturers' instructions, which may include a standing period before use.

Apply the new grouting with a plastic spreader, making sure you work it thoroughly into all the gaps. Allow it to dry and then wipe off the

■ Bathrooms benefit from good natural light; hang translucent blinds or curtains at the window to provide the necessary privacy when the room is in use.

surplus with a damp cloth. If you find that you have left too much in some gaps, wait until it is dry and then even it off with a piece of dowelling or similar material.

If the grouting is in good condition but stained, you can paint it with a special preparation available in a range of colours to match or blend in with your tiles.

The gap around the bath and the washbasin should be properly sealed to prevent water getting in behind the fittings. Existing seals will age and break up or become discoloured. The best solution is to remove them and use one of the special silicone rubber sealants now available in a variety of colours to suit your bathroom suite. They are applied straight from the dispenser and full instructions are given as to their application. But the compound is very sticky and difficult to remove once it has cured. So you must remove any excess immediately.

Because these sealants remain flexible, they are able to accommodate any movement in the fittings without cracking. The problem is that after a time black mould tends to form on them. The easiest way to deal with this is to cut out the old sealant with a sharp cutting knife and reseal the offending section.

Keeping showers working

One of the most common problems with showers is when the head becomes blocked due to excess scale, particularly in hard water areas. Since this is a gradual process, it is not always noticed until the shower becomes really weak. Regular treatment here will eliminate any serious effects.

Take the head off the hose and, if possible, dismantle it. There are a number of descaling solutions available which take varying amounts of time to work and are applied in different ways. Among these are some 'environmentally friendly' products that are less aggressive, but equally effective – and safer to use.

While tackling this problem, you may be able to descale some of the working parts of the shower itself. But be careful if you have to put any parts of a thermostatically controlled shower into boiling water. Check first with the manufacturers' instructions.

If the shower is run from your domestic hot water system and the output is weak, it may be that there is insufficient head of water. Normally the minimum is 1m (or 3ft) vertical distance from the shower head at its highest position to the bottom of the cold water storage tank in the loft. There are two ways of improving the flow rate and getting a more powerful shower.

The first is to install a pumped shower and the second to raise the tank in your loft. This will involve disconnecting and extending the rising main, which takes water to the tank, and the supply outlets (normally two) from the tank.

The tank itself will have to be moved on to a raised platform strong enough to support it. The height of this will depend on how much extra 'head' you need for your shower.

One other problem frequently encountered with this type of shower is when someone turns on another tap in the house and the shower temperature changes dramatically. This is especially likely to happen with a bath mixer tap shower or one installed from the supply pipes feeding the bath.

The only way to overcome this is to re-plumb the shower so that it takes its cold water direct from the storage tank. The hot water supply must be taken direct from the vent pipe that rises from the hot water cylinder. Ideally the shower tapping should be the first connection made above the tank.

If you are going to carry out this work, use 22mm (¾in) diameter pipe and fit bends of as large a radius as possible to give the best possible flow. This solution may not completely eliminate the problem, but it will certainly greatly improve it.

MAKING BATHROOM ALTERATIONS

If you are considering any alterations at all in your bathroom, it is worth thinking about the whole room and not just individual parts. There is little point in replacing a single fitting now if in the future you are likely to change the whole suite. Equally any amendments to the plumbing should be done altogether, rather than having further inconvenience and upheaval at some later date, when you finally decide to put in that shower you have been promising yourself.

Whereas there is usually a lot more scope in the traditionally larger bathrooms in older properties, the average small modern bathroom may not appear to offer much opportunity for changes. With a little careful thought, however, it is often possible to use the space in the room more effectively.

If, for example, you install a shower, you will find you no longer need a large washbasin as its use diminishes. Alternatively, buy a small corner bath or tub, which takes up less space than a normal bath yet still allows you to use that facility, perhaps with the addition of a shower fitted over it.

By replacing the old wc with a close-coupled version and the washbasin with a smaller model, you have already created considerably more space. This can be left to give your bathroom a more spacious feel or it may be big enough to allow you to fit a bidet or shower.

Draw up a scale plan of your bathroom and put in the fittings you would like to the same scale. This way you can estimate accurately how your ideal bathroom might work. There is a minimum recommended area of free space around fittings (see diagram) that allows easy access and safe and comfortable use. These spaces can overlap, however, since you can only use one fitting at a time.

■ Bathrooms are much easier to plan than kitchens because they contain fewer essential ingredients – usually just a bath, basin and WC, although larger rooms may have space for a bidet or a shower cubicle too. Each piece of equipment needs enough 'activity space' around it to allow it to be used comfortably and safely; the arrangements shown here suggest some workable possibilities.

When planning, it is best to leave the wc in the same position, since moving the large diameter waste pipe can be difficult. Most of the other fittings, however, can be accommodated in different positions. It may be necessary to raise the bath, however, if you propose moving it to the other side of the room. This is to give sufficient fall in the waste pipe over its new, longer run.

REMOVING AN OLD BATH

One of the first problems you are likely to come across when refitting your bathroom is that of removing the old bath. Quite possibly it is a cast-iron one and therefore very heavy and awkward. The easiest way is to break it up first, which can be done in two ways, both of which are noisy and messy.

■ Corner baths take up less floor space than is at first apparent, and can make better use of bathroom space than a conventional rectangular bath does.

First turn off the water and disconnect and remove the old taps and waste fittings. You will probably need a crowsfoot spanner to remove the taps. You can then break the bath with a sledgehammer, but make sure you have protected your eyes and your ears. Start in the middle of the sides, which is the weakest point. One snag is that there is not always enough room to get a good swing on the hammer.

The other method involves first drilling a line of 6mm (¼in) diameter holes across the bath about 25mm (1in) apart. Then drive in a tapered punch to split the bath in two. You should be able to remove these pieces – or repeat the operation, cutting it in quarters.

If you are replacing the fittings in their original position, you should find you can connect the new taps using the existing pipework. For any slight variations, you will probably find it easiest to use flexible tap connectors. If the waste pipes are of metal, it is a good idea to replace the system with plastic pipe and fittings. This is a straightforward job in most cases and certainly plastic is easier to service and looks more attractive.

FITTING A SHOWER

A shower is a very useful addition to any bathroom and will bring considerable savings in water and heating costs, not to mention the easing effect on the morning 'rush hour'. Of course, a shower can also be fitted quite easily elsewhere in the house – for example in a downstairs cloakroom. There are four basic types from which you can choose the most suitable or convenient.

Mixer tap shower

Installing this type involves replacing the bath taps with a mixer tap with a shower connection. One thing you must check is that both bath taps are fed by the cold water storage tank in the loft, with the hot tap via the hot water cylinder, of course. This means they are under equal pressure. The bottom of the tank must also be at least 1m (or 3ft) above the highest position of the shower, otherwise there will not be enough pressure for a good shower.

If the cold water tap is mains-fed, you will not be able to fit a mixer tap since the pressure difference will prevent satisfactory and safe mixing of water. New regulations also call for special measures when mixer taps are connected to the mains and you should first check those affecting your area.

With the mixer tap in place, you will have to fit the shower head, which is sometimes

■ **Left** Showers can be taken in the bath, with a shower curtain to keep splashes under control, or in a separate cubicle.

■ **Above** Careful planning can squeeze the essential bathroom components into even the most unpromising room shapes.

mounted on an adjustable rail, to the wall and also put up a suitable shower enclosure. This can be a simple screen fixed to the wall and pivoted into place, a curtain running along the bath or an enclosed curtained space.

When buying shower screens, remember that a smooth finish is easier to clean than a sculptured pattern. If you fix up curtains, these are best left fully open to dry, otherwise they will become covered in mould fairly quickly.

Thermostatic shower

This type also uses the domestic hot water supply and is subject to the same restrictions as mixer taps with regard to the feed of water. It does have the advantage that it can be positioned anywhere in the bathroom – or elsewhere – and gives a better flow and control of water temperature.

If you live in a hard water area, make sure the shower you buy is suitable for hard water and will not be affected by scale, particularly in the mixer valve.

Pumped shower

Pumped showers are becoming more popular now and have the advantage that they are not dependent on a good head of water. They provide an invigorating shower and the rose is

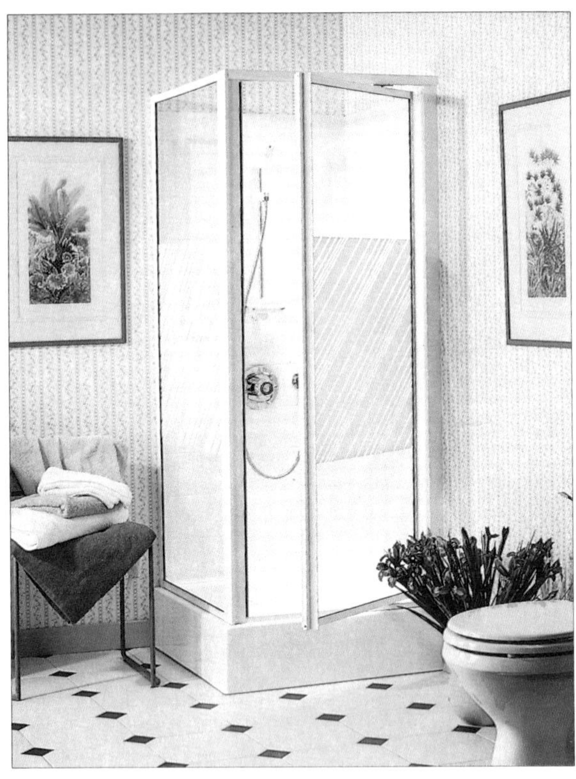

■ Shower cubicles can be bought as kits and fitted into a convenient corner (left), or can be built from scratch as part of a full-scale bathroom remodelling project (right).

usually adjustable to give variations in the pattern or volume of water spray.

These showers, which take their supply from the domestic system and cold water tank, comprise four main components – the shower head with its fixings; the mixer valve; the pump with filters and flow control valve; and the transformer. The shower head and mixer valve can either be fixed on to a wall or sunk into it with the connecting pipes concealed under panelling or tiling.

The pump motor is low voltage for safety and is usually switched on by a flow valve, which detects the flow of cold water when the shower is turned on. The pump can be positioned in any convenient location near the shower and is connected by feed pipes to the mixer valve and the water supply.

The transformer converts full mains voltage to the special low voltage required and again can be positioned in a suitable dry location reasonably near the pump.

Electric shower

This type of shower, which can be fitted over the bath or in a separate enclosure, normally takes its water supply from the mains. The water is heated electrically as it passes through the shower. Because it takes a high current, it is best installed professionally.

If you are considering buying one, remember that the hotter the shower the less water flows. The higher wattage versions give better flow

■ Matching vanity units, mirrors and wall cupboards (below) help to give the bathroom a carefully co-ordinated look.

■ The advantage of free-standing basins is that they take up very little floor area – a boon in small bathrooms. Mirrors on the walls help to make the room seem both lighter and larger.

than the low wattage ones, which in some cases do not really provide a sufficient water flow to keep you warm in a cold bathroom. Make sure you take professional advice if you live in a hard water area since some models are affected by a build-up of scale.

INSTALLING A BIDET

A bidet can be a useful addition to a bathroom if space permits. It is, however, subject to quite stringent controls under the water bye-laws to prevent any possibility of contaminating mains water by back siphonage. If you wish to install a bidet, you must inform your water supplier. The same, incidentally, applies if you want to install an additional wc or outside tap.

Bidets come in two types, the most common being the over-the-rim which can be likened to a low-level washbasin. The other, more expensive type has an ascending spray to provide the necessary rinsing facility. With either type, the waste must discharge through a separate pipe into the soil and vent pipe of your house's main drainage system.

The water supply to the over-the-rim bidet can be taken from the domestic supply in the same way as a washbasin if either separate taps or a mixing valve with two separate channels are fitted. If a single outlet mixer tap is fitted, then check valves must be fitted to the hot and cold water supply.

In the case of the ascending spray bidet, quite different regulations apply and you should check with your local water supplier before you commit yourself to fitting one.

Both hot and cold water must be supplied at the same pressure from a cistern, such as the cold water supply tank. Only if the bidet is the lowest appliance to which water is taken from the cistern can normal connections be made. This of course means the bidet must at least be on the ground floor.

For a bidet fitted on the first floor, there are two acceptable methods. One involves a separate hot water system for the bidet alone and the other the use of a check valve and a vent pipe on the hot water line that goes up higher than the cold water storage tank.

You can see from these regulations that the installation of these bidets is complicated and you are advised to take professional advice.

Creating more space

As the family grows, a once spacious house can begin to burst at the seams, making life very crowded and increasingly difficult. Perhaps an elderly relative has come to live and will need his or her own room. Or possibly having a spare bedroom will make all the difference when planned or unexpected guests arrive.

In some cases the existing space can be adapted so that, for example, a large lounge becomes a lounge-cum-dining room, leaving the original dining room free for conversion, maybe, to a ground-floor bedroom-cum-sitting room. In other cases, walls might be rearranged to change the layout of the house. Here you should first seek expert advice to ensure you are not going to affect the basic structure. Or you might decide to partition a large room to create two smaller ones.

These are just a few of the possible options available and you should consider all the various opportunities carefully before looking at other possibilities, such as building an extension. That, of course, may be your choice, but it will involve more work and greater cost.

So the basic choices available are either to convert existing accommodation, including a loft or basement if you have one, or to build on. The first option depends on whether the space is suitable for conversion and the second on whether you have the land available.

If you have complete freedom of choice then cost, convenience and looks will be the major considerations. Should you have a neighbour with a similar property that has been altered in any way, then it is a good idea to see what that conversion or extension is like inside. The new room may be the wrong shape or size or perhaps has involved altering the interior layout in some way that might not appeal. But at least it will give you some food for thought.

On the outside of the house, have a good look at the way an extension or loft conversion has affected the appearance of the property. Sometimes it can do so adversely.

CONVERTING A LOFT

It is impossible to say whether a loft conversion will be cheaper than an extension. So much depends on the type of house and therefore the amount of work involved. A local surveyor or architect should be able to give you a reasonable idea, before you go to the expense of having plans drawn up from which a builder can produce quotations.

The advantage of a loft conversion is that you do not use up any valuable garden space. The extra room will already have a roof (the existing one) and there is no need for digging foundations or getting involved in the messy building work associated inevitably with extensions.

First you have to decide what is the end use you intend for your loft space. For example, you may just want an occasional play area for the children – somewhere for them to lay out a toy village or train set, for example. Or you may want a hobbies room for dressmaking or photography. This kind of occasional use will involve little in the way of large-scale structural

■ The roof space is often completely wasted in many homes, yet careful planning and skilful construction work can create useful and attractive extra living space.

work and any conversion should be relatively quick and cheap to carry out.

If you decide you want proper habitable rooms – an extra bedroom or maybe a bathroom, for example, with all the amenities of plumbing, heating and electricity supply – then it will be a different matter altogether. Most alterations must comply with Building Regulations as far as the strength of floors, sound and heat insulation, ventilation and means of escape in the event of fire are concerned. This will obviously involve much more work and expense.

Making sure your conversion complies with the regulations is essential. So it is best to get professional advice on layout and design and to consult with your local authority at an early stage in the project. Not only will such consultation avoid problems during construction, but it will also help you to get the most practical design for your conversion and to make the best use of the space.

Checking the roof

First, though, you need to make sure your roof is suitable for conversion. Not all of them are.

Up to the 1960s, roofs were constructed on site by fixing individual timber members together. The basic shape involves a braced triangle. The sides (rafters) support the roof and the base (joists) stop the bottom of the rafters from moving outwards. They also provide support for the ceiling below. The strengthening members within the triangle (purlins) run along the roof space and hangers and struts provide extra support.

Designs vary, but all such roofs can be converted by taking out individual sections and putting additional timbers in the correct place to take the various roof loads. Looking at it from the inside, such a roof structure may seem an awkward place in which to fit a new room. But it can generally be easily adapted.

In more modern houses, the roof has probably been constructed using the trussed rafter system. Here, prefabricated triangular wooden frames span the main house walls.

If you have a roof like this, a full-scale conversion is not possible, because you cannot remove or reposition any of the timbers without seriously weakening the roof structure. However, you can improve access and lighting and use the space for storage.

Planning the work

Once the plans for the proposed conversion have been finalised and approval has been granted, you have several options as far as getting the job done is concerned.

You can do everything yourself, which is by far the cheapest method. But converting a loft from scratch is not really a do-it-yourself job. Although there are many ways in which you can save money, two important aspects – strengthening the loft floor and installing a staircase – will normally require professional help. And in some older houses, for example, there may be no felt under the roof, which might mean having to provide a waterproof roof lining.

One way in which you can save money is to use a builder to carry out the major alterations and then do the finishing work or arrange for individual sub-contractors to do it for you at a separately negotiated rate.

Jobs a do-it-yourselfer can tackle include installing windows, laying floor coverings, building plasterboard walls and ceiling, extending the power supply, plumbing and central heating into the loft and tackling the final decoration, making good and putting in fixtures and fittings.

If you do decide to undertake some of the major work, then be prepared for a long job. Alternatively, of course, you can hand the entire job over to someone else – either a loft conversion specialist or a reputable building firm. This is expensive, but it will be the quickest and easiest method.

Fire safety in loft conversions

If you are planning to add a loft conversion to an existing two-storey house, you must satisfy the following Building Regulations requirements.

- The existing stairway must be enclosed in a fire-resistant partition and must lead to an exit.
- Every existing door to a habitable room (including a kitchen but not a bathroom) opening onto the stairway should be fitted with a door closer. Any new doors should be fire doors.
- Any glazing in the walls of the enclosure or in doors opening onto it should be fire-resistant.
- The new stairway leading to the conversion can be a continuation of the existing stairway enclosure or may be in a separate enclosure that connects with the existing stairway.
- The new storey should be separated from the rest of the house by fire-resistant construction.
- Each room in the loft conversion should have an openable window or rooflight with an opening at least 850mm (2ft 9in) high and 500mm (1ft 8in) wide. The bottom of the opening must be between 600mm (2ft) and 1100mm (3ft 7in) above floor level in the case of a dormer window, and between 900mm (2ft 11in) and 1100mm above it for a rooflight. In both cases the bottom of the opening must be no more than 1.7m (5ft 6in) from the eaves of the building.

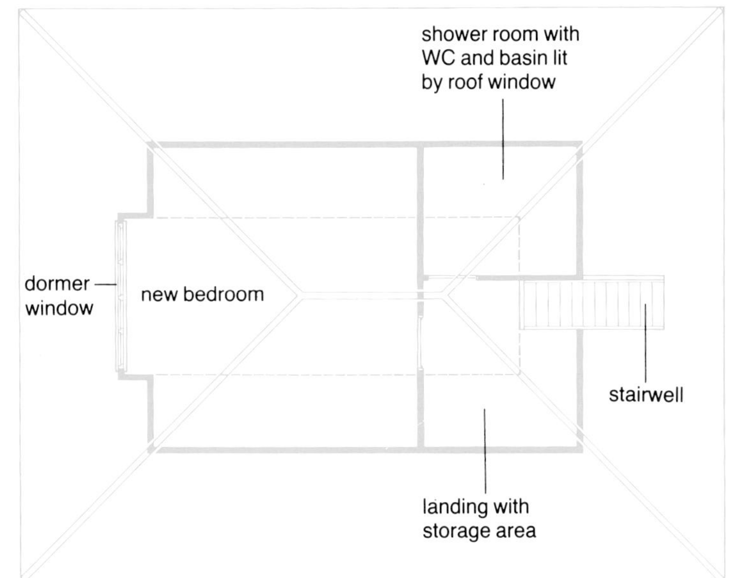

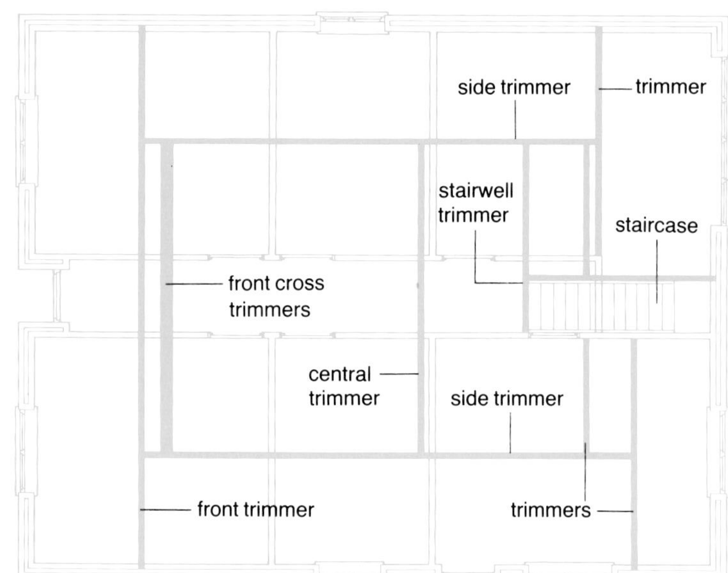

■ These outline plans for a typical loft conversion (above) show the extent of the new work, the positions of extra joists needed to support the additional loading and a cross-section through the building. Detailed plans must always be submitted for official approval before conversion work starts (below right).

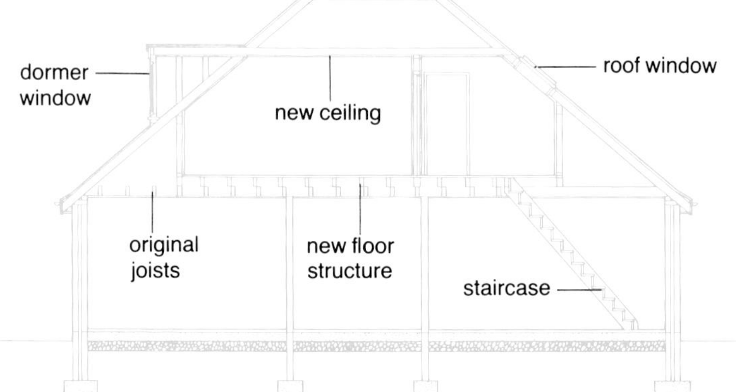

Laying a loft floor

Although you may decide to leave the job of putting down the loft floor to a builder, it is worth knowing what is involved. The main problem here is that existing roof joists stop the sides of the roof and walls moving outwards, but they are usually not strong enough to carry a floor with people walking on it.

There are three methods of strengthening the joists. The first is to bolt new joists of the same size to the existing ones to spread the load. Secondly you can install new, larger joists between the existing ones. Finally you can position a beam below the existing ceilings at right angles to the joists so as to reduce their unsupported span.

The simplest type of floor to lay on the joists is flooring-grade chipboard, which is screwed to the joists. You can, however, lay floorboards if you prefer. Do not, however, lay any flooring until other jobs, particularly any extensions to wiring and plumbing, are completed. But putting down at least some of the flooring temporarily will provide a solid platform on which to work. When putting in the flooring, it is well

■ Dormer windows projecting from the roof slope were the traditional way of lighting loft rooms, but are often not allowed on roof slopes facing a highway.

worth taking it right through to the roof edges and creating access doors in the walls of the loft room so that the eaves space can be used for storage purposes.

Once the floor is laid, put in the roof windows so you can work by natural light. Then install the plumbing, electricity and heating you require. This may involve resiting water tanks and pipe runs and this is most easily done before you start building partition walls on the new floor structure.

■ Loft windows, installed in the plane of the roof slope, are less obtrusive than dormers while admitting more light to loft rooms. They can also act as fire escapes in an emergency.

Choosing windows

There are two types of roof window – the dormer, which is built out from the roof rafters, and the skylight, which fits into the slope of the roof itself. The latter is made by specialist manufacturers and comes with a range of accessories, such as blinds and awnings.

Skylights usually have pivoting sashes so that they can be rotated right round for cleaning purposes and can be fitted working entirely from inside the roof, which makes installation less hazardous. They also provide an escape route in the event of a fire. Frames may be in hardwood, softwood or metal and the windows are supplied complete with flashings.

Putting in services

Running electricity into the loft is a straightforward operation. You can extend the upstairs lighting circuit, which will already be there in

■ A typical use of a loft conversion is to provide an extra bedroom and bathroom to cope with the demands of an expanding family.

■ Since loft windows are designed to fit between the roof rafters, there is no reason why several should not be installed side by side to increase the amount of light reaching the loft room.

the floor area of the loft. As far as the power circuit is concerned, it is a relatively simple job to run spurs from the upstairs circuit for any socket outlets you require in the roof space.

Providing cold water is also a simple plumbing job, but hot water is a different proposition. The pressure for the hot water system is provided by the cold water feed tank, which normally sits on the ceiling joists. To provide enough extra water pressure, you will have to raise the tank as high as possible by building a platform and amending the pipework.

The alternative is to provide hot water by either gas or electric instantaneous water heaters. Gas has to be installed by a competent gas fitter. You must not do it yourself. Electric heaters are different. You can install these yourself, provided you understand the job completely. If in any doubt about your abilities, employ an electrician.

If you want a shower room, there are several instant-heat fittings you can install. Or you can put in a shower cubicle. Running waste pipes should not prove too difficult, especially if the shower is positioned directly above an existing bathroom on the floor below.

Putting in walls

Your walls in the loft will be of a timber stud partition construction covered with plasterboard. These can have insulation added in the timber framing and insulating plasterboard can be used to provide additional insulation.

Once the wall framework is in position, you can complete running pipework and wiring. Then clad the walls, remembering to build in access doors to any storage areas, tanks and pipework concealed in voids in the eaves. Remember, too, to insulate any exposed pipework thoroughly.

You will need a vapour barrier of heavy gauge polythene fitted on the warmer side of the insulation – that is, under the plasterboard – to prevent moisture from inside the room causing condensation within the stud partition frame. If you are using insulating plasterboard, choose a type with an in-built vapour barrier.

The ceiling is created in a similar way. Unless you are following the angle of the sloping roof, you will need to put in new horizontal joists. These must be bolted on to the existing rafters and will form the surface on which to nail the plasterboard. Insulation can be installed on top of this as you would when insulating a standard loft space.

Providing access

You can either install a permanent staircase or fit a retractable loft ladder. Check with your local authority to see which is acceptable. A loft ladder is not usually allowed as access into a fully habitable room, although it can be perfectly acceptable for a hobbies or storage area.

The problem with a staircase is the amount of

space it takes up in the landing or room below, as well as the amount of headroom it needs. You may have to install a dormer window at the top. If there is not room for a normal staircase, there are two other possible choices.

A spacesaver staircase has a steeper pitch than normal stairs and the individual treads are specially shaped to take either the left or right foot. So you have to make sure you walk up them in the right way. Most loft conversion firms offer spacesaver stairs as an option. The other option is a spiral staircase.

BUILDING AN EXTENSION

If you decide to put an extension on the property, its positioning will be critical. You must make sure you still have access to the back of the house or garden. Existing drains will need protecting and manholes within the extension must be fitted with double-sealed covers.

If you are thinking of building on to any part of the house wall that incorporates a window, you may have to make special provisions for extra light and ventilation for the rooms affected.

■ The most important part of designing a home extension is ensuring that when it is completed it looks as much a part of the original house as possible. This involves careful matching of things like building materials, door and window styles and roof slopes and coverings.

Brick-built extension

At its simplest, your extension may just be for a ground-floor utility room. More complicated ones could involve adding on two storeys to accommodate extra bedrooms or a bathroom, with possibly a new playroom or extended kitchen situated underneath.

With this type of work, you can incorporate a timber-framed construction, which is widely used as an alternative for building modern houses. Normally, the timber frame replaces the inner blockwork skin of a cavity wall, with the outer skin remaining as brick.

A brick-built extension is an ambitious DIY project. You have to prepare proper foundations and have skill in laying bricks, plastering, roofing and so on. If you are building a kitchen or bathroom extension, extensive plumbing and electrical work may also be involved. You might, therefore, be happier to do the planning and the finishing off and leave someone else to handle the main building work.

Prefab or purpose-built extension

If all you want from your extension is a comfortable room for use in the warmer weather, then a conservatory would suit your needs. And double glazing will help make it habitable in the colder weather. Unless you can afford a tailor-made model, you will have to choose from

■ Careful attention to proportions and detail can result in an extension that blends in perfectly with the original building and its surroundings.

the range of prefabricated designs available.

The choice is between the modern and the traditional. The less expensive types have slim aluminium glazing bars, curved eaves and sliding patio doors to guarantee maximum sunlight. More expensive versions offer delightful replicas of Victorian styles with delicate framing in timber or cast aluminium, often with traditional French doors and decorative finials.

Depending on the model, some companies give you the choice of either building the conservatory yourself (with the aid of comprehensive instructions) or of opting to have it built by the supplier or an approved contractor.

You can do some of the work yourself – for example, preparing the base, the brickwork, and the final decorating – or you may choose to complete the entire installation job yourself. Pricing is flexible according to individual needs.

In order to gain the full benefit of the sun, it is advisable to build a conservatory on a south-facing wall. However, if there are other buildings or trees in the way, you may have to choose another, less sunny site.

Of course, you do not have to build a conservatory on the ground. You can construct it at first-floor level on to a suitable existing flat roof. This is a good way of creating extra space in smaller properties without the benefit of a garden. However, you must discuss any ideas you have with your local planning authority first.

CONVERTING A BASEMENT

It is relatively easy and obvious to assess what you might be able to use a basement for, if your house has one. Since it will either be completely below ground or semi-sunk, the most important consideration will be dampness.

Most often, the problem will be one of damp areas on floors, walls and ceilings. These can be treated with a brush application of a suitable waterproofing solution. If water is definitely seeping in through cracks or holes, then more comprehensive waterproofing will be needed. Condensation is sometimes the main problem, simply because the basement is so cold. The addition of some heating will solve this problem.

The next important aspect is ventilation. Clearly this will not be a major problem if the basement is to be used as a hobbies or storge area. But if you hope to create a living area, then providing a regulation size window opening is essential.

Without getting involved in very costly excavation work, a completely underground basement cannot be given windows. However, a semi-basement will probably already have a small window and it may be possible to enlarge this to comply with the regulations.

Extending plumbing and electrical requirements to the basement should not cause any problems since these services should be readily available from the floor above. And there is certain to be an existing staircase. This might be suitable or you may have to adapt or, at worst, replace it with a new one.

Depending on its overall condition, you will probably find you have to reline the walls and lay a new solid floor – or at least lay a smooth covering over the existing one.

■ Conservatories are a popular way of gaining extra living space without the complications of building a conventional extension.

■ Basement conversions face two major hurdles: keeping damp out, and letting light in. The former can be more difficult to achieve than the latter.

So practical ... and very
The Handi is particula
Beige
Green
Blue
White
"Rondette" Inset Bowls
Cut-out size 382 mm diameter
Shallow Drainer Bowl
Model DR4 1400x490
Cut-out size 1375x465 mm
are intended as a general guide only.

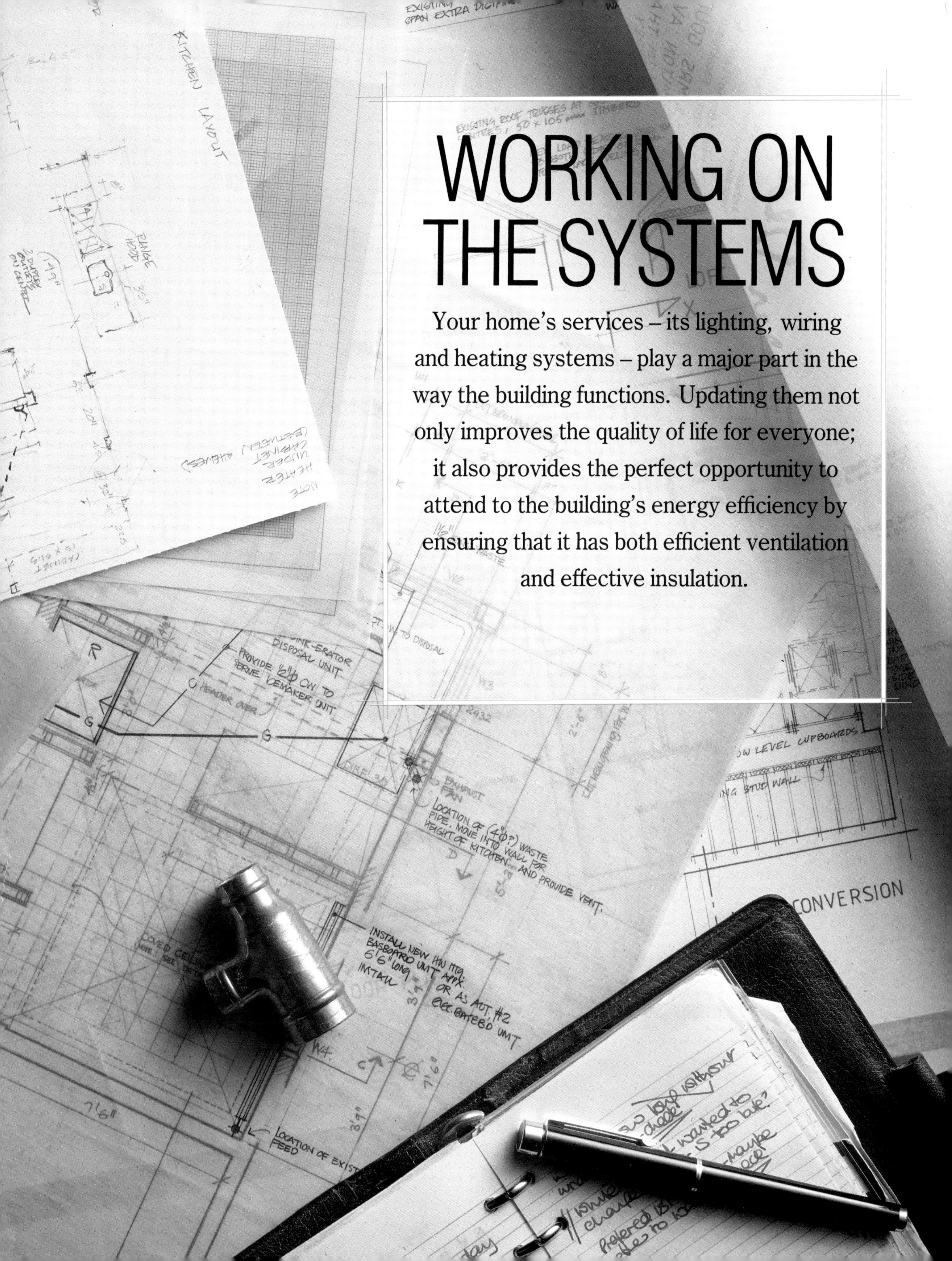

WORKING ON THE SYSTEMS

Your home's services – its lighting, wiring and heating systems – play a major part in the way the building functions. Updating them not only improves the quality of life for everyone; it also provides the perfect opportunity to attend to the building's energy efficiency by ensuring that it has both efficient ventilation and effective insulation.

Lighting

Lighting is a vital function in every home, yet all too often it is the most neglected aspect of interior design and planning. It is as important as the paint colours, wallcoverings and furnishings, which are generally chosen with such care and deliberation.

Too often just a standard central pendant, possibly backed up by a table lamp, is used to light a room. This might provide adequate illumination, but there is no atmosphere, no excitement, no subtle shadows, no contrast and no sparkle to fascinate and help you enjoy your surroundings.

Just like the decorations and furnishings, lighting needs to be planned from the start. It is not something to be added on as an afterthought once the decorating has been finished.

When you have analysed your needs room by room, you will probably find you want to put in more than one lighting circuit in some rooms. For wall, cornice and pelmet lights, aný new cable will need to be concealed. Adding extra ceiling lights will involve gaining access from the floor above. And additional table or floor-standing lamps may require more sockets to eliminate potentially dangerous trailing flexes. With any of this work, you will not want to upset decorations you have just spent much time and money putting up.

Any lighting system in the house must do two things – give you light where you want it and enhance the overall look of the room or area it affects. Choosing the right type of fitting and positioning it correctly is the key to creating a balance between light and shadow.

Uniformly bright lighting offers no contrast and the result is harsh and cheerless. Conversely, deep shadows are depressing. An acceptable level of lighting is needed throughout the room to avoid hard shadows. In addition, you will want local pools of light for tasks such as reading and sewing and for highlighting features such as alcoves or ornaments.

One basic rule is to ensure that naked bulbs are never visible, whether you are standing, sitting or lying down. Avoid this by careful choice of fittings and shades and also by thinking about the height at which lights are installed.

■ Many homeowners pay scant attention to the lighting options available nowadays, yet a well-designed lighting scheme can be a highly attractive feature of the house . . . whether viewed from indoors or outside.

■ **Right** The entrance hall is the first room your visitors will see, so make an effort to show off its features in a welcoming light. Here an array of individual track-mounted fittings turns a hallway into a miniature picture gallery.

Electrical safety

Before planning any extensions or alterations to your home's electrical wiring system, it is essential to make sure that the circuits and any protective devices fitted to the system are in good condition and capable of supplying the demand.

Start by inspecting the system controls – usually sited next to the electricity meter. In a modern home you will find a multi-way consumer unit, fitted with an array of miniature circuit breakers which provide overload protection to individual lighting and power circuits in the home. In addition, there may be another protective device fitted called a residual current device which guards against users receiving electric shocks or current leakage through poor insulation causing an electrical fire. Older homes will have rewirable fuses rather than circuit breakers, and these may be in separate switch-fuse units – a sure sign of an out-of-date system.

Next, check the condition of the circuit cables running away from the fusebox. Unless they have grey or white PVC sheathing, they should almost certainly be replaced – a job you may prefer to leave to a qualified electrician.

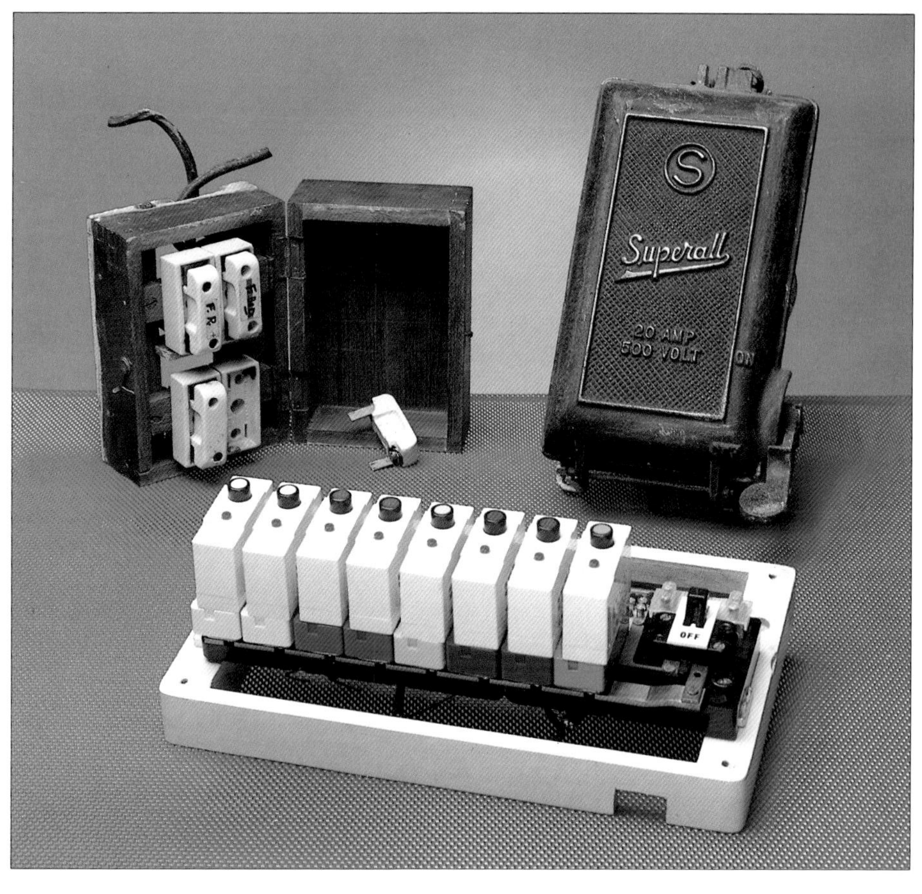

LIGHTING ACCESS AREAS

Apart from any aesthetic considerations, access and traffic areas such as entrances, halls and stairways are potentially high risk ones as far as accidents are concerned. So safety is of paramount importance when planning lighting here.

With entrances, you may want to make a specific feature of the front door by aiming a spotlight at it, illuminate a stained glass panel from inside or highlight an interesting group of plants. Consider outside lighting at low level as well, so that the path or any steps are clearly visible. Make sure, of course, that all exterior lights are fully waterproof.

Halls, corridors and stairways must be adequately lit and operated by switches at either end. Make sure each landing and flight of stairs has its own light, preferably at the top and bottom if flights are long. Individual stair treads must be clearly visible and not concealed in deep shadows.

A linear fluorescent light is particularly suitable for narrow areas, as are wall-washers directed up or down, especially if you also want to illuminate hanging pictures or objects. For good general lighting, use a row of downlights or track-mounted spotlights.

■ Good lighting in access areas is essential for safety reasons, especially on staircases where the edges of the treads must be clearly lit and visible from both above and below.

LIGHTING LIVING ROOMS

Living rooms have to cater for a range of family activities, so the lighting must be versatile. An ornate central pendant will provide an attractive feature and general lighting when lit. Back this up with wall lights in alcoves, perimeter lighting behind curtain pelmets to direct light upwards or downwards, and wall-washers to grace a long wall with diffused light.

One striking effect is to spotlight individual features of the room. To achieve this, install track lighting in different positions and add small striplights above favourite pictures. Wall-washers or spotlights should be individually switched or dimmer-controlled, so you can vary the light level at will.

Activities such as reading, sewing and homework need good localised lighting. And since the site for these activities may move around the room, plug-in lights are often the most flexible. Adjustable lights on desks can be moved to shine on the surface for writing or using a word processor keyboard, for example, again without glare being a problem. To prevent excessive glare from the television screen, provide subdued lighting behind it.

■ In living rooms, lighting has to provide background illumination, task lighting for reading and similar hobbies, and highlighting of individual features such as pictures and ornaments.

■ In dining rooms, the prime requirement is for good but glare-free lighting over the dining table, with some extra background lighting to illuminate the rest of the room and induce a restful mood. Dimmer switching can be particularly appropriate.

LIGHTING DINING ROOMS

A rise-and-fall pendant light over the dining table will illuminate both the table and guests. You will also need some background lighting such as wall-washers, pelmet lights or accent lights on pictures or ornaments to illuminate other areas of interest in the room. Dimmers can be used for both types of lighting, to cater either for family meals or more intimate occasions. Background lighting will also be needed to pick out the all-important serving areas.

LIGHTING KITCHENS

Arguably this is the most critical room in the house as far as planning lighting arrangements is concerned. It is a real workroom, which can also be used for eating, and it is occupied at different times of the day, both summer and winter. So the lighting has to be flexible to cope with the various ever-changing demands likely to be made on the room.

Overall lighting from a central pendant or fluorescent tubes should be sufficiently strong to wash the whole room with light. If you have two fluorescent tubes and control them with individual switches, you can vary the lighting as required. A pendant controlled from a dimmer will provide similar options. An alternative is to install downlights, again with optional switching or dimmer controls.

With work surfaces, the sink and the cooker, you have to be sure the lighting is strategically placed so that it illuminates the intended area and not someone's back, as can often be the case with ceiling fittings.

Wall-mounted spotlights or ceiling downlights can be adjusted to beam directly on to the work surface. Striplights below wall cupboards are also practical and effective in this respect.

Should you have a dining area or breakfast bar, then a rise-and-fall pendant that can be lowered sufficiently not to glare into people's eyes while they eat is an ideal solution. A strategically placed ceiling-mounted spotlight can make a viable alternative.

A cooker hood incorporating a light is important to illuminate a hob and an oven with a built-in light source is also essential. If you have a walk-in larder or broom cupboard, then this would benefit from some lighting – possibly a

type that is activated by a trip switch when you open the door.

Finally, do not forget that kitchens are meant to be aesthetically pleasing as well as functional, so the odd spotlight highlighting an appealing house plant or dinner service on a shelf is certainly worth incorporating into your overall lighting scheme.

LIGHTING BATHROOMS

Bathrooms should not be purely cold, clinical, functional rooms but places of relaxation, so that washing and bathing become really pleasurable activities.

If your overhead bathroom light provides a stark look, with the light glaring on all those shiny surfaces, fit a lower wattage bulb and then augment it with wall lights or washers for a softer look, maybe even with coloured bulbs.

Emphasize the mirror instead – with striplights or small, low-wattage bulbs. You can also get striplights with shaver sockets incorporated, specially for use in bathrooms.

All fittings must be safe to use in damp conditions. Lights should only be operated with a pull-cord or from outside the room. And sockets for shavers must provide an earth-free supply via a transformer.

If you enjoy reading in the bath, try a downlight positioned directly above it. But make sure that lights close to extra wet areas are properly enclosed in waterproof casings.

■ In the kitchen, it is vital to have good illumination for all work areas – the cooker, the sink and the worktops. Lighting beneath wall units is one excellent way of providing this. In addition you need overall background lighting, perhaps from directional ceiling-mounted fittings, and lighting above the table if you have room for one in the room.

■ In the bathroom, you need restful general lighting, plus good task lighting at the washbasin for shaving and making up. Make sure all fittings used in bathrooms are enclosed for safety reasons, and use splashproof types over baths and in shower cubicles.

■ In bedrooms, having some restful background lighting is a must; dimmer control is particularly effective here. You also need localised lighting for reading in bed or making up at a dressing table, and here wall and table lamps can be the perfect solution. Above all, provide two-way switching so you can turn lights on and off easily without having to get out of bed.

LIGHTING BEDROOMS

In any bedroom where you have a central pendant light, this should be under dimmer control to create a restful atmosphere. And two-way switching of all lights is important so you do not have to get out of bed to switch them off at night or on in the morning.

For reading in bed, remember to include adequate illumination. But make sure fittings are flexible so that light can be directed away from a sleeping partner. An additional task light may be required over the dressing table and wardrobes will benefit from a fluorescent tube inside to illuminate the contents.

The lighting in children's bedrooms must be flexible to cope with various activities that go on there and be adaptable as the child grows. For the youngest, good background illumination is the most important. A dimmer allows the main light to be left on very low, while youngsters go to sleep. Equally an ornamental child's night-light provides security.

A ceiling track system will cope with changing requirements and provide background or indirect lighting, as well as highlighting posters, a desk or play and storage areas. An Anglepoise or similar style lamp could provide additional light for studying and clip-on or portable spots are ideal for reading. Make sure to provide one each for the upper and lower levels in bunk beds and position them well out of the way of the bedding for safety's sake.

LIGHTING CONSERVATORIES

Conservatories are unusual because they are largely composed of glass which means that, in darkness, unwanted reflections and shadows are inevitable.

It is largely a question of experimenting with an assortment of spotlights, low-voltage lamps and even candlelight. A single light source is unlikely to be sufficient. Make sure all bulbs are well shielded to cut down reflections from the glass as much as possible.

CHOOSING BULBS AND TUBES

There are four main considerations that determine whether a filament bulb is suitable for a particular application – wattage, life rating, finish and cap fitting.

The amount of energy a bulb uses is measured in watts. The light given off is roughly in proportion to the wattage. So, for example, a 150 watt bulb will produce roughly twice as much light as a 75 watt one of the same type. The amount of electricity used is directly proportionate; that means a 150 watt bulb will use twice as much as the 75 watt one.

Bulbs can be clear, pearl or opal. Clear bulbs transmit the most light, giving brilliant illumination. But they do create harsh shadows and so are most often used where a sparkling effect is desired, such as in a chandelier.

Pearl bulbs have a frosted finish that gives a more even light with more diffuse shadows and are therefore the most popular for general lighting. Opal bulbs have a white finish and give the softest light. They also have the lowest output for equivalent wattage.

A bulb should have a life of around 1,000 hours. Double-life bulbs are intended to last for 2,000 hours, though there are fewer ratings to choose from – usually 40, 60, 100 and 150 watt.

Filament bulbs are available with either a bayonet or screw fitting, in large or small sizes.

The most common light bulb is the familiar pear-shaped GLS (general lighting service) lamp, which comes in 15, 25, 40, 60, 75, 100 and 150 watt sizes and all three finishes, although opal is comparatively rare.

Coloured bulbs

Pear-shaped bulbs are available in different shades including pink, red, amber, yellow, blue and green. And they are usually rated at 15, 25, 40 and 60 watt. They have a poor light output for their wattage, with the darkest colours being the weakest.

Mushroom-shaped bulbs are normally available in a silverlight finish (similar to opal) and in 40, 60, 100 and 150 watt ratings. Spherical bulbs, too, have an opal or silverlight finish to enable them to be used without a shade. They come in four different sizes, from 45mm up to 126mm in diameter. The choice of rating is not so wide – 25, 40 and 60 watt in the smaller sizes, together with 100 and 150 watt in the larger ones.

Candle bulbs are available in plain and twisted versions. They are mainly used in candelabras and in some decorative wall fittings. Both are obtainable in clear and pearl finishes. The plain ones are also available in opal.

Night lights are rated from 8 to 12 watts and provide continuous light at low cost for children's rooms and access areas where required.

Reflector lamps, which are used with spotlights, come in two types – ISL and PAR. The former gives a soft-edged beam and is often used for spotlights, downlights and uplighters. The ratings available are from 40 to 150 watt. PAR reflectors, which are more expensive, have a beam of exact width for highlighting specific objects. These come in 100 and 150 watt ratings.

Filament tubes are used for lighting display cabinets, mirrors and other fittings and are available with single cap (85mm long and 25 or 40 watt) or double cap (222 and 285mm and 30 or 60 watt) in either a clear or pearl finish.

Bulb life

Vibration will shorten the life of any bulb, so avoid siting light fittings near to doors and ensure they are securely fixed. You do not need to be reminded of their fragile nature.

Fluorescent tubes use less energy to produce the same light output as bulbs. The equivalent of a 100 watt bulb would be an 18 to 36 watt tube, depending on the type. However, unlike bulbs, their light output falls off considerably over a period of time – up to 25 per cent – and they may need replacing before they actually fail.

According to the type you buy, the efficiency of tubes does vary. For normal use, the options include high efficiency and poor colour or good colour and poor efficiency. The more expensive models do, however, offer good colour and

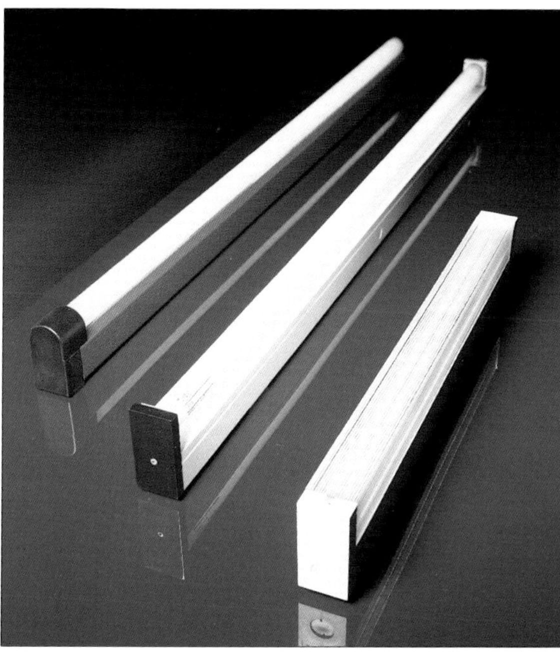

■ **Left** Light bulbs come in a wide range of types, shapes and colours. When choosing which to use where, remember to specify whether the fitting accepts bayonet cap or Edison screw bulbs, and take care not to exceed the recommended maximum wattage for the fitting or lampshade being used.

■ **Above** Track lighting offers tremendous scope and flexibility in lighting design, since different types of fitting can be mixed to create a range of lighting effects.

■ **Right** Fluorescent lights are more efficient than filament lamps in terms of the amount of light they produce, but can make rooms look cold unless care is taken over specifying the tube colour.

■ **Left** Enclosed fittings range from the simple wire-reinforced bulkhead light to globes and fittings with ornamental cut-glass shades. Recessed or semi-recessed downlighters are ideal for casting pools of light without glare.

efficiency. They come in 250, 600, 900, 1200, 1500, 1800 and 2400mm lengths and in 25 or 38mm diameters.

In each category there is usually the choice of a warm, intermediate and cold effect. Coloured tubes are also available for use with illuminated ceiling panels and in other decorative situations.

Low-energy compact fluorescent bulbs provide an alternative to the filament bulb for general use. It is claimed they last up to five times as long and use only a fifth of the energy. As they are cool-operating, they can also be used with ultra-slim fittings and types of shade that cannot take filament bulbs.

Low-energy bulbs are available in 16 and 28 watt ratings. The former falls between a 60 and 100 watt bulb, while the latter is equivalent to a 150 watt bulb. One point to bear in mind with these bulbs is that they may require a special ceiling rose, bayonet fitting or adaptor.

Fluorescent lights may seem costly to buy, but in the long-term they do pay for themselves with their long life and low running costs. It has been estimated that a fluorescent light can be up to five times more efficient than a tungsten filament lamp.

Choosing spotlights

Spotlights offer a high degree of flexibility since they can be mounted in a variety of different places, adjusted individually and controlled separately using normal switches or dimmers.

Wall-mounted spots can provide task lighting for reading or sewing, for example, or can be used to cast highlights on pictures or ornaments or throw a wash of light on to a wall or ceiling. Single spots are mounted on their own rose. Cluster spots, where two or more lights are mounted on the same rose, are also available. Ceiling-mounted spots can also be fixed on a rose, while track-mounting allows the position of the lights to be altered to suit.

Choosing a bulb for a spotlight is almost as important as choosing the fitting itself. Different width beams are available to suit different lighting effects. For illuminating an area, a precise narrow pencil beam is best. Where a less concentrated illlumination is wanted, a wider beamed bulb should be used. Framing spots, which produce a precise straight-edged beam, can be particularly effective for lighting individual ornaments.

Choosing downlights

Downlights are permanently fixed ceiling-mounted fittings that, as their name implies, direct light downwards. They can provide general illumination or task lighting and different creative effects.

Eyeball downlights are similar to spotlights mounted in the ceiling itself. Bulbs with different beam widths give some flexibility in their range of uses and beam direction is adjustable.

Flush-mounted downlights are fixed in the ceiling so that the face of the bulb is level with the surface. They are available with either fixed beams or adjustable ones that can be narrowed or broadened slightly.

With recessed downlights, the bulb is set back a few inches behind the plane of the ceiling in a brass or silver-finished metallic tube. These may require a deep ceiling void to accommodate the tube and in some cases can only be fitted into suspended ceilings.

Heating and Ventilating

Central heating provides the ideal overall system for keeping your home warm and comfortable to live in. Whereas modern homes are normally built with some kind of all-round heating, older properties may only have partial heating or in some cases none at all. If so, this should be a major consideration in any plans you draw up for the house.

Where it does exist, central heating is likely to consist of one of three different arrangements – partial, background or full.

With partial central heating, only a section of the house will be covered by the system. The other parts are either unheated or rely on isolated heaters.

A background system enables the house to be fully heated to a temperature of about 14–16°C. Where additional heat is required to boost this level – for example, in a living room – another source of heat such as a gas or solid fuel fire is used.

With a full central heating system, all the rooms in the house are heated to the desired temperature from a series of heat sources – normally radiators.

Of course, heating is also needed to provide domestic hot water for the kitchen, bathroom and possibly a cloakroom or bedroom vanity unit or shower cubicle. This is normally incorporated into the central heating system where it exists.

There are various ways of distributing heat around the home. These include hot-water radiators, fan heaters operated through the hot

■ Every room in the house needs controllable heating and adequate ventilation. In most homes this means having a central heating radiator and an openable window, but increasing use is being made of more advanced technology to remove stale air and recycle it after filtering it and heating or cooling it.

■ Solid fuel room heaters offer the comforting looks of a real fire with the bonus of greatly increased thermal efficiency. Some types can also provide central heating and domestic hot water too if they are connected to a back boiler behind the heater.

water system, electric storage radiators and skirting radiators. Ducted hot air and underfloor heating systems are normally only used when they can be incorporated into the house as it is being built.

SELECTING FUELS

The range of domestic fuels available offers a wide choice, depending on the system, the individual units and, of course, availability and supply. It includes solid fuels such as wood, coal, coke and anthracite, as well as natural gas, electricity and oil – and even solar power.

Solid fuel systems have advanced considerably from the old days of open fires. Modern boilers can be hopper-fed and only need attention once a day or less. Also, solid fuel can be delivered anywhere by road and, provided you have sufficient storage space to cope with bulk deliveries, you can take considerable advantage from off-peak summer prices.

Gas is probably the most popular form of fuel. It is clean, instantly controlled, reasonably stable in price and generally available in most areas. In more remote spots where there is no mains supply, liquid petroleum gas can be used instead. This comes in replaceable cylinders or, for larger houses, is piped into permanently installed pressurised storage tanks.

Oil provides a similarly clean and versatile domestic fuel, but it is subject to fluctuations in price. And you will need space for a fairly large storage tank, which must be accessible from the road to take the necessary deliveries.

Electricity competes with gas as the most common form of fuel. Very few homes are without a mains supply, whereas gas is still not available in some outlying areas. However, it is not as easily controlled. One popular use is with storage radiators, which can be run quite economically on off-peak electricity.

Still in its infancy as a domestic fuel, solar power cannot supply enough heat on its own in the normal British climate to run a full heating system. It is, however becoming more and more efficient as a supplier of domestic hot water in summer and for pre-heating the water ready for conventional heating in winter.

SAVING HEAT

All the heat produced by any central heating system is, of course, eventually lost to the atmosphere. To delay this, insulation is required. The better the insulation, the longer the heat will remain in the home and consequently the lower your heating bills will be. So check your installation and make sure you take all the necessary precautions to reduce unnecessary heat losses from the system.

Hot water cylinder

This must be covered with an insulation jacket, which should be 75mm (3in) thick. The cost of the jacket can be recovered in a matter of weeks. Most modern cylinders have the insulation already fitted in the form of an integral outer covering.

Loft insulation

The loft floor should be covered by at least 150mm (6in) of insulation material. Grants are available to assist in paying for this, if none exists at present. The cost of the insulation can be recovered in three to four years.

Wall insulation

If your house has cavity walls, the cavity should be filled with suitable insulation material, which must be professionally installed. The cost of this operation can normally be recovered in about five to seven years.

Double glazing

If properly installed, double glazing reduces the heat lost through windows and eliminates the 'false draught' effect caused by the cold surface of a single glazed window. New low-emission glass cuts the heat loss still further. It is difficult to calculate the cost recovery period for this, since there are many different forms and it can be expensive to fit.

Draughtproofing

It has been estimated that the air gaps present in the average house are the equivalent of having a 1 sq m hole in an outside wall. Insulation to prevent draughts is cheap to buy and easy to install, which means it is very cost-effective. Do not make the mistake, however, of sealing rooms completely.

THE SMALL BORE SYSTEM

The most common central heating system is undoubtedly the small bore type, which refers to the 15mm (½in) or 22mm (¾in) diameter pipe used. This is normally made of copper. A small feed and expansion tank in the loft supplies water to the primary circuit (unless you have a self-priming Primatic cylinder); this passes water through the boiler to the radiators and also heats the hot water cylinder.

■ A typical domestic boiler provides both hot water, stored until needed in an insulated hot cylinder, and central heating. The forces of gravity circulate water between boiler and cylinder, while a pump is used to drive water round the heating system. Cold water from a storage cistern supplies cold taps (except in the kitchen) and the hot cylinder, and a small feed-and-expansion tank tops up any losses from the heating system. The use of motorised valves on the circuit (**inset**) allows more precise control of the heating system.

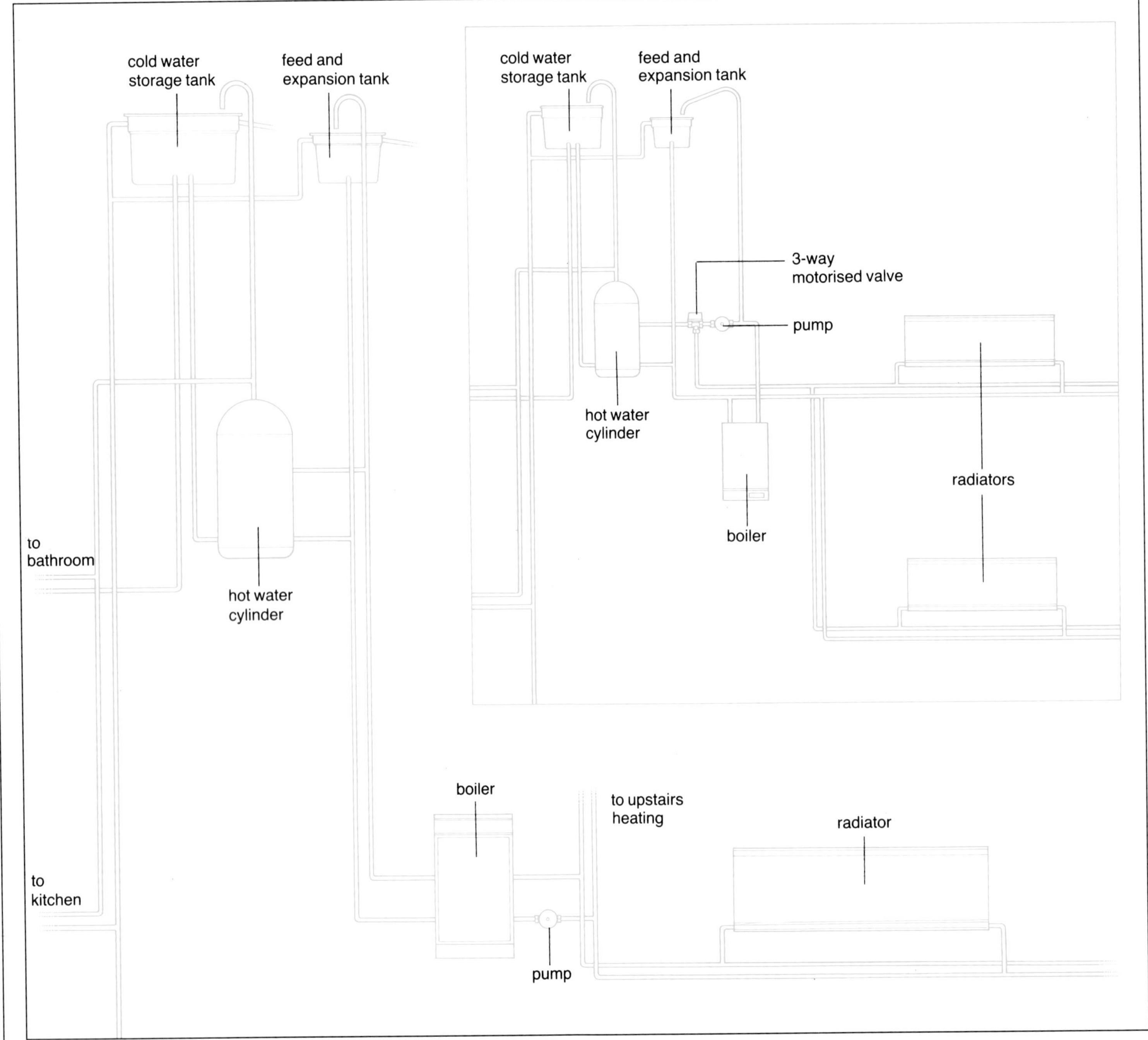

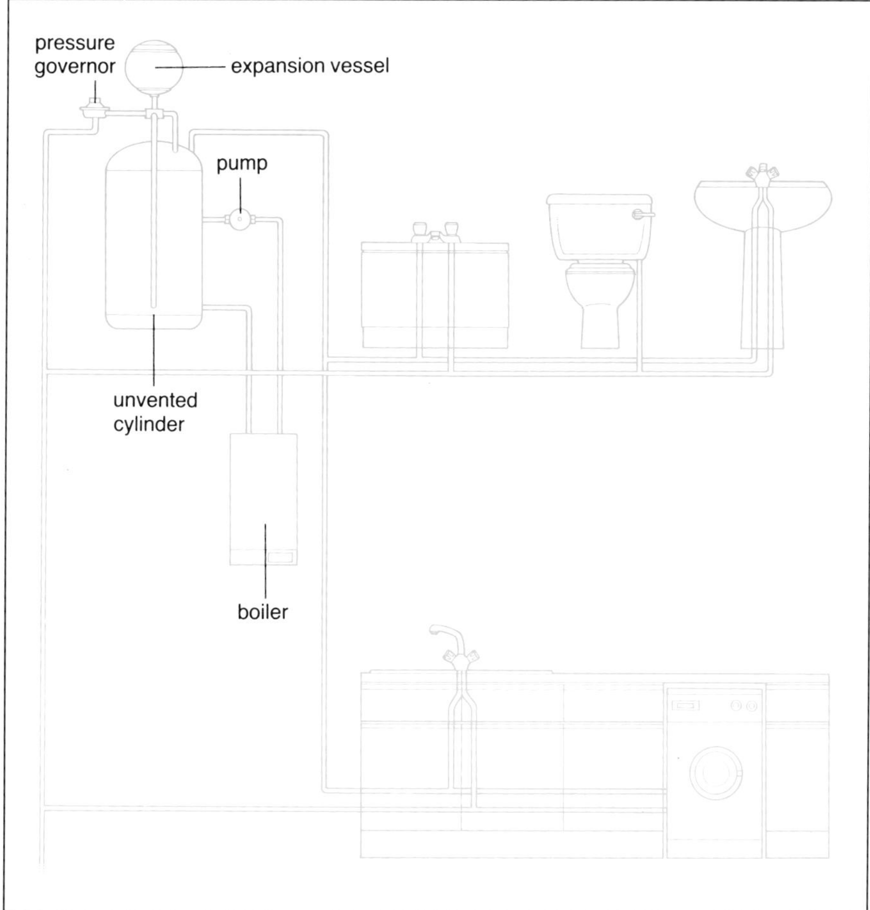

■ Pressurised hot water systems take cold water direct from the mains supply, so eliminating the need for a cold water storage cistern. However, they must be installed by professionals to ensure that they operate completely safely.

One pipe runs from the bottom of the tank to the bottom of the boiler. From the top of the boiler, another pipe runs back up, terminating in a U bend over the top of the tank. In some circuits tappings from these pipes allow water to be circulated through the calorifier in the hot water cylinder. The water flows by convection and gravity through this circuit or is pumped.

Another outlet from the top of the boiler is connected to the radiators, with the return flow entering the bottom of the boiler. At some point in this circuit a pump is fitted to provide the flow of water around the circuit. In the most sophisticated circuits, the hot water is also pumped through the calorifier instead of relying on gravity for its circulation.

There is no way that water can be drawn off the primary circuit, which is completely self-contained. Any small losses due to evaporation are made up from the feed and expansion tank, which is kept topped up by a ball-valve. This means that scale formation in the primary circuit is virtually eliminated. It is normal to add an inhibitor to the water in this circuit to remove scale and fungal build-up.

The domestic hot water cylinder is supplied from a larger cold water storage tank in the loft. From this tank, one pipe feeds all the cold water outlets except the kitchen sink, which is fed direct from the rising main. Another pipe runs to the bottom of the hot water cylinder. In the cylinder, the water surrounds the calorifier and this becomes heated. The calorifier acts as a hot water powered immersion heater.

From the top of the cylinder, a vent pipe runs up to above the cold water storage tank, terminating in a return bend over the tank. From this pipe, just above the cylinder, tappings are made to supply all the domestic hot water outlets in the house.

THE MICROBORE SYSTEM

As the name implies, this system uses very small bore pipes – 6, 8 and 10mm in diameter. The main advantage is the cosmetic effect of the smaller pipes and the ease with which they can be manipulated.

The basic system is similar to the small bore, except that radiators (and sometimes the calorifier) are fed from manifolds, which are linked to the boiler by larger bore pipes. The water is pumped around the circuit at a faster rate than with the small bore system.

ELECTRIC CENTRAL HEATING

There are two types of central heating using electricity as the sole fuel, the more common involving the use of storage radiators.

These are fairly large containers filled with heat-retaining blocks, between which are heating elements. These are normally switched on at night using low-price off-peak electricity. The heat is retained in the radiators by a sophisticated arrangement of shutters and gradually emitted during the day. In very cold conditions, a top-up may be required during the day.

Off-peak electricity is normally available between midnight and eight in the morning and a special metering arrangement is necessary, which must be installed by a competent electrician. One bonus with this arrangement is that you can also set your washing machine, dishwasher, immersion heater and other high wattage appliances to run at night, thus using the cheaper electricity.

The other type of electrical heating comes from the Economy 7 boiler. This was primarily designed to replace an oil-fired installation and comprises a large tank fitted with a number of immersion heaters. As the name implies, this boiler uses cheap off-peak electricity to heat all the water for use in the radiators during the day. A domestic hot water supply is also available from this system.

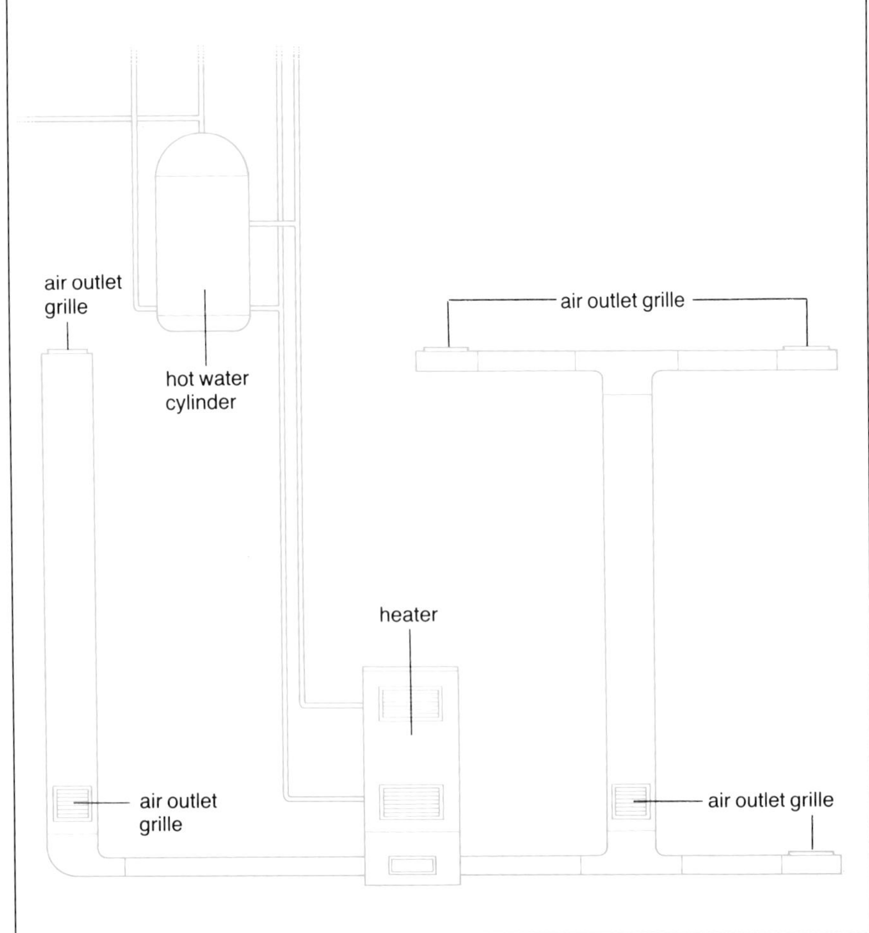

■ Hot air systems deliver warmed air to individual rooms via a network of ducts and outlet grilles, and can often supply domestic hot water too. However, installing them in an existing house can cause major disruption to family life.

TYPES OF BOILER

The traditional method of heating water is through the use of a boiler. There have, over the years, been significant advances in the design and efficiency of boilers – and the way they can be run.

Solid fuel boiler

This is the traditional type of boiler. Modern versions have eliminated much of the hard and dirty work previously associated with this fuel. One essential requirement is ample storage space for the fuel, which must be easily accessible from the road. Another is a safe means of disposing of hot ashes.

The range of solid fuel available will vary from region to region and you will have to check which is suitable for your particular model. There are some dual-purpose fuels you can use both on open fires with back boilers and some enclosed room heaters.

Wood-burning stoves have certainly been gaining in popularity recently and it may well be worth considering one of these, if you have a ready access to large supplies of wood. They can be very efficient both for providing a hot water supply and for supplying radiators.

Room heaters range from open fires with a back boiler to the more recent models, where the fire is contained behind glass doors. This latter type is designed to run a conventional 'wet' central heating system. Their fairly rudimentary controls normally incorporate a damper to control air flow to the fire.

You can also get fully enclosed, stove-enamelled boilers incorporating a hopper feed. Suitable for installation in a kitchen or similar area, they may only require attention once a day. The fuel is automatically fed from a hopper within the boiler casing.

One feature of solid fuel boilers that differs from other types is that they are not instantly controllable. This means finding some way of using up surplus heat. One answer is to install a gravity-fed domestic hot water system including a bathroom towel rail.

With all types of solid fuel boiler, the air necessary for combustion is taken from the room and the fumes have to escape up a flue. It is most important to ensure that adequate ventilation exists and it is obviously more economical if the air used for combustion is not taken from the heated air within the house. Without a proper supply of air, the boiler will not function efficiently.

If you are thinking of installing a solid fuel system, you are strongly recommended to consult your local solid fuel advisory service.

Oil-fired boiler

Oil is commonly used in rural areas where other services such as gas may be restricted. You need a large storage tank installed, which must conform to regulations concerning its siting and spillage arrangements. You may even need planning permission for this. Access from the road for the fuel delivery tanker should be made as easy as possible.

With an oil-fired boiler, a pump forces the finely atomised oil into the combustion chamber where it is fired in a pressure jet burner with the help of air. Because of the various working parts and the high powered flame, such boilers are not totally silent in operation. For this reason, you may want to site yours away from the normal living areas of the home. In most cases an external flue to roof level or internally lined chimney is needed. The burner must be serviced regularly by a qualified engineer, and the oil filter on the supply pipe from the tank should be cleaned from time to time.

All the major oil companies run very good advisory services, if you are thinking of having one of these boilers installed.

■ Central heating boilers can be floor-standing (**above**) or wall-mounted (**below**), and can have either a conventional flue that discharges into a chimney or a balanced flue that passes through the wall behind the appliance.

Gas-fired boiler

Gas is the most common fuel for central heating. Its use is strictly covered by safety regulations and it is illegal to connect any appliance to the gas supply yourself. This has to be done by a qualified gas fitter.

Excluding the combination boiler which is dealt with later, gas boilers fall into three main categories – back boilers fitted behind fires in a conventional fireplace, free-standing boilers and wall-mounted versions.

The gas fire boiler fits into a normal fireplace behind a room heater, which sometimes has a burning log or coal effect. The back boiler is powered by a separate burner and both units can be used and controlled independently. The available range of this type is now limited, since other boilers are becoming more popular.

For installation purposes, the flue must be sound and will probably have to be lined. An approved flue cap must also be fitted. The air for combustion is taken from the room unless it is a balanced-flue type, and you must therefore ensure suitable arrangements are made for adequate ventilation.

The traditional free-standing boiler was normally fitted in the kitchen, where its stove-enamelled surround enabled it to blend in with the surrounding decor. The modern free-standing boiler is normally much slimmer and can therefore fit into any convenient space – for example, in a corner or between kitchen units.

If you are fitting one of these boilers, check whether it will emit any heat into the kitchen, which may eliminate the need for a separate radiator. If a radiator is needed, it is possible to buy a 'kick space' model, which fits in the area below floor cupboard units. An electrically operated fan blows the heat out into the room.

Some of these boilers are fitted with a separate flue up to roof level, although most are now installed with a balanced flue – see below.

It is sometimes more convenient to fit a boiler away from the living accommodation. There are regulations regarding the construction of a separate boiler house and you should not forget to install sufficient insulation to avoid frost damage, should the system not be used at any time during the cold weather.

Wall-mounted boilers are now probably the most common type fitted. They are small and can be sited in any room, as convenience dictates. Most have a balanced flue, which means they are fitted on or close to an exterior wall, with the flue passing through to the outside. The air for combustion is drawn in through one part of the flue and the products of that combustion are exhausted back into the atmosphere via the other.

There are a few points to remember when considering the position for a balanced flue.

- The flue must be at least 300mm (1ft) below a window or air inlet.
- The flue must not be fitted within 300mm of the eaves, within 600mm below a balcony or in re-entrant corners of the building.
- The flue must not be lower than 300mm (1ft) above ground level or closer than 600mm (2ft) to any corner of the house.

■ Modern boiler design has produced a wide range of compact and highly-efficient designs that take up only a fration of the space of their ancestors. Even oil-fired boilers are now quiet enough to install in the kitchen instead of in a garage or outhouse.

- The flue must not be sited within 600mm (2ft) of a facing wall surface, for example in a narrow passageway.
- If the flue is within reach of passers-by, it must be fitted with a special guard to prevent anyone burning themselves on the hot metal.

Because of their small size, many of these boilers contain only a small quantity of water. These must only be used with a fully pumped system. And a special by-pass arrangement is needed to ensure continued water circulation after the domestic and central heating systems have shut down until the boiler has cooled.

All modern gas boilers are fitted with a flame-sensing device that prevents the gas from being supplied to the burner if the flame is extinguished. Most burners are lit by pilot flames, although in some cases this flame is only turned on when the burner is needed.

LPG-fired boiler

Liquid petroleum gas is available as a fuel for central heating systems, where piped gas is not connected. It is worth checking first with your local gas board whether there are plans to install gas mains in your area in the future. The price of the initial LPG installation is considerable and the running costs are higher.

The normal gas supplied is propane, which is available either in cylinders you can exchange yourself (if you are willing to handle these heavy objects) or delivered by tanker to your own permanently installed storage cylinder. The positioning of cylinders is subject to stringent safety regulations and you must check with your local supplier about a suitable location.

Most natural gas boilers can be easily adapted for LPG by a change of jets and pressure regulators. You would be well advised to insist on an economy device that ensures the pilot flame only burns when the main burner is on, thus saving fuel.

Gas combination boiler

Unvented systems are now available that do away with the conventional hot water cylinder and expansion tank. The boiler only ignites when hot water is needed, either for domestic or central heating purposes, and manufacturers claim lower operating costs. The units can often be fitted in an old airing cupboard, thus saving valuable space in the kitchen or elsewhere.

CONTROLLING THE SYSTEM

The type of control system you can install depends on the fuel you have decided to use. Since with solid fuel the heat is not instantly controllable, precise control is more difficult and you must make arrangements to use up the surplus. For this reason, while domestic hot water supply is virtually uncontrolled, central heating can be fitted with any of the fuel types discussed here.

Generally the simpler the device, the easier it is to run. But the degree of precise control over individual rooms and domestic hot water temperatures is limited. Boilers are supplied with their own control system as protection and any further controls that you may wish to fit must be compatible with this.

In any system, there are basically three aspects of control to be considered:

- The times at which the system operates.
- The basic temperature of the water.
- Whether central heating, hot water or both are required at any one time.

Timing is usually controlled by an electrically operated timeswitch. This normally gives a minimum of two periods throughout any 24 hours when the boiler is switched on. Temperature is controlled by the boiler thermostat. This switches the boiler off when the correct level has been reached and back on again when the temperature drops.

The central heating normally only operates when the pump switches on. A simple switch that is on during the winter and off during the summer will provide the basic control needed. As a simple refinement to this, a gate valve can be fitted that allows one part of the central heating system to be switched off – for example, the upstairs circuit – during the cool periods of autumn and spring when you may well want some background heat downstairs.

A system as basic as this has the following limitations:

- No control over the domestic hot water temperature.
- No control over basic room temperatures.
- The temperature of the domestic hot water will probably have to be heated above the danger level (80°C) if the rooms are to be sufficiently warmed, unless skirting radiators are used.
- No variation in basic room temperatures once the installation has been completed.
- The time switch has to be adjusted or over-ridden manually if at certain times you want different heating periods.
- The basic control for the central heating has to be operated manually.

All of these problems can be overcome by using a more sophisticated control system. Versions available are many and varied, so you must check that the one you decide to use is suitable for your own installation.

Timing for the system

For most purposes, the time period options for either the domestic hot water or the central heating offer four alternatives:

1 Off
2 On once a day
3 On twice a day
4 On constantly

In most situations, the domestic hot water will be required when the central heating is on, but you will need a separate control. For example, it may be necessary to run the central heating all day in very cold weather, during weekends or all the time with very young children about. But there is no need to have the domestic hot water heating constantly. Few people take a bath at three in the morning.

Most modern programmers enable a choice to be made as to what is running and also at what times the system switches on or off.

Temperature control

Although the boiler has its own temperature control or thermostat, this only regulates the temperature of the water in the primary circuit. To ensure that the domestic hot water is not so

■ As far as heating controls are concerned, the bare minimum any system needs includes a room thermostat (**right**) and a system programmer (**far right**). The former turns the heating system on and off to maintain a pre-set room temperature, while the latter switches the boiler and pump on and off at pre-set times.

hot that it scalds you, it should be controlled to a maximum of about 60°C.

This is normally achieved by installing a thermostat to the hot water cylinder. It fits outside the cylinder beneath the insulation jacket and is held in place by a special band. On a cylinder with built-in insulation special provision is made for a thermostat. It has a dial which you can adjust to your required temperature.

This thermostat controls a device called a motorised valve and the water feeding the calorifier flows through this. When the temperature is low, it flows through unimpeded. But when the correct temperature is reached, the valve is closed electrically by the thermostat, thus cutting off the calorifier. When someone uses hot water, the temperature in the cylinder is reduced by the cold water flowing in and the thermostat opens the motorised valve again.

Room temperature control

Not all rooms need to be heated to the same temperature. The following is a rough guide to optimum levels of heat:

- Lounge/dining room – 21°C
- Kitchen/bathroom/bedrooms – 18°C
- Hall/landing – 16°C

These temperatures are used in the initial calculations that determine the number and size of radiators fitted when your system is being designed. It will, however, be necessary to have some other form of control.

One of the most common systems uses thermostatic valves fitted to radiators in the rooms where you are likely to want to adjust the temperature from time to time. You should not fit these valves to all radiators, since the situation could arise where all the radiators are shut off at the same time and this could present problems with the flow in the circuit.

These valves can be easily adjusted and react to the temperature of the room, not the water. You can buy a radiator valve with a remote thermostat, which is fixed on the wall some distance away, thus giving an accurate reading of the room temperature.

Another popular method is to install a room thermostat. This is fitted to the wall in an area where you want to keep an optimum average temperature and where there are likely to be major fluctuations in temperatures. You should bear the following points in mind when deciding on its position:

- The room in which it is sited must be heated solely by the central heating system, otherwise another source of heat could effectively switch off the heating in the rest of the house.
- It should be positioned about 1.5m (5ft) up from the floor and away from radiators, wall lights and other forms of heat – or cold, for that matter, such as draught sources.

■ Individual thermostatic radiator valves provide better temperature control in individual rooms than a system with just a room thermostat, since each room can be heated to different temperatures if required. Some have the thermostat mounted on the valve body; others have remote sensors which eliminate the effect of the hot radiator on the valve's operation. The valve replaces the radiator's normal on/off valve.

Most thermostats have a calibrated dial with maximum and minimum settings. But other, more sophisticated models are available. One incorporates a clock and reduced temperature settings. This enables the thermostat to control the boiler to give a variety of temperatures at different times during the day. The device is useful if you are out at work, when a low level of heat is maintained, with the temperature increased when you return home in the evening.

Another type of thermosat is useful since it can automatically switch the heating on if the temperature drops to near freezing level or below, thus preventing possible frost damage. This is particularly sensible if you are spending some days away from the house.

You will see from the above that situations can arise when the domestic and central heating systems are both switched off by the thermostats. This, of course, means that the boiler is also shut off. A drop in temperature in either area causes the boiler to be switched on again, with the motorised valves opening to supply heat where it is required.

One further point to bear in mind when incorporating controls is to be aware of the possibility of one control over-riding another and so can avoid potential loss of heat at a crucial time. For example, if the boiler is programmed to come on at about four in the afternoon but the room thermostat is set very low, the system may well not switch on.

Improving air quality

Good ventilation is essential for the health of both the home and its occupants. Without a steady supply of fresh air, the interior of today's well-insulated homes would soon become stuffy and moisture-laden, concentrating unwanted smells and causing condensation to form. In addition, fuel-burning appliances such as boilers and cookers can burn improperly if starved of oxygen, causing the build-up of fumes.

The best way of providing controlled ventilation within the house is to fit extractor fans in rooms that are major sources of moisture and unwanted smells – in the kitchen, in the bathroom and in any separate toilets. These should be powerful enough to extract 60 litres of air per second in a kitchen, 15 litres per second in a bathroom, and the volume of the room within 20 minutes in separate toilet compartments. In addition, all rooms in the house should have some means of background ventilation to the outside air, to allow fresh air from outside the house to be drawn in to replace that extracted mechanically. In modern homes this ventilation is usually provided by so-called trickle ventilators let into the tops of window frames; air bricks in external walls do the same job in older homes. Each habitable room should have ventilators or airbricks with a total open ventilation area of 4000sq mm to satisfy the requirement of the current Building Regulations.

Extractor fans (above right) come in a variety of shapes and sizes, and can be installed in windows, walls or ceilings. Ducting can be used to take the extracted air to the outside where necessary.

Portable air conditioners (above) are the perfect solution to the problem of overheating in hot weather. The air in the room is drawn in over a refrigeration coil within the unit, and is then blown back into the room. At the same time as cooling the air, the unit removes moisture from it, so helping to reduce humidity levels and improving comfort. Small units of this sort simply plug into an ordinary socket outlet; more sophisticated units which can also act as heat pumps in cold weather are built in and separately wired up.

A humidifier (left) does just what its name implies, releasing controlled amounts of water vapour into the room where it is sited to counteract the dry-air effect created by many central heating systems, which can affect people with chest problems.

Insulating the Home

When you insulate your home you are effectively slowing down the rate at which heat escapes through different areas – the roof, walls, windows and floors. The longer you can keep any heat inside, the less fuel you will need to use up to keep all the rooms within the house at a comfortable temperature.

This in turn will mean lower energy bills and the money you save will soon cover the cost of the insulation materials used. When this has been recovered, which could be in less than three years in some cases, you can start counting the savings. Remember, too that you may be eligible for a grant towards the cost. So make the necessary enquiries about this with your local authority before you insulate.

From the typical semi-detached house illustrated here, you can get a good picture of where the heat escapes. This is, of course, just an example; the actual figures will be affected by a variety of factors.

The location of the house and its architecture, for example, can alter the heat loss figures – and therefore your insulation priorities. Anyone living in a country cottage with just a few small windows would see double glazing as being of less importance than the owner of a modern, fully glazed house with large picture windows. While a detached house will lose more than a semi through its external walls, with a bungalow the major area for concern will be the roof.

There are various ways in which the different parts of any house can be insulated. But in all cases, most of the jobs involved can be handled successfully by the competent homeowner.

THE LOFT

There are two DIY ways to insulate the loft. You can use rolls (of mineral wool or glass fibre) or loosefill material (vermiculite, a lightweight expanded mineral, or polystyrene granules) sold in bags. Though the two methods are comparable in terms of cost and efficiency, glass fibre blanket is the more popular.

You can also have loosefill insulation, usually mineral wool or fireproofed cellulose fibres, blown into the loft by specialist contractors.

Blanket materials are generally easier to handle than loosefill types, unless your loft contains a lot of obstructions or has irregular joist spacings. The rolls are normally 400mm

■ **Above** Insulation materials for walls include foam or chopped fibre which is blown into cavity walls – a job solely for professional installers. Alternatively the inner face of cold exterior walls can be lined with insulating plasterboard, or with ordinary board over a layer of insulation batts or rigid polystyrene.

■ **Left** For insulating lofts, blanket-type glass fibre or mineral-wool blankets are the most widely-used materials, but loose-fill materials such as expanded vermiculite are useful in lofts full of obstructions.

■ **Opposite** Pipe bandage or slip-on sleeving is ideal for insulating frost-prone pipework (top), while proprietary jackets are available for hot cylinders and cold tanks (right).

(16in) wide to match the standard joist spacing and common thicknesses are 100mm (4in) and 150mm (6in). Choose the former if there is already some insulation and simply lay it on top of the existing material. If there is none at all, then you should use the thicker blanket.

It is worth checking the thickness of any existing insulation if you move to another house. If it has been built in the mid-sixties, it could well have an inadequate layer, since 25mm (1in) was the thickness stipulated by the Building Regulations at that time. It is also worth remembering that over a period of years blanket insulation can naturally compress and shrink in thickness.

Apart from being awkward to handle, loosefill materials have another drawback. To be as effective as the blanket type, they need to be laid to a greater depth – at least an extra 25mm (1in). There are not, however, many ceiling joists deeper than about 150mm (6in), so there is nothing to contain the top of the insulation unless you are prepared to fix battens along the top of each joist. So before you commit yourself to using this type, it is advisable to check the size of joists in your loft.

Many people find that insulation materials irritate their skin, while loose fibres and the ever-present dust in the loft can also be a problem. So it is advisable to wear gloves and a face mask when laying any insulation there.

Ventilation is essential in any loft to prevent condensation forming in the winter months and causing rot in the roof timbers, as well as dampening the insulation and thus making it ineffective. This means providing extra ventilation openings at the eaves by drilling holes in the soffit boards or by installing additional airbricks in gable walls. Never pack the eaves with insulation, since this will tend to cut off the airflow. Special eaves vents are available which fit between the joists and prevent the insulation material from restricting the flow of air. In an unboarded roof, the gaps between the tiles will usually ensure sufficient ventilation.

One area that should not be insulated is the loft floor below the cold water tank. Any warmth rising from the room underneath will be beneficial in helping to prevent winter freeze-ups. But you must insulate the top of the trap door into the loft.

Thorough insulation makes it even more vital to lag all the plumbing pipes and the cold water tank, since the loft is going to be even colder in winter. The pipes can be wrapped in glass fibre bandage or moulded foam tubes. Moulded foam tubes have a slit along one side, which enables you to push them over the pipes. You then tape

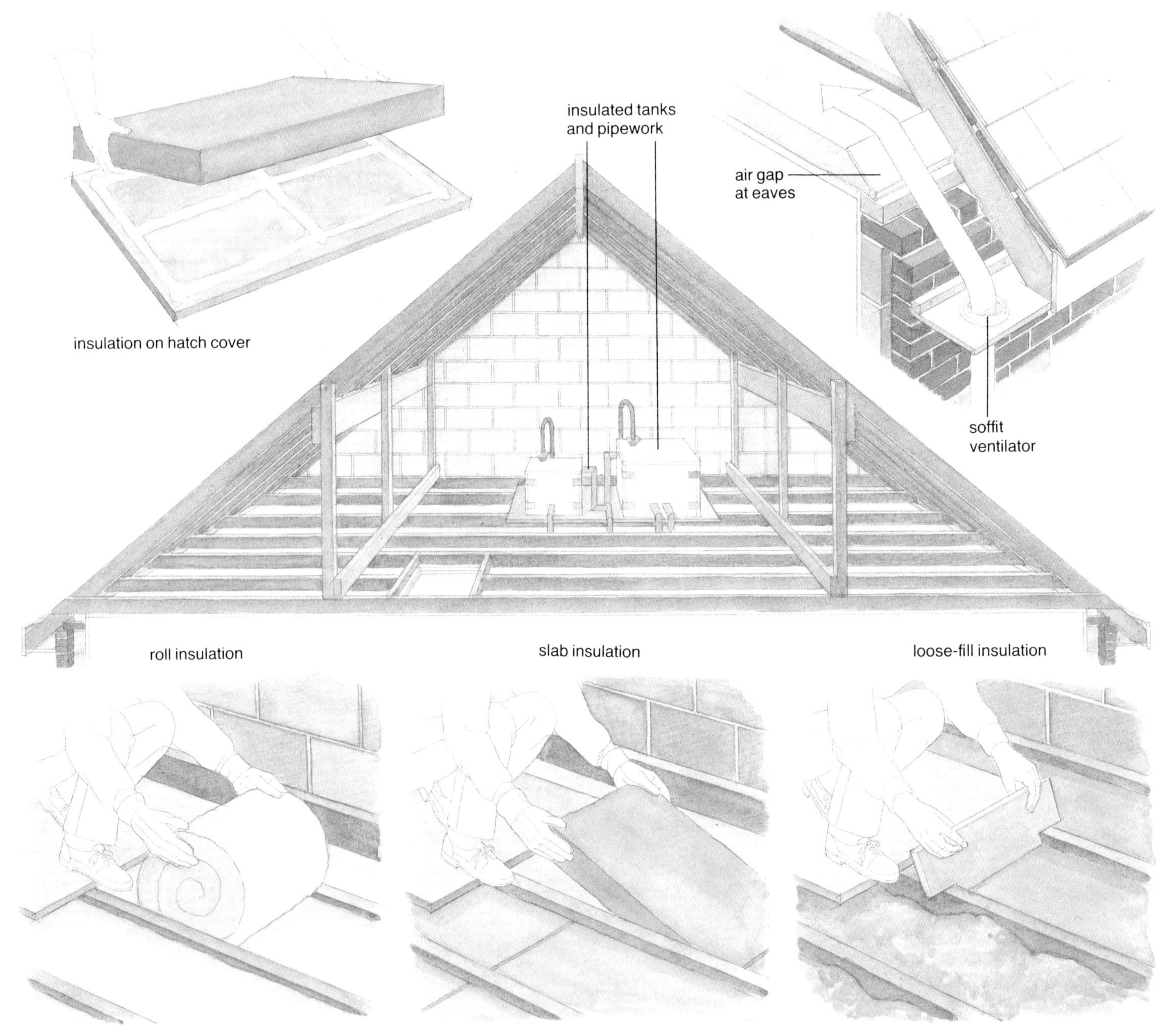

them to keep the insulation securely in place. Pay special attention to bends, making sure you do not leave any pipes exposed.

The tank can be wrapped in a purpose-made insulating jacket or glass fibre. Equally, it can be boxed in with 25mm (1in) thick slabs of polystyrene. The tank must have a 'lid' on it to prevent the possibility of the water freezing and to ensure that spiders, birds and any other creatures that have found their way into the loft do not drop into the water and contaminate it.

While on the subject of plumbing, do not forget the hot water cylinder – probably situated in the airing cupboard. A purpose-made insulating jacket is by far the best to use and you will recover its cost in a couple of months – just one indication of what an uninsulated cylinder will cost you!

THE RAFTERS

If you use the loft as an organised storage area, possibly as a hobby room or play area, then you must insulate between the rafters to keep the area reasonably warm in winter. There are two basic ways in which this can be done.

The simplest method is to use a waterproof or foil-backed building paper. This will check

■ Loft floors can be insulated by laying glass fibre blankets or semi-rigid insulation batts between the ceiling joists, or by spreading a loose-fill insulating material such as vermiculite to a uniform depth. Remember to insulate above the loft hatch, to leave clearance at the eaves for ventilation via soffit vents, and to insulate any water tanks and pipes in the loft space. Leave the ceiling beneath the water tanks uninsulated.

any draughts and rain from being blown in through the gaps between the tiles or slates. The foil-backed type reflects heat and provides a far better standard of insulation than the basic waterproof paper.

The paper is stapled to the rafters in horizontal strips. Always work down from the ridge to the eaves, overlapping each layer by a couple of inches. Remember the foil must always face inwards.

Before you fix the last strip above the eaves, tuck a layer of building paper into the eaves between each pair of joists. This will ensure that any rainwater running down the paper will drain away into the eaves. Make sure you do not block this area completely and cut off the ventilation. Staples can tear the paper and any wind blowing through the roof may extend the damage over a period of time. Therefore it is a good idea to reinforce the fixing points by firing the staple through a square of card at each fixing point.

An alternative method is to fix a proper 'ceiling' direct to the rafters using sheets of plasterboard, although this will, of course, be more expensive. First fix strips of waterproof paper, foil-backed paper or roofing felt between the rafters, followed by insulation blanket. To secure the edge of the paper or felt, use thin battens and pin through the material into the sides of the rafters. Leave an air gap of about 50mm (2in) up to the tiling battens. Finally attach the panels of plasterboard or fibre insulating board to the rafters with nails to complete the job.

FLAT ROOFS

If you are having a flat-roofed extension built, then insulating the roof is easily done at the building stage. Existing flat roofs pose more of a problem since it is not easy to get at the voids above the ceiling.

It is possible to add secondary roofing above the existing one and sandwich insulation between the two. But this is a very expensive solution and not likely to be cost-effective for many years – if ever. Should the existing roof be in need of replacement, however, then this method might be a possibility.

The term used for the construction of this type of roof insulation is 'warm decking'. The existing roof is insulated and a waterproof surface added on top. This comprises composite insulation boards with a bonded layer of roofing felt. The boards are laid on the surface

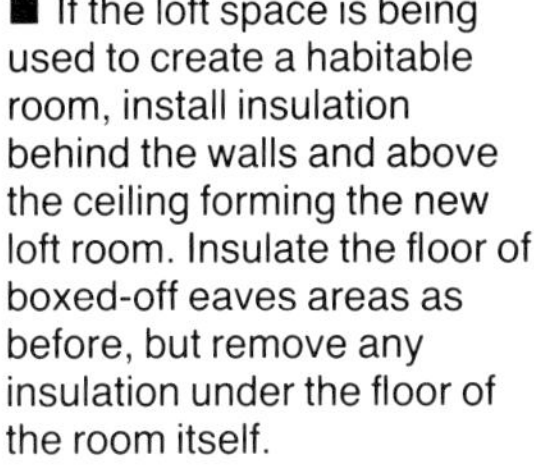

■ If the loft space is being used to create a habitable room, install insulation behind the walls and above the ceiling forming the new loft room. Insulate the floor of boxed-off eaves areas as before, but remove any insulation under the floor of the room itself.

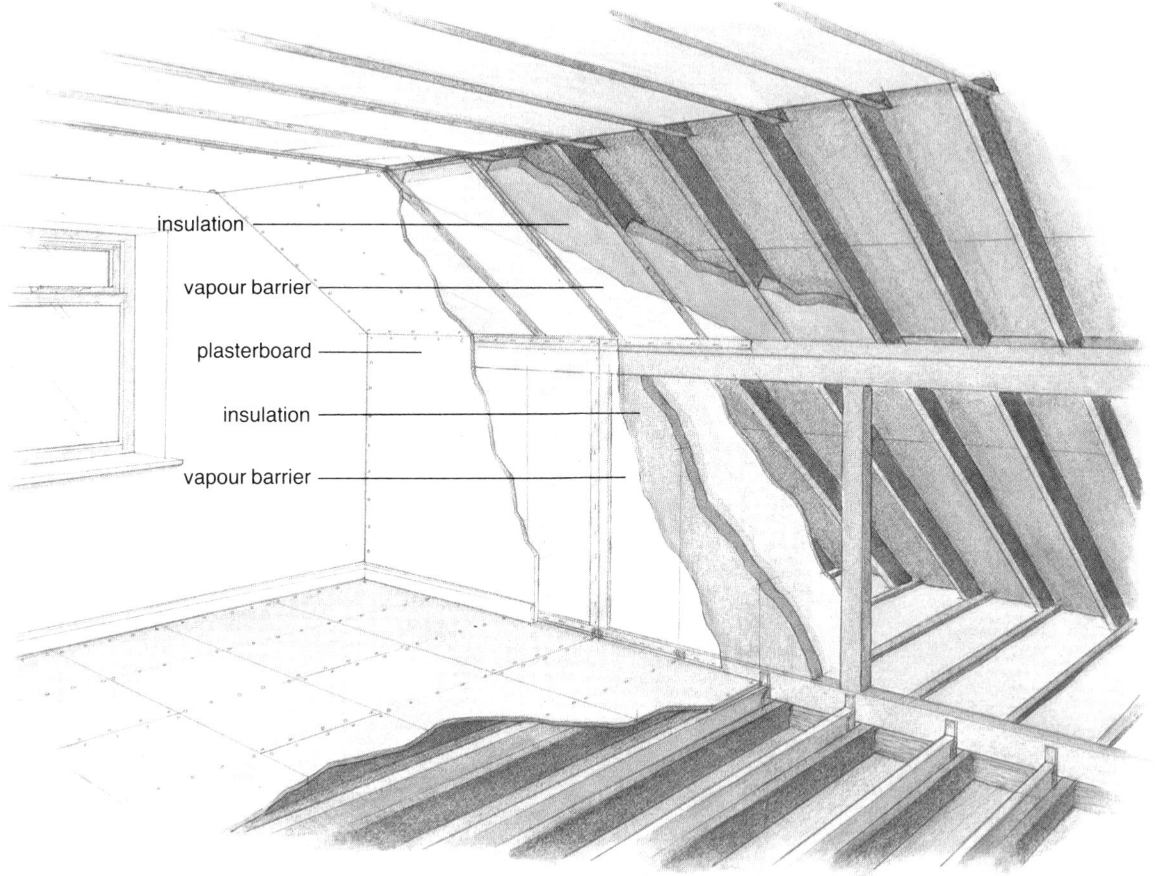

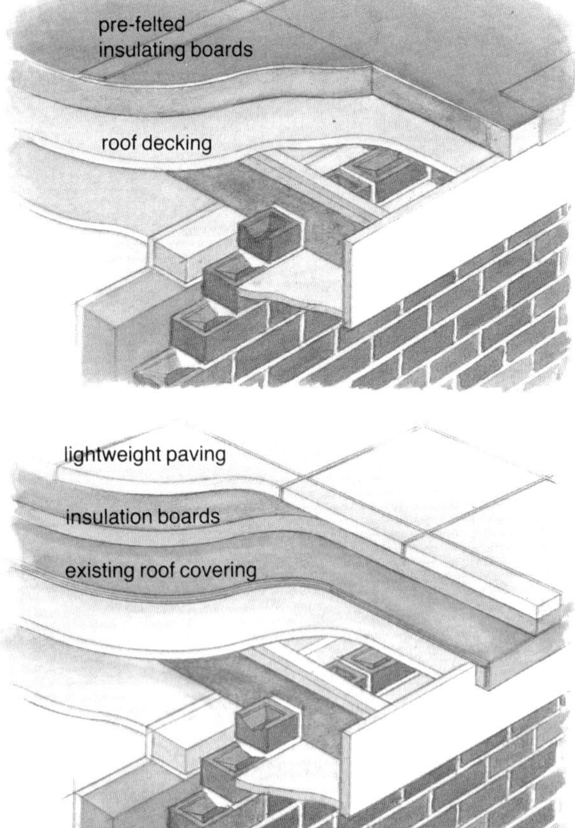

■ **Far left** If a flat roof surface is in poor condition, add insulation above the roof decking by using pre-felted insulation boards, finished with an additional layer of roofing felt.

■ **Left** If the fascia boards can be removed, slide pre-cut rigid polystyrene insulation boards into the voids between the joists.

■ **Far left** If the roof decking is in good condition, simply lay insulation slabs over it, topped with lightweight paving slabs.

■ **Left** Alternatively, add insulation below the existing ceiling and cover it with a vapour barrier and a new plasterboard ceiling.

and bonded into position. Further layers of felt are then put on to complete the covering.

Other methods should be tackled from inside the house. Taking down an existing ceiling is a fairly clean exercise if it is a modern plasterboard type, but quite a dirty job if you have to knock down a lath and plaster construction.

Polystyrene slabs or insulation blanket are fitted between the roof joists and a layer of polythene stapled to the joists. The polythene prevents condensation forming in the roof void and damaging the insulation. It also serves as a vapour barrier to moisture created in the room below which, in the case of a kitchen or bathroom, could be considerable. You can then fix a new plasterboard ceiling to the joists.

You must ensure that the roof space remains well ventilated, otherwise the roof timbers could become moist and start to rot. Allow for a 50mm (2in) gap between the top of the insulation and the underside of the roof and drill ventilation holes on both sides of the roof so that there is a continuous cross-flow of air.

An alternative method involves adding a ceiling to the interior surface, while sandwiching insulation material in between the old and new ceilings.

First you need to nail a framework of battens about 100mm (4in) below the existing ceiling. Then add insulation blanket or polystyrene slabs between the two surfaces, followed by a polythene vapour barrier and a layer of plasterboard. Alternatively, you can nail sheets of thermal plasterboard directly to the ceiling. This plasterboard incorporates a vapour barrier and a layer of rigid foam insulation.

Another option is to fix a new tongued and grooved cladding ceiling and fill the cavity above with polystyrene slabs or insulation blanket. Since wood itself has excellent insulation properties, this is a particularly effective method.

Finally, you can use a proprietary suspended ceiling comprising a framework of metal channels supporting tile panels.

THE WALLS

If your house has cavity walls, then the simplest method of insulation is to have the cavity filled. The process, which is covered in the section on external walls, is not a DIY job and should be tackled by a specialist company.

Houses with solid walls can be insulated externally (see External Walls), but more often the job is done from the inside of the house. There are various methods and the one to

■ A cheaper alternative to external wall insulation (page 76) is to add insulation on the inside of exterior walls. Either line the walls with battens and add insulation and a vapour barrier before nailing up new plasterboard, or fix insulating plasterboard direct to the wall surface.

choose depends on whether you want to retain the impression of a solid wall or prefer a decorative finish of cladding or panelling.

If the wall to be insulated has no switches, doors or windows, then the job is very straightforward. However, where these obstacles exist, then the work is much more tricky. Switches and sockets will have to be repositioned on the new wall surface and architraves and skirting removed and refixed. You will also have to cut round window and door frames.

There are several types of plasterboard you can use, but two in particular are relevant here. The one you choose will probably be determined by the type of wall being insulated.

If the wall is flat, you can use vapour-check thermal board and stick it directly to the surface with a special adhesive and secondary nail fixing. Thermal board is a standard plasterboard bonded to a backing of expanded polystyrene with a polythene film sandwiched in between.

Where the wall is uneven, you will have to put up a framework of battens to provide a level surface on which you can then fix standard (general-purpose) plasterboard. This has an ivory coloured side over which you can paint or paper directly.

All plasterboards are supplied in standard sheets measuring 2400 × 1200mm (8 × 4ft), although both 1800mm (6ft) and 2700 (9ft) lengths are available. Such board is popularly used in 9.5mm (3/8in) and 12.7mm (1/2in) thicknesses. Vapour-check insulated plasterboard comes in many sizes, with 25mm and 32mm (1in and 1 1/4in) thicknesses the commonest.

Plasterboard can be cut quite easily using either a fine-tooth tenon saw or a sharp knife, which is more convenient and less messy. Holes and other cut-outs, to accept light switches and sockets, for example, can easily be made with a pad saw or power jig-saw.

When working with plasterboard, bear in mind that it is very cumbersome and awkward to handle and you should have two people to carry it. To position it accurately on the wall against the ceiling you will have to make a 'foot-lifting' device, which you can cut from a block of wood.

Having lined the walls, you then have to replace the skirting boards and reposition any sockets and switches. Your new wall is then ready for decorating.

Using panelling

Another method of insulating walls is to panel them. You can use tongued and grooved boards or large decorative hardboard panels. Either material is quite straightforward to fix and has

the dual function of being decorative as well.

Cladding is available as either V-jointed boards in knotty pine or cedar or as pine shiplap. The boards are fixed to 38 x 25mm (1 ½ × 1in) sawn softwood battens, which are fixed 400–500mm (16–20in) centres for 9mm thick boards and 500–600mm (20–24in) centres for 12mm thick board. They can be fixed horizontally or vertically.

You must allow for a slight gap behind the boards to enable air to circulate. This will be achieved automatically where the battens are fixed vertically. With horizontal fixing, use packing pieces behind the battens. Then add insulation material between the battens.

The boards can be fixed by nailing through the faces and punching the heads below the surface. Make sure you fill the holes afterwards. An alternative is to use very thin 'lost head' nails through the tongues at an angle so that they are covered by the next board. The other option is to use special metal clips. Tap the boards firmly together as you fix them, using a wooden block between the edge and the hammer head as protection.

To finish off at ceiling level, fix quadrant moulding to conceal the sawn board edges, remembering to leave a small air gap. At the bottom, you can either leave a small gap as well or fit a new skirting board.

To fit decorative panels, you need vertical battens to provide a fixing for each edge, plus horizontal battens at 400mm (16in) intervals. If the corners are out of true, leave a small gap so that the board is positioned horizontally. You can cover this later with a piece of moulding. Again leave a small gap at the bottom for possible expansion and cover this with skirting board.

After fixing insulation between the battens, you can secure the panels either with pins (punched below the surface with holes filled) or with adhesive. Pins are really only suitable for boards with vertical grooves that resemble planking, since they can then be easily concealed within the grooves.

Where you are using wall panel adhesive, apply a generous layer to the battens and press the boards firmly in place. If a wall is perfectly flat, you can fix the panels directly to the wall surface with panel adhesive.

USING CORK TILES

Cork tiles offer a reasonable measure of insulation, but are really intended to reduce condensation on cold walls. The thicker the tile is, the better the insulation provided will be. The surface must be smooth, flat and dry and you should fix the tiles with either a contact adhesive or special cork wall tile adhesive.

Establish a horizontal line to serve as a starting point, spread enough adhesive on the wall to cover the area of one tile, then press the tile firmly in position. Butt up successive tiles closely and continue right up to the edges. Where necessary, cut tiles with a sharp knife to complete the borders and corners.

INSULATING FLOORS

A solid floor does not normally have to be insulated, since a straightforward floorcovering is sufficient to keep it warm underfoot. A timber floor, however, is a quite different matter, since it is essential that some air flows constantly beneath it to keep the joists and boards free from damp. Airbricks in the house wall are there to ensure ventilation from the outside, so never cover these over or you will be inviting trouble from rot in the floor.

Tongued and grooved floorboards are rarely draughty – apart, possibly, from at the edges below the skirting, where there is often a gap. Unless there has been acute movement caused through shrinkage, the tongues should remain in the grooves to create an effective barrier.

With square-edged boards, however, there will almost certainly be gaps at some point. If you find only the occasional one, then the simplest solution is just to plug it. This can be done by injecting a bead of flexible mastic sealant along the gap. The mastic never sets and so is able to expand and contract with any slight seasonal movement of the boards. The alternative, with larger gaps, is to fill them with wedge-shaped pieces of wood.

If you discover gaps all over the floor, you can take up the boards and relay them, butting them tightly together again (see Flooring). The problem would, however, have to be extreme to go to this trouble. Most people would settle for the simpler option of covering the complete floor with sheets of hardboard. You will have to do this anyway if you are putting a flexible covering such as vinyl or cork on the floor.

Standard hardboard is 3.2mm (⅛in) thick and ideal for living rooms and general areas. In kitchens and bathrooms it is better to use oil-tempered boards to cope with the higher moisture levels in those rooms.

The boards must be properly conditioned before you lay them so that they do not react adversely to the atmosphere of the room and possibly warp later on. To condition them, moisten the textured side with about 500ml (or

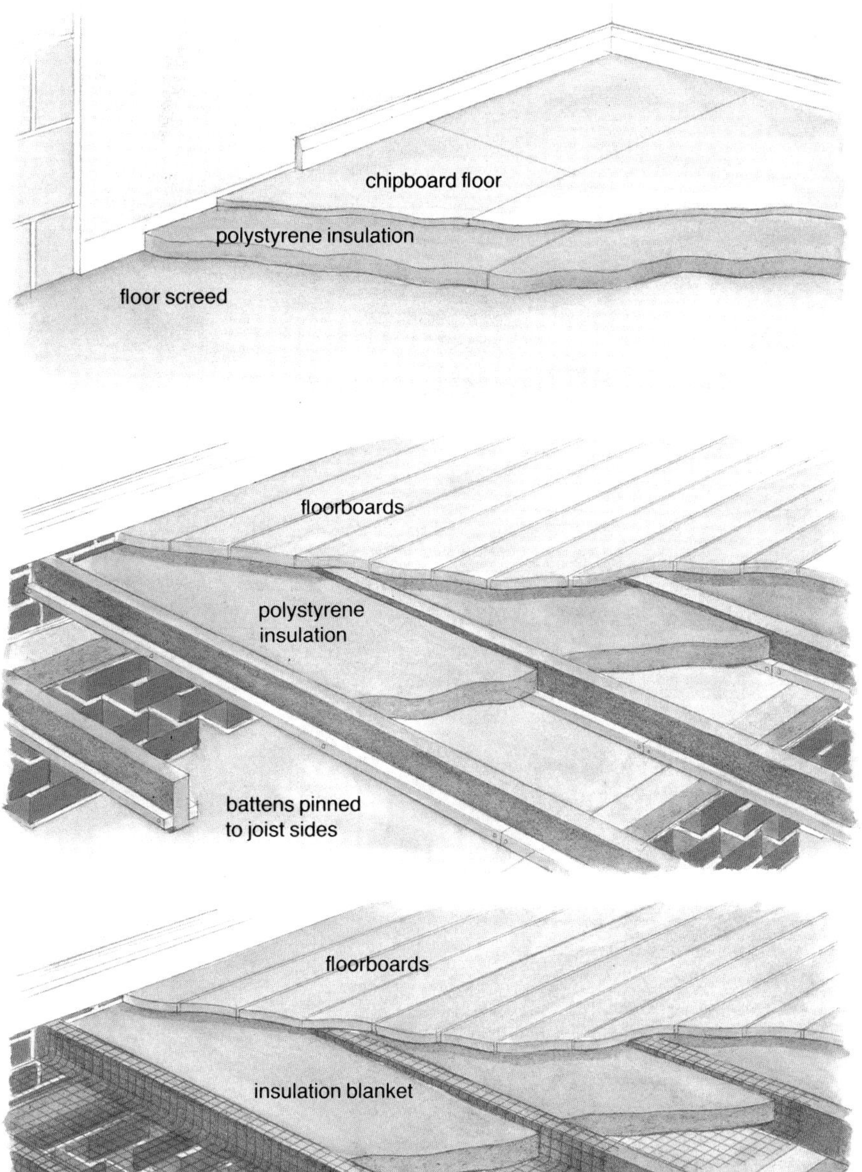

■ **Top** Insulate solid concrete floors by laying expanded polystyrene over them, followed by a new chipboard floor surface.

■ **Centre** Insulate beneath suspended timber floors either by supporting expanded polystyrene on battens pinned to the joist sides, or by stapling garden netting to the joists to support blanket insulation between them.

1 pint) of water per board. This can be sponged or sprayed on. Then stack the boards on edge for 48 hours. Use small blocks of wood to keep each board separate.

Which way up – either textured or smooth side – you lay the boards will be determined by the floorcovering you are intending to use. With carpets it does not matter. But for cork, vinyl or wood it does and you should first consult the manufacturer's instructions. Generally speaking, if an adhesive is to be used, then the textured side will provide better grip. If self-adhesive tiles are being laid, then the smooth side is the better choice.

When laying boards, you should stagger the joints between each, rather like laying a course of bricks. Cut them in half to make 1200mm (4ft) squares and start laying them against the longest wall in the room, cutting smaller pieces as necessary to complete each row.

Sealing the skirting

Although any gaps below the skirting boards can also be sealed with a flexible mastic, it is usually better to fix wood moulding. This should be pinned to the skirting, not the floor, so that the boards can still move naturally.

Insulating under floors

In extreme cases such as in a very severe climate or where the room is over a garage and therefore particularly cold, you may have to take more severe measures.

If there is enough space under a suspended timber floor to crawl into, it is quite easy to fix insulation between the joists under the floorboards. You can use rigid polystyrene, cutting it into strips and resting it on nails driven into the sides of the joists. Alternatively, you can suspend lengths of insulation blanket between the joists using garden netting stapled to the joists as support. If there is only a narrow space under the floor, you will have to lift all the floorboards first. This will inevitably cause a lot more disruption within the room concerned.

This method is the best way of insulating rooms above cold, ground-floor areas such as integral garages.

Insulating concrete floors

With concrete floors, to add insulation you will have to raise the existing floor level significantly. The work involves laying 50mm (2in) thick rigid polystyrene boards over the concrete and then putting down sheets of flooring grade chipboard or a fine concrete screed on top. The effect will be to raise the floor level in the room by about 70mm (2¾in).

Obviously here you will have to strip the room completely, repositioning skirting boards (which will anchor the new floor surface in place), trimming the bottom of the doors and adding a sloping filler strip at the thresholds – unless, of course, you are treating adjacent rooms in a similar way.

Reducing draughts

A house that has not been draughtproofed can never be kept really warm and comfortable. And there is nothing more unpleasant than icy cold draughts whistling around you on a cold winter's night.

Although such work can be time-consuming, it is not expensive. In fact, under normal circumstances you can look forward to recovering the cost of adding full draughtproofing to a house within three years.

Plan any work sensibly, since there are circumstances in which it is not advisable to eliminate all draughts completely. In kitchens and bathrooms, for example, you will want to seal off major draughts, but should leave minor ones to help ventilate the area and combat condensation. And you must remember that a boiler in the kitchen needs some ventilation for it to operate safely and efficiently.

Fuel-burning appliances need ventilation, so you should consult your fuel supplier for advice before applying any draughtproofing in areas where these are sited.

In rooms that are heated by electricity or central heating radiators, it is still advisable to leave the odd window untreated, since the normally small amount of draught from this will ensure that the room does not become stuffy.

When you are working out what draughtproofing materials you need, doors and windows should be top of the list. But do not forget other areas such as letterboxes, keyholes and, of course, those major culprits like floors and any disused chimney flues.

For window and door frames, you will find there is a variety of different materials to choose from, the simplest and cheapest being self-adhesive foam and brush strips. Supplied in rolls, they are simply stuck to the appropriate place on the frame so that the door or window closes against them.

Other, more expensive devices include V-shaped lengths of plastic, phosphor bronze or aluminium, which are pinned to the frame. The door or window then compresses the V shape when shut, sealing out any draughts.

For the bottom of doors you also have several options. All are simple and quick to fit, although some are more sophisticated and effective than others.

The basic type is a strip of wood, metal or plastic housing a rubber, brush or plastic insert that grazes along the floorcovering when the door is closed to form a sound seal. You just cut it to length and pin or screw it to the door. If you have the type with pre-drilled screw holes, you should trim where necessary from both ends to ensure the remaining holes are evenly spaced. You can, of course, drill new holes in the strip if you have to.

There is also a rise-and-fall excluder, which will lift above the floorcovering as the door opens and then fall back into place when the door is closed. Another type comes in two parts, one fitting to the bottom of the door and the other to the threshold. The two parts interlock when you close the door.

■ Draughtproof sliding sash windows by pinning on proprietary excluders down the edges and across the meeting rail. Check that the window still slides freely.

■ Use self-adhesive foam excluders to draughtproof casement windows and doors, sticking the strips into the rebates so they are fully compressed when the window or door is closed.

On the front door, make sure you fit a letterbox flap and keyhole cover. Newspapers left in the flap can let in quite a draught, but you can overcome this problem by fitting a special excluder. This comprises a plastic frame housing brushes, which will mould themselves around any shape pushed through them.

Sealing fireplaces

A disused fireplace can be a source of considerable draught and heat loss from the room. If you want to retain the appearance of an open fireplace, the simplest method is to push some glass fibre blanket up into the throat of the flue, leaving a small air space so that it remains ventilated. Remember, of course, to remove this if you ever decide to use the fire.

A more permanent solution is to seal the chimney stack outside by removing the pots and replacing them with paving slabs. If you do this, you will have to incorporate a couple of airbricks in the top of the stack to provide ventilation.

Inside the house, you can of course block off the fireplace opening with plywood, bricks or breeze blocks. Again, allow for ventilation by incorporating a ventilator; one about 100 × 50mm (4 × 2in) should be sufficient.

FITTING DOUBLE GLAZING

Exactly how much heat double glazing will save is debatable; much depends on the number and size of the windows in the house. It is generally estimated that about 10–15 per cent of heat goes out through the windows of the average house and that this can be halved with an efficient, well-installed system.

Double glazing is not a short-term investment. Its initial cost will take many years to recover. However, it will make the house much more comfortable by reducing draughts and cold areas around the windows.

Whereas most people install a system to reduce heat loss, in some cases insulation against unwanted outside noise is the main objective. For thermal insulation, an optimum gap of 18mm (¾in) is needed between the two panes of glass, whereas for good sound insulation the gap should be about 100mm (4in).

Where the combined benefits of thermal and sound insulation are required, it is better to concentrate on the noise aspect. The slight reduction in thermal efficiency that results from increasing the gap between the panes of glass to improve the sound insulation is not likely to be noticed in terms of overall comfort.

Buying double glazing

There are two ways to obtain double glazing. The most costly is to get a specialist company to install hermetically sealed units – generally the most efficient. Installation involves taking out the existing window frames and installing new ones. The outside appearance of the property will consequently be altered – slightly or drastically, depending on the type of replacement window frames you choose.

The second, much cheaper method is to fit secondary glazing, which is available as a DIY kit. The advantage here is that the existing windows remain in place so that the outside appearance of the house is unaltered. This type is fixed on the inside, either to the existing window frames or to the surrounding walls of the window reveal.

■ Secondary double glazing consists of panes of glass fixed on the inside of the existing window to create a barrier of still, insulating air between the two panes. The secondary glazing may be fixed, hinged or sliding; avoid fixed panes in rooms where the window may have to be used as an emergency escape route.

The simplest and cheapest DIY system uses a clear, durable sheet of film, which you can fix in minutes. Cut the film to the overall size of the window, with an allowance of 50mm (2in) all round. Then fix double-sided adhesive tape or PVC strip around the frame and secure the film to this around the edges. Finally heat the film with a hair-dryer to remove all the wrinkles, leaving a perfectly smooth surface. Trim off any excess film with a sharp knife.

A slightly more sophisticated type involves a magnetic system that uses clear rigid plastic instead of glass, but still requires no clips, screws or other similar fixings. You cut the plastic sheet to the size of the window frame and then fix steel strip, which comes in rolls, around the outside of the frame. Apply the matching magnetic strip around the perimeter of the plastic sheet and position this so that the two strips meet. The magnetism will hold the glazing in place.

Conventional double glazing kits are similar in principle and vary only in detail. A framework of PVC or aluminium accepts the glass and this assembly is then fixed either direct to the existing window frame or to the walls of the windows reveal. The glazing panels can be fixed, hinged or sliding. Hinged or sliding panels will give access to any windows you may want to open, whether side or top hung.

You will have to buy the glass separately, since this is not supplied with the kit. The correct thickness – either 3 or 4mm – will be specified by the manufacturer in its literature. Details for measuring the overall dimensions of the glass required will also be given and you must follow these instructions very carefully.

With some kits, ordering the right units can prove quite a headache. It is best to study the various manufacturers' leaflets first and then make your shopping list. Measure the windows accurately and then refer to the literature to establish exactly what you need.

Often you will find horizontal channels come in one pack and the vertical ones in another, with all the fittings in a third. It gets more complicated with sliding units, where an additional frame pack is supplied.

In terms of materials, the choice is between PVC and aluminium frames. Since both perform equally well, your decision is likely to be purely an aesthetic one.

■ Sealed-unit double glazing is factory-made to the size required, and consists of two parallel panes of glass sealed together round their edges to trap a layer of inert gas between the panes. The glass can be clear, coloured, patterned or given the appearance of leaded lights by placing lead strips on the inner face of one pane.

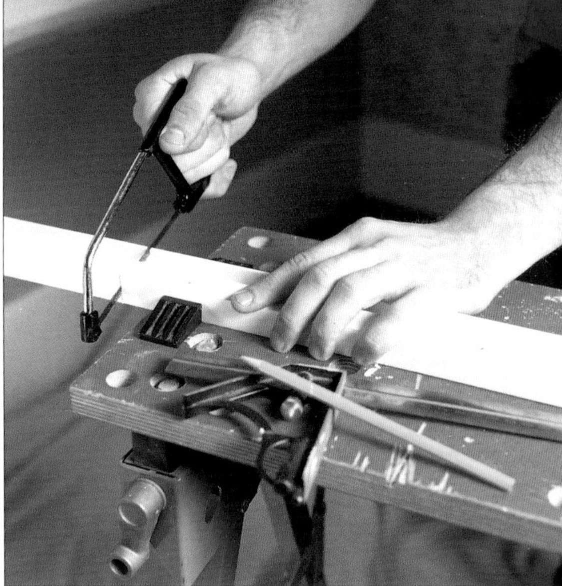

Assembling & fitting

There is generally no problem in fixing the double glazing frames to an existing timber-framed window; metal frames, however, are more awkward. If the system you chose is suitable for fixing to metal, then you will need either self-tapping screws or you will have to install a secondary timber frame around the window on which to mount the system.

It is a relatively straightforward job mounting the double glazing directly on to the window frame. Fixing it into the window reveal, where necessary, can be quite difficult, since rarely will a reveal be exactly square. But it is essential to ensure your secondary frame is perfectly square if the panels are to slide, hinge or close properly.

Check the existing handles and stays. If they project too far, they will prevent you fitting your system to the window frame. If you do not want to fix the glazing to the window reveal, then you will have to change them.

The different systems are all assembled and fitted in a similar way. Bear in mind, however, that if you want a hinged system, you will need to construct a timber framework on which to mount the secondary glazing and then hang the whole assembly on brackets fixed to the window frame.

Provided both the existing window frame and the double glazing you have put up are both well sealed, the problem of condensation between the two layers of glass can largely be avoided. A point worth noting is that it is advisable to install your system on a day when the air in the room is cold and dry. If damp air is trapped inside the cavity, inter-pane misting will be a constant problem in the future.

■ **Far left** Start fitting sliding secondary glazing by cutting the side tracks to length. Then screw the side, top and bottom tracks to the frame or reveal (**left** and **below left**). Next, measure and cut to length the channels that frame the glass (**right**), and fit them to the panes (**bottom left**). Finally, lift the panes into the tracks and check that they slide freely from side to side.

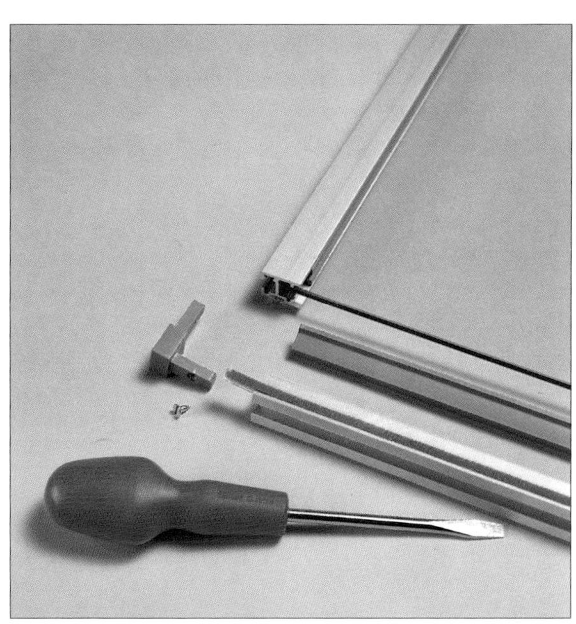

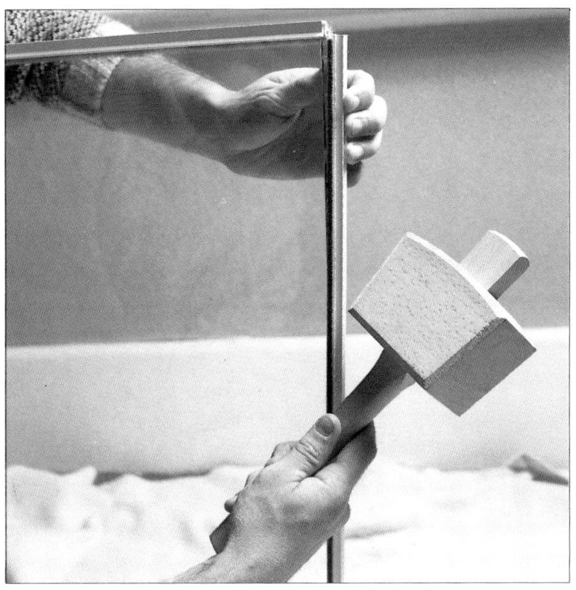

apple
tree
LAWN
MAN-
HOLE
COVER
REMOVE TWO EXISTING
CONIFER SAPLINGS

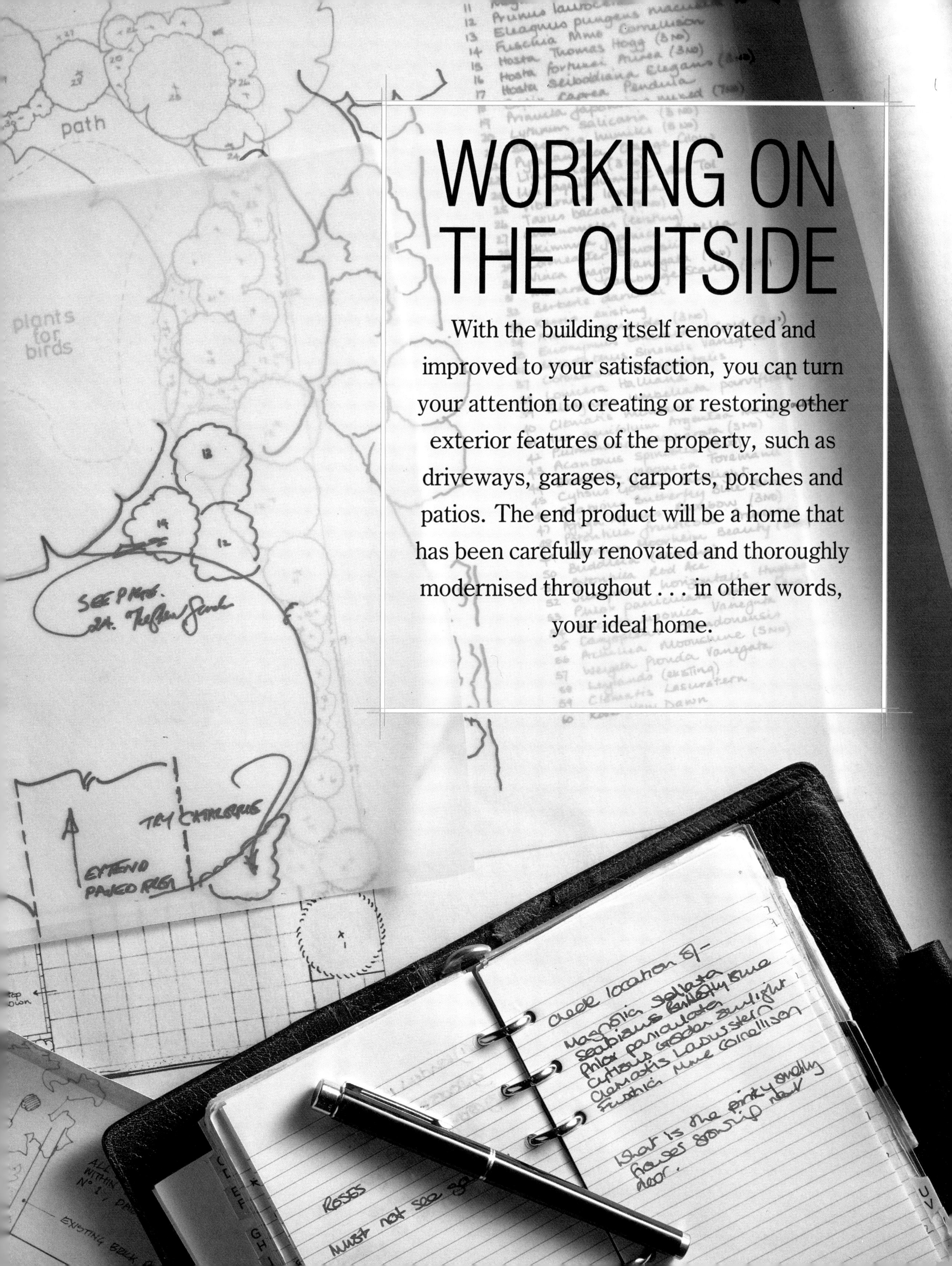

WORKING ON THE OUTSIDE

With the building itself renovated and improved to your satisfaction, you can turn your attention to creating or restoring other exterior features of the property, such as driveways, garages, carports, porches and patios. The end product will be a home that has been carefully renovated and thoroughly modernised throughout . . . in other words, your ideal home.

Garages and Carports

It is obviously desirable to get cars off the road – and even better if you can have them securely locked away under cover. At the very least, your property should have a hard standing for a car, caravan or boat, preferably with a roof over it to create a carport. Ideally, though, you will have a garage where your car can be kept protected from the elements and out of reach of car thieves or vandals.

If you have a garage, it is worth spending some time checking it for faults – leaking roofs and deteriorating or poorly operating doors are the main problems. With carports, faults are normally few. But you need to keep an eye on the condition of the covering if you are not to loose roofing sheets during autumn or winter storms. With an unprotected area of hard standing, all that can happen is that it may crack or the surface break up.

If you decide to build or extend a garage, remember that this will give you scope for providing additional facilities such as a do-it-yourself workshop or hobby area, or space for storing garden equipment, laundry appliances or a large chest freezer.

■ Since the family car became an essential rather than a luxury, many homes have been built with the garage as an integral part of the house structure. It may be built out to the front of the house (**above** and **right**) or positioned alongside it (**left**). Such integral garages often have an internal door giving access direct to the house, avoiding a dash to the front door on wet wintry nights. The traditional pair of side-hung timber doors is still found on many older properties (**right**), but up-and-over doors are now the norm for most homes.

CARRYING OUT ROOF REPAIRS

If you discover a leaking roof, check from the underside to see if you can trace the source of the leak during rain. This can be particularly difficult with a felt-covered flat roof, especially if the underside is lined, as it should be, with insulating material.

The problem, as has already been discussed in the section on roofs, is that rain can enter at one place and travel a considerable distance along roofing joists before it shows itself as a damp patch on the garage ceiling.

With a leak in a felt-covered flat roof, scrape away any stone chippings from the affected area. Then paint the roof with flashing strip primer, which is a bitumen-like product, and allow this to dry. The process takes a few minutes, while the primer changes from brown to black. Then stick a patch of metal-faced, self-adhesive flashing strip over the hole or crack and bed it down well.

The same method of repair can be used for pitched roofed garages, where metal or cement-based corrugated roofing sheets have developed holes. However, this is only a temporary measure, since you should eventually change the sheets for new ones.

If the garage is attached, leaks often develop

■ **Right** To repair a corrugated garage roof, free the fixings securing the damaged sheet so you can slide it out. Buy a sheet of replacement roofing to match the profile of the existing roof sheeting, and cut it to length using a jig saw and a guide batten. Then slide the new sheet into place, drill holes for the new fixings and secure it to the roof joists. If you suspect that the old sheeting contains asbestos, contact your local authority for guidance on its safe disposal.

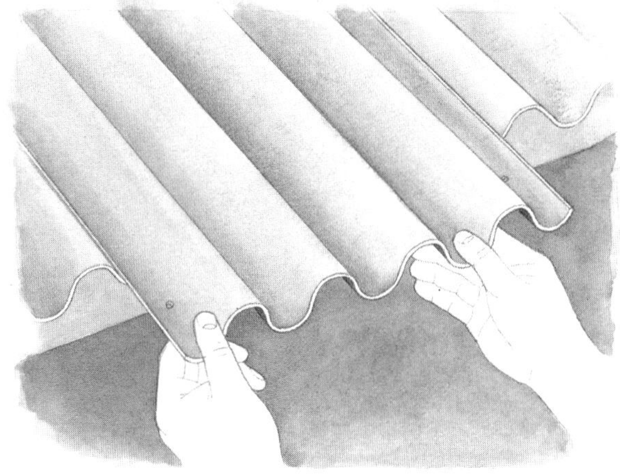

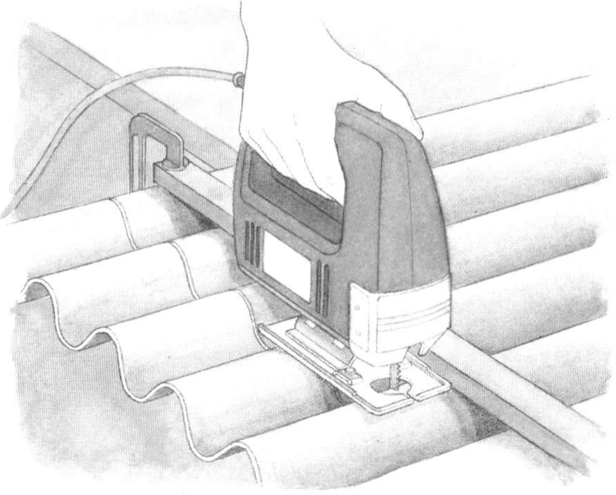

between the roof and where it joins the house wall. You may also spot the effects of differential movement between the house and the garage where the two buildings meet if the foundations were not built deep enough.

There is little you can do about this. If the building is showing no signs of cracking elsewhere, you might as well leave it. Fill any gaps with non-setting mastic and cover the joint with a self-adhesive flashing strip, which should be able to absorb the movement.

The usual roof covering for a carport is clear

corrugated plastic sheeting. If this starts to leak, it is often a sign that the plastic has become brittle and is nearing the end of its useful life. So be prepared to strip the roof and fix new sheets.

In the meantime, you can extend the life of the roof by sealing any leaks with self-adhesive waterproof tape, which you just press down over the hole or split. If the damage is extensive, replace individual sheets with new ones with matching corrugations.

CARRYING OUT DOOR REPAIRS

Among the common problems with hinged doors, gaps may appear between the frames and the surrounding masonry. You can seal these using non-setting cartridge mastic. If the doors are difficult to open and close, oil or grease the hinge cups.

Look out, too, for rot in the doors or sagging due to loose joints or rot in the door frames, especially round the lower hinge position. You can carry out minor repairs to the doors and frames by cutting out the rot and using a two-part wood filler.

A more satisfactory method of repair would be to insert a new piece of timber or, better still, fit new doors or frames. Repairs are similar to those described for exterior doors.

Up-and-over doors are sometimes made of wood, which is of course prone to rot. Most types, however, are of non-rusting metal. The main problem with either type is usually in the mechanism itself. Moving parts should be oiled from time to time and the channels in which the door gear slides kept well greased. If a door comes off its channel, you may need to adjust the lifting cables. If a door is dented, you may be able to fill the dent; otherwise you may have to replace it with a new one.

EXTENDING A GARAGE

If you have a timber or brick-built garage, it is quite feasible to consider extending it to incorporate extra facilities. The work will involve adding to the base and building on the extra section to match the existing structure. Check first with your local authority, however, on the question of whether planning permission will be needed for the extension work.

If you have a prefabricated concrete garage, it will not be so easy to extend it, unless a similar model is still available from the manufacturer. In that case, all you need do is extend the base and bolt in extra wall and roof sections.

It is more likely, though, that your particular

■ A sweeping driveway not only provides an imposing approach to the house. It also allows ample off-road parking space for visitors, and makes it easy to turn cars round without the need for reversing out of the drive onto a busy road.

■ **Above** Gravel is one of the most attractive drive surfaces, conjuring up an image of country-house carriage drives. It also acts as an excellent burglar deterrent. However, it needs regular raking and treating with weedkiller to keep it looking good.

■ **Above right** Paving of various types is one of the most popular surfaces for drives. For durability, the slabs should be laid in a continuous mortar bed over a concrete base; if they are simply laid over a sand bed the weight of the car will shift and crack them.

model will be out of production. Here the only choice will be to demolish the existing garage and erect a new one, either prefabricated or built in the traditional manner.

LAYING A HARD STANDING

You do not normally need planning consent for a hard standing in the front garden. But you will need permission from the highway authority to create an access on to the road, if the hard standing opens on to a trunk or classified road. You will also need permission if you live in a listed building or in a conservation area.

Make the hard standing as large as possible – about twice the car's length and double its width. This will give you enough space to open the car doors easily and enable front garden gates to open inwards. It will also allow people to pass comfortably by the car when it is parked without scraping the bodywork.

Concrete is practical, but not very attractive. You lay it as for a garage base, as described below. It can be made more attractive with a surface covering of asphalt, as can an existing area of old but sound concrete.

Alternatively, concrete blocks or bricks can be used and here you have the chance to create some interesting patterns. These materials are available in a range of colours. Laid on a 50mm (2in) deep bed of sand over hardcore, they are ideal for a hard standing.

Paving slabs can be used if well-bedded in mortar over a concrete base. If they are simply loose-laid over a sand bed, they will soon shift and crack under the car's weight.

BUILDING A GARAGE

By building your garage, you give yourself the opportunity to create so much more than just somewhere to keep a car. It will form an excellent additional storage area for items like bicycles and garden furniture. It can provide a utility area for a washing machine or dish-washer. It will also be somewhere to put a large freezer if this will not fit indoors.

Above all, it makes an excellent workshop. And if you build it large and airy enough, it can also make a playroom for the children or a games room for the whole family.

If you want a plain, value-for-money garage with no frills, then a prefabricated design is a good choice. If you have special requirements or want the garage to fit a certain size or shape of plot, then a purpose-built brick or concrete block garage will be your only option. In the latter case, you can at least be sure of creating a building that will match the style of the house.

When choosing a prefabricated garage, dimensions (length and width) will have to be based on the manufacturer's module size, which is generally about 600mm wide. So its eventual length and width will be fixed to 600mm increments. And the wall finish will be what is available from the manufacturer; the most common are pebbledash, simulated brick and plain concrete.

You can normally choose from a pitched roof or one that is more or less flat, but in fact slopes to the end or one side. A pitched roof looks more attractive, especially if tiled to match the house, and offers useful extra storage space. But it is more expensive.

An extra door for access at the back or side of the garage is often useful and additional windows are important if the garage is to be used as a workshop or utility room. The entrance door will usually be an up-and-over type, either plain or panelled, and made from steel, timber or glass-reinforced plastic. Side-hung doors are an alternative.

With a prefabricated garage, you will need to prepare a concrete base, whether the garage is to be assembled by the manufacturer or yourself. Normally a 100mm (4in) thick layer of concrete laid over a 100mm thick layer of hardcore will be sufficient.

You should make the base 150mm (6in) wider than the garage on all sides and dig out the edges to 200mm (8in) deep to give an extra thickness of concrete to support the walls. Peg out timber boards around the slab to support the concrete while it sets and to make it easy to level off the slab.

All manufacturers offer a garage erection service, although you will save money by doing the job yourself. First you have to lift the wall panels into place and bolt them together. Window and door frames slot in as necessary and are linked by lintels that bolt to the sides of the adjacent wall panels.

Depending on whether the garage has a flat or pitched roof, you next have to fit either roof joists or trusses on to wall plates. You then complete the structure with corrugated fibre cement roofing sheets or with battens and roof tiles, according to the roof type.

After fitting the up-and-over door, you seal the exterior by injecting non-setting mastic between the individual wall panels. On the inside, you have to rub mortar into the joints between the panels.

With a purpose-built garage, you will at least be getting one to suit your requirements exactly. Equally it will enhance the value of your property, although it will cost more to build than a prefabricated type. By choosing the materials and style of building carefully, you can effect a perfect match to the house.

If you build the garage against the side of the house, you will get one wall for nothing and save some space. And if you knock a hole for a door in the wall between the house and garage, you will have direct sheltered access.

■ Detached garages are common on older properties where space was less at a premium than today. Modern versions can be brick-built, or constructed from pre-fabricated panels supplied in kit form.

■ Carports provide an economical way of creating a shelter for a car, caravan or boat, and can do double duty as a covered play area for children or even somewhere to hang washing to dry in wet weather. Most consist of lightweight roof structures supported on slender poles, and are often built off the house wall.

However, the door must have a half-hour fire rating, be fitted with a metal door closer and there must be a non-combustible step between the house and garage in case of spills of flammable liquids.

If you have the space, it can be a good idea to build a detached garage – and even better if you can build a double one, even if you have only one car at present. The extra room will be useful and family needs change remarkably quickly. It may not be many years before you become a two-car household.

Obviously, it is preferable to build a double garage widthways. But if you do not have the space for this, you will have to build it lengthways to take two cars in line.

The minimum internal width of a single garage should be about 2.5m (8ft) – and ideally 2.75m (9ft) or more. The minimum length should be about 5m (16ft 5in) and preferably at least 6m (19ft 8in). It is difficult to make a garage too big!

Single thickness brick or block walls strengthened with piers at regular intervals are suitable for this type of garage. If you are going to use it as a workshop or playroom, however, it would be better to build insulated cavity walls. The roof should be insulated, too.

BUILDING A CARPORT

If you already have a hard standing, all you have to do is put a roof over it to create a carport and thus keep the worst of the weather off the car.

Apart from the restrictions mentioned for a hard standing, you are unlikely to need planning permission. Building regulation approval will not be needed as long as at least two sides are open and the floor area is not greater than 30sq m. If you are in doubt, check with your local authority before starting work.

You can make your own carport by using timber or metal posts to support a light timber grid framework that will form the roof of the structure. While the posts will support one side of the frame, the other side can be attached to a 100 × 50mm (4 × 2in) timber wall plate bolted to the house wall.

To complete the structure, screw lightweight corrugated plastic roofing sheets or twin-wall polycarbonate sheets to the roofing framework. Build the roof with a slight fall away from the house and ensure you allow a minimum headroom under the carport of about 2.5m (8ft 2in).

If the DIY approach does not appeal, you can buy carport kits, which are available in aluminium or steel and wood.

Porches

A porch is an invaluable addition to a home. It helps stop cold winds blowing into the house every time you open the front door, conserves heat and increases security. It also forms a small extension where you can park a pram or bike, take off and store wet clothes, boots and shoes and stand umbrellas.

TYPES OF PORCH

In its simplest form, a porch can just be a canopy over an entrance door. This at least will give some protection to callers to the house and provide a shield for the front door against the worst of the weather.

The roof canopy can be supported by a simple timber framework fixed to the house wall above the door or by pillars or posts at the front outer corners.

One refinement you can make is to fill in between the pillars and the wall with trellis panels, on which climbing plants can be grown. This gives some additional protection. You could go even further and enclose the sides with panes of glass and fit a glazed door to the front, thereby creating an enclosed porch.

With some styles of property, the front door

■ **Left** If the house has a recessed porch, it is often possible to fill in the front of the recess to create an enclosed lobby. However, care must be taken to match the architectural style of the house.

■ **Below left** With this type of double porch, infilling can lead to visual disaster and is best avoided.

■ **Below** Building a porch out from the front of the house can create a pleasant additional feature if care is taken over the design and detailing of the extension.

is recessed from the front wall or sited below a concrete canopy. In either case it can be quite easy to create an enclosed porch simply by filling in the recess with glass panels and a door or by building curtain walls beneath the canopy.

Where the house has a canopy extension to bay windows at the front, you can also quite easily create a porch by adding a curtain wall and door. The result will blend very well with the style of the property. That is very important. As far as possible, any porch you construct should look an integral part of the original house design and not an obvious afterthought.

■ Older properties offer a wide variety of porch designs, from the simple overhanging canopy to more elaborate designs. Often the overhanging roof provided a pleasant place for the occupants to sit out and watch the world go by.

To allow the maximum amount of light into the hallway, you may want a porch with floor-to-ceiling glass. Alternatively, you may prefer to incorporate low walls of brick, stone or timber. Matching the materials you use for these walls to blend with the overall style of the house is an important factor.

With a modern house, or where the property has bay windows with flat roofs, it may be acceptable to have a flat-roofed porch. If your house has a sloping roof, it is better to plan a pitched roof porch, with slates or tiles to match those on the house.

The size of the porch may be governed by the recess being filled in. If you are building a porch as an extension to the front of the house, subject to planning regulations you can make it as wide and deep as you like.

In fact, it may be better to go beyond what could strictly be termed a porch and make it into a cloakroom, incorporating a downstairs wc. Or it could be divided to incorporate a garden store, bike shed or fuel storage area.

PLANNING A PORCH

Porches are subject to the Town and Country Planning Acts (dealing with the appearance of the building) and the Building Regulations (concerned with the method of construction). These regulations are constantly changing, so you should check your own plans with the local authority to make sure your proposed porch meets current requirements.

In recent years, the regulations have been considerably relaxed. At present, if the porch has a floor area of less than 30sq m (or 320sq ft) Building Regulations approval will not be required. However, you will have to get approval if the porch is to incorporate a wc or fuel store or if it will enclose airbricks, drain inspection covers, gullies or similar facilities.

Planning and building rules

Planning rules exist to exert some degree of central control over changes people want to make to their properties; in other words, they govern how things look, in relation to the original building and to its surroundings. Building rules are little concerned with appearances; their task is to ensure that what is built is properly constructed using suitable materials and techniques. Both are under the ultimate authority of Parliament, but are administered by local authority planning committees and building control officers, who have the legal power to enforce compliance with the rules.

Most porches will be classed as 'permitted development' and will be exempt from planning approval unless you have already extended your house and used up your permitted development allowance (see above right). Certainly infill porches will not need planning permission.

BUILDING A PORCH

When it comes to building a porch, you have the choice of going for a tailor-made design or buying a prefabricated building. You must

■ The best way of adding a porch to your house is to make the most of existing architectural features, by picking up the line of existing eaves or windows to create a structure that looks part of the original building (**above** and **top left**). If you have the space to build a more substantial porch (**top right**), try to echo the materials and style of the main house in its architectural design.

decide whether you want to carry out the construction yourself or employ a builder.

If you choose a prefabricated building, most manufacturers offer an erection service. If you employ a builder, choose a reputable firm, get written quotations and check examples of similar jobs done in your area. And always agree the quotation, starting and completion dates and payment schedules in writing before any work commences.

Obviously, the choice in prefabricated porches is limited. But if you can find a suitable design in a manufacturer's catalogue, you should get good value for money.

If you decide on a tailor-made design, you have complete flexibility as far as styling and materials are concerned. By looking at styles of others in your area, you may be able to design the porch yourself. Otherwise you may need to employ an architect. If you are using a builder, he may have a design department to take care of this aspect of the job.

When designing a porch, do not forget it must have its own dpc and must not bridge the dpc in the house wall. The floor must incorporate a dpm and the junction between the porch walls and the wall of the house must also be damp-proofed, as must that between the roof and the house wall.

INSULATING A PORCH

It is certainly worth insulating a porch. Glass areas should be double-glazed and brickwork should be of cavity wall construction with insulation batts built into the cavity.

Timber walls should be similarly insulated, with a polythene vapour barrier between the inner and outer cladding. Alternatively, insulating plasterboard can be used for wall lining. This can be used to line the ceiling as well.

FINISHING OFF

The porch will need an interior light and ideally an exterior light, too. So put in the necessary wiring for this during construction.

You might also want to incorporate heating in the porch, especially if it contains a cloakroom. So at the building stage either extend the central heating system or incorporate wiring for electric heaters.

Security is a very important factor, so make sure the porch is fitted with a high security lock. In the case of an open porch, make sure the house door is really secure. The danger here is that a partially enclosed porch may allow an intruder to work on the house's main front door in comparative privacy.

Patios

Whatever size of garden you may have with your house, you should try to make the best possible use of it. One very useful facility is a patio, which not only acts as a link between the house and the garden but also creates another functional area for a whole range of activities.

PLANNING A PATIO

The greatest influence on planning will be the primary use of the patio. For example, will it be used mainly as an outdoor room whenever the weather is fine, with chairs and tables where you can sit and read, eat alfresco meals, sunbathe at leisure and entertain your friends?

You need to decide whether you want a permanent, built-in table and seating set or whether you want movable furniture. The same decision needs to be made with regard to a barbecue. Do you want a built-in one or will a portable barbecue be suitable? In either case, a built-in table may prove useful.

If children are likely to play on the patio when the ground is wet, a large area of unobstructed paving would be most suitable. You may even need a timber structure like a pergola to support a removable canvas awning or a plastic roof, so that the patio can be used even when it is raining. You will also need a large, unobstructed area if you are going to site a washing line or a rotary clothes line on the patio.

The size of your patio may well be governed by the area available. With large gardens,

■ Whatever materials you choose to create your patio, aim for an overall effect that blends in naturally with the garden by using curves and broken edges rather than stark-looking squares and rectangles.

where there are no space restrictions, the size could depend on how many people are likely to use the patio at any one time. Bear in mind, for example, peak usage such as summer evening barbecue parties. It is impossible to make a patio too big – unless it dominates the garden. But it could easily be too small. If you are likely to use sunloungers on the patio, the minimum satisfactory size is about 4m (13ft) square.

In many cases the aspect of the patio will depend on the outlook at the back of the house. But sometimes it is possible to build the patio out from the back of the house to take advantage of other factors. You may want it south-facing for sunbathing, east-facing to catch the morning sun or west-facing for catching the last of the sun in the evening.

For such activities as eating out, it is a good idea if part of the patio is in shade for some of the day. It is usually best to keep it alongside or fairly close to the house, where you can link it with paving so that it is not too far to carry food and other items.

■ If you can incorporate different levels in your garden design, you will create a much more interesting effect. Adding lighting – low-voltage types are the safest – will allow you to enjoy it by night as well as during the day.

For privacy, you may want to build screen walls, fences, pergolas and awnings into the design. These will have the added advantage of offering a degree of wind protection.

If the ground slopes away from or towards the house, some excavating will be required to create a level area on which to build your patio. Although this will involve making steps and putting up retaining walls, these will enhance the patio's appearance.

It is very important to allow for rainwater to drain away. So build the patio with a slight slope – about 25mm (1in) in 3m (10ft) – away from the house. In the case of ground sloping towards the house, you will have to slope the paving

Casting ready-mixed concrete

Ready-mixed concrete is one of the most versatile building materials available to the do-it-yourselfer. Not only is it an essential ingredient of many building projects, in the form of strip or raft foundations set in the ground to support walls and other structures. It is also a constructional material in its own right, and can be used to create many outdoor features such as patios, paths and drives.

The main drawback with concrete is without a doubt its appearance. This obviously does not matter when it is used for something that is largely hidden, such as a foundation slab, but where the material is on show its looks become more important. There are two ways in which the appearance of large expanses of concrete can be significantly improved; colour and surface texture.

Colour can be affected to a certain extent by careful choice of the sand used as part of the formula, and more drastically by the use of pigments, while the finish given to the slab can add a strong element of visual interest to the project.

In principle, laying concrete in the form of a patio, path or drive is little different from casting a slab foundation. However, there are several specific points to bear in mind over and above the straightforward casting technique.

Firstly, order all the ready-mixed concrete you need for the job in one delivery. If you use several batches of concrete for a large project, slight differences in shade will be impossible to correct.

You may want to create shapes rather more elaborate than straightforward rectangles and squares. Fortunately, concrete can do this easily so long as you are prepared to spend some time setting out the formwork in the shape you require.

As you plan the layout of your project, watch out for obstacles such as manhole covers and drainage gullies. You will need to plan the levels of your new surfaces carefully unless you are willing to move or reposition the obstacle.

Large areas of concrete cannot be laid as continuous slabs, or they will crack due to expansion and contraction. This means dividing the work up into bays, each separated from its neighbour by an expansion joint of hardboard or bituminous felt if the concrete is laid as a continuous operation. If it is laid in alternate bays, board or felt joints are not needed; a simple butt joint will suffice.

■ When the delivery arrives, try to have it delivered direct to where it is needed via the chute on the delivery lorry.

■ Use barrow to transport loads to areas the chute cannot reach. Protect glazed doors with a sheet of hardboard.

■ Spread the concrete using a garden rake and a shovel. Work it well into the sides and corners of the formwork to avoid hollows.

■ Cast the slab in easily managed bays no more than 3m (10ft) long and compact the mix down well with a tamping beam.

■ Lay the next bay in the same way, finishing off with a sawing to-and-fro action of the beam to level the surface of the slab.

■ When you have compacted the slab, apply the finishing texture. For a smooth, polished surface use a steel float.

away from the house and towards a central gully connected to a large soakaway – a pit filled with rubble that can be paved over.

Avoid complicated shapes that involve cutting lots of slabs. For the same reason plan the size of the patio carefully to incorporate standard sizes. When you have got a rough design, peg it out with canes and string and see if it can be improved. Check that there is enough space for sitting out, see which areas are in shade at those times you are most likely to use the patio and work out where screening will be required.

When you have done all this you can prepare a detailed plan on squared paper with a predetermined scale. This will help you estimate and order exactly the materials you require.

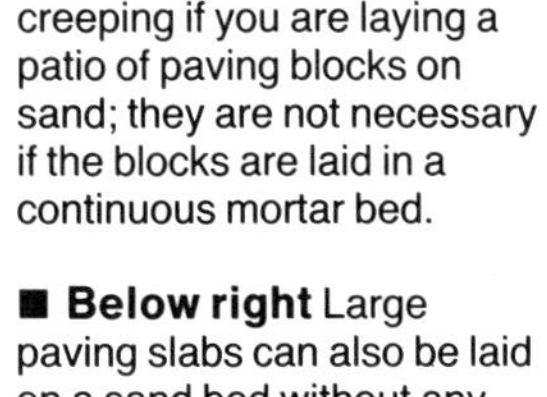

■ **Below** Fit edge restraints to stop edge blocks from creeping if you are laying a patio of paving blocks on sand; they are not necessary if the blocks are laid in a continuous mortar bed.

■ **Below right** Large paving slabs can also be laid on a sand bed without any edge restraints, but crazy paving must be laid in a continuous mortar bed to stop the paving from subsiding.

LAYING FOUNDATIONS

When building a patio, you must provide a good base. A layer of hardcore will give a substantial foundation that acts as a stabiliser between the soil and the paving material.

Remove any top soil to a depth of at least 150mm (6in) or as deep as required to get the final surface of the patio 150mm (6in) below the dpc level of the house. Apply a weedkiller over the surface of the excavated base.

Firm the soil and spread a covering of hardcore to a depth of 100mm (4in). Then ram this down and level it, remembering to allow a slight fall from the house. Spread ballast – a mixture of sand and gravel, also called combined aggregate – over this to provide a smooth, compact surface. This type of base can be used under mortar, sand or concrete – the next layer, depending on what surface material you have decided to put down.

Paving slabs can be laid on an overall bed of mortar or on five spots per slab. Use a mix of one part cement to five parts builders' sand mix and, if spreading it, make sure it is 25–50mm (1–2in) thick. Use the same mix dry to brush in between the paving. Water it in with a can fitted with a fine rose.

Sharp sand for block pavers should be laid about 60mm (2½in) thick. Position the pavers so they are butted tightly together about 10mm (or ½in) higher than required. Use a plate vibrator (which can be hired) to work the blocks down to the correct level. Spread fine dry sand over the pavers, then vibrate again to settle the sand into the cracks and lock the blocks in place. Brush away excess sand.

Concrete should be laid 100mm (4in) thick over the hardcore base. A mix of one part cement to six parts of combined aggregate (ballast) will be suitable for a patio area.

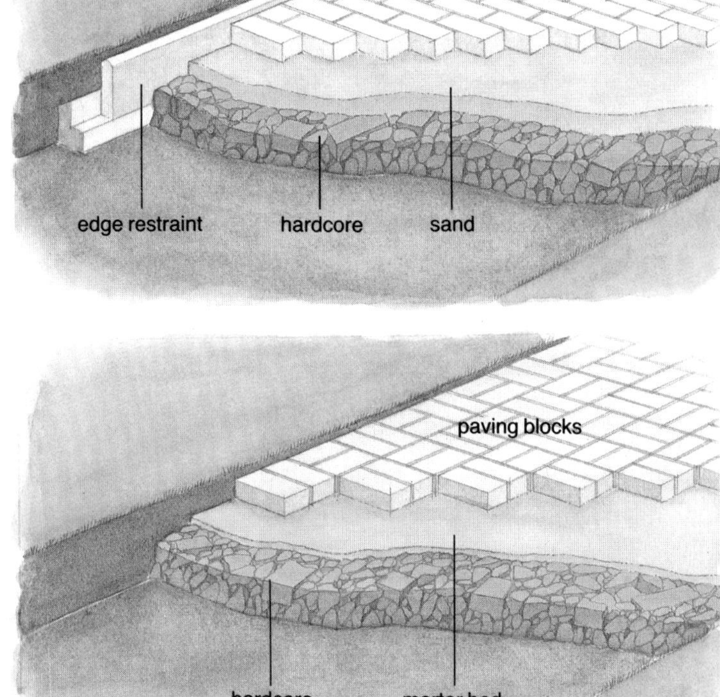

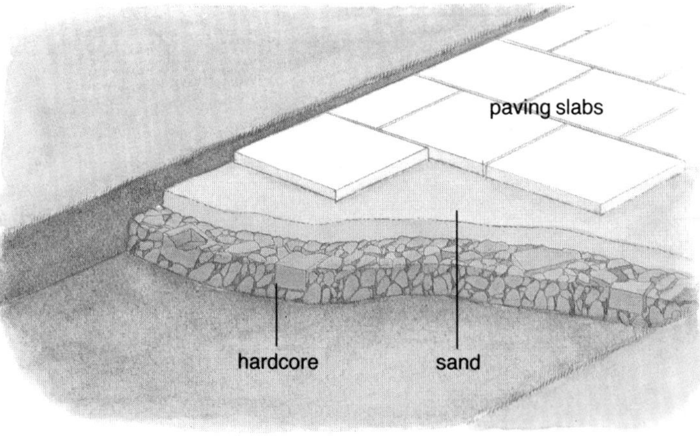

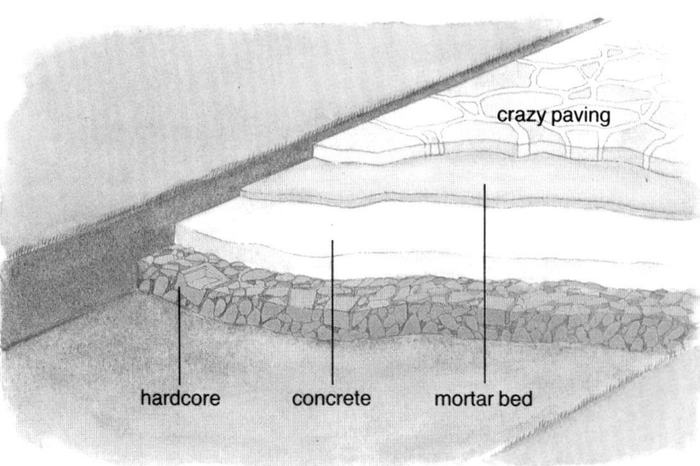

Conclusion

Having put so much thought, time and effort – not to mention money – into renovating and improving your home, you should certainly be proud of your achievements. But that is not the end of the story. If you do not take measures to look after and protect what you have done, soon you might have to start all over again.

By going through the book, you will have gained a good working knowledge of what is involved in the general maintenance and upkeep of a property. You will also have realised that the time, effort and cost expended in looking after a house is small in comparison to what is involved in putting any faults right.

Take a simple example such as a wooden window frame. Always keep an eye on it and make sure it is well painted or varnished. Every few years you should give it an 'overhaul' by rubbing down and redecorating it. This way, you should have no trouble with it.

Compare the cost of replacement to a small amount of materials and an hour or two of your time, which is all regular checking will involve. If, through neglect, you fail to notice putty or paint cracking, moisture will get in and attack the frame itself. You may be lucky to get away with minor repairs. Alternatively you might have to replace the whole window.

The simple fact of the matter is that to inspect a house that is in good condition takes very little time or effort. With binoculars you can view the roof and chimney stack in close-up. Walls you can check from ground level. Gutters, downpipes and drains you should inspect on a rainy day to see if there are any drips or overflows. And check closely any wood or metalwork for early signs of rot or rust.

COPING WITH EMERGENCIES

Of course, even the most diligent householder can be caught out. But with constant inspection you should be able to avoid major problems and expense. A damp patch appearing on a wall should signal a quick search for the source of the trouble outside. Prompt action will eliminate the defect before it does any real damage.

To this end it is well worth while keeping a 'first-aid' box of repair materials alongside your tool kit. There is a vast array of tapes, compounds and other waterproofing materials available, many of which can also be used in wet conditions to make immediate repairs.

MAINTENANCE CHECKLIST

FAULT	CAUSE
Chimneys and flashings	
1 Cracked, damaged or leaning pot.	Old age, failed flaunching.
2 Cracked or missing flaunching.	Damp penetration, frost damage.
3 Faulty pointing on stack.	Damp penetration, frost damage.
4 Damaged brickwork on stack.	Damp penetration, frost damage.
5 Damaged flashings round stack.	Old age, wind damage.
6 Dampness penetrating stack.	Porous masonry, failed flashings.
Pitched roofs	
7 Loose or missing ridge tiles.	Failed mortar, wind damage.
8 Out-of-position tiles or slates.	Failed fixings, wind damage.
9 Missing tiles or slates.	Failed fixings, wind damage.
10 Damaged tiling battens or felt.	Missing tiles, rot, wind damage.
Flat roofs	
11 Torn or cracked roofing felt.	Wind damage, temperature extremes.
12 Blistered roofing felt.	Protective chippings missing.
13 Torn or damaged flashings.	Old age, wind damage.
14 Puddles standing on roof.	Rot causing decking to sag.
Gutters and eaves woodwork	
15 Overflows from guttering.	Blockages, gutters sagging.
16 Leaks from joints in gutters.	Failed brackets or joint seals.
17 Rot in eaves woodwork.	Failed protective coating.
External walls	
18 Large cracks or bulges in wall.	Subsidence, failed wall ties.
19 Damaged brickwork and pointing.	Old age, frost damage.
20 Cracked or hollow rendering.	Moisture penetration, frost damage.
21 Damaged wood cladding/tile hanging.	Rot, physical or wind damage.
Doors and windows	
22 Rot in door and window frames.	Failed paint or missing putty.
23 Doors binding in frames.	Damp penetration, paint build-up.
24 Casements binding in frame.	Paint build-up, failed joints.
25 Sashes binding in frame.	Paint build-up, broken sash cord.
26 Cracked or broken glass.	Accident, slamming, failed joints.
Damp, rot and woodworm attack	
27 Internal dampness at ground level.	Failed or bridged damp course.
28 Internal dampness elsewhere.	Penetrating damp, plumbing leaks.
29 Rot in structural timbers.	Penetrating damp, poor ventilation.
30 Woodworm damage.	Lack of preservative treatment.
31 Condensation.	Poor insulation, poor ventilation.
Wall, floors and staircases	
32 Cracks in wall/ceiling surfaces.	Old age, subsidence, damage.
33 Holes in wall/ceiling surfaces.	Physical damage.
34 Loose or damaged floorboards.	Failed fixings, overloading.
35 Creaks in floorboards or stairs.	Loose boards or treads, overheating.
36 Loose staircase handrail.	Old age, physical damage.

ACTION	MATERIALS
Chimneys and flashings	
1 Hack off old flaunching, reset or replace old pot and renew flaunching.	New pot, bricklaying mortar.
2 Hack off and replace old flaunching; coat with waterproofing sealant.	Bricklaying mortar, waterproofing sealant.
3 Chisel out areas of failed pointing and replace with new mortar.	Bricklaying mortar.
4 Cut out damaged brickwork and replace with new bricks and pointing.	Replacement bricks, bricklaying mortar.
5 Refix loose flashings, patch holes and repair tears with flashing tape.	Mortar, mastic, flashing repair tape.
6 Repair flashings as necessary, then apply waterproofing sealant to brickwork.	As 5, plus silicone waterproofing sealant.
Pitched roofs	
7 Hack off old mortar, then bed old or new ridge tiles in place on new mortar.	Bricklaying mortar, replacement tiles.
8 Push tiles or slates back into place, securing with nails or lead/zinc strap.	Fixing nails, metal retaining straps.
9 Fit replacement tiles or slates, securing with nails or lead/zinc strap.	Replacement tiles/slates, fixing nails.
10 Cut broken batten back to joists and replace; patch in new roofing felt.	New tiling battens, felt, fixing nails.
Flat roofs	
11 Stick or nail down damaged roofing felt and cover with patch of new felt.	Roofing mastic, felt, fixing nails.
12 Make cross-cut into blister, stick down resulting tongues and cover with patch.	Roofing mastic, felt, fixing nails.
13 Refix loose flashings, patch holes and repair tears with flashing tape.	Mortar, mastic, flashing repair tape.
14 Strip old roof covering and decking, renew decking and re-felt roof surface.	New decking, roofing felt and fixings.
Gutters and eaves woodwork	
15 Clear blockages; fit new gutter brackets to realign gutter to correct fall.	Replacement gutter brackets, fixings.
16 Undo joints if possible and repair/replace seals; otherwise seal with mastic.	Bituminous mastic or new joint seals.
17 Fill or cut out and patch rotten wood, using new preservative-treated timber.	Filler, new wood, fixings, preservative.
External walls	
18 Professional help essential to discover structural cause and advise on action.	Rebuilding, replacement wall ties.
19 Cut out damaged brickwork and replace with new bricks and pointing.	Replacement bricks, bricklaying mortar.
20 Hack off damaged rendering to sound edge, then re-render with new mortar mix.	Rendering mortar, bonding agent.
21 Strip affected area as necessary, then replace damaged cladding or tiles.	Matching timber/tiles, fixings, paint.
Doors and windows	
22 Cut out rotten wood, replace with filler or new wood; replace missing putty.	Filler, new wood, replacement putty.
23 Strip paint and plane down door edges to improve clearance, then repaint.	New paint system.
24 Strip paint and plane as 23, remake weak or sagging casement joints, repaint.	New paint system, joint reinforcement.
25 Remove sashes, strip and plane as 23; fit replacement sash cord at both sides.	New paint system, replacement sash cord.
26 Hack out old putty, remove and replace damaged pane.	New glass, glazing sprigs/clips, putty.
Damp, rot and woodworm attack	
27 Remove damp bridges from outside walls; install new chemical damp course.	Damp course injection fluid, mortar.
28 Locate and rectify source of moisture penetration; repair plumbing leak.	Fillers, sealers, mastics, pipe repair kit.
29 Cut out and replace affected timber; get expert advice for treating dry rot.	New preservative-treated wood, fixings.
30 Treat or replace affected timber; apply woodworm fluid to all exposed wood.	Woodworm fluid treatment, new wood.
31 Improve level of heating, insulation and ventilation in affected areas.	Insulation materials, extractor fan.
Walls, floors and staircases	
32 Hack out loose material and fill cracks with plaster or interior filler.	Plaster or filler, joint tape.
33 Cut back to studs/joists and patch hole with plasterboard offcut and plaster.	Plasterboard, plaster, joint tape.
34 Refix loose boards; lift and replace split or otherwise damaged boards.	New fixings, replacement boards.
35 Add extra fixings to secure floorboards to joists and treads to risers.	New fixings.
36 Replace loose fixings or fit new components in place of damaged parts.	New fixings, replacement components.

The same applies to domestic plumbing. Although draining down a leaking pipe will stop the immediate problem, if you have pipe repair materials to hand you will be able to stop the leak and restore the system to full working order in a matter of minutes.

Equally, if you have a temporary repair kit, which could include a two-part repair compound, two-part adhesive tape or a pipe clamp, effective emergency measures can be achieved in seconds without having to turn off the water.

Another useful emergency aid is a sheet of tough polythene, which makes excellent temporary glazing or roof cover. Keep some thin battens and wire nails to hand so that the sheet can be anchored quickly to a door or window frame in the event of a problem.

It is also a good idea to keep a can of aerosol filler handy. This can quickly fill any gap that you discover is letting in the elements. And it can also be used to refix the odd loose slate or tile securely in position.

Your home's log book

As you carry out the gradual repair, restoration and renovation of your home, it makes sense to try to keep track of what you have done by keeping a log book. This will record everything from the materials and fittings you used to the builders and other professionals you employed, and will also be a very useful asset to a future buyer.

You can set up your house log book using a standard A4 or foolscap folder containing lined, blank and graph paper (for drawing scale plans), with divider tabs to split it into sections. Do this either by the type of job involved (building, decorating, plumbing and so on) or by the room or area of the house concerned. The folder (or a matching box file) can be used for manufacturer's leaflets and other useful bits of literature. How detailed your notes are is up to you, but you should at least always record things like quantities of materials used, to save you having to work them out again when you repeat the job.

KEEPING A CHECK

To protect your home and your pocket, give it a regular check-up. The most important time to do this is in the autumn.

At this time of year the weather should still be mild enough – and dry enough – for any outside jobs to be completed in relative comfort. It is very unpleasant to have to work outside in really cold weather – and it is not always possible or advisable to do so with certain repair materials in adverse or extreme weather conditions.

With the pre-winter check taken care of, you should be fairly confident that the house is able to withstand the worst the weather can throw at it. Every house has to put up with some barrage from the elements. Rain, snow and wind batter the roof, walls, windows and doors while, from below, the all-round attack is completed by moisture in the ground rising to do its worst to the structure.

Make sure you keep this book not only as a basic reference for specific projects but also as a reminder for all the various aspects of your home you should keep your eye on. If you go back through the different sections, you can make a list of the points to watch for when you do your pre-winter inspection.

Get into the habit of carrying out routine maintenance checks and any subsequent work needed so that everything is kept in sound condition. It is a good idea to devote a morning or a day each month to checking and doing small jobs, such as touching up chipped paint, oiling hinges, testing that stopcocks are not jammed and other similar aspects of the general 'working' of your home.

Your house is almost certainly going to be the largest investment of your life. For most people it is the tangible proof of the effort they have made to obtain security for themselves and their family. In many ways, it represents their wealth and safeguard against illness, unemployment and other potential pitfalls in life.

Having worked so hard to improve the property – to modernise it and to make it a comfortable and pleasurable place in which to live – you will also have increased its value. Possibly the amount of that increase will surprise even you.

So make sure you safeguard this, the centre of family life, by insuring it adequately. If you have any doubts about its worth, get it valued by at least two local estate agents or surveyors. It is important to get several valuations, since occasionally a property can unwittingly be over- or undervalued.

Should your insurance cover not represent the true value of the property then, in the event of a claim, you could find yourself not receiving sufficient finance to meet any necessary repair or rebuilding costs.

Your house is your home and it is there to be enjoyed over the years you remain in it. By working on it, changing it, improving it and caring for it, you will gradually impress your personality on it. With the help of this book, you will also create the home you have always wanted.

Index

A

B

C

D

E

F

G

H

I

J

K

L

M N O

P

Acknowledgements

Photographs

Page 11 (bottom), 13 (top) and 17 (bottom): Elizabeth Whiting Associates. Page 18 (bottom) and 23 (bottom): Robert Harding Picture Library. Page 24 and 25 (top): Elizabeth Whiting Associates. Page 25 (bottom) and 44 (bottom): Robert Harding Picture Library. Page 45 (top and centre): Rentokil Ltd. Page 73 (top): Robert Harding Picture Library. Page 74: Rentokil Ltd. Page 76 (top): External Wall Insulation Association. Page 76 (bottom): National Cavity Insulation Association. Page 100 and 101: Robert Harding Picture Library. Page 103: Rentokil Ltd. Page 104: Richard Burbidge Ltd. Page 110: Elizabeth Whiting Associates (Jarvis Woolgar). Page 122: Marshall Cavendish Ltd. Page 123: Elizabeth Whiting Associates. Page 126 and 127 (bottom right): Elizabeth Whiting Associates (126 top left: Maggie Colvin. 126 centre: Lucinda Wright). Page 127 (far right): Robert Harding Picture Library. Page 129: Marshall Cavendish Ltd. Page 140 and 141: Franke UK Ltd. Page 142 (top): In-Sink-Erator. Page 143 (top): Robert Harding Picture Library. Page 143 (bottom): Wickes Building Supplies Ltd. Page 144: Magnet plc. Page 145 (top): Elizabeth Whiting Associates. Page 145 (bottom): AEG (UK) Ltd. Page 147 (bottom) to 149: Alno (UK) Ltd. Page 150 (bottom): Shires Bathrooms Ltd. Page 154 (top): Elizabeth Whiting Associates. Page 154 (bottom): Wickes Building Supplies Ltd. Page 155 and 156 (top): Elizabeth Whiting Associates (155: Carolyn Warrender). Page 158 (top): Svedbergs (UK) Ltd. Page 158 (bottom): Armitage Shanks Ltd. Page 159: Robert Harding Picture Library. Page 160 (top and centre): Wickes Building Supplies Ltd. Page 160; (bottom): Svedbergs (UK) Ltd. Page 161 (top): Robert Harding Picture Library. Page 162: Elizabeth Whiting Associates. Page 164, 165 (bottom) and 166: The Velux Co Ltd. Page 169 (bottom) and 172: Elizabeth Whiting Associates. Page 173 (top): Marshall Cavendish Ltd. Page 173 (bottom): Elizabeth Whiting Associates. Page 174 (top): Robert Harding Picture Library. Page 174 (bottom) and 175: Elizabeth Whiting Associates. Page 176 (top): Robert Harding Picture Library. Page 176 (bottom) and 177: Elizabeth Whiting Associates (176: Leila Corbett). Page 178 and 179: Marshall Cavendish Ltd. Page 180: Robert Harding Picture Library. Page 181: Trianco Redfyre Ltd. Page 185 (top): Potterton Myson Ltd. Page 185 (bottom) and 186: Trianco Redfyre Ltd. Page 187 and 188: Potterton Myson Ltd. Page 189: Marshall Cavendish Ltd. Page 190 and 191: Robert Harding Picture Library. Page 198 to 201: Marshall Cavendish Ltd. Page 215: Hozelock Ltd. Page 216: Robert Harding Picture Library.

All other special photography by David Markson, LBIPP. Chapter openers by David Parmiter. Styled by Victoria Furbisher.

Illustrations

Pages 30 to 37: Richard Phipps. Page 38: Steve Cross. Page 39: Richard Phipps. Page 42: Steve Cross. Pages 44, 48 and 49: Richard Phipps. Pages 50 to 59: Steve Cross. Pages 62 to 68: Ed Stuart. Pages 69 to 91: Rob Shone. Pages 94 to 109: Richard Draper. Pages 111 to 125: Ed Stuart. Pages 128 to 132: Richard Draper. Page 133: Richard Phipps. Pages 134 to 137: Richard Draper. Page 139: Andrew Green. Pages 146 and 151 to 153: Ed Stuart. Pages 157, 164, 182 to 184, 192 to 195, 197, 205 and 217: Andrew Green.